Another Politics

Another Politics

Talking across Today's Transformative Movements

CHRIS DIXON

With a Foreword by Angela Y. Davis

University of California Press

University of California Press, one of the most distinguished university presses in the United States, enriches lives around the world by advancing scholarship in the humanities, social sciences, and natural sciences. Its activities are supported by the UC Press Foundation and by philanthropic contributions from individuals and institutions. For more information, visit www.ucpress.edu.

University of California Press
Oakland, California

Library of Congress Cataloging-in-Publication Data

Dixon, Chris, 1977–.
    Another politics : talking across today's transformative movements / Chris Dixon; with a foreword by Angela Y. Davis.
        pages   cm
    Includes bibliographical references and index.
    ISBN 978-0-520-27901-8 (cloth : alk. paper)
— ISBN 978-0-520-27902-5 (pbk. : alk. paper)
— ISBN 978-0-520-95884-5 (e-book)
    1. Radicalism.   2. Social movements—Political aspects.   3. Social change—Political aspects.   4. Anti-racism.   5. Feminism.   6. Criminal justice, Administration of.   7. Anarchism.   I. Title.
    HN49.R33D58   2014
    303.48′4—dc23
                                                                2013045365

Manufactured in the United States of America

23   22   21   20   19   18   17   16   15   14
10   9   8   7   6   5   4   3   2   1

In keeping with a commitment to support environmentally responsible and sustainable printing practices, UC Press has printed this book on Natures Natural, a fiber that contains 30% post-consumer waste and meets the minimum requirements of ANSI/NISO z39.48–1992 (R 1997) (*Permanence of Paper*).

For Tim Young and Ruth Sheridan, beloved anarchist mentors who taught me how to carry a new world in my heart

A lot of our movements are shaped defensively, necessarily. It can be easy to set our dreams only on the horizon of what seems possible in circumstances largely controlled by oppressive systems. It feels like radical work to actually stretch our imaginations and recenter ourselves in the long arc of what we need to survive.

ADRIENNE MAREE BROWN

Contents

Illustrations

Foreword

ANGELA Y. DAVIS

As a member of the jury for an important social justice prize in 2013, I had
the opportunity to hear presentations by emissaries from fifteen phenom-
enal organizations chosen as finalists for the award. They had come from all
over the world—Africa, the Middle East, Asia, Europe, as well as Central
and North America—to speak about their leadership and organizing strategies in relation to a wide range of movements, including economic justice,
food sovereignty, HIV/AIDS, and prison education. Together they were a
vibrant microcosm of global social justice activism.

After two days of presentations and the final announcement of the prize
winners, we learned that early on, the competitive context within which
they had been summoned had pretty much dissolved. It had become almost
irrelevant, many of the organizers said, which ones would emerge as the
winners. Without exception, they agreed that the opportunity to share histories, analyses, and strategies was far more valuable than the fact that
some might receive the prize and others might not. Given the plethora of
issues—homelessness, mass imprisonment, homophobia, the suppression
of indigenous rights, racist violence, and repressive immigration policies are
only a few of them—around which contemporary organizations and movements revolve, and the tendency for activists to move in circles that reflect
their particular interests, there are not many opportunities to exchange
ideas and experiences on a sustained basis and within broader contexts. This
was a weekend of rich interaction across the usual dividing lines and I came
away from it wishing that activist groups could more frequently engage
deeply in these kinds of exchanges.

Shortly after the meeting on the social justice prize, when I read Chris
Dixon's *Another Politics*, I realized that he had staged, recorded, and analyzed many more insightful conversations with contemporary radical

activists than I could have imagined. This book not only allows the reader to feel a part of these conversations about radical movements of today, it also helps all of us to identify key points of convergence and possible future directions for social justice movements in our part of the world. In this impressive documentation of the experiences, theories, and strategies of contemporary radical activism in North America, Dixon records the contributions of people associated with a range of movements in Atlanta, Montreal, New Orleans, New York, the San Francisco Bay Area, Toronto, and Vancouver. As a long-time scholar/activist Chris Dixon is well aware of the dangers of positioning himself as the all-knowing academic masterfully analyzing his subject matter—in this case, the activist community of which he himself is a member. He is, of course, a stellar academic, but in this book he is more concerned about collective experiences and communities of resistance than about his individual scholarship. As he points out, he neither writes about, nor even for, movements and their participants; rather he writes with those movements. He consciously avoids a stance that establishes the author as final arbiter. Thus when he informs his readers that he has uncovered three main political directions influencing many radical movements today—antiracist feminism, prison abolition, and new anarchist approaches to organizing—he means that he has engaged in conversations with activists across many regional and national borders and these three important themes have emerged. Given that opportunities for these activists and organizers to meet directly with each other are rare, Dixon allows them to exchange ideas through the interviews he stages in the major cities of North America.

The conversations that animate this book urge us to take seriously new modes of politicization that have recently emerged through, for example, the Occupy Wall Street campaign and the student uprisings in Quebec. For bystanders who operate under the assumption that the Occupy movement was a failure because it did not produce a new political party or a permanent national or international organization or even a coherent political agenda, this book provides important lessons regarding the ongoing significance and the continuing legacies of Occupy. For those closer to the movements detailed here, and who thus realize that the closure of the encampment phase was just that—the closure of a phase—it clearly enunciates the way Occupy pointed to new modes of creating political community.

While highlighting new approaches to organizing, Dixon does not forget to place these efforts within a political context that acknowledges radical movements of the past—socialism, anti-colonial campaigns, anti-racist and feminist organizing, and queer movements. He and his interviewees are especially interested in what he calls the anti-authoritarian current that runs through many contemporary movements, but that has been especially deepened by the emphasis in these movements on anti-racist feminism, prison abolitionism, and new forms of anarchism.

In previous decades feminism was assumed to be confined to circles of theorists and activists who have embraced feminism as their primary political identity. Although this idea of feminism still lingers today, at least since the emergence of women of color feminism in the 1980s, which insisted that gender and race (as well as class and sexuality) are always interwoven and enmeshed, these approaches—often abbreviated as intersectionality— have deeply influenced radical theories and practices. Dixon takes these developments seriously, confirming—with the help of his various activist cohorts—that anti-racist feminism has informed and indeed transformed most of the important radical movements of our time. The anti-authoritarian current, Dixon's primary concern, has been especially and extensively influenced by anti-racist feminism. He refers, for example, to Elizabeth "Betita" Martinez, one of the pioneering figures in the emergence of anti-racist feminism, whose intervention in the aftermath of the 1999 anti-globalization mobilizations in Seattle, "Where Was the Color in Seattle," helped to stimulate dialogue on internal hierarchies, especially with respect to race and gender, within organizations and movements. And although people familiar with academic feminism are expected to be familiar with the Combahee River Collective—the pioneering black lesbian feminist organization of the late 1970s—this history has not necessarily entered the broader activist mainstream. Even as Chris Dixon engages with current developments at the level of grassroots activism, he allows these conversations to unfold against a valuable and rich historical backdrop.

Prison abolitionism has acquired particularly public visibility during periods of major crisis in the prison system. As Dixon points out, during the 1970s, prison abolition was associated with the Attica Uprising, and during the late 1990s and early 2000s, it emerged as an alternative to the ravages associated with the prison industrial complex—soaring prison populations reflecting self-evident racial disparities and increasing trends toward the exploitation of prisoners for the purposes of generating profit. Because most activist efforts during both eras, aside from explicitly abolitionist campaigns, called for prison reform (reflecting the way that prison historically has always presented itself as a putative solution to problems of its own creation), abolition emerged as a way to imagine strategies to address the prison crisis that did not reproduce the very problem prison activism sought to solve. Although the abolitionist movement of the 1970s clearly emphasized its ties to demands for far-reaching economic, political, and social transformation, it was not until the second era of prison abolitionism that the broader revolutionary dimension was clearly brought to the fore. What might have remained a relatively marginal movement, entirely focused on issues related exclusively to incarceration, revealed its immediate relevance to a range of other issues—education, housing, jobs, et cetera.

Dixon also insists on the role that anarchism has played in helping to define twenty-first-century radical political activism. Having himself grown to political maturity within anarchist movements, he points out that while these movements should be situated within the broader anarchist tradition, they have been especially influenced by the contributions of radical pacifists and by the direct action strategies and participatory democracy associated with civil rights organizations like the Student Nonviolent Coordinating Committee. This "reconfigured anarchism" insists on non-hierarchical leadership models and prefigurative politics. The Occupy assemblies reflected these non-hierarchal approaches to leadership and helped to popularize prefigurative methods of community-building.

What is most interesting about these three directions—antiracist feminism, prison abolition, and reconfigured anarchism—are the crucial ways they have mutually influenced each other, constituting what Dixon calls the anti-authoritarian current, and in the process giving rise to entirely new approaches to movement-building in the twenty-first century. These approaches are employed across a great spectrum of radical political organizing. As he points out in the introduction, "anti-racist feminism provides a set of politics and practices for understanding interrelated systems of oppression and exploitation, linking interpersonal and systemic forms of domination, and elaborating intersectional strategies for social transformation. Prison abolitionism contributes an analysis connecting state violence and dominant social relations, a nonreformist approach to strategy, and experiments aimed at reducing harm and resolving conflict without resorting to the state. And reconfigured anarchism supplies nonhierarchical practices, prefigurative values, and a confrontational orientation."

This book is a valuable orientation for those who are interested in understanding and taking part in contemporary activism. It reorients those who are accustomed to older approaches to organizing in a way that clearly acknowledges the importance of other, earlier modes of struggle, while emphasizing new work "in the space between our transformative aspirations and actually existing social relations." It is a much-needed guide to the twenty-first century for all of us who believe that people's movements are the key to a habitable future.

Acknowledgments

Writing a book is an odd activity. It takes a long time, involves a lot of solitary labor, and requires an almost fanatical level of dedication. Following dominant social myths, it can be quite tempting to understand this as a process of realizing some sort of "individual genius" through personal excellence and hard work. But like all products of human activity, a book grows out of a dense web of sociality and is nourished by a lot of invisible labor. At least that was my experience. While working on this book, I was reminded again and again about the relations of care and collaboration that we develop in spite of the systems that so often dominate our lives.

Whatever weaknesses this project has (and I'm certain there are some important ones) are my responsibility. Whatever strengths it has, however, come largely from the contributions of others. The trouble is that it would take another book-length piece of writing to do justice to the many efforts that have nurtured this project. Since I don't have that kind of space, I offer some acknowledgments here that I hope at least indicate the scope of sociality and otherwise invisible labor involved in this book.

Let me start with the most significant contributions. This book would simply not have been possible without the generosity, reflections, and work of all of the organizers I had the pleasure of interviewing: Sarita Ahooja, Ashanti Alston, Clare Bayard, Jill Chettiar, Rosana Cruz, Mike Desroches, Rayan El-Amine, Francesca Fiorentini, Mary Foster, Harjit Singh Gill, Tatiana Gomez, Harjap Grewal, Stephanie Guilloud, Rachel Herzing, Helen Hudson, Pauline Hwang, Rahula Janowski, Tynan Jarrett, Sharmeen Khan, Brooke Lehman, RJ Maccani, Andréa Maria, Pilar Maschi, Sonya Mehta, Amy Miller, Rafael Mutis Garcia, Michelle O'Brien, Adriana Paz, Lydia Pelot-Hobbs, Leila Pourtavaf, Paula Ximena Rojas-Urrutia, Joshua Kahn Russell, Sophie Schoen, Mac Scott, Jaggi Singh, David Solnit, Mick

Sweetman, James Tracy, Harsha Walia, Marika Warner, Jennifer Whitney, and Ora Wise. (Unless otherwise noted, comments from these individuals in this book are based on our recorded conversations. A complete listing of these interviews is in the bibliography.) I also wish to acknowledge Megan Adam, Margot, Monami Maulik, Derrick O'Keefe, and Andrea Pinochet; although I didn't bring their interviews into this book, what they shared helped me think more clearly about another politics.

I didn't know most of these people before I started this project. What's more, I'm a really shy person. So, in connecting with people to interview, I benefited from the advice and support of a wide circle of friends and comrades. I especially want to thank the individuals of this circle who went "above and beyond" in providing me with places to sleep, feeding me delicious vegan food, introducing me to others, and/or helping to orient me in cities I didn't know well: Stephanie Guilloud, Helen Hudson, Pauline Hwang, Karl Kersplebedeb, Helen Luu, RJ Maccani, Amy Miller, Michelle O'Brien, Jaggi Singh, Harsha Walia, Jennifer Whitney, and Lesley Wood.

In addition to the people I interviewed, there were many others who contributed insights, questions, and challenges that influenced this book. I want to underline my appreciation for comrades from the AKA Autonomous Social Center, Catalyst Project, Collectif de recherche sur l'autonomie collective, the Halifax Radical Imagination project, the Institute for Anarchist Studies, *Left Turn*, Team Colors, and *Upping the Anti* for helpful discussions. My work here particularly benefited from conversations and exchanges I had with Max Bell Alper, Jen Angel, Kazembe Balagun, Dana Barnett, Liat Ben-Moshe, Doug Bevington, Bekki Bolthouse, Chris Borte, Sam Bradd, Sean Burns, Karen Button, Irina Ceric, Ingrid Chapman, Aziz Choudry, John Clarke, Carolyn Cooley, Aaron Dankman, Alex Day, Bryan Doherty, Nick Dyer-Witheford, Rami Elamine, Kenyon Farrow, Amie Fishman, Craig Fortier, Caelie Frampton, Sara Galindo, Louis-Frédéric Gaudet, David Gilbert, Harmony Goldberg, Cindy Gorn, Debbie Gould, Andrej Grubacic, Sean Haberle, Candida Hadley, Max Haiven, Ryan Harvey, Heather Hax, Adam Hefty, Mostafa Henaway, Walter Hergt, Ben Holtzman, Craig Hughes, Chris Hurl, Johanna Isaacson, Sayyida Jaffer, Sandra Jeppesen, George Katsiaficas, Shailagh Keaney, Tom Keefer, Gabe Keresztesi, Alex Khasnabish, Emma Kreyche, Mette Kruger, David Langstaff, Joseph Lapp, Clarissa Lassaline, Sasha Lilley, Jeremy Louzao, Rachel Luft, Matthew Lyons, Angus Maguire, Andrea Marcos, Sara Matthiesen, Jamie McCallum, Molly McClure, Mike McGuire, Geoff McNamara, Gavin Mendel-Gleason, Lara and Paul Messersmith-Glavin, Cindy Milstein, Hilary Moore, John Moore, Tamara Myers, Madeleine

Nerenberg, Clare O'Connor, Jose Palafox, Shiri Pasternak, Alex Patterson, Justin Paulson, David Peerla, Brigitte Pelletier Cisneros, Justin Podur, Chanda Prescod-Weinstein, Torie Quinoñez, Billie Rain, Manju Rajendran, Khalida Ramyar, Michael Reagan, ander reszczynski-negrazis, Ted Rutland, Rachel Sarrasin, gabriel sayegh, Rebecca Schein, Alan Sears, Andy Sernatinger, David Shulman, Matt Silburn, Marina Sitrin, Sonja Sivesind, Laurel Smith, Trudi Smith, Josh Sonnenfeld, Pavlos Stavropoulos, Joshua Stephens, Suzy Subways, AK Thompson, Brook Thorndycraft, Brian Tokar, Shelley Tremain, Max Uhlenbeck, Kevin Van Meter, Camilo Viveiros, Ryan Wadsworth, Theresa Warburton, Carl Wassilie, Andrew Willis Garcés, Sasha Wright, Eddie Yuen, Rafeef Ziadah, David Zlutnick, and Marla Zubel.

My thinking in this book was also significantly shaped through my involvement in activism and organizing over the last twenty-three years. I offer much love and appreciation to all of those with whom I had the privilege to collaborate in the Steller Action Group, DIRT!, Evergreen Animal Rights Network, Evergreen Political Information Center, Direct Action Network, Alaska Action Center, Colours of Resistance, Corvallis Action on Globalization, Wrench, Graduate Student Solidarity Network, Student and Worker Coalition for Justice, Long Road Collective, Sudbury Against War and Occupation, Occupy Sudbury, Sudbury Coalition Against Poverty, and Indigenous Peoples Solidarity Movement—Ottawa.

I would additionally like to recognize the mentors who nurtured me. When I was in my early teens in Anchorage, Tim Young and Ruth Sheridan cultivated my passion for justice, introduced me to radical politics, and helped me to understand myself in a long lineage of struggle. While I was an undergraduate student activist in Olympia, Washington, Peter Bohmer, Larry Mosqueda, and Therese Saliba encouraged me to think and act with critical analysis, careful intention, and long-term dedication. During my time as a graduate student in Santa Cruz, California, I learned how to teach with the mentorship of David Brundage, Julie Guthman, Pamela Perry, and Mary Beth Pudup. At various times, Iain Boal, Roxanne Dunbar-Ortiz, Max Elbaum, Gary Kinsman, Mark Leier, and Tony Vogt also offered me crucial guidance and encouraged me to take risks.

This book started out as a PhD dissertation in the History of Consciousness program at the University of California, Santa Cruz. I was incredibly lucky there to have a dissertation committee of distinguished activist intellectuals who are also genuinely good people. I thank Paul Ortiz for his insight and constant encouragement, and for putting forward such a vibrant model of engaged scholarship. I also offer my deep appreciation to Angela Davis, who first showed me what it means to be a movement intellectual; I feel very privileged to have benefited from her advice and sharp mind. The mentorship I received from Barbara Epstein, all the while, was never anything less than exceptional; she was my advocate from the moment I started graduate school, and consistently provided support, critical nudging, invaluable conversations, companionship, and an orienting compass for me to keep sight of my political priorities while ambivalently working in the academy.

I also wish to express my sincere gratitude to staff and readers of the University of California Press. Niels Hooper miraculously understood my vision for this book right away and, almost without me noticing, helped me to take it further. Kim Hogeland cheerfully answered all of my questions, including some very unusual ones, and assisted me in keeping track of countless details while preparing the materials for this book. Stephen Duncombe and Max Elbaum, who served as readers, offered comments that helped me not only to improve my manuscript, but also to better understand its purpose and promise. Caroline Knapp carefully copyedited this manuscript, making it considerably more consistent and readable. Last but not least, Dore Brown expertly guided me through the final stages of the publishing process

I am grateful, as well, to those people who generously allowed me to use their photos in this book: Clare Bayard, Mark Brown, Adam Elliott, Caelie Frampton, Robin Markle, JJ Tiziou, Thien V., and Edward Hon-Sing Wong. Locating and getting permission to use these photos would never have happened without the assistance of Marque Brill, Stefan Christoff, John Clarke, Craig Fortier, Rachel Herzing, Eli Isaacs, Jacob Klippenstein, Vikki Law, RJ Maccani, Angus Maguire, Eli Meyerhoff, Cindy Milstein, Bhavana Nancherla, Dan Sawyer, David Solnit, Mayuran Tiruchelvam, Harsha Walia, and Chanteal Winchester.

This book benefited from lively discussion and collaborative thinking at every stage. I thank the editors of *Anarchist Studies, Left Turn, Upping the Anti,* Znet, and various book collections to which I have contributed for providing me with spaces to develop aspects of this writing. Thanks too to all who organized and participated in my workshops, panels, and talks at Brown University, the Evergreen State College, Laurentian University, Towson University, University of Victoria, University of Washington, the AKA Autonomous Social Center in Kingston, the Emma Goldman Finishing School in Seattle, Last Word Books in Olympia, Libertalia Autonomous Space in Providence, Red and Black Café in Portland, Space 2640 in Baltimore, Wooden Shoe Books in Philadelphia, the 2003 Social Movements and Social Transformation conference at Cornell University, the 2004 Activist Scholarship conference at the University of Michigan,

Left Forum conferences from 2005 to 2012, Renewing the Anarchist Tradition conferences in 2007 and 2010, the 2008 National Conference on Organized Resistance, the 2008 Great Lakes Political Economy Conference at York University, the 2008 Radical Philosophy Association conference at San Francisco State University, sessions hosted by the Society for Socialist Studies at the 2009 and 2011 Canadian Congresses of the Humanities and Social Sciences, the 2010 U.S. Social Forum, Montreal Anarchist Bookfairs in 2010 and 2012, the 2011 North American Anarchist Studies Conference, the 2011 Study in Action conference at Concordia University, the 2012 Colloque/Happening des Employées et Employés de Syndicats Étudiants in Montreal, and the Take Back Democracy! and Taking Back the University conferences at Carleton University in 2012 and 2013.

There were three other essential forms of sustenance for this book that I wish to highlight. One was money. I was able to carry out my initial research and writing with the assistance of a Canadian Studies Graduate Student Fellowship, a UCSC Humanities Alumni Fellowship, a UCSC Oakes/ Humanities Dissertation Fellowship, and several travel grants from the History of Consciousness department and the UCSC Institute for Humanities Research. I'm grateful to all of these programs for supporting my project.

Music was another source of nourishment. My writing process had an epic soundtrack that included Asian Dub Foundation, Babyland, Baroness, Blaqk Audio, Converge, From Monument to Masses, Front 242, Fugazi, Godspeed You! Black Emperor, Gossip, Heaven Shall Burn, Iron Maiden, Judgement Day, Massive Attack, Metallica, Neurosis, Pelican, Refused, Russian Circles, Sepultura, *Shels, Tegan and Sara, and Tesa. And when I wasn't at my computer, KPFA's Against the Grain kept my mind stimulated; thanks to Sasha Lilley and C. S. Soong for maintaining such a shining example of left radio broadcasting.

One other form of sustenance was bodily care. Since I was eleven, long-distance running has been a constant in my life. It is also closely connected to my writing process. But this wasn't always smooth or easy, as I had several running injuries over the course of completing this book. My physiotherapists Angele Carriere and Amy Fahlman consistently worked miracles to get me running again. I offer them my deep gratitude. On this note, thanks too to my longtime friend Luc Mehl, who regularly reminded me about the wonders of outdoor endurance activities and the importance of striving to live our dreams.

Finally, I would like to acknowledge the special crew of people who kept me going during my book-writing journey. My mother, Karen Henderson, who first taught me to write and to run, gave me steady support; although we live far apart, her love was always readily available. My best friend, Andrea Dewees, has stood by me for over twenty years, bringing her own special intensity and building with me a radical Alaskan identity. My families of choice—the Barnholden-Kinsmans (Gary, Patrick, and Mike), the Calvert-Maddens (Nora, Scout, and Ursula), and the Shotwells (Hudson, Janet, Gordon, and Vivien)—offered abundant care and delight. My dear friends Dan Berger, Andy Cornell, Chris Crass, Scott Neigh, Maia Ramnath, James Rowe, and Emily Thuma all provided extensive feedback on this book, repeatedly reminded me about its importance, and supported me in more ways than I can possibly list here. My treasured friends Sharmeen Khan and Kim Marks sustained me with their political wisdom, rebellious spirits, and enduring love. Above all, my partner, Alexis Shotwell, accompanied—and, at times, carried—me through the writing process for this book. Her brilliant mind, visionary radicalism, fierce love, and contagious joyfulness lifted me at every step. I feel so very fortunate to have her loving companionship, and I look forward to our further adventures together.

Introduction

Those of us who are not interested in starting a political party, and have even shied away from cadre organizing of any kind, have found it hard to articulate what exactly it is we would want to see on the local, regional, or even national level, much less how we might organize towards such a goal. . . . We know we are critical of the non-profit world—increasingly integrated into the corporate model—as a major vehicle for structural social change. We are critical of the centralized political party structure, whether it be the neoliberal Democrats or the small leftist "revolutionary sects" that continue to operate in near anonymity around the country. On the other side of the spectrum, the frustrating anti-organizational and sectarian tendencies within many of the contemporary anarchist movements, coupled with the predominantly white subcultures surrounding them, have left much to be desired. The alternative for many of us has been to continue to identify with a broad-based, but still rather vague, political tendency—sometimes described as the "anti-authoritarian, anti-capitalist, non-sectarian left."

Max Uhlenbeck

Occupy Homes Minnesota members and others support the Ceballos family in their struggle against a housing eviction in Minneapolis, Minnesota, on July 29, 2013. (Photo by Mark R. Brown, markrbrownphoto.com)

WE ARE IN A MOMENT of tremendous crisis and possibility. Recent years have seen a sustained global economic slump that has caused tremendous suffering for many, especially the poorest and most marginalized. The ecosystems that sustain life on the planet are in undeniable danger, as is evident from superstorms to melting polar icecaps. In the overdeveloped world, there has been a massive expansion of policing, prisons, militarized borders, and detention facilities, all of which have particularly targeted working-class people of color and migrants. The U.S. government and its allies are regularly carrying out devastating military interventions around the globe, creating a crisis of nearly unfathomable proportions, especially in the lives of people in West Asia and North Africa. In a word, ruling systems and institutions are undermining life and life-making on the biggest scale in human history.

And yet, seemingly against all odds, possibility is in the air. In the face of crisis, we see plenty of fear, but also yearnings worldwide for different ways of organizing our lives and societies. In 2011, these yearnings burst into action in cities such as Tunis, Cairo, Madison, and Madrid as people seized public spaces and collectively challenged ruling elites. These initial actions opened a wide space for movement and mobilization: in New York, Occupy Wall Street turned a park into a protest encampment, inspiring hundreds of similar occupations across the continent and widespread public discussion of inequality; in Quebec, hundreds of thousands of students waged a combative six-month strike against tuition hikes, ultimately delegitimizing their government; and across the Canadian context, tens of thousands of Indigenous people and their allies mobilized in opposition to proposed national legislation, generating a resurgence of anti-colonial resistance. In these and many other places, ordinary people are stepping onto the stage of history. A new spirit of radicalism is blooming.

In this moment, many are searching for fresh political approaches with powerful visions and practical possibilities for action. This book examines one leading set of efforts, deeply intertwined with recent upsurges, to develop a relevant radical politics in the United States and Canada. In the following pages, I explore the anti-authoritarian, anti-capitalist, nonsectarian left: a tendency composed of activists, organizers, fighters, and dreamers who share overlapping politics. We use many labels to describe ourselves—including "abolitionists," "anarchists," "anti-authoritarians," "anti-capitalists," "autonomists," and "radicals"—and some of us avoid political labels entirely. What we are developing together has the potential to remake our movements, our lives, and, ultimately, our society.

THE ANTI-AUTHORITARIAN CURRENT

Those who share these politics come from many circumstances. Some of us have direct experiences with exploitation and oppression while others experience relative forms of privilege; most of us contend with some of each. Some of us were born in the United States or Canada and carry the advantages of citizens; others were born elsewhere, came here through struggle and hardship, and live precariously as "noncitizens." Some of us are settlers whose ancestors immigrated from other places, some are descendants of those who came here in chains, and some are native to this land. Most of us were designated as "girls" or "boys" when we were born and many have come to dispute those fixed categories. Some of us are racialized as Arab, Asian, Black, Indigenous, and/or Latino, and others benefit from being classified as "white"; some cross these boundaries.

Some of us grew up poor or working-class and others have had more access to economic resources and middle-class—and in some cases, owning-class—lives. Some of us have come to understand our sexual desires through the dominant category "straight" and others have come to understand them as lesbian, gay, bisexual, and/or queer. Some of us move through a world constructed to fit our bodies and abilities, and some, often marked as "disabled," have to struggle for a world that accommodates us. Some of us come from cultural and spiritual traditions that fit within the prevailing norms of Christianity and others—Buddhists, Hindus, Jews, Muslims, and others—don't. We are from cities, suburbs, small towns, reservations, and reserves. We find ourselves, in short, located in different places amidst social relations of power that organize our lives for the benefit of some and at the expense of others. We also exceed these relations, generating new identities and collectivities.

Across our differences, we are forging a shared politics through struggle. We believe in the power of people to fight for justice and dignity, and to shape history in the process. We oppose all forms of domination, exploitation, and oppression, and we maintain a critical stance towards the state. We carry a rich democratic vision of everyone being able to directly participate in the decisions that affect them in their relationships, homes, communities, workplaces, schools, and elsewhere. We believe in the equality of all people and we struggle on the basis of solidarity and cooperation. We ground ourselves in the day-to-day work of building mass movements capable of fundamentally transforming the world. We see the importance of developing organizations and institutions to advance our movements, and we favor organizing approaches that involve building collective power to challenge ruling institutions. We struggle with thorny social hierarchies as they play out in our movements and in society more generally. We try to build the world we would like to see through the ways in which we struggle.

We are skeptical of political approaches based on purity, understanding that there are no easy answers and that we all have to get our hands dirty in the process of organizing for radical social change. We attempt to avoid dogmatism and sectarianism in our work and strive to engage in respectful dialogue with other sectors of the left and communities in struggle. We try to develop horizontal organizing that isn't subcultural, ways of transforming social relations that aren't flaky or individualized, organizations that foster movements rather than fracture them, ways of strategically fighting systems, organizing spaces that we can enter as whole people, modes of struggle that improve the lives of ordinary people while building emancipatory capacities and moving us toward a new world, and visionary politics rooted in liberatory dreams.

Our efforts have wide scope and significance. They traverse migrant justice, anti-militarism, prison abolition, feminism, labor struggles, anti-racism, environmental defense, anti-austerity, economic justice, student democracy, and queer radicalism, among other areas. As part of this, we have been building initiatives that reflect our politics, including the No One Is Illegal and Rising Tide networks, national organizations such as Critical Resistance and INCITE! Women of Color Against Violence, and networks around publications such as *Make/Shift* and *Upping the Anti*. We are also involved in initiatives which less explicitly enunciate our politics but are no less important in developing them: radical anti-poverty groups, women's centers and other feminist institutions, community-based racial justice organizations, Indigenous and international solidarity efforts, workers' centers and labor unions, environmental justice groups, post-disaster grassroots reconstruction efforts, Public Interest Research Groups on Canadian campuses, and national student activist organizations such as the Student/Farmworker Alliance and United Students Against Sweatshops. And this just scratches the surface.

Generationally, we tend to be young, mostly in our twenties and thirties, although some of us are older. In most large cities, we number in the hundreds and, in a few cases, the thousands. Outside major urban areas, there are smaller but still significant concentrations of us. Many of us have jobs with nonprofit organizations or unions, others are students of one sort or another, some work as professionals (especially educators, health care providers, and legal advocates), and quite a few of us try to piece together a living in the low-wage service sector. All of us attempt to structure our lives in ways that allow us to dedicate much of our time to our political activities.

Together, we are a political current that cuts across a range of left social movements in North America. However, there is no consensus about what we call ourselves, and we have only a general sense that we even exist as something that can be named. For shorthand, I call us "the anti-authoritarian current." This is not a self-description that everyone associated with these politics would choose. Nor is this current the only political tendency with a claim on the term "anti-authoritarian." What I discuss here is one current in a growing landscape of North American anti-statist, anti-capitalist politics composed of various anarchist and left communist tendencies. I'm certain that, through further collective reflection, those of us in this current can develop more precise terms to describe ourselves.[1] We're not there yet, though, so I use the inadequate terminology that is presently available.

While the anti-authoritarian current is in a certain sense new, this doesn't mean that it materialized out of thin air. As I discuss in chapter 1, this current comes out of dense lineages of movement and struggle. In recent decades, it has particularly grown as a result of the convergence of a variety of anti-authoritarian politics and broader-based movements. Three political strands have been especially important: anti-racist feminism, prison abolitionism, and anarchism. The convergence of these and other strands has provided crucial space for the mutual articulation and influence of anti-authoritarians and popular struggles in ways that have transformed both.

ANOTHER POLITICS

A significant part of what defines the anti-authoritarian current is what it is *not*. As Max Uhlenbeck points out in the epigraph, those in this current are attempting to create a political space that is not bound up in the parties or party-building of liberals, Leninists, or social democrats; nor in the non-profit and agency sectors, all too often constrained by foundations, state funders, and grant cycles; nor in the insularity and aversion to strategy and structure of much contemporary anarchism.

Anti-authoritarian activists and organizers are working to make something *other*—"another politics." I use this term to describe shared politics, practices, and sensibilities in the anti-authoritarian current. It came into somewhat wider use in the United States with the "Another Politics is Possible" delegation and workshop track at the 2007 U.S. Social Forum.[2] In using the name "another politics," those organizers highlighted the influence of the Zapatista rebels in Mexico and their *Otra Campaña*.[3] Like "anti-authoritarian," the term "another politics" is not something that all or even many in this current would necessarily choose. In the Canadian and U.S. contexts, though, I think it's useful because it gestures, poetically, to something in process and unfinished, something that consciously pushes beyond currently available political categories, and yet something that can be shared, held in common.

Another politics has no party line. Indeed, it is a politics suspicious of "correct lines" offered by identifiable leaders and centralized organizations. Still, it does have key features. Based on my interviews with organizers and drawing on other attempts at self-definition, I see four core principles to the politics of the anti-authoritarian current:[4]

1. *Struggling against all forms of domination, exploitation, and oppression.* Sometimes associated with "anti-oppression politics," this means developing approaches and analyses to challenge and transform hetero-patriarchy, racism, colonialism, capitalism, ableism, and the state. In concrete terms, this involves strategically making central the struggles and perspectives of those most affected by systems of exploitation and oppression. It also entails what Montreal migrant justice organizer Sarita Ahooja called, in my interview with her, "reorganizing ourselves socially"— consciously working, through political education and struggle, to shift relations of privilege and oppression as they play out in our movements.

2. *Developing new social relations and forms of social organization in the process of struggle.* Often called "prefigurative politics," this is about trying to manifest and build, to the greatest extent possible, the egalitarian and deeply democratic world we would like to see through our means of fighting in this one. This principle informs the types of organizations we build, the organizing methods we favor, and the kinds of relationships that we nurture in struggle. It also frames, as Toronto prison abolitionist Marika Warner described in conversation with me, "the way that we interact, the way that we try to be aware of what is going on for people, and really try to make room for people to show up whole at that table."

3. *Linking struggles for improvements in the lives of ordinary people to long-term transformative visions.* Another politics seeks to ground movement-building in everyday struggles while cultivating liberatory possibilities. The consistent question here is the one New York housing and HIV/AIDS organizer Michelle

O'Brien shared with me: "What's the connection between concrete activities and vision?" In general terms, we try to forge this connection through fighting in the world as it is—engaging with where and how people are struggling, including around reforms—while organizing toward the world that we want. This vision-based work also includes building counterinstitutions to meet people's immediate needs while furthering transformative movements.

4. *Organizing that is grassroots and bottom-up.* Another politics prioritizes grassroots organizing, which New Orleans criminal justice reform organizer Rosana Cruz defined in discussion with me as "bringing people together in ways that link them in a long-term struggle and build their power." At the most basic level, this involves developing relationships and working with people in workplaces and communities of various kinds in order to confront and change the social relations and institutions that rule their lives. Alongside this, another politics prioritizes horizontal organizing practices, such as directly democratic decision-making, training to develop people's confidence and competence, and participatory political education. We carry this out through democratic membership organizations, general assemblies, and collectives linked to broader movements, among other forms.

These features are neither entirely new nor unique. When it comes to social movements, hardly anything ever is. But the ways in which the anti-authoritarian current is bringing them together indicate an increasingly sophisticated politics with powerful implications. The story of this politics is thus incredibly rich. It's also largely untold. As Oakland prison industrial complex abolitionist Rachel Herzing observed, "if you struggle to be taken seriously and therefore to take your own selves seriously, there can be less of a value on documenting your history." This is certainly true for another politics. One aim of this book, then, is to document the anti-authoritarian current and, in this way, encourage the seriousness that our movements deserve.

My other aim is to preserve hard-earned lessons and challenging discussions across recent cycles of struggle. In the pace of movements and mobilizations, years can sometimes feel like decades and, with frequent activist turnover, we all too easily end up repeating similar mistakes and debates over and over again. One solution to this, as San Francisco direct action organizer David Solnit proposed, is to develop "humble continuity"—ways to carry lessons and challenges across movement experiences, and share them respectfully. I seek to do that here.

Throughout this book, I examine lessons and challenges using two main themes. The first is "against-and-beyond," a term I take from radical theorist John Holloway.[5] This formulation offers us a way to see, side-by-side, the two foundational aspects of another politics: our "against" is our active opposition to all forms of domination, and our "beyond" is our work to build new social relations and forms of social organization through struggle. The challenge is how to consistently link "against" and "beyond" in the practical work of building movements and fighting for justice.

If we take this challenge seriously, we inevitably come face-to-face with a tension at the heart of radical organizing. Joshua Kahn Russell, an Oakland-based ecological justice organizer, summed it up well: "If we're idealistic enough to believe that another world is possible, then we have to be realistic enough to actually live in the world that exists and not in the world we'd like to exist in." The challenge, growing out of this, is how to work in the space *between* our transformative aspirations and actually existing social realities. We have to figure out how to be "in this world but not necessarily of it," as veteran organizer and former political prisoner Ashanti Alston suggested. This is the second main theme that I use in this book.

Like so much else in these pages, these themes come out of discussions within the anti-authoritarian current. What I present and argue here, as I explain in more detail below, is based on extensive interviews with fellow organizers across the United States and Canada who have generously shared their ideas and experiences with me. I have also drawn on magazines, meetings, online exchanges, books, protests, activist events, trainings, late-night conversations, and many of the other ways that we engage in reflection and dialogue. This book is my attempt to collect much of the knowledge that the anti-authoritarian current is developing. My hope is that, using this knowledge, we can deepen our ideas, strengthen our practices, and honestly discuss the significant challenges that we face.

WHERE I COME FROM

As should be clear, I write as an anti-authoritarian organizer, not a disinterested outsider. For more than two decades, my life has been embedded in this current and its tensions, contradictions, and insights. I grew up as a white guy in a middle-class home in Anchorage, on traditional Dena'ina Territory. With some of my friends, I stumbled into radical politics at age thirteen, about the same time that we discovered punk rock. This was just as the U.S. government was launching the first Gulf War in 1991, a moment which radicalized a whole generation of anti-authoritarians. In the following years, my friends and I cut our teeth organizing as high school student activists around student power, environmental issues, anti-militarism, and labor solidarity. As part of this, I immersed myself in the anarchist tradition with its steadfast rejection of the state, capitalism, and all other forms of domination. Through anarchism, I began to develop a critical understanding of the world and a link to a history of radical struggle.

My politics deepened when I went to Evergreen, a university in Olympia, Washington, that holds a well-deserved reputation as a school for rabble-rousers. While there, I was fortunate to develop friendships with an energetic crew of anarchist-oriented student activists, including many queer women. With this crew, I got involved in animal rights activism, protested U.S. sanctions against Iraq, helped to organize a regional activist conference, participated in one of the first U.S. student groups against the prison industrial complex, campaigned against Nike's use of sweatshops, and contributed to a men against sexism project. I also co-led a successful campaign to have U.S. political prisoner Mumia Abu-Jamal as the commencement speaker for my graduation ceremony, causing a national controversy. Like many young anti-authoritarians in this period, I was deeply influenced by women of color feminism with its analysis of how systems of oppression intersect and must be fought accordingly. In anti-racist feminism, I found experiences and vision that strengthened my anarchist politics.

In 1997, my friends and I traveled to Vancouver to participate in "crashing the summit" of the Asia-Pacific Economic Cooperation (APEC), a free-trade agreement among a number of Pacific Rim economies, including the United States and Canada. We joined activists at the University of British Columbia in reclaiming space, camping out in the middle of campus and using school buildings to organize. On the first day of the summit, in what became known as "SprayPEC" in Canada, police hosed down protestors with pepper spray. But the protests succeeded in generating an expansive public discussion. I took particular inspiration from the ways in which Vancouver activists grounded their efforts in solidarity with Indigenous resistance and movements in the global South. This made sense to me based on what I was learning about the Zapatistas, who were quickly becoming a touchstone for anti-capitalists worldwide. My experience at the APEC protests was the beginning of my relationship with the left in Canada and what would come to be called the global justice movement.

Two years later, I collaborated with other organizers along the West Coast in launching the Direct Action Network (DAN). This organization, developed along anti-authoritarian lines, would become the organizing hub for mass direct action against the Seattle ministerial of the World Trade

Organization (WTO). Following months of intense organizing, on November 30, 1999, DAN's rhetoric of "shutting down the WTO" became a stunning reality when mass blockades and street disruptions effectively halted the first day of the ministerial. The rest of the week was a blur of direct actions, late-night meetings, and police confrontations as the thousands of activists present in Seattle quickly learned a whole lot about our capacities and what we were up against. Combined with collective action by a coalition of delegates from the global South inside the meetings, our efforts ultimately led to a stalled ministerial and a delegitimized WTO. Our experience was reflected in recurring graffiti throughout the week: "We are winning!"

Following the Seattle protests, the mainstream media suggested that we had launched something new called the "anti-globalization movement." But many organizers knew better. Those of us who had been involved in movements before Seattle understood that the WTO protests, although significant, were part of a much longer arc of resistance to colonialism and capitalism. Many of us were also growing increasingly aware of the limitations of our efforts in Seattle. As my comrade Stephanie Guilloud, a leading DAN organizer, would later write, "We were not building a long-term resistance movement: we were mobilizing for a protest."[6] And in the process, we clearly overlooked some fundamental issues. Longtime activist and writer Elizabeth "Betita" Martinez, in a widely circulated article, posed one question with which many of us were grappling: "Where was the color in Seattle?"[7] This intervention and others inspired widespread discussions about not only racism, but also other social hierarchies at play in the movement as well as questions of organizing and strategy.

I saw these post-Seattle discussions as vital and, with others, tried to broaden and advance them. As part of this, I helped to build Colours of Resistance (COR), a network across Canada and the United States that sought to develop feminist, multiracial, anti-racist, anti-authoritarian, anti-capitalist politics in the global justice movement.[8] An important feature of COR was the way we tried to enact our politics, with women of color activists taking leading roles in all areas of work and with caps on the proportion of white people and men participating. Although COR was little more materially than an informal network mediated through email lists and a website, it did build relationships among activists and organizers across North America grappling with similar questions as we tried to combine our politics with grassroots organizing. In significant ways, the origins of this book lie in my experience helping to facilitate COR. Through my involvement, I came to see the outlines of a shared, movement-oriented, anti-authoritarian politics and I came to have a critical appreciation for all of the people building this approach.

In 2002, I started graduate school in the History of Consciousness department at the University of California at Santa Cruz. My hope was to use university resources to assist movement work and to further the discussions I saw developing in an increasingly coherent anti-authoritarian current. This book is based on the PhD dissertation I researched and wrote between 2006 and 2010 for this program. While in Santa Cruz, I also organized rank-and-file initiatives with and against my union, participated in the direct action protests that shut down San Francisco's Financial District after the United States invaded Iraq in 2003, worked in a solidarity campaign with predominantly Latino/a campus service workers, participated in direct action against military recruitment, and helped with immigrant justice organizing, particularly in actions against border vigilantes in 2005 and during the massive spring demonstrations of 2006. I also worked as a teaching assistant in activist-inspired courses and mentored many younger student radicals. These experiences made it all the more clear to me that those of us aging on the left should do all we can to support up-and-coming activists.

In 2007, my life circumstances changed dramatically as I moved with my partner to Sudbury, Ontario, so that she could take a job. Known for its giant smokestacks and ecologically devastated landscape, Sudbury is a small mining city located about 250 miles north of Toronto. Although it has a distinguished history of militant labor organizing, Sudbury isn't an easy place to build movements these days. The few working-class organizations that have survived the last three decades of neoliberal assault are barely holding on, most people struggle to make ends meet, and there is a pervasive sense of resignation. Living there was eye-opening for me. I worked as part of a very small crew of activists involved in anti-war and Indigenous solidarity organizing. I also participated in solidarity actions with striking miners and a support campaign for John Moore, a local Indigenous man fighting a racist conviction that had sent him to prison for a decade for a crime he didn't commit. These experiences helped me see the limitations of forms of radical activism from big urban centers, which often don't get very far in smaller cities and rural areas. They also convinced me of the central transformative potential of struggles based in the lives of ordinary, nonactivist people.

During my five years in Sudbury, I wrote much of what appears in this book. I also developed a habit of traveling regularly in the United States and Canada, conducting interviews, giving presentations and workshops for activists, organizing sessions focused on movement-building at left gatherings, assisting with various activist projects, and spending time talking with hundreds of people involved in many movement sectors. In addition, I worked as a guest editor and copyeditor for the U.S. activist magazine *Left Turn* and an advisory board member with editing responsibilities for the Canadian radical journal *Upping the Anti*. I also joined the collectively run Institute for Anarchist Studies, which provides grants to people writing about anti-authoritarian ideas and organizing as well as running several activist publishing projects. Together, these activities have helped me to sustain a continental perspective of the anti-authoritarian current.

In September 2011, I was at a meeting of the Institute for Anarchist Studies in New York just after Occupy Wall Street had started. When several of us went to Zuccotti Park, we experienced a thriving encampment with lots of determined, newly politicized people. As I then traveled along the West Coast on speaking tour, I encountered activists enthusiastically engaging in or preparing for occupations wherever I went. And after I returned to Sudbury, a group of mostly young people, inspired by what they were seeing elsewhere, set up an occupy encampment. I helped with that month-long initiative, experiencing both the amazing sense of possibility and some of the frustrating day-to-day challenges. When the encampment folded, some occupiers began holding meetings with some of us longer-time activists about direct action anti-poverty organizing. This eventually led to the resurrection of the Sudbury Coalition Against Poverty (S-CAP), which has since made a name for itself in Ontario through combative organizing with poor people for entitlements and against austerity.

Participating in the occupy movement, working with S-CAP, and then experiencing the Quebec student strike in 2012 inspired me. They also all demonstrated to me the vitality of bottom-up organizing and the continuing relevance of another politics. After moving to Ottawa, Ontario, in mid-2012, I felt this further through my participation in Idle No More. This book is my humble contribution to these and other ongoing efforts for social transformation.

MY RESEARCH AND WRITING APPROACH

Given my history, it should come as no surprise that my approach in research and writing puts the ideas and experiences of anti-authoritarian activists and organizers at its center. I follow this approach for two connected reasons. First, as an activist, I'm politically committed to helping this current flourish and, as part of that, I wish to foreground insights from a broad range of people working within it. This book is principally meant to be a useful tool, documenting and fostering discussions. In my experience, opportunities for seriously reflecting on political work and sharing it with others are unfortunately rare. I hope for the reflections collected here to open more such opportunities.

Second, as a researcher, I think we can learn the most when we look to activists and organizers as producers of vital knowledge about social movements and social relations. "Social movements," as scholar-activist Robin Kelley writes, "generate new knowledge, new theories, new questions. The most radical ideas often grow out of a concrete intellectual engagement with the problems of aggrieved populations confronting systems of oppression."[9] We have much to gain when we understand activists and organizers as experts about the struggles in which they are engaged. And we can gain even more when we join them on the frontlines. In this way, I side with left historian Barbara Epstein when she says, "I believe that in general one can learn more about a movement from the inside than from the outside, and that a position of engagement and critical identification tends to be more fruitful than objectivity achieved by maintaining a distance."[10]

With this kind of "critical identification," I write as both an activist and a researcher—an activist-researcher. This means that I deliberately include myself in what I discuss. When I refer to the anti-authoritarian current, I don't write of "them" but "us." Throughout this book, I take up shared aspirations, questions, and uncertainties as my own. At the same time, I recognize that my role gives me a lot of power: I set the framework for understanding another politics in this book and I make interpretive claims about the statements and activities of others. While I don't see a way to get around this, I do think it's possible to navigate it. This requires honesty, intentionality, humility, and accountability, all of which I have tried to build into my research and writing practice.

My approach draws on lessons I have gleaned from movement-based researchers, including both academics and independent intellectuals.[11] I have learned a lot from research methods known as "ethnography" (analyzing lived culture by experiencing it), "participant observation" (understanding how and why people do what they do by participating in it), and "oral history" (gathering history by inviting and listening to people's stories). However, none of these methods has fully satisfied me, largely because they still rest on inside/outside distinctions between movements and researchers. What does it mean to write and reflect not *about* or even *for* but *with* movements? This is a question I have tried to resolve practically through this book.

The core of my approach is identifying and engaging key movement discussions. Ranging from conversations about day-to-day organizing to large-scale debates about strategic direction, these discussions constitute what I call "movement-generated theory"—the self-reflective activity of people engaged in struggle.[12] This activity is frequently collective and enormously generative. In choosing to focus on it, however, I'm in no way arguing for uncritical celebration of whatever anyone says or does as part of movements. Rather, I am advocating for taking activist ideas and practices very seriously. In building movements and challenging injustice, anti-authoritarian organizers are collectively crafting complex visions, strategies, organizational forms, and organizing methods, all of which deserve critical attention.

Some of this critical attention requires thinking historically. Too often those of us engaged in movements take particular ideas and practices for granted, as if they've always existed. But consensus decision-making processes, collective structures, direct action tactics, and anti-oppression politics, to take just a few widely-used forms, all have histories. And as products of historical circumstances, there is absolutely nothing fixed or eternally "correct" about them. One key to taking activist ideas and practices seriously, then, is historicizing them—understanding their origins and trajectories. In this way, we can begin to develop a "history of the present," a genealogy of ways of thinking and acting that circulate in contemporary movements.[13] This kind of historical orientation guides my approach.

Following this approach, my research for this book involved two main sources. The first was written work, including zines, flyers, pamphlets, magazines, online discussions, journals, websites, correspondence, notes from meetings and events, and books. The second source for my research was interviews. I traveled to six different parts of the United States and Canada and conducted forty-seven in-depth interviews with a broad range of activists and organizers. I spent about a week each in Montreal, New Orleans (with a brief side-trip to Atlanta), New York City, the San Francisco Bay Area, Toronto, and Vancouver. I selected these cities based mostly on promising organizing work that I'd heard about or witnessed. While I knew that there was no way that they would represent all manifestations of another politics, I decided that this set of cities would at least give me a broad view of what was happening in larger urban areas. In all places, I tried to immerse myself in ongoing political work and activist communities. I spent most of my time conducting interviews, attending meetings and events, talking with organizers, and participating in protests.

Before visiting each city, I identified people to interview by asking for suggestions from well-connected activist friends and acquaintances all over North

America. These requests generated dozens of suggestions per city. I sorted through these suggestions with four criteria. First, I looked for organizers who might be understood as "anti-authoritarian" using the principles mentioned above. Second, I looked for people who were involved in grassroots organizing outside, or in addition to, activist scenes. Third, I looked for organizers who were reflective about their work, had strong critical analysis, and had deep political commitments. Fourth, I tried to get a broad cross-section of people in a given city, specifically in terms of race, gender, class, sexuality, political history, current work, and organizational affiliations. I also focused on anti-authoritarians younger than thirty-five, since another politics has manifested itself most distinctly among activists radicalized during the last two decades. In addition, I prioritized people whose ideas we rarely see in writing. Using these criteria, I picked ten to twelve people per city to approach about being interviewed and, of these, I usually managed to sit down with at least seven.

From the beginning of this project, I was clear that the people with whom I talked could never represent all anti-authoritarians. I had other priorities. I aimed to interview organizers who had sophisticated insights to offer and shared a politics based on grassroots organizing against all forms of domination. I also worked from the assumption that people who directly experience exploitation, oppression, and marginalization frequently have some of the most innovative ideas about how to organize and struggle. In these ways, my criteria seem to have worked well. Of the people I interviewed, two thirds identified as women or transgendered, half were people of color, nearly half came from poor or working-class backgrounds, and over a third identified as queer. In addition, fourteen were immigrants or children of immigrants. At the time of the interviews, only ten people were older than thirty-five and six were parents.

My approach to interviews was two-sided. I saw them as opportunities both to gather insights for sharing and to create space for intentional reflection in the lives of very busy organizers. In many cases, people whom I interviewed thanked me for giving them a chance to think through their work aloud and, in a couple of cases, I heard later that my visit to a particular city had helped to inspire longtime comrades to engage in deliberate collective discussions. I came to realize that many of us, as activists and organizers, have the experience of talking about our work, but far too rarely do we more deeply explore the political assumptions underlying our efforts, what we believe we are accomplishing (rather than what we want to accomplish), what we've learned through our work, how we've made changes based on what we've learned, and what those lessons mean for our visions for change.

My practice of conducting interviews was a work in progress. I sharpened my interview questions as the people with whom I spoke shared their own thoughts and priorities. My way of doing interviews was thus an ongoing process in which I incorporated things I had learned from previous conversations, listened to different ideas, and engaged in collaborative thinking. Even as my questions changed, the core themes I introduced were generally quite consistent: organizing approaches, anti-oppression politics, conceptions of leadership, organizational forms, movement strategy, and sustainability in political work.

As much as I could, I tried to let this book develop out of the interviews. Early in my research, I realized that the themes of politics, strategy, and organizing were central to how many organizers were thinking. Other topics, such as prefigurative politics, developed over time because they came up so consistently in interviews whether or not I asked about them. More topics became clear to me as I selectively transcribed the interviews and saw consistent ideas that a majority of people discussed. Of course, I understand that my politics and priorities were constantly present, even more so in this finished book. I have attempted, however, to reflect accurately and responsibly the insights that everyone shared with me. I have also attempted to emphasize the collective character of these ideas since they almost always come out of collaboration and struggle. In this way, I tend to think about what I share in this book as not so much individual brilliance, but rather the brilliance of our movements.

HOW THIS BOOK WORKS

This book is organized into three parts followed by a concluding chapter. The chapters in Part I lay out the background and political content of another politics. In chapter 1, I trace the radical traditions and movements that have led into the contemporary anti-authoritarian current, including anti-colonial struggles, socialist initiatives, feminist upsurges, anti-racist organizing efforts, and queer mobilizations. I highlight how anti-racist feminism, prison abolitionism, and anarchism have converged in another politics in recent decades, and look at other movements that have shaped and been shaped by the anti-authoritarian current.

Chapter 2 focuses on the politics bound up in the foundational "against" of this current. I describe the synthetic political approach at the heart of another politics, which flexibly draws on a wide set of theories and experiences. Borrowing a mode of analysis from *Upping the Anti,* I give an overview of the four "anti's"—the main formulations of "against"—in the anti-authoritarian current: anti-authoritarianism, anti-capitalism, anti-oppression, and anti-imperialism. I argue that these "anti's" have intertwined in important ways to lay the basis for the politics in this current.

In chapter 3, I turn to the reconstructive dimension of another politics, the foundational "beyond" that builds from prefigurative ideas and practices that organizers regularly use. Another politics, I suggest, rests in the contradiction of this approach. On the one hand, entirely liberated social relations are never fully possible in the context of domination. On the other hand, developing new social relations is crucial as part of building visionary movements. With this tension in mind, I survey popular prefigurative forms in the anti-authoritarian current: nonhierarchical decision-making structures, efforts to develop more caring ways of relating, and activities aimed at transforming dynamics of privilege and oppression. I also examine common pitfalls in prefigurative work.

The chapters in Part II look at emerging anti-authoritarian thinking on the question of strategy. Chapter 4 discusses some of the formidable obstacles to this type of thinking: fixating on principles over plans, fetishizing particular tactics, and organizing in crisis modes. I argue that more and more organizers are struggling to move past these obstacles and, in the process, are using a "movement-building" orientation. By this, I mean a way of approaching political work that is about moving beyond insular activist spaces, connecting with popular struggles, and building broad-based movements capable of engaging ordinary people.

With this orientation, anti-authoritarians are beginning to develop a strategic framework of "in the world but not of it." This framework, as I explain in chapter 5, is based on organizing in the world as it is while cultivating strategies toward the world that we want. I explore how anti-authoritarians are beginning to relate to reform struggles—fights to win improvements within the existing system. Long a source of controversy and confusion among radicals, such struggles can be opportunities to ground ourselves in day-to-day realities while pushing beyond what is considered "possible." I also investigate anti-authoritarian efforts to construct the infrastructure of a new society, particularly through counterinstitutions. Steering past subcultural isolation and limited service provision, these sorts of initiatives suggest modes of relating to people's immediate needs that also advance transformative movements.

The chapters in Part III explore pressing practical issues for the anti-authoritarian current. In chapter 6, I look at organizing specifically, examining how anti-authoritarians are increasingly distinguishing "organizing" from "activism" and, with this, developing an "organizing orientation."

This orientation, I argue, focuses attention on how to bring ordinary, non-activist people together and build collective power toward social transformation. I discuss the implications of this orientation and how it concretely manifests in anti-authoritarian political work. In addition, I highlight instructive challenges that anti-authoritarian organizing raises for more traditional organizing models.

Chapter 7 turns to the issue of leadership. In movements influenced by anti-authoritarian ideas, leadership has long been something to completely reject. I investigate this tendency, the problems that it creates, and how organizers are increasingly talking about and crafting anti-authoritarian practices of leadership and leadership development. I examine these practices in detail, arguing that they can help us increase accountability, transform dynamics of privilege and oppression, and deepen democracy in our movements.

In chapter 8, I focus on how anti-authoritarian organizers are grappling with questions of organization and organization-building. Looking at the problems and possibilities of available organizational forms—from parties to nonprofits, cadre formations to affinity groups—organizers are creating a "movement-building approach" to organization, centering not so much on idealized models as on organizational features that we are working to cultivate. I lay out this approach and also explore some of the organizational longings, mostly unfulfilled but nonetheless illuminating, that consistently come up in the anti-authoritarian current.

My concluding chapter argues that another politics is a project in motion—it is growing, experimenting, and consolidating. In the process, it's staking out a political pole and opening a political space, both efforts that have crucial implications for the landscape of left politics in the United States and Canada. I also suggest that the anti-authoritarian current, as it is, is not enough to make large-scale social transformation. Those of us in the current will have to push beyond where we are right now. To this end, I synthesize core lessons from organizers featured in the book and pose what I see as the biggest questions facing another politics.

While explaining how this book works, I also want to acknowledge its limitations—or at least those that have struck me while writing it. For one, my engagement with the anti-authoritarian current here primarily draws on the experiences of people based in large metropolitan areas. I'm certain that some of what I share has relevance for organizers in other contexts, but to speak adequately to the unique circumstances of suburbs, smaller cities, and rural areas would require a different book, one that I hope to see in the future. In addition, this book foregrounds the shared perspectives and activities of anti-authoritarian organizers on either side of the U.S.-Canada border. With a few exceptions, I don't discuss the important differences between these nation-state contexts (or regions within them) nor the impacts of those differences on movements. This, too, would require a different book. Finally, my account of another politics, in large part, does not include the vibrant Francophone anti-authoritarian milieu in Quebec. My inability to speak French kept me from interviewing many Francophone organizers and hindered my efforts to learn Quebecois movement history. So, I decided to focus on Anglophone Canada and the United States. Thankfully, more knowledgeable and rooted activist-researchers in Quebec are developing sharp analyses of their milieu.[14] There is much to learn from this.

WALKING WE ASK QUESTIONS

There are only a few things we can say with complete certainty. Most of what I write in this book doesn't fall into that category. So, I offer the words in the following pages with both audacity and humility. Writing with social movements, if it is going to make any difference in the world, has to be audacious. It has to sum up complex issues and histories, to make claims based on diverse experiences. At the same time, this audacity is perilous. In discussing the ideas of grassroots organizers in the civil rights movement, historian Charles Payne observes, "Generalizing about the beliefs of these people risks oversimplifying them."[15] This, in fact, is a constant danger in writing with movements: turning multidimensional perspectives and events into flattened representations.

Another risk is treating movements as objects. All too often researchers—academics especially—make use of movements in order to prove or advance specific theories. Used this way, the words and actions of people in struggle become significant mainly in terms of how they confirm an individual researcher's agenda or argument. Perhaps the biggest danger of all, though, is losing sight of dynamism. Writing with movements is like taking a photo of a human body in rapid motion. The snapshot captures the physique but misses the movement—the contracting muscles, pounding blood, and deep inhalations. The photo may be expertly composed, but it still only shows one angle of perspective within a split second of motion.

Conscious of these perils, I write with humility. Based on my conversations and experiences, I offer some propositions for understanding and doing another politics. All the while, I try to avoid flattening out complexities, sweeping up ideas into overarching theories, or mistaking snapshots for movements in motion. In doing this, I draw on a formulation from the

Zapatistas: "*preguntando caminamos,*" roughly translated as "walking we ask questions." As I understand and use it, this is an approach based not on certainties but ongoing collective inquiries. It suggests that those of us in struggle can produce vital knowledge together through a shared practice of asking about and reflecting on our circumstances. "Walking we ask questions" isn't about erecting ideological edifices, gaining scholarly acclaim, or assuaging individual activist egos; it's about continually learning as we travel together on a path toward another world.

I wrote this book with a few audiences in mind. First and foremost, this is for activists and organizers, particularly those who in some way identify with another politics. To you, I offer this book as my contribution to ongoing conversations. I hope this helps us to become more reflective, imaginative, and effective in our organizing. This is also for those who care about achieving greater justice, peace, equality, and ecological sustainability in the world, and who engage in action, whether electoral campaigns, union drives, or community clean-ups. To you, I offer this book in order to share some of the insights that another politics has to offer and to push us all to think and act more intentionally, lovingly, and synthetically. Let's go deeper together. And finally, this is for those who are interested in social movements and social change. To you, I offer this book to suggest that we can learn the most about movements, social relations, and perhaps humanity itself by participating in collective fights for justice and dignity. I invite you to join me in the process of learning from and through struggle as we walk and ask questions.

PART ONE

Politics

1. "Fighting against amnesia"

Movement Histories of Another Politics

> In part, capitalism and oppression rule through what we call "the social organization of forgetting," which is based on the annihilation of our social and historical memories . . . . This social organization of forgetting is crucial to the way in which social power works in our society. We no longer remember the past struggles that won us the social gains, social programs, and human rights that we now often take for granted.
>
> Gary Kinsman and Patrizia Gentile

Indigenous activists and allies march as part of an Idle No More national day of action on January 11, 2013, in Vancouver, British Columbia. (Photo by Caelie Frampton)

AT ONE POINT DURING my conversation with Clare Bayard, she beautifully laid out the essential basis for any discussion of movements and radical politics. As an organizer and educator with the Catalyst Project in San Francisco, Bayard assists activist groups all over the United States with political education and organizational development. Based on her experience, she has a finely honed appreciation for history-telling and a grounded understanding of how rarely it happens, even in movement spaces. "I'm always trying to fight against this historical amnesia of 'this is just the moment that exists by itself,'" Bayard explained.

This sort of amnesia—an experience of the present detached from the past—is pervasive in North America, common in schools, politics, and media. As activist-scholars Gary Kinsman and Patrizia Gentile suggest, systematic forgetting is deeply connected to the organization and administration of power in our society. Given this, it's not terribly surprising that movements—and writings about them—are frequently afflicted by historical amnesia. Resisting forgetting is rarely easy, even for those of us engaged in collective struggles for justice and dignity. Remembering requires conscious, dedicated work.

This chapter is an effort to fight against amnesia. Over the last decade, there has been a lot of talk about the "new radicalism" or the "new anarchism."[1] While I don't deny that there is a quality of newness to recent anti-authoritarian activity, the backstory is much more complicated. Another politics bears the imprints of many previous political experiences and traditions. It has also been importantly shaped by the more recent convergence of a variety of radical politics and broader-based movements. To properly understand the contemporary anti-authoritarian current, then, we have to look at the histories that have produced it and continue to animate it.

There isn't a linear story to tell here. When it comes to movements, there rarely is. I've found that a more useful way to understand the histories leading into the anti-authoritarian current is to trace influential strands of politics and struggle.[2] These strands weave in and out, often intertwining in unexpected ways and sometimes temporarily receding from view. In this chapter, I sketch a brief history of the more significant, longer running strands that have shaped another politics. In looking closely at these, we can see how past movements have catalyzed and carried constellations of ideas and practices that are still widely used by activists today. With this sketch in hand, I then turn to three particularly crucial strands that have converged in recent decades: anti-racist feminism, prison abolitionism, and anarchism. This convergence, in my view, has laid the basis for what is emerging as another politics in the United States and Canada, shaping its development through movements and mobilizations from the early 2000s into the present.

STARTING POINTS

Many movements and lineages of struggle have created visions of social transformation and revolutionary strategies to achieve those visions. What has historically distinguished anti-authoritarian politics is its determination to fight colonialism, capitalism, and the state-form (and, over time, other systems of oppression) *while* putting liberatory visions into practice. This two-part orientation, the combined "against" and "beyond" that I discuss more in the following chapters, is the anti-authoritarian kernel that has been nourished through many seasons of struggle.

We should begin with Indigenous resistance to European colonization. Anti-authoritarian politics, in significant but mostly unexplored ways, strongly resonates with certain lineages of anti-colonial struggle across the globe. Such resistance is over five hundred years old, stretching from the Arawak peoples' efforts to survive after the invasion led by Christopher Columbus to eighteenth-century fugitive African slave communities in what is now Brazil to contemporary struggles of the Ogoni in Nigeria and the Kanien'kehaka (Mohawks) across Ontario, Quebec, and New York.[3] Many Indigenous peoples have sustained forms of social organization without— and, at times, against—state structures and capitalist relations, and some continue to do so.[4] While non-Indigenous movements have historically had an uneasy relationship with this strand of resistance, it has impacted them nonetheless, especially in Canada and in some regions of the United States. More than any other lineage of resistance in North America, Indigenous struggles for self-determination have consistently challenged the territorial control of nation-states, offered a living alternative to private property, and foregrounded colonialism as an ongoing system of domination.

We can trace another strand from abolitionism, the movement to abolish slavery and free slaves of African descent. Abolitionism grew out of the efforts of enslaved Black people to resist slaveholders and slaveholder institutions throughout the Americas. In the late eighteenth century, it emerged more coherently as a movement through the diligent efforts of Black and white anti-slavery activists. In North America, abolitionists organized speaking tours and conventions, published newspapers and pamphlets, and assisted with direct action initiatives such as the Underground Railroad. Their efforts also inspired a wave of groundbreaking feminist political activity. Drawing on Christianity, the radical wing of the abolitionist movement combined commitments to confronting slaveholding forces, enacting values of racial equality, and overturning the white supremacist social order. Ultimately, the movement managed to spark a civil war with impacts that still echo into the present.[5] Abolitionism also helped to inaugurate a tradition of Black freedom struggle that has carried powerfully through subsequent movements and steadily highlighted race as a key social fault line.[6] As well, it has left an enduring legacy of morally charged radicalism oriented toward egalitarian principles rather than seemingly fixed realities of oppression.

We can trace yet another strand from nineteenth-century Europe, where working-class movements emerged on an unprecedented scale. Growing out of labor struggles, these movements created the context for a socialist milieu with a vibrant patchwork of organizations, campaigns, and publications. Radicals in this milieu were united by the goal of achieving a society beyond capitalism, but they differed on how to get there. Indeed, the second part of the nineteenth century saw major debates around this question among socialist revolutionaries, most famously between Karl Marx and the anarchist Mikhail Bakunin. While many in the developing Marxist tendency looked to seize state power as an instrument to create an egalitarian society, anarchists aimed to abolish state power and develop nonstate ways of organizing societies. "The marxians argue that only dictatorship—theirs, of course—can establish the people's freedom," wrote Bakunin. However, "no dictatorship can have any aim other than lasting as long as it can . . . : freedom can be conjured only by freedom, that is to say, by uprising by the entire people and by free organization of the toiling masses from the bottom up."[7] This stance, fundamental to anarchism, is a prefigurative one: the means (popular struggle and deeply democratic organization) must be consistent with the ends (a free and egalitarian society). It has had a lasting influence.

Another important source of debate in the socialist milieu had to do with the centrality of capitalism and class. Many socialists argued that capitalism is the primary system of social domination and that all other forms of oppression have developed from it. Some socialist dissidents challenged this idea, suggesting that forms of oppression based on race and gender have their own autonomous logics even as they dynamically interact with capitalism. During the first part of the twentieth century, these debates concerned what were frequently known as the "National Question," the "Negro Question," and the "Woman Question" among communists, though they often went by other terms among unaffiliated socialists and anarchists. At times, they created spaces for innovative forms of anticapitalist organizing and thinking against patriarchy and racism. For the most part, however, these were unresolved debates in the socialist milieu, including its anti-authoritarian wing. They would come up again and again in subsequent upsurges of struggle, and continue to remain central today.[8]

The late nineteenth and early twentieth centuries were times of massive strikes, widespread organizing in factories and communities, regular street clashes between workers and police, and growing revolutionary sentiments.

In the midst of all this, anarchism emerged as an important political current in working-class movements. What distinguished anarchists from other radicals in these movements was their opposition to capitalism, landlordism, and the state as fundamental forms of domination, as well as their commitment to self-management, mutual aid, and social equality. Anarchism quickly developed a global character. Propelled by migration and circulations of struggle, it came to flourish not only in Europe but also in the Americas, Asia, Australia, and, to a limited extent, Africa. This era's anarchist politics and movements, at their best, represented a nonstatist form of socialism rooted in working-class and peasant communities. They generated a political strand that has woven through many subsequent antiauthoritarian efforts.[9]

FOUNDATIONAL EXPERIENCES

During the first decades of the twentieth century, this politics found something of a home in the Industrial Workers of the World (IWW), a militant labor union active in the United States and Canada. Founded in 1905, the IWW organized expansively, developing campaigns among textile workers in Massachusetts and New Jersey, teamsters in British Columbia, lumber workers in the northwestern and the southeastern United States, miners in Nevada and northern Ontario, and many others. Through this work, the IWW crafted new forms of bottom-up organizing, particularly among those whom other unions considered "unorganizable." And they sought to enact their values—democracy, equality, and solidarity—in the form of their organizing efforts, whether by resisting racial segregation and antiimmigrant sentiments, organizing women workers, or insisting on direct democracy and direct action.[10] In line with this, radicals in IWW described one of their core aims as building "the new society in the shell of the old."[11] This continues to be an influential prefigurative formulation.

The IWW declined significantly as it faced state repression during World War I and as many radicals gravitated into Communist parties during the 1920s and 1930s. By the 1940s and 1950s, however, a new anarchist-influenced current was emerging. Inspired by the Christian radical Leo Tolstoy and the Indian anti-colonial leader Mohandas Gandhi, small circles of faith-based activists combined elements of anarchism and socialism with a deep commitment to nonviolence, known as pacifism. They built organizations such as the Fellowship of Reconciliation (FOR) and the War Resisters League (WRL). They also formulated a prefigurative politics based on living and acting in accordance with their radical values. As part of this, they used the tactic of civil disobedience (intentionally breaking laws to show that they are unjust) and a Quaker decision-making practice called "consensus" (making decisions through collective deliberation and unanimous consent).

While the United States and its allies faced off with the Soviet Union in the Cold War, these small groups of radical pacifists steadfastly resisted militarism and helped lay the basis for the much broader peace movement that began to emerge in the late 1950s. Drawing on the legacy of abolitionism, some of these activists also helped to shape a new upsurge in the Black freedom struggle that would eventually become known as the civil rights movement. Although they had participated in struggles against racial segregation beginning in the early 1940s, white and Black organizers from FOR and the WRL played especially crucial roles in advising African American community activists in Montgomery, Alabama, when these activists launched a landmark boycott campaign to desegregate buses in 1955. In the following years, radical pacifists ran influential nonviolence workshops throughout the southern United States and assisted in developing the strategies that would come to define the movement.[12]

As much as civil rights movement activists adopted practices from radical pacifism, they also reinvented them. This was especially true in the wing of the movement associated with the Student Nonviolent Coordinating Committee (SNCC). Growing out of the wave of southern student sit-ins to desegregate lunch counters, SNCC was founded in 1960 by mostly young African Americans with assistance from two older Black radicals, FOR activist James Lawson and longtime community organizer Ella Baker. SNCC grew into an organizational center for anti-racist direct action and community organizing across the South during the first part of the sixties.

Part of what distinguished SNCC from other leading civil rights organizations was its commitment to a kind of participatory democratic practice and nonhierarchical organizational culture. Early on, Baker described this as an "inclination toward *group-centered leadership,* rather than toward a *leader-centered group pattern of organization.*"[13] Instead of relying on charismatic leaders, SNCC activists tried to organize in ways that rested on broad, egalitarian participation and collective problem-solving and decision-making. With SNCC, this was no lofty political commitment; it grew out of the experiences of organizers working to build unity and power in Black communities under the constant threat of racist violence.

SNCC also worked to enact a transformative culture, often known as the "beloved community," in which people organized together in racially integrated groups on a basis of equality and respect. In their efforts, they attempted to challenge and change social relations of white supremacy, particularly racial segregation. While there were real limitations on how much SNCC activists could achieve given the tremendous historical weight of racism, they made an enormous contribution to organizing Black communities in the South and to undermining white supremacy. They also offered, by example, a revolutionary vision of how people could relate with one another, individually and collectively. SNCC, along with others in the civil rights movement, inspired and galvanized people across the United States and north of the border as well.[14]

THE THIRD WORLD EXPLOSION

As the Black freedom movement erupted in the United States, a wave of anti-colonial resistance was radiating across the Third World. This wave grew out of liberation movements that won national independence in Latin America during the nineteenth century and in Asia and Africa during the twentieth century. These movements, from Bolivia to India, developed new forms of revolutionary struggle and consciousness, often drawing on—and reshaping—socialist politics.[15] In the period following World War II, these efforts accelerated and spread. By the early 1960s, the world was on fire: the Vietnamese resisted French and then U.S. military occupations, the Cubans overthrew a U.S. puppet dictatorship, and the people of Angola fought Portuguese colonial rule, among many other struggles. In these circumstances, recently decolonized countries and anti-colonial movements crafted a set of politics and sensibilities of Third World liberation that circulated widely.[16]

Black freedom struggles in North America and anti-colonial struggles in the Third World, mutually influencing each other, propelled racism and colonialism onto the center stage. This confluence significantly catalyzed the movements of the period known as "the sixties" (really, the late 1950s through the mid-1970s). As part of this, revolutionaries across the globe combined elements of socialism, anti-racism, and anti-colonialism into a more generalized form of anti-imperialism that became a leading political orientation on the left.[17] This orientation was very generative politically, but it also had problems. One was that it associated effectiveness and militancy with hierarchical, highly masculinized forms of organization. Pushing aside the nonhierarchical practices and culture that SNCC had developed, this association deeply influenced the central leadership structure that many revolutionary organizations came to use.

The Black Panther Party for Self-Defense (BPP) played a key role in honing and popularizing this anti-imperialist orientation and its organizational prescriptions. Launched in 1966 in Oakland, California, the BPP combined confrontational challenges with state authorities, organizing in African American communities, and the development of needs-based counterinstitutions. As their popularity grew, BPP chapters sprang up all over the United States. With their success, the BPP also faced intense state surveillance, harassment, and violence, which compounded the already-strong tendency toward centralization in the organization.[18] It is a testament to their courage and vision that they managed to sustain a powerful prefigurative dimension in their work while contending with this targeted disruption.[19]

Ashanti Alston, who was active in the BPP and then in the underground Black Liberation Army, described this dimension in his experiences:

> It [the BPP] gave me, and a whole lot of us, a way to start transforming our lives into what we envisioned a revolutionary life would be—one in combat against this system, and at the same time, [one focused on] creating the kind of new society that we wanted. That's pretty much what we were doing. The free breakfast programs, the free clothing programs, the free clinics was also our way of getting people to envision, in the richest country in the world, the possibility that all of this could be, should be, must be free. And that was heavy stuff. And I know them programs, way more than our guns, was what attracted so many especially Black people to the Party.

These programs, carried out by dedicated Panther volunteers, provided free meals, clothes, and healthcare in Black communities across the United States. And they weren't simply social services; building on longstanding African American traditions of mutual aid and echoing the IWW, the Panthers called them "survival programs pending revolution."[20] These programs met immediate popular needs, challenged social relations of scarcity and subordination, and laid infrastructure for a new society. At the same time, the BPP created a context for people to reimagine and transform themselves.[21] As Alston recalled, there were broad discussions in the BPP about "the new man" and "the new woman," as well as efforts to develop common expectations about how people should treat one another. "In a way," he pointed out, "we were augmenting Black cultural, even religious, traditions of 'brother/sister,' and the survival/liberatory aspects of Black communal church." These were crucial contributions.

Taking inspiration from the BPP, activists in the United States and Canada launched Asian, Black, Chicano, First Nations and American Indian, poor white, Puerto Rican, Québécois, and other liberation movements.[22] In various ways, they drew on the BPP model to build organizations oriented to both fighting the system and serving their communities. Together, their efforts transformed social relations of white supremacy, which many activists understood as deeply connected to capitalism, while also foregrounding the importance of struggles by racially oppressed people. As well, these movements developed a collective revolutionary imagination and concrete relationships of solidarity that linked struggles from Havana to Harlem, Algiers to Montreal, Beijing to Oakland, Hanoi to Toronto.[23]

LIBERATION MOVEMENTS MULTIPLY

These anti-racist movements created a context for the emergence of other liberation struggles in the United States and Canada.[24] The civil rights movement, particularly the wing associated with SNCC, was especially crucial in catalyzing the student movement. Starting in the early 1960s, leading white student activists began looking to southern organizing as a source of inspiration. In the United States, many of these activists joined Students for a Democratic Society (SDS). In Canada, many were or became involved in, first, the Student Union for Peace Action and, later, groups affiliated with the Canadian Union of Students and Students for a Democratic University.

Through experiences of campus occupations, activist conferences, and community organizing experiments, student activists worked to create their own participatory democratic practices in which everyone had a say in decisions. Growing out of their vision of a more thoroughly democratic society and their understanding of the movement in the southern United States, these activists also developed collective sensibilities that favored embodying their values in their work and relationships. And as student radicals helped to launch the movement against the war in Vietnam, they brought these practices and sensibilities with them.

By the late 1960s, such prefigurative commitments were widespread in the New Left, as the convergence of sixties movements is often called. In 1969, former SDS president Greg Calvert posed a question on the minds of many young radicals: "What are the embryonic forms of revolutionary society which must be created, however embryonically, as we work?"[25] Activists across North America developed answers to this question through all sorts of practical experiments, including institutions such as food co-ops and underground newspapers, revolutionary formations such as collectives and national organizations, new ways of organizing daily life such as housing co-ops and intentional communities, and countercultural values that emphasized freedom, self-determination, and cooperation.[26]

There were also strains in the New Left. Activists grappled with combining efficacy and liberatory aspirations in the face of daunting challenges of strategy and direction. Some, in the search for effectiveness, turned to Leninist forms of politics and organization with very limited space for prefigurative concerns.[27] In the late 1960s, this turn took one or another of two main forms. Some radicals, through groups such as I Wor Kuen, the October League, and En Lutte, chose to focus on building revolutionary parties through mass organizing.[28] Others, through groups such as the Black Liberation Army, the Front de libération du Québec, and the Weather Underground, turned to forms of armed struggle in the hopes of advancing further waves of mass movement.[29] The BPP, SDS, and other groups experienced splits along these and related lines.[30]

Both orientations—party-building and armed struggle—grew out of activists' dedication to social transformation and shared desires for more seriousness and organization. They had substantial impacts as well. The party-builders contributed to organizing work in communities and workplaces, and the armed groups managed to create instability for governing institutions. But these orientations also had real limitations. Indeed, while debates between the two camps were often bitter, they shared striking similarities: they were based on troubling vanguardist revolutionary models, they frequently romanticized anti-imperialist movements in the Third World, and they often formulaically sought to import forms of organization and strategy from elsewhere. Most importantly, both orientations became more and more disconnected from the societies in which they struggled, and neither managed to build the revolutionary movements that they wanted. In their successes and their failures, however, they posed a key question: How can radicals, as small minorities in North America, take action that meaningfully moves toward large-scale social transformation? This question remains pressing.

The women's liberation movement developed out of another problem in the New Left: its failure to live up to its stated commitment to egalitarianism.[31] One of the most striking ways this manifested was that, in New Left groups, men dominated highly valued leadership roles while women were frequently relegated to less-valued secretarial and caregiving work. Inspired by the Black freedom struggle, predominately white women activists started consciousness-raising groups to discuss these kinds of experiences of oppression in not only left organizations but also society more generally. These efforts blossomed by the late 1960s into a movement that named its enemy as patriarchy and began to develop a shared feminist politics. Activists in the movement created bookstores, publications, and organizations. They turned violence against women into a political issue, and built rape crisis centers and women's shelters. They also targeted institutions perpetuating and profiting from patriarchy, such as beauty pageants, bridal fairs, and even Wall Street.

Many in the radical wing of the women's liberation movement worked against the cultures and organizational models that they had experienced in other movements. They challenged dominant ideas of leadership, decision-making, and organizing, and began developing nonhierarchical approaches. Working in small groups, they built relationships with one another through shared experiences and used informal kinds of consensus to make collective decisions. They also introduced new ways of thinking about what counts as politics. With the slogan "the personal is political," feminist activists claimed what were previously considered private, everyday experiences in women's lives (sex, child-raising, housework) as arenas for collective action. The movement thus challenged not only patriarchal relations, but also many prevailing assumptions on the left.

These efforts, while groundbreaking, had their problems too. Sometimes opposition to hierarchies in the movement manifested as feminists "trashing" (publicly denouncing) those who took on leadership roles or who were designated as leaders by the media. Other times it manifested as a general rejection of formal structure and organization, a practice that frequently contributed to informal leadership cliques rather than equal participation in organizing.[32] And even as feminist activists brought a new quality of attention to the ways in which power relations are reproduced in movements, many who were white and class-privileged overlooked how they were implicated in relations of race and class. Women of color feminists, as I discuss further below, pushed at these limitations and sparked crucial movement debates. As the women's liberation movement wrestled with these challenges, activists insisted on bringing their values and aspirations into their lives. This is a vital legacy.[33]

Like the women's liberation movement, the gay and lesbian movement was nourished by a broader context of liberation struggles. Although there were earlier sparks in San Francisco and elsewhere, a widely acknowledged initial flashpoint for this movement was the Stonewall riots in New York City in 1969, when Black and Puerto Rican drag queens, lesbians, and gay street people physically resisted a police raid of the Stonewall Inn, a gay bar. Riots continued for several nights afterward.[34] In the aftermath, people radicalized by these events joined with gay and lesbian activists influenced by their experiences in other liberation movements. Together, they formed the Gay Liberation Front (GLF), which aimed to transform heterosexist relations and other systems of oppression. The GLF model quickly spread across the United States and Canada as activists formed similar groups along with publications, social clubs, and cultural institutions. In significant ways, they struggled for self-determined public spaces like bars, bathhouses, and streets. As well, gay and lesbian activists disrupted and demonstrated against a whole range of institutions that sustained heterosexism, such as the American Psychiatric Association with its listing of homosexuality as a mental illness.

The gay and lesbian movement faced some challenges similar to those of the women's liberation movement. In particular, activists struggled with internal hierarchies of race, gender, and class, and these dynamics motivated autonomous lesbian and people of color organizing efforts. Nevertheless, the politics that the movement developed were uniquely transformative. They challenged conventional gender roles, notions of family, and ways of relating sexually. Many lesbians also combined these politics with those they were encountering and creating in the women's liberation movement to challenge what they saw as patriarchy buttressed by "compulsory heterosexuality."[35] In fighting these forms of domination, the movement opened up new possibilities for gender, sexuality, kinship, and political action. It laid the basis for an explosion of trans and queer identities, communities, and practices that many radicals are continuing to explore and expand today.[36]

ANTI-RACIST FEMINISM

The liberation movements of the 1960s created new possibilities, posed new questions, and activated new collectivities. Even as the pace of movement activity began to slow in the United States and Canada by the mid-1970s, activists were building on these very recent and powerful experiences. In doing so, they developed innovative radical initiatives that drew on some of the best features of previous movements while trying to move past their problems. Indeed, the three major movement strands that have converged in the contemporary anti-authoritarian current have their beginnings in this period.

The first of these strands is usually known as anti-racist or women of color feminism. This politics had roots in earlier movement experiences, particularly the overlap between abolitionism and nineteenth-century feminism and, in the early twentieth century, feminist or woman-oriented efforts within anti-racist struggles. It bloomed in the liberation movements of the 1960s and came into its own in the 1970s and 1980s. And although this politics took many routes, they all started in a similar place: radical women of color, many of them lesbians, criticizing the ways in which existing movements failed to account for their experiences of oppression. In the United States, these discussions often began in broader, mixed-gender organizations, such as SNCC, the BPP, the National Welfare Rights

Organization, and the Young Lords, in which women of color sometimes created their own caucuses. In both Canada and the United States, they also happened within the frequently white-dominated spaces of the women's liberation movement, including women's centers, International Women's Day events, and more informal groups.

While radical women of color never completely left these mixed contexts, many launched autonomous formations. During the 1970s, activists in the United States started organizations such as the Third World Women's Alliance, Women of All Red Nations, and the National Black Feminist Organization. In the Canadian context, autonomous organizing blossomed in the 1980s with groups such as the Black Women's Collective and the National Organization of Immigrant and Visible Minority Women. In these and other initiatives, radical women of color engaged in activism related to health and reproductive rights, interpersonal and police violence, anti-poverty and labor organizing, and immigrant rights, among other issues. Coming together in groups, conferences, publishing collectives, and social scenes, these activists began creating shared politics grounded in their lives and struggles. Through these collaborations, they also constructed the category "women of color" as a new, radical political identity.[37]

The Combahee River Collective, a Black feminist group in Boston, offered one of the most influential articulations of these emerging women of color feminist ideas in a 1977 statement. They wrote, "We are actively committed to struggling against racial, sexual, heterosexual, and class oppression, and see as our particular task the development of integrated analysis and practice based upon the fact that the major systems of oppression are interlocking."[38] This "integrated analysis," which subsequent efforts have developed further, suggests that the ways that women of color simultaneously experience systems of oppression illuminate the interconnections among these power relations in everyone's lives. In other words, social relations of capitalism, racism, patriarchy, and heterosexism operate with and through each other—they are "interlocking." Following from this, truly revolutionary politics is necessarily a multilayered fight against oppression.[39]

This form of analysis has circulated widely over the last few decades. Partly, this is thanks to a cohort of women of color feminist scholars and others who have struggled to make space for these ideas in frequently hostile academic contexts. Drawing on early movement conceptions, these scholars' writing, teaching, and organizing efforts have elaborated what has come to be called an "intersectional" analysis.[40] Many students have become familiar with this through the "race, class, gender" trio in humanities and social sciences classes.[41] By various names, this integrated analysis has permeated many activist contexts too, although often more rhetorically than practically. It is now commonplace for radical groups to indicate their commitments to "fighting all systems of oppression," and many draw on vocabulary from women of color feminism to talk about power.

Anti-racist feminist efforts have also crafted vital prefigurative ideas and practices. Here, again, the Combahee River Collective offered an evocative framework: "In the practice of our politics we do not believe that the end always justifies the means. Many reactionary and destructive acts have been done in the name of achieving 'correct' political goals. As feminists we do not want to mess over people in the name of politics. We believe in collective process and a nonhierarchical distribution of power within our own group and in our vision of a revolutionary society."[42] This gets at one invaluable contribution of women of color feminism: a desire for a way of doing politics that doesn't treat people as objects or instruments—a politics that doesn't "mess people over" in its own name. With this desire, many radical women of color have tried to hold a space for a politics based in love, a politics through which we all can become more whole human beings.[43] These aspects of women of color feminism have become much more widespread over the years and have strongly influenced the anti-authoritarian current.

These aspects also resonate with other formulations of prefigurative politics. The ways in which women of color activists have enacted them, however, have offered an important innovation. This is because women of color feminist organizing has developed, in theory and practice, a specific understanding of coalition and difference. In this understanding, coalition is neither about setting aside differences nor about understanding differences as necessarily pitting people against one other. Instead, women of color feminists have put forward a model of coalition that is about working *across* differences: acknowledging how we are situated in systems of oppression and exploitation, building bridges from where we stand in order to fight for a better world, and indicating transformative ways for people to relate with one another.[44] Activists generated this model through early women of color organizations, such as the Coalition of Visible Minority Women in Toronto, which brought together women coming from diverse backgrounds.[45] Radical women of color also honed this model through participation in often uneasy collaborative efforts with men and white women, such as the series of mid-1970s defense campaigns in the United States for Joan Little and other women of color facing criminal trials for using lethal force to protect themselves from sexual violence.[46] This model of coalition has thus been central to women of color feminism, which has, in turn, introduced it into broader movement contexts.

Over the last decade, one of the most crucial conduits for circulating these politics has been the organization INCITE! Women of Color Against Violence. Now with chapters and affiliates across the United States, INCITE! grew out of a 2000 conference at the University of California, Santa Cruz called "The Color of Violence: Violence Against Women of Color." Initially intended as an intervention in the anti-violence against women movement, the organization has since blossomed into a vital space for further developing integrated analysis and practice.[47]

Through conferences, publications, and collaborative organizing efforts, INCITE! has connected more university-based thinking around intersectionality with community-based work. Groups connected to INCITE!, as part of this process, have introduced important new modes of struggle against oppression. For example, the Brooklyn-based INCITE! affiliate Sista II Sista pioneered community organizing methods focused on young working-class women of color, including collective forms of leadership development, political education through storytelling, and public interventions in interpersonal and state violence.[48] Meanwhile, INCITE! has also articulated an influential critique of what they call the "nonprofit industrial complex"—the circuit of state funding, foundations, and nonprofit organizations—as containing and undermining radical movements. As part of this, individuals and organizations involved with INCITE! have begun to explore alternatives to these forms of funding and organization.[49] I describe this in more detail in chapter 5.

Along with other radical women of color activists and initiatives, INCITE! has helped to elaborate a set of politics and practices based on an intersectional analysis that includes an oppositional stance toward capitalism and the state, especially state violence against women of color. These politics and practices have had a wide influence across movements, including reproductive justice organizing, the immigrant rights movement, anti-violence organizing, radical queer activism, domestic worker organizing, and the occupy movement.[50] As I discuss in the next chapter, women of color feminism has also significantly shaped how many in the anti-authoritarian current think about power relations and organizing.[51]

PRISON ABOLITIONISM

A second crucial strand leading from the 1970s into the contemporary anti-authoritarian current is prison abolitionism, a set of politics aimed at the complete elimination of institutions of incarceration. In significant ways, this strand grew from the movement for the abolition of slavery as well as other mobilizations against racialized social control. The long Black freedom struggle has consistently challenged white supremacist institutions of confinement, from slave ships to prisons, and put forward powerful visions of a post-abolitionist society.[52] As well, this strand draws on groundbreaking socialist (particularly anarchist) contributions in the early twentieth century that identified prisons as mechanisms for silencing dissidents and maintaining class relations in capitalist societies.[53]

While these earlier experiences provided important resources, the struggles of the 1960s and 1970s were really the crucible that formed prison abolitionist politics. Amid the explosion of liberation movements, this period saw the widespread radicalization of prisoners, particularly incarcerated people of color. Current and former prisoners, such as George Jackson, Malcolm X, and Eldridge Cleaver, came to play leading roles in Black liberation politics especially. As governments responded to movement successes with repression, more and more radicals found themselves behind bars. Movement-based defense campaigns for leaders facing or serving prison time became commonplace.

In these circumstances, prisoners started organizing, built organizations, and engaged in mass collective actions. Perhaps the most high-profile of these actions was the rebellion at Attica Correctional Facility in upstate New York in 1971, during which prisoners forged an alliance that took over the prison for five days before being bloodily quashed by police. The events at Attica quickly became a compelling symbol, inspiring waves of subsequent uprisings and strikes. Across the border in Canada, a major focus of attention was Millhaven Maximum Security Prison in southern Ontario, where prisoners staged a hunger strike in 1976 that quickly spread nationally and mobilized supporters on the outside.[54]

A broad prison abolitionist politics emerged from this confluence of struggles and events during the 1970s. It brought together prisoner organizing efforts, revolutionary formations, prisoner support campaigns, radical pacifist initiatives, and feminist collectives. In 1976, the Prison Research Education Action Project (PREAP), an abolitionist collective, offered a sharpened version of these politics in their *Instead of Prisons* handbook. "The oppressive situation of prisoners," they asserted, "can only be relieved by abolishing the cage and, with it, the notion of punishment."[55] Toward this end, PREAP put forward an ambitious "three-pronged abolitionist ideology: (1) Economic and social justice for all, (2) concern for all victims and (3) rather than punishment, reconciliation in a caring community."[56] This ideology, they believed, would be the basis for building wider alliances and, ultimately, a prison abolitionist movement. It would take years more for this to fully happen.

During the 1980s, prison abolitionism mostly faded from view as "law and order" politics initiated by ruling elites strategically shifted prevailing public discussions about crime and punishment. The so-called "war on drugs"—with longer prison sentences, vast new prison construction, and huge injections of government funding into policing—transformed the landscape of criminal justice in the United States and, more recently, in Canada. This transformation, still in progress, has led to skyrocketing rates of incarceration, which disproportionately affect racialized communities, poor people, and those who don't fit within dominant gender norms.[57]

In opposition to this expanding carceral system, small networks of dedicated activists inside and outside prisons carried on organizing. Some came together around publishing projects that spanned prison walls, such as *Bulldozer/Prison News Service* in Canada and *Prison Legal News* in the United States.[58] Others focused on supporting political prisoners, many of them serving decades-long sentences for their movement activities in the 1960s and 1970s.[59] Still others developed campaigns to change particularly oppressive conditions inside prisons, such as prolonged forms of isolation, pervasive sexual assault, and lack of access to adequate health care. Radicals involved in these initiatives nurtured prison abolitionist visions.[60]

The 1990s saw the emergence of a movement against what activists increasingly called the prison industrial complex (PIC), the interlocking set of institutions and social relations based on surveillance, policing, and imprisonment.[61] This movement blossomed out of enduring prison activist networks of the 1980s, efforts to end the death penalty in the United States, and rapidly growing organizing against police violence in communities of color.[62] In 1998, the radical edge of this movement came together at an ambitious abolitionist conference in Berkeley, California, called Critical Resistance (CR), which subsequently led to the founding of an organization of the same name.[63] Since then, individuals and groups affiliated with and inspired by CR have played a vital role in the movement against the PIC, whether through CR chapters in places such as Oakland or New Orleans or through organizations such as End the Prison Industrial Complex in Kingston, Ontario.[64]

CR and allied groups have revitalized and reinvented prison abolitionist politics in North America. Mobilizing the broader analysis of the PIC, they have expanded abolitionism to target not only prisons, but also other institutions of incarceration, including immigrant detention centers and youth correctional facilities.[65] As well, they have elaborated a longstanding radical critique of policing as a form of social control, especially in low-income communities of color. And drawing on women of color feminism, they have developed a sophisticated understanding of carceral institutions within the broader arrangement of power in our society. As CR writes, "The PIC depends upon the oppressive systems of racism, classism, sexism, and homophobia. It includes human rights violations, the death penalty, industry and labor issues, policing, courts, media, community powerlessness, the imprisonment of political prisoners, and the elimination of dissent."[66] And in turn, they argue, the PIC is crucial for maintaining existing relations of exploitation and oppression. This new generation of prison abolitionists proclaims that just, safe, and healthy communities are only possible in a world without cages and cops.[67]

These anti-PIC organizers are refashioning at least two key abolitionist approaches.[68] The first is a strategic framework based not on reforming institutions of incarceration, but getting rid of them altogether. In the words of CR, "Our goal is not to improve the system even further, but to shrink the system into non-existence."[69] For many organizers, this means fighting construction of prisons and other detention facilities and helping incarcerated people get out and stay out. Secondly, abolitionists have begun to imagine and enact, in necessarily limited ways, a world beyond punishment and prisons. A central question here is the one posed by writer and activist Victoria Law: "How do we keep our communities and ourselves safe without relying on the police?"[70] Motivated through collaboration with anti-racist feminists in the anti-violence against women movement, abolitionists have started to explore alternatives to state-based strategies for dealing with violence in communities and interpersonal relationships.[71] As I suggest in chapter 5, this prefigurative approach has opened small but significant spaces for organizations and communities to work on reducing harm and resolving conflict without resorting to cops and courts.

Self-consciously drawing on the struggle against slavery, CR and allied groups have created a political context in which "abolitionist" has become a much more widely used radical identification. The politics associated with this identification fundamentally challenges the legitimacy of the state to regulate, police, and punish people. In this way, it has opened into a critique of all forms of state violence and their deep interconnections with gender, race, and class relations.[72] At the same time, this politics has provoked activists and organizers across North America to imagine and build organizations, institutions, and ways of relating that aren't oriented around the state.[73] In these ways, abolitionists have played a crucial role in the anti-authoritarian current as they have begun to construct a broadly anti-statist politics with anti-capitalist undertones, grounded in community-based racial justice struggles and, increasingly, feminist and queer organizing.[74]

RECONFIGURED ANARCHISM

The other major movement strand that has converged in the contemporary anti-authoritarian current is anarchism. This is a reconfigured anarchism, however. While it draws on the broad anarchist tradition, it owes just as much to the values-based actions of radical pacifists of the 1950s, the direct action and participatory democracy of SNCC, the confrontational ethos of the New Left, and the transformative ideas and organizing practices of the women's and gay liberation movements. These influences produced something that wasn't altogether new but also wasn't entirely the same as the anarchist politics popular much earlier in the twentieth century.

Starting in the late 1970s, the nonviolent direct action movement, sometimes known as the "anti-nuke movement," played a pivotal role in this reconfiguration. Emerging through mobilizations against nuclear power and the nuclear arms race, this movement explicitly drew on a model of confrontational nonviolence from the southern Black freedom movement and the nonhierarchical practices and sensibilities of feminism. The movement took its name from its main tactic: large-scale civil disobedience organized through "affinity groups," a form derived from the anarchist movement in Spain in which five to fifteen people work together collectively. For deliberation and coordination among these groups, activists in the movement developed the model of the "spokescouncil," composed of delegates from affinity groups. For making decisions, they used a kind of formalized consensus process that they called "feminist process."

Well into the 1980s, movement activists organized large blockades and protests against nuclear power facilities. Through their actions, they helped swing public sentiment against nuclear energy, but their more long-lasting contribution was the bundle of politics and practices that they fused together. In this bundle, civil disobedience became closely linked with affinity groups and consensus, all within a feminist-influenced anti-authoritarian politics that aimed for nonviolent revolution. Prefigurative politics was also essential to this bundle. Through trainings for unlearning oppressive behavior, counterinstitutions such as co-ops, and directly democratic organizing practices, activists explicitly saw themselves as building forms of organization and community that prefigured a new society.[75]

Movements in the 1980s and 1990s added to this bundle. During the 1980s, queers and allies launched groups such as ACT UP and AIDS Action

Now! that used a direct action approach in grassroots struggles for AIDS funding, research, and treatment. They combined this approach with queer sensibilities and a dramatic sense of urgency about the AIDS epidemic as not simply a health matter, but a social and political crisis. In this context of struggle, they crafted a distinct style of militant confrontation through images, slogans, occupations, and street protests that grabbed media attention and won consistent victories. They also developed a prefigurative politics of sexuality and health, opening spaces for people collectively to create new relations and practices of desire, expression, and care. While much (but not all) of this direct action AIDS activism subsided in the 1990s, its contributions have continued to reverberate through subsequent direct action organizing and radical queer activism.[76]

At the same time, something crucial was going on in forests on the West Coast. The radical wing of the environmental movement, represented by Earth First! (EF!) and already a decade old in 1990, was beginning to develop a political perspective that combined environmentalism with social justice. EF! activist Judi Bari, a working-class mother and former union organizer, was leading the way in the midst of a growing campaign to save two-thousand-year-old trees in the Headwaters Forest in Northern California.[77] Drawing on lessons from the nonviolent direct action movement, the Headwaters EF!ers organized a broad-based campaign that involved large-scale civil disobedience actions and community organizing, including creating alliances with loggers through the IWW. The Headwaters experience inspired many and, by the mid-1990s, EF! groups were engaged in confrontational campaigns across Canada and the United States. In often remote wilderness areas, tight-knit groups of EF! activists further fused consensus decision-making, affinity groups, and direct action as they used their bodies to protect ecosystems. Through these experiences, EF!ers nourished a strongly prefigurative movement culture based on working together collectively, sharing resources equitably, challenging power relations, and supporting one another through repeated arrests.[78]

The bundle of ideas and practices welded together through these movement experiences influenced and was influenced by the anarchism of this period. Indeed, anarchists were deeply involved in all of these movements, just as these movements introduced many people to anarchist politics. By the early 1990s, many activists understood anarchism—or radical activism more generally—to mean this bundle, along with a commitment to egalitarianism, mutual aid, and freedom as well as a far-reaching critique of domination.[79] The glue that largely held it all together was a shared counterculture and template of activities. The mostly young people involved in

1990s anarchism were connected through a series of predominantly white and middle-class subcultural scenes, often rooted in punk rock. They set up local Food Not Bombs groups, supported U.S. political prisoners such as Mumia Abu-Jamal, engaged in confrontational direct action, worked to inject art and imagination into activism, organized large gatherings, and developed a network of bookstores and political spaces known as infoshops.[80]

This period also saw important attempts to break out of the anarchist subcultural milieu and build broader movements. Anarchist publications such as *The Blast!* in Minneapolis intentionally tried to move beyond punk scenes and connect with community-based struggles. The U.S.-based Love and Rage anarchist network, which started in 1989 and solidified into a formal membership organization in 1993, began to identify strategic priorities, wrestled with key political questions around white supremacy, and attempted to construct a continental revolutionary anarchist federation. Anarchists also organized two groundbreaking Active Resistance conferences—in Chicago in 1996 and Toronto in 1998—that explicitly foregrounded themes such as community organizing and movement-building. All of these efforts, in different yet overlapping ways, tried to develop anarchism in the United States and Canada into a more intentional orientation toward popular struggles.[81]

Meanwhile, movements were growing elsewhere that would come to further reconfigure North American anarchism. A revolt against neoliberalism was brewing, especially in the global South. Building on legacies of anti-colonial and anti-imperialist struggles, this started in the 1980s with widespread popular mobilizations against austerity measures mandated by the International Monetary Fund. By the early 1990s, meetings of neoliberal institutions such as the World Bank and the World Trade Organization (WTO) faced massive protests from Bangalore to Berlin.[82] Then, on January 1, 1994, the Zapatista Army of National Liberation stepped onto the world stage by seizing seven cities in Chiapas. *"Ya basta!"* ("Enough!"), they said in opposition to the Mexican government and neoliberalism. Bringing together aspects of left radicalism and Indigenous Mayan traditions, the Zapatistas offered an autonomous politics based on listening and dialogue, building democratic power from below, and creating self-governing communities.[83]

The Zapatistas also facilitated transnational connections among movements. In 1996 and 1998, they sponsored face-to-face global *encuentros* (encounters) that served as key meeting points for what was to become the global justice movement. The second of these led to the formation of the Peoples' Global Action (PGA) network. The PGA brought together massive movements in the global South, such as the Landless Workers' Movement in Brazil and the Karnataka State Farmer's Movement in India, along with generally smaller organizations in the North, to develop horizontal links in the struggle against neoliberalism. This network was a key node through which an emerging anti-capitalist current in the global justice movement was able to engage in discussion and planning. The PGA hallmarks, developed through early conferences, came to define this anti-capitalism in anti-authoritarian terms. They included a rejection of "all forms and systems of domination and discrimination," "a confrontational attitude," "a call to direct action," and "an organisational philosophy based on decentralisation and autonomy."[84]

As the new millennium approached, anarchism in the North and autonomous movements in the South were increasingly connected. In the United States and Canada, anarchist-influenced activists were deeply inspired by the Zapatistas and were some of the first to work with the PGA. Following the example of their European counterparts, many began organizing around the PGA's calls for "global days of action" involving coordinated international protests against institutions of neoliberalism. And though there were previous summit protests, it was the week of successful protests against the 1999 WTO ministerial in Seattle that grabbed significant attention. Anarchists played leading roles in planning and coordinating the mass blockades and street battles in Seattle, combining the bundle of direct action tactics, consensus decision-making, and affinity groups with the politics circulating through the PGA.[85]

In the wake of the successful disruption of the Seattle ministerial, this enhanced bundle of practices and politics came to characterize an anti-capitalist current in North America. Bringing together veterans of 1990s anarchism and newer radicals, this current rapidly carried movement coalitions and momentum into other demonstrations against major summits and meetings. The next few years saw showdowns between protestors and police from Los Angeles to Quebec City, and North American activists also traveled to mobilizations at major summits elsewhere in the world.[86]

Through the global justice movement, thousands of people participated in anti-authoritarian approaches and politics. At the same time, this cycle of struggle provided opportunities for activists to wrestle with their own limitations in the context of a growing movement. Longtime radical and writer Elizabeth Martinez raised some of these with her widely circulated essay "Where Was the Color in Seattle?"[87] This critical intervention and subsequent ones fostered widespread discussion. While the conversations were most visible around the racial composition of summit mobilizations, they opened up a range of crucial issues: how to understand the relation between global justice mobilizing and community-based organizing; how to build strategic and broad-based movements in Canada and the United States and link them to other movements across the globe; and how to confront hierarchies of race, gender, class, age, and experience as they were being reproduced in movement spaces.[88]

As activists influenced by anarchism grappled with these issues, some began to develop more complex political approaches. These combined anti-authoritarian, anti-capitalist politics with an orientation toward organizing to build popular power and broad-based movements.[89] Even as the global justice movement waned in the early 2000s, many activists took these increasingly sophisticated politics with them into other struggles and movements. Indeed, some of the most successful anti-authoritarian projects and formations today come from this strand. One example is the network of No One Is Illegal collectives across Canada, which works to challenge borders by organizing with migrant communities in their struggles with the Canadian state. No One Is Illegal collectives ground their efforts in an anti-capitalist, anti-colonial politics, emphasizing the connections between migrants from the global South and Indigenous peoples in North America. Their work, as I discuss further below, is impressive.

Since the late 1970s, anarchism in the United States and Canada has functioned as a carrying case for a growing bundle of ideas and practices. These include a rejection of social relations based on domination, a commitment to enacting liberatory visions in the here and now, and a set of non-hierarchical organizing approaches, direct action tactics, and alternative institutional models. Activists continue to develop and make use of this bundle in a wide variety of movements. Anarchism, in this way, is a live political strand in North America, influencing how many activists and organizers understand the state and capitalism—and fight for alternatives.

DIGGING IN AFTER SEPTEMBER 11, 2001

Anti-racist feminism, prison abolitionism, and anarchism have significantly contributed to contemporary anti-authoritarian organizing and politics. Although still distinct, these strands have been major routes through which people have come to participate in the anti-authoritarian current, and they have also offered overlapping sets of movement experiences and radical ideas that have laid the basis for another politics. Since the early 2000s, these politics have developed through further waves of movement and mobilization.

This recent history is framed by the events of September 11, 2001. In the aftermath of the attacks on the World Trade Center, the U.S. government declared an open-ended "war on terror" and, with the collaboration of the Canadian government and other allies, invaded Afghanistan. Less than a year and a half later, the U.S. government launched a war of occupation in Iraq. During this period, activists of many political stripes, anti-authoritarians among them, leapt into anti-war organizing, especially to mobilize for what became marches of historically unprecedented sizes in the first months of 2003.

Many anti-authoritarians sought to carry energy and organizing models from the global justice movement into the anti-war movement, but this was surprisingly difficult. One reason for this was the sudden rightward shift in the political climate; in response, most unions and other progressive organizations retreated from confrontational protests, breaking the coalitional efforts that had made the global justice movement so dynamic. Many activists also struggled to make sense of what was happening, since there had previously been only limited discussion about imperialism in the mostly white sections of the global justice movement. Speaking about this in a 2004 interview, San Francisco organizer Clare Bayard observed, "This hole reflected a weak spot around understanding world histories of colonialism, white supremacy in relation to European and U.S. economic and political development, and the relationship between self-determination struggles by colonized peoples and the fight against global capitalist entities."[90] While anti-imperialist analysis eventually became more widespread among anti-authoritarians, its initial absence hamstrung organizing efforts.

Organizationally, the anti-war movement also presented a challenging situation. At its height, the movement was dominated by, on the one side, sectarian organizations that aggressively claimed the mantle of anti-imperialism and, on the other side, broad peace coalitions that shied away from discussing imperialism or using confrontational tactics.[91] In this context, anti-authoritarians largely concentrated on supporting soldiers who refused to fight, struggling against military recruitment in schools, and using direct action to disrupt institutions linked to war-making. They also created organizations within the anti-war movement, such as Bloquez l'empire / Block the Empire in Montreal, Direct Action to Stop the War in San Francisco, and the Pittsburgh Organizing Group. Through these efforts, they tried to foster political approaches based on the power of ordinary people to undermine militarism.

The anti-war movement never completely disappeared. By 2005, however, it had significantly shrunk. In the United States, the protests against the 2004 Republican National Convention in New York City were arguably the last gasp of hope for carrying the momentum of the global justice movement into a large-scale anti-war movement. While the demonstrations there were massive, the movement wasn't substantially reinvigorated. Since then, anti-war initiatives have carried on. Examples include the long-running movement publication *War Times*, the organization Iraq Veterans Against the War, and support efforts for GI resisters such as the War Resisters Support Campaign (in Canada) and Courage to Resist (in the United States), all of which have involved anti-authoritarians. National organizations and local activist groups have also continued. But while hardworking, all of these initiatives have remained fairly small.[92]

The middle of the first decade of the twenty-first century was a bleak time for the left. Amidst the "war on terror," national politics in both Canada and the United States moved decisively to the right. Neoliberalism was in full swing and inequality grew, gains of previous left movements were aggressively rolled back, immigrant and racialized communities faced intensified attacks, institutions of imprisonment and detention dramatically expanded, and climate change was distressingly evident yet largely ignored by policymakers. In 2005, the U.S. government also launched a campaign of repression, dubbed the "green scare," against environmental activists allegedly involved in the sabotage efforts of the Earth Liberation Front; this had a chilling effect on some sections of the anti-authoritarian current.[93] In these circumstances, most struggles were defensive, and activists grappled with marginalization, demoralization, and exhaustion.

While the global justice and anti-war movements had ebbed, they left behind layers of committed anti-authoritarian organizers with experience and skills. During this difficult time, many of them dug into longer-term initiatives. Building on earlier discussions, they focused on organizing to develop popular power and broad-based movements. Many of the organizations profiled in this book were born or nourished through these efforts: INCITE! affiliates, Critical Resistance chapters and other abolitionist groups, No One Is Illegal collectives, campus-based chapters of the new Students for a Democratic Society, base-building organizations such as Young Workers United in San Francisco, the Anti-Poverty Committee in Vancouver and other economic justice groups, radical collectives such as Another Politics Is Possible in New York City, and dozens more initiatives. In a period of reaction, anti-authoritarians fought hard, sometimes won victories, and steadily sustained a space for radical ideas linked to grassroots struggles. These experiences generated many hard-earned organizing lessons.

LEARNING THROUGH CRISIS AND CONFRONTATION

Some of the most important learning experiences of this period came out of instances of large-scale crisis and confrontation. One of these was Hurricane Katrina in 2005 and its aftermath on the Gulf Coast, particularly in New Orleans. As with many so-called natural disasters, the real catastrophe of Katrina grew out of ongoing disasters of poverty, racism, and other forms of structural violence and inequality, combined with a tremendously destructive storm. The outcome was a devastated city, a collapse of essential services, and tens of thousands of displaced residents. Those people hardest hit were overwhelming poor and Black. Meanwhile, the state was quickly present as a repressive force (in the form of police and military forces) and miserably inadequate as a force for relief.

Radicals from New Orleans and elsewhere attempted to organize and build in this context. As I discuss in more detail in chapter 5, the city was host to a whole range of grassroots relief and reconstruction efforts, and several were distinctly anti-authoritarian. Local INCITE! and Critical Resistance groups stepped up their organizing to challenge intensified racist policing, fight ongoing displacement under the guise of reconstruction, and relate to the survival needs of primarily low-income people of color. At the same time, a small crew of radicals launched the Common Ground (CG) collective, which quickly began coordinating volunteers to distribute supplies, clean up toxic areas, and provide medical services. Thousands of predominantly white activists came from all over the continent to participate in CG's efforts.

Given the influx of white activists into predominantly Black neighborhoods, there were predictable tensions that emerged around race and accountability, among other issues. After spending several months in New Orleans, anti-racist organizer Ingrid Chapman summed these up well: "Many white middle-class folks started projects without establishing any system of accountability to the people the projects impacted and/or sought to serve."[94] Although there were efforts to confront these problems, they were never fully resolved. Through post-Katrina work, however, a significant cross-section of activists and organizers gained new skills in responding to popular needs, learned lessons about the challenges of building community-based organizations, and developed deeper understandings of the intense realities of capitalism, racism, and disaster.[95]

The extraordinary U.S. immigrant rights mobilizations of 2006 offered another learning experience. Amid growing anti-immigrant sentiment and open organizing by racist border vigilantes, Republican Congressman Jim Sensenbrenner proposed a bill in late 2005 that included provisions for further militarizing the U.S.-Mexico border, substantially raising penalties for undocumented immigrants, and criminalizing anyone found to be helping them. In response, immigrants and supporters began organizing protest marches that, in many cases, also involved sizeable work stoppages and school walkouts. The first of these, in Chicago, involved at least one hundred thousand people, and more and more actions rapidly unfolded across the United States, culminating with coordinated marches in two hundred cities on May 1, called "A Day Without Immigrants." Altogether, more than five million people, the vast majority of them Latino/a, participated in these actions over a two-month period. In effect, this was a general strike against the Sensenbrenner bill, which subsequently floundered.[96]

These mobilizations catalyzed a combative wave of organizing propelled primarily by young Latino/a activists. As right-wing lawmakers have proposed and sometimes passed draconian anti-immigrant measures in Arizona and other states in recent years, they have been met with this wave of resistance, which links activist organizations and dense social networks in immigrant communities. Dramatic civil disobedience actions by undocumented activists, such as the "No Papers No Fear" bus tour across the southern United States in 2012, have demonstrated the growing audacity and power of this movement. And anti-authoritarian organizers and groups have participated in much of this organizing, especially in California and the U.S. Southwest. In the process, they have been learning key lessons about border regimes and racism, as well as the capacities of people outside of self-identified activist communities to organize and fight back.[97]

These are lessons anti-authoritarians have been learning in Canada too, where migrant justice struggles, generally smaller than those in the United States, have ratcheted up over the last several years. Initiated in Montreal in the early 2000s, No One Is Illegal (NOII) spread to other major cities and began engaging in aggressive campaigns against deportations. In 2003, NOII-Montreal collaborated with other organizations in launching the Solidarity Across Borders (SAB) network around a set of far-reaching demands, including regularization for all undocumented immigrants. In a major undertaking in 2005 that raised the bar for migrant justice organizing nationally, SAB coordinated a 120-mile march from Montreal to Ottawa to build support for its demands. Two years later, NOII-Vancouver's ongoing organizing sparked a high-profile fight in support of Laibar Singh, a paralyzed refugee from India. In a stunning December 2007 action, some two thousand people, largely South Asian, blockaded the Vancouver International Airport to stop Singh's impending deportation. And starting with an "Education not Deportation" campaign in 2006, NOII-Toronto launched a multi-year fight for Toronto to become a "solidarity city" where all people can access city services regardless of immigration status. Organizing across sectors and services, they finally won in 2013.[98]

In the Canadian context, there has also been a surge of Indigenous land struggles that have profoundly affected the anti-authoritarian current. Since the early 2000s, the Secwepemc people have resisted the expansion of a ski resort on their lands in south-central British Columbia, with Vancouver-based activists offering ongoing support.[99] In 2006, people from Six Nations, a confederacy of First Nations also known as the Iroquois, set up a blockade to prevent a suburban development on their land in south-western Ontario. For nearly a month, hundreds of people, including a contingent of non-Indigenous activists, regularly participated in the occupation. Struggles at Six Nations, sometimes quite confrontational, have continued since.[100] Recent years have also seen sustained Indigenous resistance in Ontario and Quebec to resource extraction, government interference in community decision-making, and infringements on territorial sovereignty.[101] As well, Indigenous communities in British Columbia have been steadfastly fighting proposed construction of the Northern Gateway Pipeline, which would transport oil from the Alberta tar sands through their traditional territories.[102]

All of this flared up dramatically in late 2012 when the governing party of Canada proposed a sweeping set of bills aimed at restructuring governance and rights of First Nations. Sparked by Indigenous women activists in Saskatoon and fueled by social media, a movement calling itself Idle No More rose up in opposition. Over a two-month period, Indigenous people and allies organized hundreds of educational events, protests, ceremonies, marches, and road and railway blockades across North America.[103]

Idle No More and recent land struggles have produced widespread public discussion and controversy in Canada. Many non-Indigenous anti-authoritarians have been involved in these efforts through groups such as the Indigenous Peoples Solidarity Movement. Activists have been especially impacted by Indigenous assertions of sovereignty that call the state into question. As I explain in the next chapter, these experiences have significantly shaped how anti-authoritarians in the Canadian context understand colonialism and self-determination, and have also opened up important discussions about solidarity organizing.

The situation in the U.S. context is different. Certainly, there are distinguished histories of Indigenous struggle, including recent collaborations with non-Indigenous anti-authoritarians. For sixteen months in 1998–99, radical environmentalists built an inspiring coalition with Native American communities and others to resist highway construction through Mendota Mdewakanton Dakota territory near Minneapolis; together, they held their ground in what was called the "Minnehaha Free State."[104] Since the mid-1990s, settler activists have taken stints living with Dineh families in northeast Arizona to support their resistance to relocation as the Peabody Coal Company seeks access to the coal reserves beneath their land.[105] Still, colonial relations are heavily obscured in the United States and, as a result, anti-colonial struggle remains fairly abstract for most non-Indigenous anti-authoritarians. But many activists are learning lessons from south of the border, as Indigenous movements in countries such as Mexico and Bolivia are gaining ground. Increasingly, activists are looking north too, first toward the mobilization in Vancouver against the 2010 Winter Olympics, which brought together thousands of activists under the slogan "No Olympics on Stolen Land," and more recently toward Idle No More.[106]

FAST-MOVING MOBILIZATIONS

The last few years have seen more and more fast-moving mobilizations. Many of these have emanated from movements with strong participation from anti-authoritarians or have made extensive use of anti-authoritarian ideas and practices. One example is the rapidly growing climate justice movement, which brings together campaigns and organizations engaged in struggles around global climate change. After a downturn in radical environmental organizing in the early 2000s, a newer generation of anti-authoritarians has taken up the tradition of Earth First! with slogans such as "system change, not climate change." This movement particularly took off in the lead up to the 2009 United Nations Climate Change Conference in Copenhagen, as activists in a number of North American cities began organizing to build popular consciousness and put pressure on policymakers and energy companies. Some activists also traveled to the Copenhagen conference for a week of direct action protests.

This organizing led to new initiatives. Through coalitions such as the Mobilization for Climate Justice West in the San Francisco Bay Area, activists have worked to foreground communities, often racialized and poor, experiencing the major consequences of a carbon-based economy. Struggles against oil refining in Richmond, California, mountaintop removal coal mining in southern Appalachia, and oil extraction on traditional Indigenous territories in Alberta have thus emerged as frontline fights. Since 2011, the climate justice movement has also held a series of well-attended activist conferences and civil disobedience actions in Ottawa and Washington, D.C.

Drawing considerable media coverage, these convergences have brought thousands of new activists together and developed a constituency for the movement, especially on university campuses. Meanwhile, activists in the radical wing of the movement have built the Rising Tide North America network, which has dozens of local chapters. The climate justice movement has received increased attention in recent years with protests and Earth First!-style blockades against the proposed Northern Gateway Pipeline, and the construction of the Keystone Pipeline, running from the Alberta tar sands to Texas. Together, these efforts suggest a possible renewal of direct action environmentalism.[107]

Another example of recently reinvigorated resistance is the movement against the PIC, in which abolitionists have played a central role. Since 2010, there have been historic hunger strikes involving thousands of prisoners in Georgia and California, and smaller numbers in other states, protesting their conditions of confinement. Activists associated with CR have offered consistent support to these efforts, often working with families of hunger strikers and other prisoner activists. Abolitionists have also spearheaded campaigns against prison construction, most recently through initiatives such as Decarcerate PA (Pennsylvania) and Californians United for a Responsible Budget. Combining community organizing and creative protests, these broad-based efforts aim to pressure state lawmakers to shift spending priorities away from prisons and jails and toward communities. In Canada, the government's closure of farms at six prisons in 2010 led to direct action protests with substantial community support in Kingston, Ontario. There have also been more and more activities across Canada associated with Prisoners' Justice Day, August 10, supporting prisoners' struggles and commemorating people who have died in prison.

This movement has also been at the center of mobilizations against racist police violence, particularly police murders of people of color. In 2008, a Montreal police officer killed Honduran immigrant Fredy Villanueva, catalyzing riots and then more sustained organizing through activist groups such as Montréal-Nord Républik. Similarly, the 2009 murder of African American man Oscar Grant by a transit cop in Oakland led to a series of riots and a surge of anti-police organizing that would come to decisively influence Occupy Oakland. The 2012 Florida killing of Black youth Trayvon Martin by George Zimmerman, though Zimmerman was not a police officer, was consistent with this longstanding pattern of racist criminalization and violence. In response, activists organized dozens of rallies, marches, and vigils across North America. Although episodic, these struggles tap into a wellspring of outrage against the criminal justice system, especially among poor and working-class racialized people. As I mentioned earlier, over the last several years there has also been significant growth in experiments with community-based alternatives to cops and courts. These efforts demonstrate the widening reach of abolitionism. Together with ongoing organizing against prisons and policing, they signal an increasingly radical movement.[108]

To date, perhaps the most widespread use of anti-authoritarian ideas and practices has been within the occupy movement. Launched in September 2011 in New York City, occupy was initially the scheme of an assortment of anarchists and other activists, some with experience from the global justice movement. In the midst of a global economic crisis, they sought to turn critical attention to Wall Street, which they saw as symbolizing inequality and immiseration. With recent experience protesting city budget cuts in the "Bloombergville" tent city and a widely-circulated communiqué from the radical magazine *Adbusters*, these activists set up the Occupy Wall Street (OWS) encampment in Zuccotti Park near Wall Street. They also began using and popularizing many of the practices associated with anarchism, including directly democratic decision-making in general assemblies, alternative institutions such as camp-based kitchens and clinics, and confrontational direct actions including disruptive street marches and bank occupations.

OWS activists were riding a movement wave. Indeed, if the global justice movement was born with the Zapatistas, the occupy movement grew out of the Arab Spring of 2011. Starting in Tunisia, this was the blossoming of popular struggles against dictatorships (often U.S. client regimes) in North Africa and West Asia. The most spectacular was the sustained occupation of Tahrir Square in Cairo by tens—and sometimes hundreds—of thousands of determined protestors in opposition to the Hosni Mubarak regime, which they eventually overthrew. This occupation, in early 2011, also played a mutually inspirational role with the occupation of the Wisconsin state capitol by thousands protesting Governor Scott Walker's proposed legislation limiting collective bargaining rights for unions. And these initial actions inspired the rapid growth of movements in many other countries, such as Spain and Chile, occupying central public spaces with protest encampments. Beyond a shared set of tactics, the threads linking these movements are commitments to direct democracy, criticisms of existing political and economic systems, impatience with traditional party-based politics, and audacious willingness to engage in mass action.[109]

When OWS activists set up their encampment, they were building on all of this. What surprised nearly everyone, occupiers included, is that they managed to hold Zuccotti Park for two months and to develop such broad support. Inviting participation from "the 99 percent" and naming the enemy as "the

1 percent," OWS tapped a deep reservoir of public outrage about inequality and initiated a long-suppressed discussion about class. They also catalyzed a movement, as activists in hundreds of other cities, inspired by what was happening in New York, set up their own occupy encampments with general assembly models from OWS that they largely learned about through social media. These encampments brought together a wide range of people, including longtime radicals, newly politicized activists, houseless people, organizers from established left organizations, curious bystanders, and people with farfetched ideas looking for an audience.

Not surprisingly, most occupy encampments experienced a lot of chaos and conflict. However, they also opened a broad organizing space from which occupiers launched all sorts of creative initiatives. In addition to sustaining mass meals and tent cities, most occupy encampments engaged in frequent street protests and many allied with ongoing struggles, in some cases joining union picket lines, marches against police violence, and other efforts. Taking this further, occupiers in cities such as Atlanta, Minneapolis, Portland, and Rochester began organizing to physically resist housing evictions of local residents. In a strategically brilliant move, Occupy Baltimore teamed up with the Black-led Baltimore Algebra Project to occupy the proposed site for a youth jail, starkly calling into question state funding priorities. And capturing the imagination of the movement, Occupy Oakland organized a one-day "general strike" on November 2, 2011, that saw some thirty thousand people participate in work stoppages, street demonstrations, and a successful blockade of the port. In the movement's largest coordinated action, occupy encampments all along the West Coast organized a daylong blockade of ports the following month.

All of this activity, as in other moments of upsurge, created opportunities for activists to grapple with limitations and develop new capacities. The People of Color Caucus of OWS played a crucial early role in this process, raising challenges around racism and other systems of oppression in a predominantly white and often male-dominated context. Their work was motivated by the conviction, as caucus member Manissa McCleave Maharawal recounts, that "OWS absolutely *needed* to prefigure a world in which oppression within the movement, as well as racial justice as connected to economic justice outside of the movement, was an integral part of the analysis."[110] Linked to this, the occupy movement also saw discussions about how to relate with the police, enact anti-colonial principles, balance meeting survival needs with organizing, ensure safety and accountability in movement spaces, and work in alliance with more established organizations. Some of these rich discussions continue.

While most of the occupy encampments were evicted by early 2012, their energy has carried into other initiatives. These include Occupy Our Homes, a network that grew out of anti-eviction organizing in various cities; Strike Debt, a campaign of resistance to all forms of debt; and Occupy Sandy, a grassroots relief effort that OWS activists launched in the 2012 aftermath of Hurricane Sandy. More generally, the occupy movement touched the lives of hundreds of thousands of people in North America, introducing many to anti-authoritarian politics and practices. The encampments generated broad layers of newly-politicized activists and renewed discussions about organizing and movement-building.[111]

The occupy movement also contributed to a continental atmosphere of upsurge. Shortly after the encampments ended, tens of thousands of students in Quebec waged a remarkably determined six-month strike against tuition hikes. Rooted in a longer history of student mobilizations in Quebec, the strike was significantly propelled by a student association that had grown out of the global justice movement experience. With this history as well as inspiration drawn from more recent upsurges, the student movement's effectiveness was built on direct democracy in general assemblies and combative direct action, both within a broad organizing strategy. The students in Quebec, in a sense, deepened and extended some of the best aspects of the anti-authoritarian current.[112] This bodes well as more mobilizations erupt and people continue to use and refine anti-authoritarian ideas and practices. If 2001 marks a time when anti-authoritarian organizers began digging in, perhaps 2011 marks a shift into widened and accelerated struggles.

CONVERGENCE

The anti-authoritarian current, like nearly all movement-based radical tendencies, has grown out of dense political lineages and histories of struggle. Three strands in particular have increasingly intertwined in this current as it has developed through movement experiences since the early 2000s. Anti-racist feminism provides a set of politics and practices for understanding interrelated systems of oppression and exploitation, linking interpersonal and systemic forms of domination, and elaborating intersectional strategies for social transformation. Prison abolitionism contributes an analysis connecting state violence and dominant social relations, a nonreformist approach to strategy, and experiments aimed at reducing harm and resolving conflict without resorting to the state. And reconfigured anarchism supplies nonhierarchical practices, prefigurative values, and a confrontational orientation.

politics bears the imprints of all of these strands, as well as oth-
important, however, not to exaggerate the connections or coher-
among them. These strands are distinct and, at times, in tension with
another. Indeed, they have different, if overlapping, political vocabularies and approaches. As a result, there are crucial unsettled questions among
them that come up again and again in movements: How do we understand
the primary systemic forces we seek to transform? Where exactly do healing and individual change fit into organizing efforts to challenge these systemic forces? How can we most productively manifest our visions through
our organizing work? What kinds of organizations are the most useful for
advancing our fights? How should we judge the effectiveness of our struggles? What is the role of militant confrontation in our movements? As I
discuss in the following chapters, debates around these and other questions
are ongoing.

Despite differences, these strands are substantially converging. As anti-
authoritarians, most of us come out of one or more of these radical lineages.
We braid them together as we work collectively and build relationships
across politics, campaigns, and movements: anarchist labor organizers draw
on analytical frameworks from women of color feminism, radical queer
activists use community-based models for dealing with violence developed
by anti-racist feminists and prison abolitionists, and migrant justice activists build on anarchist organizing methods. In this convergence, the development of the anti-authoritarian current is moving in two directions. On
the one hand, deep political affinities across these strands are enabling relations among them. On the other hand, these relations are creating the basis
for shared politics. I turn to these now.

2. "Defining ourselves in opposition"
The Four "Anti's"

In redefining what we're for, it always helps to understand what
we're against.

Maia Ramnath

Members of Rising Tide and other activists protest proposed export terminals
for coal, oil, and gas in Portland, Oregon, in July 2013. (Photo by Adam Mills
Elliott)

WHEN I ASKED LEILA POURTAVAF how she described herself politically, she
had a thoughtful response. "I don't often call myself an anarchist," she said,
"but I do use a lot of terms like 'anti-capitalist,' 'anti-authoritarian,' 'anti-
imperialist'—I come up with a lot of 'anti's.'" At the time I interviewed her,
Pourtavaf was deeply involved in organizing in Montreal, primarily with the
radical queer group Anti-Capitalist Ass Pirates and the local No One Is Illegal
collective. The "anti's" she mentioned are, in fact, at the heart of NOII-
Montreal's basis of unity, which asserts, "No One Is Illegal acts to expose and
educate against injustice from an anti-capitalist, anti-imperialist, anti-patriar-
chal, anti-authoritarian, and a queer positive perspective, while asserting a

vision for open borders and social and economic justice."[1] And Montreal activists aren't the only ones to emphasize "anti's." In New Orleans, organizer and health care worker Jennifer Whitney shared similar sentiments. "I don't like always defining myself as 'anti,'" she said, "but my politics are anti-authoritarian, anti-capitalist, anti-imperialist, anarchist, and internationalist."

These "anti's"—these ways of naming what we're against—are widespread among those working to develop another politics. Part of what characterizes the anti-authoritarian current is that we aren't shy about naming what we reject. Still, many of us share a reluctance to identify simply in these terms. As activists and organizers, we often talk about the limitations of a politics that is just about refusal and we frequently strive to develop affirmative visions in our work. These impulses point to a vital feature of another politics: a fusion of rejection and affirmation, pushing against and beyond existing social relations and structures.

While a politics based on rejection alone is insufficient for building the movements that we need, the negative is still essential. Longtime activist and radical journalist Francesca Fiorentini stressed this point in a way that resonated with others: "I think negativity in some ways mobilizes people . . . . Defining ourselves in opposition is not necessarily positive, but it can be empowering and be a form of clarifying what a political entity wants by agreeing on what it does *not* want." Our collective refusal, that is, can help anchor and guide us, particularly when we are consistently told that there are no viable alternatives to what we see around us.

Defining ourselves in opposition is the starting point of this chapter. As I suggested in the introduction, a core feature of the anti-authoritarian current is a rejection of all forms of domination, exploitation, and oppression. What are the sources of this rejection? What brings them together? And how do we translate this rejection into relevant analysis and political practice? Using an approach offered by the activist journal *Upping the Anti*, I engage these questions by exploring the "anti's" that converge in another politics: anti-authoritarianism, anti-capitalism, anti-oppression, and anti-imperialism.[2] I argue that what holds them together is a synthetic political approach. By "synthetic," I mean the way that organizers, in developing another politics, are drawing on the analyses and experiences of a range of radical political traditions and movements. After laying out this synthetic approach, I explore the four "anti's" individually, emphasizing that each comes out of the histories I traced in the last chapter. I also describe the core features of these "anti's" as they are used in the anti-authoritarian current. Together, I suggest, they define the "against" so central to another politics.

Before continuing, I want to offer a word of caution. In talking about another politics, it can be tempting to abstract ideas from actions. Jaggi Singh, who worked with NOII-Montreal, pointed this out very usefully: "If you read the basis of unity of No One Is Illegal, we describe ourselves as anti-authoritarian, but it's not something we need to specially advertise. What's more important is the on-the-ground work that we're doing, the actual organizing that we're doing—putting our anti-authoritarian ideas in practice. There's an expression I've always liked: 'The action is in the organizing.' Your politics is in the organizing as well." In other words, politics in the anti-authoritarian current can't be separated from practices—from the day-to-day work of developing campaigns, facilitating training sessions, knocking on doors, leading meetings, resolving conflicts between allies, planning events, organizing childcare, building organizations, engaging in direct actions, and so much more. It's crucial to bear this in mind. Otherwise, we run the risk of tearing political formulations from the soil where they're rooted, treating them as fixed objects rather than dynamic aspects of ongoing struggles, and seriously misunderstanding their significance.

A SYNTHETIC APPROACH

Those who are developing another politics identify politically in many different ways and through a variety of legacies of resistance. We call ourselves abolitionists, anarchists, anti-capitalists, autonomists, feminists, horizontalists, radicals, and many other things. Most of us draw eclectically on a variety of influences and traditions. Part of the reason for this, it seems to me, is that we are trying to stay critical, avoid dogmatism, and find what actually works. Political traditions, even at their best, offer us only approximations for making sense of a messy, constantly changing world. Organizer and researcher Andréa Maria captured this sentiment well: "There's nothing interesting or life-giving or useful about a static tradition. Traditions are actually only useful insofar as they're about moving along—not necessarily even evolving, just moving and dynamic. I deal with anarchism that way."

The search for the "dynamic" gets at what I understand as a synthetic approach to politics in the anti-authoritarian current. To be clear, though, this doesn't mean that anti-authoritarians avoid aligning ourselves with traditions. Maria certainly sees herself as working within the anarchist tradition, as do many others in this current. Nor is this to suggest that anti-authoritarians unthinkingly draw on a contradictory hodgepodge of ideas and practices. This synthetic approach is, rather, an eagerness to learn from diverse traditions and movements even while being critical of them. That is, many are turning to this sort of critical synthesis because we yearn for deeper, more nuanced analysis. Sharmeen Khan, a longtime organizer and editor of *Upping the Anti* in Toronto, discussed this in her own evolving politics: "It's like reading a Harlequin novel—things are very simple, right? Black and white things. And then you get into the dirtier stuff, right? And then you want to get into the kinkier material. It's kind of like growing up and developing a deeper analysis."

There is something else here too. One way I understand the approach to politics in the anti-authoritarian current is as an ongoing search for alternatives to what we might call "correct line" politics. The "correct line," as formulated by Chinese communist leader Mao Zedong, refers to the set of ideas that "correctly reflect the laws of the objective external world," which of course assumes that there is only one set of ideas that accurately describe social reality.[3] Among those influenced by Mao in North America, having the "correct line" has often been elevated to primary importance. Veteran activist Max Elbaum, one of the U.S. radicals who turned to Maoism in the 1970s, recalls, "Mao declared that 'the correctness or incorrectness of the ideological and political line decides everything,' and this dictum was quoted endlessly."[4]

Correct line politics is not limited to Maoism. Radical theorist John Holloway traces this tendency back, in the socialist tradition, to Karl Marx's collaborator Friedrich Engels. Engels, argues Holloway, played a leading role in developing so-called "scientific Marxism" in which "Marxism is objective, certain, 'scientific' knowledge of an objective, inevitable process." This led to "a distinction between those who know and those who do not know, a distinction between those who have true consciousness and those who have false consciousness." When we assume this distinction, warns Holloway, "Political debate becomes focused on the question of 'correctness' and the 'correct line.'"[5] And just this sort of debate is all too common on the left.[6]

The problem with all of this is that correct line politics assume that working for social transformation is mainly a matter of having the "right" analysis and imparting it to everyone else. This became clearer to me in conversation with Montreal organizer Sophie Schoen, who suggested that, at the most basic level, people don't join movements because we tell them how to think, but because we suggest how they can participate. We don't build movements, in other words, by hitting people over the head with our predetermined "correct" politics, but rather by engaging together in collective struggles around common aspirations. Developing and discussing politics is vital, without a doubt. However, our politics have to be grounded in the dynamism of social relations and social struggles, not sealed off in sanctified "lines."

We might understand the key difference here as between "prescriptive" and "revelatory." These are terms offered by Stephanie Guilloud, an organizer with Project South in Atlanta. She used them to describe two often conflicting approaches she has encountered on the left. I understand "prescriptive" to gesture more to correct line politics: this approach *prescribes* what we should think and do based on a predetermined "right" analysis. In contrast, I understand "revelatory" to mean a more open-ended, synthetic approach based on the revelations—undetermined and uncertain—that we experience together through the process of struggle. That is, collective struggles *reveal* things to us about our movements, our world, and ourselves—things that we previously didn't or couldn't know.

In the notion of the "revelatory," we hear echoes of the Zapatistas. Instead of ideological certainties and "correct lines," the Chiapas-based rebels have offered an approach of collectively asking questions, of exploring and experimenting together.[7] In this way, writes U.S.-based collective El Kilombo Intergaláctico, the Zapatistas "have taught the left that that dogmatism of idea and practice, the insistence on an ideology or model that transcends history and the decision of those in the present, always accompanied by a refusal to move, re-analyze, change, adapt, transform, is, in fact, a conservatism."[8] This is the basis of the synthetic political approach in the anti-authoritarian current.

This synthetic approach opens up space for a complex range of identifications among activists. Rayan El-Amine, a former organizer with the Arab Resource and Organizing Center and Direct Action to Stop the War in San Francisco, offered one example:

> I'm an organizer who is committed to doing nonhierarchical organizing and that sees movement-building as critical in this country at this time. I'm also committed to doing non-sectarian movement-building with an emphasis on anti-imperialism and anti-racism. Much of my analysis has developed over time but it originally comes from a Marxist understanding of the world. That's still there; its part of my politics and part of the way that I sometimes look at theory, but I've also integrated a nonhierarchical, anti-authoritarian practice of my politics. Nonhierarchical spaces are where I'm most comfortable organizing and participating. None of these ideas or practices are pure; they're cross-pollinated with different currents. I wouldn't say that I'm a socialist in the classical sense, even though I believe in socialism and equality and most of the things that come out of Marxist theory. But I'm also really committed to the post-Seattle, post-Zapatista, nonhierarchical, horizontal organizing that feels much more liberatory on all sorts of levels than how classical Marxist groups organize. This approach

challenges all sorts of oppressions, some that even exist in progressive organizations that I've been involved with here in this country but also where I'm from, in Lebanon.

El-Amine's particular identifications don't represent everyone in the anti-authoritarian current. But his emphasis on nonhierarchical organizing that "challenges all sorts of oppression" is widespread. Just as common is the way that El-Amine pulls together various political influences. This is the synthetic approach in practice. It doesn't mean that El-Amine or other anti-authoritarians have no central political orientation, but it does suggest openness in how we develop our politics.

This approach is closely tied to the nonsectarianism that El-Amine stressed. Sectarianism is derogating other people or groups because they don't share our political perspective or they aren't part of our organization. Usually this involves us thinking that we have a monopoly on the truth and therefore sidelining or smearing those who think otherwise. Sectarianism is often associated with Leninist groups claiming that their particular "line" on any given issue is the right one and that everyone else is counterrevolutionary. However, there are sectarians of all political stripes, including anarchists, and all can damage movements.

San Francisco anarchist organizer Rahula Janowski, a former member of the anti-imperialist collective Heads Up, was very self-critical in this regard: "I have developed a lot, politically, since I stopped being so sectarian . . . . [Part of that shift is] being able to work with, learn from, teach people who are Third World Marxists. For years, it was like, if you're not an anarchist, I might work in a coalition with you, but I'm not going to treat you very well; I'm not going to see you as someone I can learn from. I don't think I was unique in that; I think it's pretty common." Janowski, in this way, gestured to a kind of nonsectarian practice and sensibility—a willingness to work alongside and dialogue with people in other parts of the left.

This nonsectarianism is vital to the synthetic approach of another politics. I see it as a practical rejection of correct line politics. But it is no simple matter. The tricky balance is between open dialogue and principled debate. After all, even as the anti-authoritarian current is learning from other experiences and traditions, it's also staking out a politics that has real differences with other left tendencies. While activists and organizers have various feelings about how exactly to navigate this, one consistent stance I've seen is an emphasis on listening and a skepticism toward the kind of agonistic debate that has characterized a lot of conversation on the left.

This stance clearly flows from the revelatory orientation highlighted by Guilloud, with its emphasis on open-ended, nonprescriptive political dialogue. At the same time, this stance comes alongside a growing confidence among anti-authoritarian organizers that it's possible to learn from others while staying grounded in our core political commitments. As Janowski put it, "people refer to it more as a fusion politics, and I'm into that while still feeling very firmly rooted in being an anarchist, being anti-authoritarian. [I learn] so much about organizing, about strategizing, about what different communities might look like from people of other tendencies . . . . I think that maybe people feel like, if you are open to other stuff, you will lose your mooring. I don't think it has to be like that." Others might express this differently, but the underlying combination of rootedness and openness is widely shared.

Nonsectarian practices and a synthetic politics are still very much a work in progress as we try to develop approaches appropriate to our organizations and movements. Indeed, the synthetic approach cannot be disconnected from specific experiences: it has developed in different circumstances and with different influences across the anti-authoritarian current. For example, activists and organizers in the U.S. South describe how the long lineage of the African American freedom struggle powerfully influences their politics, organizing practices, and coalition work. And in Vancouver and Montreal, anti-authoritarian organizers, especially those involved in migrant justice and Indigenous solidarity work, have been learning from anti-imperialist (often communist) politics in migrant communities and anti-colonial traditions of struggle in Indigenous communities.

In each of these cases, the synthetic approach that has emerged is only partly ideological, based on the exchange and development of political ideas. Just as much, it has emerged through day-to-day relationships that organizers have built together in struggle—relationships based on care and respect, sometimes challenging disagreements, and shared experiences of fighting against injustice. Through both ideas and relationships, this synthetic approach makes possible the convergence of influences and experiences that forms another politics. The four "anti's," to which I now turn, are at the heart of this convergence.

ANTI-AUTHORITARIANISM

"Anti-authoritarian" is the term that I use, in a general way, to talk about the current propelling another politics. Politically, though, this term has a more specific meaning. As the first "anti" that defines another politics, anti-authoritarianism is a politics that opposes social relations of hierarchy and domination. Such relations manifest themselves in systems, institutions, communities, and individual relationships. Fundamentally, they are based on what anarcha-feminist writer and activist Starhawk calls "power-over": "the entitlement and ability of some groups to control others, extract their labor or resources, and impose sanctions or punishment."[9] Relations based on "power-over"—in states, wars, borders, workplaces, prisons, schools, neighborhoods, families, and other sites—constrain and curtail dignity, freedom, and justice. Anti-authoritarianism calls into question "power-over" in all of its manifestations.

Those in anti-authoritarian current tend to feel this strongly and intimately. As Andréa Maria put it, "There's ways in which [anti-authoritarianism] just speaks to a fundamental revolt that I've always felt against injustice and oppression, hierarchies, and also just being told what to do." In this way, she described it as "a stance of always being critical of oppressive systems and always being willing to deconstruct things even if that means that your privilege is going to get deconstructed along with that, and always seeing things on both a systemic level and on the level of the personal—where there's this interplay between them that's never simple but where you're always going back and forth between them."

This basic rejection of hierarchy and domination significantly comes out of anarchism. But anti-authoritarianism is not the same as anarchism. Indeed, the relationship between the two is complex for those in this current. Some claim the anarchist tradition without hesitation, others define themselves against it, and others see it as largely irrelevant. Some organizers criticize the Eurocentricism of anarchism, at least as it's usually understood.[10] Harsha Walia, a Vancouver-based migrant justice organizer, emphasized this, along with the way that "anarchists love ascribing the label 'anarchism' to forms of organizing and models of resistance which are not explicitly anarchist, such as Magonistas or Zapatistas or other Indigenous worldviews. The very attempt to appropriate those cultural contexts and box them into the existing framework of anarchism is quite oppressive. This is why I prefer the term 'anti-authoritarian,' as it conveys a richer tradition of diverse ideologies, communities, and practices, including some which are often contradictory with each other."[11] Many also criticize, to use the words of writer and organizer Roger White, the "overwhelmingly white, youth orientated, scene-based, political phenomenon" of anarchism.[12] This critique opens into questions about the racial and class character of anarchist politics in the United States and Canada, particularly as it has been connected in the last three decades to punk subcultures.[13]

With these criticisms in mind, some anti-authoritarians argue for reclaiming and reinventing anarchism—challenging its limitations, moving it out of subcultural scenes, and rooting it in popular struggles. Others distance themselves from anarchism while carrying anti-authoritarianism into grassroots organizing work. David Solnit, a longtime direct action organizer in the San Francisco Bay Area, leaned toward this view: "A lot of the 'capital-A' anarchist stuff honestly doesn't feel that hopeful to me. So I work in the spaces where people are actually engaged in some kind of concrete movement or struggle with some anti-authoritarian politics and practice, which I see as much more hopeful."

The anarchist tradition, meanwhile, is just one source of anti-authoritarianism. Many in this current have come to a rejection of hierarchy and domination along other political routes. As I described in the last chapter, these include anti-racist feminism, prison abolitionism, autonomous movements in the global South, and Indigenous struggles for self-determination. Organizer Paula Ximena Rojas-Urrutia, in her life and work, brings together many of these perspectives. Born in Chile and having lived in both the United States and Latin America, she worked with INCITE! affiliate Sista II Sista in New York and, as part of this, was involved in organizing against police violence. In Rojas-Urrutia's view, autonomous movements in Latin America offer crucial lessons for the North American left. Among such movements, she writes approvingly, "the emphasis is on the people's struggle for autonomy, not gathering power to topple the state and take it over. Revolution is about the *process* of making power and creating autonomous communities that divest from the state."[14]

While certainly not the same, these various routes to anti-authoritarianism have a lot in common. Across them, I see three central features—sometimes consistent practices, always defining aspirations—of anti-authoritarianism as it manifests in another politics. The first is a rejection of the state, or at least the most repressive aspects of it, such as the police, the military, and immigration authorities. In this sense, it's no coincidence that some of the most dynamic activity in the anti-authoritarian current comes from those fighting prisons and borders, both of which are sites where the state comes into direct contact with people's lives. As Montreal organizer Jaggi Singh pointed out, "We can sit around and proclaim, 'Smash the state!' or 'No borders!' But what does that mean tangibly? One way that 'smash the state' becomes meaningful, as a valid demand, is when you do migrant justice work because you find out what the state actually means, with clear day-to-day examples, and how it actually affects people negatively."

Our rejection of the state also means refusing state-based social change approaches and looking, instead, to visionary alternatives. Rosana Cruz, who organizes with formerly incarcerated people in New Orleans, explained, "I'm not trying to replicate El Salvador or even South Africa. I don't believe in replicating the models of the state, regardless of what you call it . . . . I feel like a lot of people spend a lot of time philosophizing over the politics of where we're going when, in reality, we need to start fantasizing—doing the guided meditation of what a self-determined community would look like—and work from that vision." This hostile stance toward the state, along with this search for visionary alternatives, is essential to anti-authoritarianism. We inevitably engage the state as we fight to defend or gain concessions (public education, welfare programs, environmental protections) but we try to reject its logic.

The second feature of anti-authoritarianism is often called "nonhierarchical" or "horizontal" organizing. This involves developing and practicing alternatives to "top-down" models based on a few people making decisions and everyone else following them. Helen Hudson, an organizer and health care worker in Montreal, talked about this as organizing in ways that are "radically democratic insofar as they try to include people in decisions to the degree that they're affected by the outcome." As I discuss in the next chapter, these horizontal organizing practices take many different forms—collectives, general assemblies, democratic membership organizations—depending on the circumstances in which organizers are working. But the underlying commitment to rigorous deliberation and democratic decision-making is quite consistent.

The third feature of anti-authoritarianism is a critique of vanguardism. Related to sectarianism, vanguardism is when an organization or party seeks to direct a struggle or movement according to its political priorities. Vanguardism is often linked to the work of the Russian revolutionary Vladimir Ilyich Lenin and those who draw on him. The role of the vanguard party, in Lenin's view, was to bring political consciousness to the working class and guide it through revolutionary struggle into building a socialist state.[15] And vanguardism has continued to be attractive for many on the left. For anti-authoritarians, however, this directive model of revolutionary leadership comes up against our rejection of hierarchy and domination. We're critical of models based on one group of people generating the revolutionary vision and strategy for everyone else. Toronto-based anti-prison organizer Marika Warner put it plainly: "Oppressed people don't need to be told how to win their own liberation." This isn't to deny, of course, that we all have much to learn from one another, but that shared learning is significantly different than one group presenting all of the answers and calling the shots. For this reason, we support nonvanguardist approaches based on bottom-up democracy.[16]

ANTI-CAPITALISM

The second "anti" in another politics is anti-capitalism. Capitalism is a system of social relations based on dispossession, exploitation, and alienation for the benefit of a small minority. It is founded on continuously dispossessing people of our means of subsistence (land, food, shelter) and turning these into things (commodities) exchanged for money. As part of this, individuals and companies in capitalist society privately own property and means of production (things that we use to do work, such as workplaces, machines, materials). Without means to sustain ourselves or produce anything, most people have to sell the one thing we do have, our labor, in exchange for money that we can use to buy what we need. Our labor, in a capitalist society, thus becomes an object separate from us; we are alienated from our own capacities to make and create—to *do*—as these capacities are channeled into work over which we have little or no control. Meanwhile, those few people who own the means of production direct our work and profit from it; they exploit us by taking the difference between what we produce and what we're paid, and using it for their own benefit.

Capitalism has to expand continuously or it will go into crisis. In this and other ways, it is inextricably linked with colonialism, which I discuss later in this chapter. Through this expansion, more and more people are separated from our means of subsistence and forced to work for money, and more and more things in our lives are turned into commodities (water, medicine, knowledge) to be sold to us. This constant growth of capitalism has devastating consequences for ecosystems around the planet as "resources" (petroleum, plants, animals) are extracted and sold and environmental degradation (pollution, deforestation, species extinction) is treated as an "externality," something irrelevant to the cycle of profit-making.[17]

Anti-capitalism opposes capitalist social relations. This "anti" in another politics comes from several overlapping sources. Some organizers draw on longstanding socialist political traditions, including Marxism and anarchism. Others have developed anti-capitalist politics through struggles against borders, prisons, environmental destruction, militarism, poverty, the mainstreaming of queer politics, university restructuring, animal exploitation, and cuts to public services. Some have come into anti-capitalism through experiences in the labor movement with union organizing campaigns, workers' centers, and labor solidarity work. Still others have been influenced toward this analysis by Indigenous land struggles. However, the last three decades of resistance to neoliberalism have probably played the most important role in shaping anti-capitalism within another politics. While not everyone in the anti-authoritarian current has participated in these struggles, most have been influenced by them.

Neoliberalism is an ideology and set of practices that is about deepening and extending capitalist social relations. Its tools include so-called "austerity" measures (slashing spending on development projects, welfare, health care, and other social programs), privatization (selling off public institutions and resources, such as schools and water, so that they can be run for profit), and deregulation (gutting laws that regulate business, such as environmental, health, and labor standards). Since the late 1970s, ruling elites have used this ideology and its tools to reshape the global economy. This process has happened especially through international institutions such as the International Monetary Fund (IMF) and the World Trade Organization (WTO), free trade agreements such as the North American Free Trade Agreement (NAFTA), and individual governments. Most of all, it has been pushed by the U.S. government.[18] With the worldwide economic crisis that started in 2008, ruling elites have aimed to intensify and accelerate many aspects of this thirty-year assault.[19]

None of this has occurred without struggle. Neoliberalism has generated fierce resistance across the globe, as I described in the last chapter. Some of the initial waves of this resistance, emanating particularly from the global South, gave birth to the global justice movement at the turn of the twenty-first century. More recent waves have developed through popular struggles against austerity, such as students mobilizing to challenge university cuts, workers pushing back against union-busting, and occupy actions seizing public space to highlight economic inequality. Anti-authoritarians have played leading roles in these struggles and have also been significantly shaped by them.

One of the most important effects of this resistance is a reinvented and reenergized anti-capitalism.[20] The rise of neoliberalism was framed by the famous slogan of then British Prime Minister Margaret Thatcher: "There is no alternative." Capitalism, we were told, is here to stay and there is nothing else. The fall of the Soviet Union seemed to confirm this. And yet struggles against neoliberalism have managed to call neoliberalism into question and to offer, at their best, a resolute challenge to capitalism.[21] These efforts have moved anti-capitalism from what had often become, in the United States and Canada, an abstract ideological commitment into something else—a living, breathing politics at least partly embedded in popular struggles. This is no small achievement.

The difficulty is that this resistance to neoliberalism, for all it has contributed, hasn't yet offered a lot of deep thinking about what capitalism is and how we should go about fighting it. What does anti-capitalism mean in North America today? This is the question with which many anti-authoritarian organizers are grappling. In trying to answer it, a lot of us have drawn on lessons, both good and bad, offered by the global justice movement. Two main aspects of the anti-capitalism in another politics emerge from this experience. Though they are more like aims than like fully formed features, they nonetheless indicate the direction of this "anti" in the anti-authoritarian current.

The first is an effort to think and act against capitalism as a system. This is hard. A major reason why targeting summits was—and, in some cases, continues to be—compelling is that protests against institutions offer a focus for anti-capitalist politics. Such protests have won victories too. The significance of this became clearer to me in conversation with Stephanie Guilloud, a leading organizer for the 1999 Seattle protests. The protests against the WTO, she emphasized, "delegitimized that particular institution." But, she added, "they didn't delegitimize capitalism .... That is a large and daunting system." Activists involved with the occupy movement have faced a similar difficulty in their targeting of Wall Street and individual banks.

Capitalism, in short, isn't an agreement or an institution. It's a system of social relations: it has a history, it has changed over time, and it's neither natural nor inevitable. And though resilient and difficult to physically confront, capitalism is not invincible. As something constantly created through social relations, it is also something we can undo.[22] That is, capitalism can be resisted, undermined, and displaced through collective action. But, as many in the anti-authoritarian current have discovered, this requires us to think well beyond the scope of what we know. Guilloud posed the relevant question: "How do we move systematically against this system and the conditions it creates?"

While the anti-authoritarian current has yet to develop adequate answers to this question, some initiatives have begun to suggest promising possibilities. The Coalition of Immokalee Workers (CIW) in southern Florida, for example, organizes Latino/a immigrant farmworkers who pick the tomatoes that supply some of the biggest fast food corporations in the world. Combining horizontal organizing and strategic campaigns, they have built broad alliances and won major concessions from Taco Bell, McDonald's, and Burger King. They've accomplished this, in part, through understanding and showing the exploitation of farmworkers in a systemic context.[23] What the CIW is fighting against is local and particular, and also tied to enormous global forces; like every instance of dispossession and exploitation, it is one manifestation of capitalist social relations. Organizers are learning that, if we're smart and strategic, we can dig in and fight in any of these instances and contribute to anti-systemic struggle against capitalism.

The second aspect of anti-capitalism in another politics is an expansive view of where capitalism "happens." Socialists of many stripes have generally understood the formation of capitalism as involving an historic dispossession of people from their lands and other means of subsistence. This dispossession—"primitive accumulation" as it is often called—incorporated vast resources into capitalism and forced people to sell their labor for wages.[24] Once primitive accumulation was over, by this analysis, the workplace became the primary site of exploitation and struggle. Workers who are paid a wage, according to this view, are the main agents of struggle as they fight over their working conditions and pay.[25]

Anti-capitalists in recent movements have highlighted an alternative way of thinking about capitalism, one which has deeply influenced another politics. From this perspective, primitive accumulation is an *ongoing* process: dispossession is expanding and deepening as, globally, more and more of the ways we sustain ourselves (public space, seeds, health care) are incorporated into the circuit of profit-making and more and more of us are forced to sell our labor (and more of it) in order to buy what we need to live.[26] At the same time, this perspective calls into question the centrality of waged labor. Capitalism, in fact, has always depended on the labor of people who are not getting paid a wage for their work, whether they are slaves harvesting sugar and cotton, women caring for their families and communities, or incarcerated people working in call centers or factories. As unwaged workers, these people can play key roles in disrupting and displacing capitalist social relations.[27]

This is all to say that, for another politics, the workplace and the wage don't define anti-capitalism, even as they remain crucial. Our challenge is to see capitalism as a system based on both dispossession *and* exploitation, both waged *and* unwaged labor.[28] Many in the anti-authoritarian current are developing this understanding out of our experiences as we try to articulate the connections between, for instance, workers' centers and defense of welfare entitlements, Indigenous land struggles and union fights, or campaigns against housing evictions and prison construction. Together, we're developing a much broader understanding of where anti-capitalist struggle is (everywhere) and who is best positioned to fight (all of us).

ANTI-OPPRESSION

The third "anti" in another politics is anti-oppression.[29] This refers to a set of politics and practices aimed at confronting and transforming intersecting systems of exploitation and oppression. As sets of social relations, these systems include capitalism, patriarchy, heterosexism, racism, and ableism. Capitalism concentrates wealth and power in the hands of a small owning (or "ruling") class, awards some prestige and material privilege to a middle (or "coordinator") class, and renders most people working-class or poor with very little material security and social standing. Patriarchy forms some people into men and other people into women, punishes those who don't conform to these categories, and gives social and material power to men. Heterosexism privileges sexual relations and identities based on sex between men and women and constructs other kinds of sexual relations and identities as deviant. Racism, which manifests as white supremacy in North America, classifies (or "racializes") people of particular ethnicities and with particular physical features as Arab, Asian, Black, Indigenous, and/or Latino, and others as "white." At the same time, this system privileges those who are "white" and subordinates those who are "nonwhite." Ableism sets norms for bodies and minds, and stigmatizes, medicalizes, and devalues people who don't fit within these norms. It also facilitates a physical and social infrastructure (buildings, forms of communication, transportation modes) that produces some people as "normal" and others as disabled.

All of these social relations are set in history, which means that they have changed over time, their previous consequences affect us today, and they carry dense sediments of collective memory and forgetting. As well, these social hierarchies all operate through complex webs of ideas (what is "natural," who is "normal"), everyday practices (talking, having sex, child-rearing), socially organized violence (intimate violence, targeted assaults of individuals, sexual violence, policing, war-making), and institutions (families, schools, workplaces, prisons, hospitals, borders). And these systems, each with their own specificities, are all fundamentally based in granting some people privileges while oppressing and marginalizing others. Together, their effect is to sustain a wider systemic dynamic through which a small number of very wealthy people wield enormous power over a deeply divided majority.[30]

Anti-oppression, as it is developing among activists and organizers, is based on an understanding of these social relations as shaping and mediating each other. This politics carries the legacies of a wide range of movements, including anti-colonial and anti-racist struggles, working-class and socialist movements, waves of feminist activity, the interrelated liberation movements of the 1960s and 1970s, radical queer activism, disability justice organizing, and others. But the single most important influence on anti-oppression politics in the anti-authoritarian current is anti-racist feminism. Indeed, for many activists, anti-oppression politics is an effort to carry radical women of color feminist ideas into a set of principles and practices.

The experience of the global justice movement also looms large here. Debates following the Seattle mobilization shaped anti-oppression politics in ways that are still very present. A catalyst for these debates, as I mentioned in the last chapter, was Elizabeth Martinez's article "Where Was the Color in Seattle?" In this piece, Martinez observed that those present in Seattle were "overwhelmingly Anglo," and she suggested that "understanding the reasons for the low level of color, and what can be learned from it, is absolutely crucial if we are to make Seattle's promise of a new, international movement against imperialist globalization come true." In exploring these reasons, Martinez highlighted the prevailing dynamic of marginalization in the predominantly white organizing leading up to the protests. This was reflected, she argued, in who was chosen to speak on behalf of protestors, how resources were distributed, who made decisions, how issues were framed, and who was comfortable in organizing spaces.[31]

What Martinez wrote resonated with critical discussions that were already starting in the movement. And while she was principally addressing race, Martinez's intervention opened up space for others to raise questions related to other power relations.[32] In this space, organizations, networks, and individual activists were able to explore how forms of oppression manifest themselves even in spaces committed to liberatory values and practices. Anarchist politics and sensibilities offered a foundation for this exploration, as many understood their opposition to hierarchy and domination to mean fighting all systems of oppression.

This is the context in which activists increasingly began to talk about "anti-oppression politics." Sharmeen Khan, a leading anti-oppression trainer in Canada, remembered that she first encountered this term in an anti-oppression workshop during the Seattle WTO protests. After the Seattle actions, these sorts of trainings became more and more common as individuals like Khan and groups like the Challenging White Supremacy Workshop in San Francisco began traveling widely to offer them.[33] Many organizations and mobilizations also systematized and adopted "anti-oppression principles."[34] These forms have since become ubiquitous in many movement contexts.

While the term "anti-oppression" continues to be popular, there are actually a variety of ways that organizers talk about these politics and practices. Some prefer the language of "intersectionality" since it more clearly indicates the influence of women of color feminism. Particular organizations have also developed their own terms. Sista II Sista, an INCITE! affiliate in New York, created an analysis around what they call "a braid of oppression" made up from strands of capitalism, racism, patriarchy, and heterosexism. "We choose to work from the braid of oppression," they explain, "because it makes our analysis and strategies stronger; after all, a braid is harder to cut then its individual strands."[35] LA COIL (formerly the LA Crew), a collective of organizers in Los Angeles, uses the term "unbreakapartability" to illustrate the ways that systems of oppression, together, "create a different experience than a simple sum of their parts." As part of this analysis, they argue, "we must struggle against all oppressions simultaneously" and "we must learn lessons from movements and organizational forms and visions fighting these oppressions and combine them into practices, visions, and methods of resistance that build something greater than the sum of their parts."[36] The Catalyst Project, a political education and movement-building center in San Francisco, has popularized the idea of "collective liberation" as an affirmative way to talk about transforming interconnected power relations. This term also emphasizes, in the words of Catalyst organizer Chris Crass, "how my liberation is connected to the liberation of all people" and how systems of oppression deform even those of us who experience privilege.[37] These formulations, each with their own specificities, name a common set of politics and practices in the antiauthoritarian current.

Anti-oppression, as it manifests in another politics, has three core features. The first is an understanding of power relations as fundamentally intertwined. As part of this, activists refuse hierarchies of oppression, in which one system is seen as more important than others. Sonya Z. Mehta, who worked as a labor organizer with Young Workers United in San Francisco, explained, "Capitalism is one pillar of oppression, and that's also why I identify as anarchist and anarcha because I believe that patriarchy and racism are just as intense, and they hold up this system together." Mehta, like many in the anti-authoritarian current, doesn't see capitalism as the primary system from which all relations of exploitation and oppression develop, but rather as one pillar in a group of connected systems.

A consistent difficulty here is how to highlight connections without treating all systems of oppression as the same. "It's important to talk about oppression as a concept," argued Montreal organizer Helen Hudson, "but also specific forms of oppression—transphobia, sexism, racism, ableism, and others—and the particular ways in which those things play out. There are commonalities, but there are also important differences." Radical queer activist-scholar Gary Kinsman echoes this: "Sexism is not racism and is not heterosexism, even though they are made in and through each other and are connected to class relations in a broad sense." There is a danger, he warns, "of flattening out the differences in the social organization of the various forms of oppression in developing a common anti-oppression politics."[38] We need to understand the histories that have shaped the systems that we fight, how these systems reinforce one another, and where we can best work to disrupt and transform them.

The second feature of anti-oppression is a commitment to confronting the ways in which people replicate power relations in movements and in day-to-day lives. This comes from an understanding that, even as we fight social hierarchies, they have shaped us and we participate in reproducing them. In the words of New York prison abolition organizer Pilar Maschi, "We're trying to break down the system, and it lies in all of us." With this understanding, the challenge is to deal with these power relations as they infiltrate even our most intentionally liberatory spaces. As I discuss in the next chapter, anti-authoritarians are tackling this challenge through consciousness-raising about oppressive dynamics and creating intentional organizational structures to shift power relations. For activists, these are often the most visible and common practices associated with anti-oppression politics.

The third feature of anti-oppression is a focus on transforming systems of domination in broader society. In this regard, San Francisco organizer Clare Bayard posed the central question we face: "How do we shift the fundamental power relationships that our society is built on?" The primary way that anti-authoritarians have tried to answer this question politically is by making the struggles of those who are exploited and oppressed—working-class people, people of color, women, gender-nonconforming people, queers, disabled people, among others—central in our movements, organizations, and campaigns. The basic idea is that these struggles, particularly when they combine, can potentially rupture power relations and open new ways of relating and organizing.

This focus also emphasizes solidarity as a political practice across power differences: those who experience privilege in a given context offering support, on a basis of equality and respect, to those who experience oppression in that context. How to enact this sort of solidarity is a topic of ongoing discussion. After all, developing solidarity in practice opens demanding questions concerning strategy, leadership, and organizing. And yet, as activists and organizers, we try, learning and grappling with these questions as we go. Anti-oppression names the political space within which we wrestle with these challenges while working to transform the organization and administration of power in our society.

ANTI-IMPERIALISM

The fourth "anti" in another politics is anti-imperialism. Imperialism is a system through which countries in the global North dominate countries in the global South economically, politically, culturally, and/or through outright military force. It is built on the historical foundation of European colonialism, the subordination and plunder of Indigenous peoples in Africa, Asia, Australia, and the Americas by European powers such as England, Spain, and France. This vast dispossession, beginning in the fifteenth century, was essential to the development of capitalism, as resources and people's labor (often in the form of slavery) were incorporated into emerging circuits of exploitation and profit-making. Racism, meanwhile, was key in legitimating this whole process.

Through colonialism, European powers carved up the globe into colonies, territories over which they claimed ownership and control. In some cases—Australia, southern Africa, and the Americas, in particular—the European powers sent some of their own populations to "settle" colonies. Through this process, European settlers developed societies, economies, and forms of government that were based on systematically stealing Indigenous peoples' territories and, at various times, killing or forcibly assimilating them into settler cultures. This continues today in settler states such as the United States, Canada, and Israel. Through enslavement, murder, and theft, colonialism has fundamentally shaped the current world system of nation-states.

While most territories held by European powers gained independence by the middle of the twentieth century, imperialism has continued colonial relations in more indirect ways. Dominant countries now rarely claim colonies, but they sustain power over formerly colonized countries through finance and trade, politics and aid, media and popular culture, and policing and military intervention. The United States, as the leading imperialist power since the end of World War II, has played a central role in shaping and sustaining these relations.[39]

Anti-imperialism, as it is developing in another politics, opposes imperialism and the colonialism that it rests upon. This "anti" draws on a lineage of struggle significantly anchored in the long memory of Indigenous peoples worldwide who have fought colonialism for centuries. As well, this lineage comes out of movements that resisted and eventually defeated formal European colonialism in Latin America, Asia, and Africa during the nineteenth and twentieth centuries. The experiences of 1960s-era movements also had a deep impact on anti-imperialism. As I discussed in the last chapter, people of color struggles in North America and liberation movements in the Third World, together, created a context in which revolutionaries across the globe came to see themselves as anti-imperialists. For radicals in the United States and Canada, these experiences pointedly opened what would become a persistent question of international solidarity: How can activists in the overdeveloped world best support the liberatory struggles of those in the global South?

During the 1980s, the Central American solidarity and anti-apartheid movements attempted to answer this question practically in the United States and Canada. The Central American solidarity movement allied with popular movements in countries such as El Salvador and Guatemala, where the U.S. government was aiding dictatorships, and Nicaragua, where the U.S. government was trying to destabilize the left-wing Sandinista government. The anti-apartheid movement supported the struggle in South Africa against white minority rule, known as "apartheid," which had developed out of British colonialism and was tacitly supported by the U.S. government. Activists in these movements built solidarity committees, coalitions, and campaigns involving students, faith-based institutions, labor unions, and community groups. Their efforts provided important aid to movements abroad and thrust Central America and South Africa into public discussions in North America. It is widely believed that the Central American solidarity movement effectively prevented the U.S. government from engaging in an outright military invasion of Nicaragua. The anti-apartheid movement, especially through its boycott and divestment campaign, contributed to the eventual success of the South African movement in toppling formal white rule.[40]

While these movements opened up many positive ways for activists to engage in solidarity activities, they also revisited longstanding difficulties for anti-imperialism. In particular, their experiences underlined two troubling patterns in international solidarity efforts. One is a tendency toward charity, which mobilizes through well-intentioned guilt and pity for "those poor people over there," and reproduces relations of power and paternalism between those in the North and those in the South. The other is a tendency toward adulation, which treats revolutionaries and popular movements in the South as politically superior, and shapes solidarity work in the North as a kind of cheerleading.

As people living in countries responsible for vast human suffering, we shouldn't be surprised by how compelling these tendencies are. But we also need to recognize that neither gets us very far. Both locate "real" suffering and struggle as happening elsewhere, and both avoid wrestling with thorny power dynamics necessarily bound up in solidarity work. Ultimately, both create a flattened anti-imperialism in which those in the global South are objects—either of our charity or our adulation—rather than dignified and imperfect people with whom we can collaborate on the basis of mutual equality and respect, conscious of the power differences between us.

The Zapatistas, since their emergence in 1994, have helped to interrupt these tendencies. On the one hand, they have refused solidarity-as-charity—whether in the form of discarded clothing or of paternalistic sentiments—with their own vision of dignity.[41] On the other hand, they have refused solidarity-as-adulation with humility, humor, and a consistent unwillingness to be anyone's vanguard.[42] The Zapatistas have thus introduced something that has developed more broadly through the global circulation of struggles against neoliberalism: solidarity as a two-way relationship of support, accountability, and transformation between people fighting for another world.[43] As part of this, anti-authoritarians have grasped onto—and continue to grapple with—a suggestion from Zapatista representative Subcomandante Marcos: "*haces el Zapatismo donde vives*" or, in English, "be a Zapatista where you are."[44] In the United States and Canada, organizers have used this formulation as an antidote to the tendency for radicals to get transfixed by faraway struggles in ways that make it harder to see similarly pressing struggles much closer to where we live. Solidarity, by this understanding, is necessarily about recognizing and practically building the connections between struggles "away" and "at home" in a common project of social transformation.

This notion of solidarity is still mainly an aspiration for anti-authoritarians. However, we can see its practical expressions in initiatives such as Tadamon!, a Montreal-based collective that supports liberatory struggles in the Middle East while also foregrounding Indigenous struggles in North America, and Movement for Justice in El Barrio, an immigrant-led organization in New York that combines radical community organizing with consistent support for poor people's movements in the global South.[45] In inspiring this kind of solidarity, the efforts of the Zapatistas combined with the experience of the global justice movement have reframed anti-imperialism.[46]

Anti-imperialism in another politics has been deepened, as well, through our experiences struggling against wars of occupation in Afghanistan and Iraq over the last decade. As I discussed in the last chapter, these experiences in the anti-war movement offered a political education for activists about the connections between capitalism and colonialism, and introduced the political vocabulary of anti-imperialism to many in the anti-authoritarian current.

Anti-imperialism in another politics has also been shaped by our participation in struggles against the Israeli occupation of Palestine.[47] While some anti-authoritarians have long been involved in this work, more were galvanized by the upsurge of struggle in Palestine known as the Second Intifada, between 2000 and 2005.[48] Amidst this wave of resistance, international activists collaborated with Palestinians to launch the International Solidarity Movement (ISM) in 2001. People from around the globe have since joined the ISM for stints of weeks and months in order to nonviolently support Palestinian struggles—attempting to stop Israeli demolition of Palestinian homes, accompanying Palestinians through Israeli checkpoints, and joining Palestinian farmers in efforts to access their fields in areas where they have been denied access by Israeli soldiers or settlers.[49] Some who have gone from North America have also developed connections with like-minded activist groups in Israel, particularly Anarchists Against the Wall.[50]

These experiences and ties have created a much broader awareness in the anti-authoritarian current about struggles in the region. Like others involved in Palestine work, many anti-authoritarians have begun to understand Israel "as a colonial, settler state based on a system of apartheid resembling apartheid South Africa," as described by Toronto-based organizers Adam Hanieh, Hazem Jamjoum, and Rafeef Ziadah.[51] Building on this foundation, activists and organizers have increasingly focused on the call, first made by 170 Palestinian organizations in 2005, for boycott, divestment, and sanctions (BDS) against Israel.[52] The BDS campaign is explicitly modeled on strategies that helped to topple apartheid in South Africa, and activists have taken it up in labor unions, on university campuses, and through consumer boycotts and popular education work. In these efforts, anti-authoritarians work through organizations such as the Coalition Against Israeli Apartheid in Toronto and Queers Undermining Israeli Terrorism in San Francisco, and international networks such as Al-Awda, the Palestine Right to Return Coalition, and the International Jewish Anti-Zionist Network.[53]

The apartheid framework, growing out of the experiences of South Africa and Palestine, has influenced how some in the anti-authoritarian current think about imperialism and other power relations on a world scale. As Montreal organizer Jaggi Singh put it, "You can't ever understate the fact that we live in a reality of global apartheid." Those of us in the global North are socially and geographically separated from those in the South, even as the resources and the labor that sustain our lives frequently come from them. "We're living on the other side of the apartheid fence," continued Singh. "But on this side of the Third World/First World apartheid wall, there are still other walls that exist from within, which are mostly invisible ones; but sometimes they're visible too—such as gated communities and gentrified neighborhoods." In this way, anti-authoritarians have used apartheid as an analytical tool to link inequalities and separations *between* countries to power relations *within* countries. While there are real differences, there are also key continuities. One of the most glaring is between imperialist relations among nation-states and colonial relations within settler states.

Indigenous struggles in North America have made these colonial relations more visible while sustaining vital forms of anti-colonial politics. As I explained in the last chapter, such struggles have deeply affected the anti-authoritarian current, especially in the Canadian context, influencing how many activists understand imperialism. Longtime organizer Andréa Maria expressed this growing sentiment: "A key area in North America—particularly in Canada, it's different in the United States—is dealing with the colonial present and addressing decolonization. To me, that's part of anti-imperialism." This means seeing colonialism in North America not as something that happened long ago, but rather as a process, shaped by history, that continues today. And this also poses a fundamental question: What would it mean for the inhabitants of this continent, both Indigenous and settlers, to overcome colonial relations?[54] These concerns are increasingly making anti-colonialism into what Montreal organizer Sophie Schoen aptly called "a basic stance" for anti-authoritarians. This stance is literally about acknowledging the ground on which we struggle as the starting point for anti-imperialism.

Taken together, these histories and recent experiences have shaped a particular formulation of anti-imperialist politics in the anti-authoritarian current. This formulation has two core aspects. The first is a base-level commitment to self-determination for everyone, both in North America and elsewhere in the world. Self-determination fits solidly within anti-authoritarian politics as it rejects "power-over" and emphasizes people building power together to decide their own circumstances collectively.[55] It also brings in an analysis that connects the "colonial present" of the settler states that we inhabit to the imperialist relations that they produce. Ora Wise, a Palestine solidarity organizer in New York City, stressed this sort of analysis for U.S.-based activists: "We need to ground our Palestine work in a decolonization framework, and that means decolonize here too."

This "decolonization framework" is usefully provocative. It pushes us to imagine what it would mean to end the U.S. and Canadian governments' occupations everywhere, including in North America. For settler activists, this framework also pushes us to grapple with our responsibilities on both fronts. Winnipeg organizer Paul Burrows describes this as being "committed to international solidarity both at home and abroad." In the Palestine solidarity work with which he is involved, he explains that he and his comrades "feel that it would be hypocritical to advocate self-determination for Palestinians without acknowledging that we ourselves live on stolen land, and that colonialism and genocide continue within Canada to this day."[56] For the anti-authoritarian current, the challenge is to tangibly and consistently develop ties between these fronts of struggle.[57]

The second core aspect of this "anti" is a willingness to leap into the messiness of actual anti-imperialist struggles while staying critical. As we work in and alongside such movements, we face consistent challenges. One is how to relate to struggles that manifest as national liberation movements seeking to build new states or seize power in existing ones. Anti-authoritarians tend to have deep reservations about movements oriented toward state power. And yet, in a system of global apartheid, not all nation-states are equal. What's more, national liberation movements, whether in Palestine or Puerto Rico, engage millions of people in resistance and open imaginative space for new liberatory possibilities. This is where it gets messy, as Ora Wise pointed out: "For me, it's about recognizing that there is a progressive element to a national liberation struggle in that they are trying to overthrow a colonial power. But, as we see from the Palestinian Authority and countless other historical experiences throughout the world, there is an almost automatic process of, once gaining state power, reactionary forces coming to the surface."[58]

The formulation of anti-imperialism in another politics, as Wise indicated, supports struggles against colonialism and imperialism without stepping away from the difficult questions about where such struggles take us. But as Jaggi Singh stressed, these are not questions that activists can somehow contemplate in the abstract, but rather live discussions in anti-colonial and anti-imperialist movements, with which we must engage.[59] There are no easy formulas for any of this, other than critical engagement with the messiness. But there is promise here. "When you bring anti-imperialism and anti-authoritarianism together," argued Andréa Maria, "you get a much more nuanced politic as long you apply it to specific situations." In combining these two "anti's," she continued, "you start having to talk about support for different movements, support for different aspirations and political goals and strategies that go along with those. And that's actually where true politics . . . begins."[60]

AGAINST

These four "anti's" define the "against"—the collective refusal—at the heart of another politics. This "against" is both simple and multifaceted. At the most basic level, anti-authoritarians oppose "power-over." We reject a relation based on some people having control over others, and we struggle against the organization and administration of our lives for the benefit of a few. We oppose all forms of exploitation and oppression with their specificities and interconnections. We fight these relations as they are produced and reproduced through ideas, practices, and institutions. Our "against" thus takes us from refusal of a power relation to confrontation with vast and complex systems and their intertwined histories of violence, dispossession, and domination.

In asserting this "against," the anti-authoritarian current draws on dense and tangled histories. Consciously or not, we work with analyses and aspirations developed through previous experiences of struggle, such as nonhierarchical organizing practices, intersectional understandings of power relations, and a commitment to self-determination. At the same time, we challenge certainties that have been widespread on the left, such as correct line politics, vanguardist orientations, and claims about the primacy of capitalism. The synthetic political approach is essential here, as it enables us to pull on different traditions, histories, and political identities even as we try to recognize their flaws and build on their strengths.

We should understand each of the four "anti's," even as they tug on strands of history, as live formulations within the anti-authoritarian current. In this sense, they're not so much set lines as they are anchor-points for dynamic politics and practices. Activists and organizers use and modify them as core principles that are also open questions: To what extent do we need to relate to the state as we engage in collective struggles for liberation? How do we effectively undermine capitalist social relations in ways that foster collectivity? What does an intersectional political practice look like? How do we get to decolonization? Another politics lies precisely in our attempts to grapple with these and other pressing questions opened by the "anti's" in the messy, complicated circumstances in which we struggle.

Defining ourselves in opposition, as Francesca Fiorentini suggested, brings clarity. The "against" in another politics helps us determine where we come from, stake out where we stand, name our enemies, and identify important questions we face. As crucial as it is, however, the "against" represents only one half of our politics. I now turn to the other.

3. "Organizing now the way you want to see the world later"

Prefigurative Politics

On the one hand, it is necessary to engage in oppositional politics to corporate and state power by taking power. Yet if we only engage in the politics of taking power, we will have a tendency to replicate the hierarchical structures in our movements. So it is also important to "make power" by creating those structures within our organizations, movements, and communities that model the world we are trying to create.

Andrea Smith

Kids and caregivers make magical amulets at the 2012 Allied Media Conference in Detroit, Michigan, as part of a Kid's Track program organized by members of the Intergalactic Conspiracy of Childcare Collectives, a network of radical childcare collectives and caregivers. (Photo by Robin Markle, Philly Childcare Collective)

IN MY CONVERSATION with RJ Maccani, he emphasized the essential reconstructive aspect of another politics. Drawing on his extensive organizing history in New York—with Critical Resistance, Regeneración Childcare, the Challenging Male Supremacy Project, and many other initiatives—Maccani observed that "there's a lot of prefigurative work going on and there's a lot of this organizing around new social relations, prioritizing stories, listening, and trust-building." This work grows out of a shared commitment to what is frequently called "prefigurative politics."[1] This term names activist efforts to manifest and build, to the greatest extent possible, the world we would like to see through our means of fighting in this one. Examples of such efforts include using directly democratic methods of making decisions and building institutions through which people can self-organize to meet popular needs.

While Maccani and his comrades in New York have well-developed vocabularies for talking about this work, the practice of prefigurative politics is not unique to them. Indeed, the combination of the oppositional and the reconstructive is foundational for another politics. This politics brings together refusal of domination with affirmative commitment to building new social relations and forms of social organization in the process of struggle. It aspires to fuse the "against"—our rejection of ruling relations and institutions—with the "beyond"—our creation of new ways of being, relating, and doing. This chapter focuses on the second aspect, the "beyond."

Prefigurative politics can seem hollow, naïve, or simply impractical. In the United States and Canada, the kinds of efforts most often called prefigurative tend to be associated with marginal and insular activist subcultures, and generally function on small scales.[2] For the most part, these are genuine limitations. Part of the promise of another politics, however, is that organizers are attempting to ground prefigurative ideas and practices in community-based work in ways that can grow much more widely and deeply. There are plenty of tensions in these efforts, but also crucial emerging possibilities.

One useful way to explore the reconstructive dimension of the anti-authoritarian current is to start from the tensions, which I understand through a linked contradiction and challenge. The contradiction is this: on the one hand, developing entirely liberatory social relations is never fully possible in a context of domination; on the other hand, developing such social relations is crucial to building visionary movements capable of transforming the world. In other words, the new modes we create for living, relating, and organizing always come up against the dominant social order. We can't bring a new world into being as long as current systems call the shots. And yet we can't bring a new world into being unless popular move-ments can envision and create something new here and now. Prefigurative activities, in sum, are always constrained and always necessary.

This leads to the challenge, as posed by journalist and organizer Andréa Maria: "How do you work in the disjunction between what is and what you want?" That is, how do we push at the bounds of what is possible while understanding that we will come up against limitations imposed by the existing organization and administration of power? How do we struggle in that space of contradiction with a sense of hope and possibility?

In this chapter, I explore how anti-authoritarians wrestle with this chal-lenge practically as we organize in broad-based movements. My main focus throughout is on what I understand as prefigurative praxis. By this, I mean the ways people in struggle both put prefigurative aspirations into practice and develop, from our practices, those prefigurative aspects that are already present. With this focus, I unpack the range of activities that get lumped under the label "prefigurative" and look at forms of prefigurative activity that are especially widespread in the anti-authoritarian current. I also point to some consistent dangers in these activities and suggest that, in grappling with these dangers, organizers are working in the disjunction between "what is" and "what we want."

UNPACKING PREFIGURATIVE POLITICS

Like the "anti's," prefigurative politics has developed out of interconnected histories of struggle. The anti-authoritarian current, as I traced in chapter 1, draws on reconstructive ideas and practices that activists have crafted over the last two centuries and especially the last few decades—from aboli-tionism to labor radicalism, feminism to the occupy movement. Across these experiences, prefigurative formulations have often built on previous ones. Individual organizers (and, in some cases, particular organizations) have played key roles here, carrying ways of doing and thinking with them as they've traversed movements. Together, these overlapping experiences and formulations have created the foundation for prefigurative politics in the anti-authoritarian current.

For many activists, the term "prefigurative politics" has thus come to define a commitment to putting vision into practice through struggle. Sonya Z. Mehta, a former organizer with Young Workers United in San Francisco, succinctly summed up this understanding: "prefigurative organ-izing means organizing now the way you want to see the world later." The core idea here is that *how* we get ourselves to a transformed society (the means) is importantly related to *what* that transformed society will be (the ends). The means *prefigure* the ends. To engage in prefigurative politics, then, is to intentionally shape our activities to manifest our vision. While useful in this general conceptual way, though, the term is much less precise for describing particular practices. As anarchist activist-scholar Andrew Cornell points out, "it has been applied to such a variety of activities that it can prevent us from clearly distinguishing between different forms of action and the value we believe they hold."[3]

There are, in fact, a few kinds of activity that tend to get lumped together under the label "prefigurative." Perhaps the most widely recognized of these forms is practicing countercultural lifestyles that in some way point toward a better society. Whether vegetarianism, collective living, or nonmonogamous relationships, such lifestyles generally involve efforts to "live our values"—to bring day-to-day ways of living into line with radical aspirations. People with a wide variety of political commitments engage in this kind of activity, and it is not necessarily linked to organizing efforts and collective action.

A second form of prefigurative praxis is building and running counter-institutions, such as food co-ops, free community health clinics, and land trusts. At their best, counterinstitutions address popular needs (such as food, health care, or housing), drain support from dominant institutions, bolster broader movements, and offer venues for people to practice democratic and egalitarian ways of working together. I discuss such institutions in more detail in chapter 5. A third kind of prefigurative activity is organizing—bringing people together in ways that build their collective power—with a horizontal orientation. This orientation aims to foster people's capacities for critically analyzing the world, taking initiative with competence and confidence, engaging in strategic action, and democratically running their own affairs. I examine this form of praxis in chapters 6, 7, and 8.

A fourth kind of prefigurative praxis is creating and practicing more egalitarian modes of interacting within movement contexts. This is probably the most common way that anti-authoritarians experience and understand prefigurative politics. I focus on this fourth type of activity in what follows.[4]

NONHIERARCHICAL DECISION-MAKING

The most widely used form of prefigurative praxis in the anti-authoritarian current, as in many previous movements, is nonhierarchical decision-making. Montreal organizer Jaggi Singh, active with the migrant justice network Solidarity Across Borders, laid this out very clearly:

Solidarity Across Borders meets monthly to figure out the broad orientations of our campaigns and then delegates the organizing work together. The community assembly structure is prefigurative of something that's key to eventual organization on a mass scale: the community council, what was called the *soviet* during the Russian Revolution. In the Kabylie area of Algeria, their local forms of direct democracy are embodied in a horizontal community structure called the *aarsh*. In Guatemala there are base communities. The Iroquois have the longhouse. In each situation, there are cultural differences, and I don't want to make this look monolithic; there are differences between each local example of horizontal decision-making that I'm mentioning. As well, those examples are much more rich and deeply rooted in local organizing contexts and long-term histories of struggle and resistance. But they are inspirations, and in my terrain of struggle, the open assembly structure—with delegation, transparency, and openness within certain shared principles—is prefigurative of how we should organize in other situations: in the workplace, in communities, in schools, in the neighborhood. People meeting and figuring out things directly . . . . That's all prefigurative of what we mean by "base democracy," "grassroots democracy," "popular democracy," or "direct democracy."

This idea of direct democracy is key. Anti-authoritarian organizers try to use methods of making decisions in which everyone concerned has a say, all involved are accountable to the broader group as they carry out decisions, and everyone shares a sense of collectivity. Rahula Janowski, who was part of the Heads Up collective in San Francisco, expressed a widely shared perspective: "The world I want to live in is one where people collectively make decisions about the day-to-day operations of our lives; everybody is able to participate, and 'able' means both that they're allowed to and that they have the capacity—the skills, the time, the access. That's the world I want to live in, so the way I want to struggle for that world is by trying, as much as possible, to do that now in the spaces where I can."

There are both political and practical reasons for this approach. As I mentioned in the last chapter, nonhierarchical process rests on a critique of top-down decision-making structures in which only a few people call the shots, as well as on a vision of a society in which all people can participate in making decisions to the extent that they are affected by them. Nonhierarchical process is also a useful tool in our organizing work. Like many organizers before us, anti-authoritarians have come to find that participatory decision-making can help build trust and a common sense of purpose, open spaces to create new ideas and ways of doing things, and develop skills for working collectively and democratically.[5] This kind of decision-making process is thus both a tool and a vision, a means and an end. We use it regularly in our communities, organizations, and movements.

Nonhierarchical process in the anti-authoritarian current takes different forms. The longstanding model of consensus decision-making is especially popular. In the formal version of this model, group members make proposals that are then discussed collectively. Together, the group refines proposals based on any concerns that members express. A person designated as a "facilitator," usually a rotating position, prepares a meeting agenda in advance, guides the group through the process, and checks for consensus, meaning unanimous agreement. Any group member who strongly disagrees with a decision can "block" consensus, in which case the proposal must be discussed further, postponed, or abandoned.[6] What many activists appreciate about consensus decision-making is that it makes it difficult for a majority to force decisions on a minority, encourages collective problem-solving through discussion and compromise, and aims to equalize participation. In the anti-authoritarian current, most small groups and collectives use some form of consensus.

Another popular form of nonhierarchical process, particularly in big meetings, is the general assembly. In this model, everyone has an opportunity to speak and make proposals, and decisions are made through a modified form of consensus or a general vote. The practice of assemblies, in one form or another, has been and continues to be common in liberatory movements across the globe, most recently in the occupy movement and the Quebec student movement. As many activists have learned, assemblies can create dynamic spaces for popular deliberation and decision-making in large meetings even when people present don't share a common background.

These forms of decision-making are works in progress with their own consistent challenges. Consensus can come up against major problems when a meeting is very large, when those present don't have a shared group identity or goal, or when meeting participants have uneven familiarity with the decision-making process. Actively participating in a general assembly, as Montreal organizer Sophie Schoen pointed out, usually requires speaking in front of a large group. Not surprisingly, those (often men) who have been socialized to feel entitled to voice their opinions tend to be more comfortable with this kind of participation. Consensus-based meetings and assemblies can also be incredibly time-consuming, leading to situations in which those who are able to stick around the longest are able to have the final say.[7] More generally, nonhierarchical decision-making structures can obscure leaders and leadership in groups, a problem I discuss in chapter 7.

As organizers grapple with these and other challenges, we work in the disjunction between what is and what we want. Rahula Janowski's comments go to the heart of this: the ability to have a voice in nonhierarchical decision-making is about both process (a structure of interacting) and capacity (the things everyone needs in order to participate). The idea of capacity is a way of recognizing that we all come into organizations with very different kinds of skills and experiences, resources of available time, and levels of confidence. Often these differences are related to our class backgrounds, how we are racialized, our genders and sexualities, whether we are disabled, and other ways we are positioned in existing social hierarchies. They're also about how long we've been involved in movement work.

Bringing the question of capacity into nonhierarchical process means acknowledging these differences, creating intentional practices for helping people to learn skills and develop self-confidence, and creating structures that allow for different time commitments and levels of involvement. Anti-authoritarian groups are experimenting with a variety of ways of doing this, including "buddy" systems that team up more experienced organizers with less experienced folks as well as skills-building and political education programs. These are attempts to model and move toward what we want without forgetting where we currently stand.

Even as we work with these challenges, we shouldn't lose sight of how these processes help us move toward the world that we want. Used with intention and attention to context, directly democratic models are powerful and transformative; they tap into the enormous potential for people to learn from one another, make well-considered collective decisions, and collaborate through discussion and action.

NEW WAYS OF RELATING

In describing the values associated with nonhierarchical process, many anti-authoritarians use a term from Latin America: *horizontalidad* or "horizontalism." Drawing on her experiences with movements in Argentina, activist-scholar Marina Sitrin explains, "*Horizontalidad* does not just imply a flat plane for organizing, or nonhierarchical relationships in which people no longer make decisions for others. It is a positive word that implies the use of direct democracy and the striving for consensus, a process in which everyone is heard and new relationships are created."[8] What Sitrin importantly highlights here is that nonhierarchical process is closely connected to creating new modes of relating—new ways of living, loving, and struggling together. This is central for prefigurative praxis in another politics.

Constructing new ways of relating can be controversial. In many parts of the left, talk about how we relate is viewed with confusion, suspicion, and even contempt. Certainly, talk along these lines is too often insular and individualized. Yet as Montreal migrant justice organizer Tatiana Gomez pointed out, serious attempts can be smeared with these sorts of labels too. Discussions about how we relate, she observed, are "sometimes even thought of as 'less important,' 'less relevant,' 'flaky,' 'hippie.'" Gomez argued that these kinds of dismissals have a gendered dimension to them since, in the context of patriarchal relations, the undervalued work of sustaining relationships is generally associated with women. This is a crucial point.

How we relate matters. It affects how inviting and resilient our movements are, how effective and transformative our struggles are, and what sorts of new possibilities we can create. Developing another politics, for many anti-authoritarians, means developing another way of *doing* politics—one with neither the masculinized "hardness" that so often dominates the left nor the self-engrossed individualism that dominates much discussion of how we treat one another. But what does this look like in practice? There are three relational formulations I have consistently encountered among organizers doing very different sorts of work in different regions of North America: "wholeness," "affective organizing," and "being nice." These ideas, as they are linked to practical efforts, point to small yet significant ways that activists approach developing new social relations.

The first of these is a desire for all people to be able to enter movements as "whole people." Atlanta-based organizer and educator Stephanie Guilloud posed this as a question: "How do we come to these spaces [of struggle] as our whole selves?" Marika Warner, who was active in anti-prison and radical women of color organizing in Toronto, talked about this in relation to her work with the Prisoners Justice Action Committee. For this group, she said, prefigurative politics is "an undiscussed mandate" that shapes "the way that we interact, the way that we try to be aware of what is going on for people, and [the way that we] really try to make room for people to show up whole at that table."

This notion of wholeness grows from women of color feminism, with its rejection of politics that fragment people's experiences of power relations into separate issues associated with race, class, gender, sexuality, and disability. What radical women of color have frequently crafted instead are political spaces that allow for the complex realities of their lives as they are shaped by multiple forms of oppression—spaces that they can enter as whole people. Warner discussed this in relation to her efforts with others to start a Toronto affiliate of INCITE! Through the space that they were creating together, she said, "We're prefiguring a society where women will be healthy and where women of color won't have to be meek or have to pretend or have to shut ourselves down." Efforts like these have much to teach all of us about creating collectivities in struggle. In particular, they suggest that we develop spaces in which we can work with the complicated ways that we all carry relations of privilege and oppression with us.

This concern with wholeness also delves into very intimate aspects of people's lives. Life under systems of domination is toxic for everyone, although in different ways and with different effects. Many people experience abuse and other kinds of violence, and live with trauma. Lots of us endure a barrage of daily social messages telling us that we're inferior, worthless, or simply wrong. Most people struggle with anxiety and depression. As Oakland-based organizer Joshua Kahn Russell put it, "We're all psychologically scarred"—and these scars are deeply connected to how power is organized and administered in our society.[9]

In these circumstances, Guilloud asked the relevant question for everyone who seeks to transform the world: "How are we holding and understanding, and then moving and shifting with broken, broken people, including ourselves?" That is, organizers must relate to the ways that all people are wounded, sometimes deeply, while also moving them into collective action. Entering our work as whole people also means allowing space for the battered and broken parts of ourselves, and understanding struggle itself as a process through which we can recover or create some sense of wholeness.

In doing any of this, care is key, which I think accounts for the increasing popularity of a second relational formulation: "affective organizing." "Affective" means having to do with emotions. Its pairing with "organizing" draws on *política afectiva* or "affective politics," a term from Latin American autonomous movements. This is a political approach aimed at building relationships of genuine care in the process of struggle.[10] To be sure, this is nothing new for movements; people have long nurtured collective feelings of love while fighting injustice. Nor is this unique in our everyday lives; the capacity to build caring relationships with one other is an enduring and hopeful characteristic of humans and many other animals. Affective organizing is about recognizing and deliberately fostering these feelings and relationships as essential ingredients for transformative struggle.

Affective organizing grows from a critique of a prevailing mode of left political work. Paula Ximena Rojas-Urrutia, who was active with Sista II Sista and INCITE! in New York, described this mode as "based on a macho revolutionary standard of struggle in which commitment is measured by how 'tough' you are, how much you can sacrifice family and love in order to focus on the revolutionary process." While she traced this standard to a particular idea of armed struggle, it has been and continues to be widespread across the North American left. As Rojas-Urrutia pointed out, "Some U.S.-based organizers, including feminists of color, seem to romanticize this 'old-school' revolutionary model, equating militaristic talk and dress, top-down chains of command, 'tight security,' long hours at meetings every night, and personal-life sacrifice with being truly revolutionary."[11]

Affective organizing in another politics names a space in which activists are trying to create alternatives to this "macho revolutionary standard." One part of this, building from feminism particularly, is recognizing and valuing an often overlooked activity in our movements: the labor of care, sometimes called "reproductive labor." Rojas-Urrutia described this as the "other kind of work that makes society run," which involves "caring for others—not just parenting, but taking care of each other, taking care of our elders, our children, or anyone who needs it." Usually associated with women, she argued, "that invisible labor isn't accounted for in these models [that dominate left political work]."[12] And yet this labor—whether in the form of preparing food, mediating conflicts, or nurturing burnt-out activists—is fundamental for building and sustaining movements.

In the anti-authoritarian current, organizers are attempting to be more intentional and explicit about caring labor. One example is the increasing popularity of building collectives that provide childcare for parents, particularly working-class mothers of color, while they are involved in organizing work. Anti-authoritarians have created these sorts of collectives in Baltimore, Chicago, Montreal, New York, Philadelphia, San Francisco, and other cities, often collaborating with community-based organizations. Childcare collectives are an important way for activists to contribute caring labor, develop alliances, and support critical organizing efforts. Such collectives practice a different set of social relations around care in terms of who does it (not only parents, and especially not only mothers) and how it is organized (collectively rather than individually).[13] While there is much more to be done to make movements into spaces where kids can thrive, such collectives are significant initial steps.[14]

This kind of activity is just one of the experiments of care being practiced in the anti-authoritarian current. Others include collective households with shared homemaking tasks and organizations that designate and rotate caregiving responsibilities. Much of the time, this work continues to be less valued and to fall disproportionately on women, but these are exciting experiments worth developing further. Ultimately, they hold the promise of building what activist and theorist Silvia Federici calls "self-reproducing movements"—movements that prioritize their own reproduction and reorganize caregiving in ways that weave into and transform the caring labor that permeates our society.[15]

Affective organizing also grows out of frustrating and demoralizing interpersonal experiences we've had on the broad left, including within the anti-authoritarian current. Indeed, one of the most common topics in my discussions with organizers was how vicious activists can be toward one another. As Montreal organizer and nurse Helen Hudson said, "We're not that principled or caring in the way we treat each other." James Tracy, a housing organizer in San Francisco, put it more bluntly: "We can be our own worst enemies on the left."

Why is this? Certainly, how we treat one another is deeply influenced by dominant social relations. Through these, we learn to see compassion as scarce, to look out for our loved ones and ourselves first, and to relate to other people based on what we can get from them. At the same time, how we relate is shaped by the circumstances in which we struggle. Speaking in broad terms, Tracy observed, "We haven't been part of a leftist movement that's made a long-lasting impact in a really long time, so it's a lot easier to point at other people for their deficiencies—for how they're not political enough, they don't have the correct line." In short, prevailing ways of relating and self-protective efforts easily feed into sectarian and even malicious behavior, all fueled by circumstances in which our movements are frequently embattled. While this is understandable, it doesn't make for healthy movements. As Tracy asked, "How the hell are you going to build our movement if you're alienating everyone who wants to roll up their sleeves and work and collaborate and share ideas and perspectives?"

A commitment to affective organizing means resisting these alienating tendencies while working to create movement cultures based on care and trust. Much of this approach can be summed up in a third relational formulation, what some organizers simply call "being nice." Others use more negative terms. Harjit Singh Gill, an Oakland-based social worker and board member of the Institute for Anarchist Studies, called it "not being a fucking asshole."

This deceptively simple notion is deeply prefigurative. For one, it suggests dealing with political differences with respect rather than contempt. In Gill's words, "I don't see a reason to be mean-spirited, because we're all in this for a reason. Even if we disagree, we're all in this fight together. This is a situation where we really need to remember the old song, 'Which Side Are You On?' Are you on the side of working people and the majority of the planet? Then, okay, let's figure this out." This focus on recognizing our common aspirations grows out of the synthetic political approach I described in chapter 2. In no way does it mean overlooking political differences or avoiding debate, but it does suggest approaching disagreements with an eye on shared values and aims.

"Being nice" also means developing new habits of being in which we appreciate and support one another. San Francisco organizer Rahula Janowski talked about this as shifting "to being really nice to people—asking them how they're doing and asking if they need help and offering them the help they need or just sympathizing with them if they're having a struggle." This generally involves lots of sharing and listening to one another's stories in both more formal situations (such as meetings) and less formal ones (such as meals). It also involves intentional mentorship, in which more experienced organizers offer encouragement and support to less experienced organizers, a topic I discuss further in chapter 7.

These new modes of relating are, of course, easier said than done. As organizers, we struggle with the often harmful ways we have been socialized to treat one another and with how to develop more healthy and liberating practices. And if we're succeeding, we're grappling with these things inside movements that are fighting against injustice. We face important questions, then, about how to combine our attempts to develop new social relations with our efforts to challenge existing social relations. One crucial example of this has to do with healing. Many involved in developing another politics believe that prefigurative praxis has to relate in some way to how we are damaged by systems of domination.[16] But what is the role of healing in relation to organizing? When and how should it happen?

Some anti-authoritarians argue for making healing a central feature of movements. Montreal organizer Helen Hudson articulated this view:

> Through my involvement in gender centers, I've counseled a lot of people dealing with personal trauma, some of whom were also organizers and others who were not. I've noticed that taking action to address not only your own oppression, your own trauma, but also the way that same oppression is manifested more broadly in society can be really empowering, really healing. Some radical communities seem more willing to make space for that than others. I mention this because the gender centers example is perhaps overly obvious. But even radical spaces that don't explicitly place healing at the center of their praxis, can—and I think should—foster that type of self-awareness and empowerment.

From this perspective, work around healing is a powerful basis for developing consciousness and taking action against structural forms of violence. As well, this perspective sees healing as crucial for welcoming and sustaining people's participation in movements. Many who hold this perspective argue for bringing an orientation toward healing into most or all aspects of political work. In Hudson's words, "I think the degree to which movements can be healing—and the degree to which there's space for that, for it to be messy but still okay—is directly proportional to the sustainability of the movement and the ability for people to stay involved."

Others in the anti-authoritarian current emphasize the importance of healing work but think it should be separate from organizing work. As Atlanta organizer Stephanie Guilloud suggested:

> The individual healing process from racism, internalized oppression, queer oppression, and the like, is a messy, complicated, difficult process for people . . . . Maybe we need a space that's all queer or maybe we need a space that's all men or male-born folks to just sort of hash some of this stuff out. Maybe we do, maybe we don't. But the process of internal healing does not confront the institutions of white supremacy or patriarchy, and we just have to be real about that. So, there are two different processes, absolutely linked—because we know that in order to confront those institutions, we have to work individually and with groups. In order to work collectively or in group, we have to be engaged in some kind of process with ourselves to be part of that group and part of our own wholeness and to be part of a community that can hold us, if that's possible. But the point of being in that group is not to do the individual healing work at all. And to treat groups like that—that is wrong. The purpose of group work is to direct outwards and confront institutions, build alternatives, and create spaces. Our purpose within collective work must be to externalize our responses to oppression and violence.

This perspective also understands healing as a necessary foundation for engaging in struggles to change society. However, it sees healing and organizing (what Guilloud calls "working in group") as different processes that must happen in different spaces. Those with this perspective warn that orienting most or all political work around healing focuses our attention inward, away from the structural forces that we must confront. Guilloud concluded, "If the group allows itself to get stuck in people's pain over organizing collective action—not to devalue people's pain—but if the group finds purpose in handling pain and internal process to heal from one thing or another, whether it's oppressor or oppressed, you're done; the group will fall, and I have been a part of that imbalance too many times."

Both of these perspectives have something vital to offer. The first illuminates how new ways of relating that we create in movements can help us understand our individual experiences of trauma in the context of power relations, and become more whole people. The second highlights how our attempts to develop new social relations through healing processes, if we're not clear about their role, can undermine our efforts to challenge and change society.

In their tension, these two perspectives bring us back to the disjunction of prefigurative praxis. We want a world in which people are healthy and whole, caring labor is valued and shared equitably, and we treat each other with trust and tenderness. Our efforts to develop these features in our movements are crucial in modeling more liberatory ways of relating and sustaining organizers for the long haul. But in the world that is, prefigurative practices are not enough to fundamentally transform dominant social relations. No matter how well we treat one another inside our movements, the social forces that shape how we relate continue to exist and must be fought. We can't lose sight of the fact that the new social relations we are developing are ones we want to see in our broader society, not just in our movements.

TRANSFORMING POWER RELATIONS

One of the most significant and consistently challenging modes in which organizers in the anti-authoritarian current are trying to create new ways of relating is anti-oppression practices: efforts to transform power relations in movements. Although not usually understood as a form of prefigurative praxis, anti-oppression politics has an important reconstructive dimension to it.[17] As we saw in the last chapter, a key insight in this "anti" is that social relations of heterosexism, white supremacy, ableism, patriarchy, and capitalism, among others, not only exist "out there" in the wider society, but also "in here" in our movements. This leads to the difficult question, as posed by Paula Ximena Rojas-Urrutia: "How are we replicating domination in the way that we're struggling?"[18]

This is a pressing concern for anti-oppression politics, and one that comes up again and again in the anti-authoritarian current. The core idea is that we have to contend with how power relations are reproduced in our communities, organizations, and interpersonal relationships. The prefigurative promise, meanwhile, is that our movements can be spaces in which we develop liberatory, egalitarian ways of interacting and being. Importantly, we understand that power relations, whether in activist groups or broader society, don't change through good intentions or wishful thinking; they change through agitating and organizing. In the anti-authoritarian current, this work of transforming power relations happens in a number of different ways.

The first of these is developing consciousness around privilege and oppression. This means locating ourselves within hierarchies of race, class, gender, disability, and sexuality. How, if at all, do we benefit from these hierarchies? How, if at all, are we oppressed? And how are these dynamics at play around us? Montreal-based organizer Mary Foster, who was deeply involved in international solidarity efforts and organizing against repressive state measures, talked about herself in these terms: "I'm hoping to even begin to grasp the kind of privileges I have on the basis of my race and my class and then to work to confront those privileges as part of my broader work against hierarchies and power." With this kind of investigation, we can critically reflect on how we participate in reproducing power relations as well as how we might disrupt these relations and help develop new ones.

Within the anti-authoritarian current, common modes of building anti-oppression consciousness are through trainings, individual and collective study, and discussion. Anti-oppression workshops, combining presentations and participatory exercises to spark critical reflection, are probably the most frequently used of these modes. Many activists and organizers also learn from being involved, for better and worse, with "calling people on their shit"—confronting individual behavior or organizational dynamics that perpetuate oppressive relations. Through this consciousness-raising work, we struggle with the ways that we are shaped by "what is," in an effort to manifest new ways of being and relating. We learn, as Oakland activist Harjit Singh Gill put it, "how to be better people."

The second main way that anti-authoritarians work to transform power relations is by creating organizational structures that challenge and shift dynamics of oppression and privilege. Echoing Rahula Janowski's comments earlier in this chapter about capacity, New York activist Brooke Lehman pointed out that "not everybody is coming to an organization with an equal amount of time and ability . . . . Not everybody is coming with the same level of confidence in their voice based on privilege and opportunity or knowledge." Lehman thus emphasized building structures that are "self-reflective and responsive to privilege within the group." Veteran organizer and former political prisoner Ashanti Alston spoke about this in relation to his experiences in Anarchist People of Color groups. "We're going to experiment and develop practices that allow for maximum participation," he said. "We're going to be conscious as we come, as we engage or encounter (*encuentro* as the Zapatistas would say), about who we even silence."

Practices with this focus are widespread in the anti-authoritarian current. Some groups, such as United Students Against Sweatshops, use identity-based caucuses (women-identified and men-identified, people of color and white folks, and so on) so that marginalized groups can structurally intervene in decision-making; in the occupy movement, these also sometimes took the form of working groups.[19] Some organizations, such as INCITE!, intentionally develop formations for people who have a shared experience of a particular form of oppression. Some groups develop tools to regulate the composition of who speaks in meetings, whether by prioritizing contributions from members who are traditionally marginalized (a procedure sometimes called "progressive stack") or limiting the number of comments that all members are able to make. Some organizations, such as Solidarity Across Borders in Montreal, designate "resource people" who are trained in anti-oppression work and peer education; these individuals act as allies and advocates for anyone in the group who is experiencing oppressive dynamics.

With these and other practices in the anti-authoritarian current, our consistent concern has to do with "who we even silence," as Alston put it. As more and more organizers have taken up this concern, we've also started to think in increasingly proactive ways about how, in our groups, to build and support the participation and initiative of those of us who are often kept on the margins—queers, people of color, women, disabled people, and working-class folks. This approach involves what is sometimes called "leadership development"—skills-training, political education, and confidence-building—which I explore in chapter 7.

The third main way this anti-oppression work happens in another politics is through how organizers orient group cultures and priorities. Sometimes this comes up in our conversations about the kinds of movement spaces that we're creating. Talking about her work with Critical Resistance, for example, Pilar Maschi said, "We need to make this a comfortable space and have the culture be reflective of people most impacted." This formulation of "most impacted" or "most affected" is a central one in the anti-authoritarian current.[20] Among organizers, it has become shorthand for describing those who, in a given situation, most directly experience oppression. Depending on the circumstances, those most impacted might be low-wage workers, women, houseless folks, people who are imprisoned or detained, Indigenous people, migrants, and/or transpeople, among many others.

The core of this notion is that those who take the brunt of domination frequently have the most insight into what needs to change in order to achieve justice and equality. The other idea here is that genuine social transformation happens when those targeted by power relations play a leading role in challenging those relations. Consequently, those most impacted, as Montreal organizer Jaggi Singh put it, "should be the ones that determine responses, determine the nature of struggle on all levels."

A consistent way that anti-authoritarian groups cultivate this orientation is by trying to put those most affected at the center of analysis and strategy. When we are organizing with directly impacted communities, this often means striving to ensure that the campaign or organization is genuinely reflective of those communities. Oakland-based organizer Rachel Herzing described this approach in Critical Resistance, where "there's a kind of a value around bringing in, developing leadership among, and keeping involved people who are most impacted by the prison-industrial-complex."[21] Adriana Paz similarly discussed this in the context of her work with Justicia for Migrant Workers, a migrant worker organizing collective in Vancouver: "We really try to encourage, in our group, members that are coming from the affected communities. And that's just mostly Latinos, but also Punjabis, Filipinos, and Chinese. That is going to define what the organizing culture and style of your group is going to look like."

In other cases, anti-authoritarians work in groups that offer solidarity to directly impacted people—whether fired textile workers in Montreal or African American youth facing police harassment in Oakland—but are mostly not made up of those people. In these circumstances, organizers frequently try to set priorities with some direction from those most affected in a given struggle, though how exactly to do this is a topic of intense discussion.[22] Additionally, some anti-authoritarian efforts, such as men against patriarchy groups, explicitly focus on people who are relatively privileged organizing similarly privileged people to participate in struggles for justice and equality. In these situations, organizers attempt to bring in the analysis generated by those most affected, to deepen understanding and indicate possibilities for strategic action.

As more and more activists and organizers are working to enact anti-oppression politics, it is increasingly clear that efforts to transform power relations are full of pitfalls. One of the most debilitating of these is getting fixated on particular forms of talking rather than how those forms are connected to practical activities. This is especially stark when organizers—particularly those who are relatively privileged—master specialized anti-oppression vocabulary without substantially changing how their organizations function. Using a specific set of terms isn't enough. And particularly when such terms rely on an assumed university education, they can perpetuate exclusion based on class.[23]

To put anti-oppression politics into practice in our groups, we have to wrestle with hard questions in an ongoing way: How do we remain consistently mindful of power dynamics and shift them? Who has the opportunity, capacity, and support to take initiative? How do we determine our priorities and develop strategy? Who gets recognition and for what work? How do we hold people accountable? These aren't just questions for discussion; we have to create practices to move on them. Otherwise, we're participating in a transformation of "talk" and perhaps individual consciousness, but not a deeper transformation of structures and orientation.[24]

Even with their pitfalls, anti-oppression practices are crucial. On the one hand, they are our attempts to struggle in the world that is—a world structured by social relations of oppression and exploitation. On the other hand, they are our attempts to manifest and model the world that we want—a world built on egalitarianism, solidarity, and self-determination. Because of the yawning gap between these two worlds, it's easy not to notice what such practices regularly accomplish. In fact, organizers have used them to shift the consciousness, structures, and cultures of many activist groups. As a result of these efforts, there is substantially more space—not enough, but more—in left movements to identify power relations and work to transform them.

DANGERS

Organizers make use of these prefigurative forms unevenly, and often they're more aspirations than realities. Still, it is significant that anti-authoritarians are increasingly focusing on and developing these forms. Prefigurative practices are also important contributions to visionary left organizing more generally. But they're not without their challenges. With each, organizers encounter the tension between dominant social relations and often small attempts to develop liberatory social relations. Working in this disjunction, we face very real dangers.

One danger is treating certain prefigurative forms as somehow preset or eternally correct. For instance, many activists understand "nonhierarchical" more or less to mean "consensus" or "general assembly." Similarly, "anti-oppression work" is frequently equated with facilitating or participating in anti-oppression workshops, and such workshops are often the knee-jerk response to any manifestations of oppressive dynamics in groups.[25] While understandable, this recipe-like focus on specific forms is a mistake. No form works in all times and places, and some forms can be counterproductive in certain situations. To take one example, insisting on using strict consensus process in a very large meeting when participants don't have a shared goal is likely to lead to unproductive tensions rather than united action. Rather than mimicking preset models, we should be developing practices and structures that make sense in our particular circumstances.

A related danger is seeing specific forms of prefigurative praxis as "things" that, as individuals, we either "have" or "don't have." This danger is perhaps most pronounced in the case of anti-oppression politics, which activists all too often understand as a package of directions about how individually to treat people. Sharmeen Khan, a leading anti-oppression trainer based in Toronto, said that she frequently encounters this perspective. "I try to do [a training] in ways where it's engaging and really critical and people are thinking about things," she explained. "But so many people are just like, 'I know we're bad. Tell me how I can stop being bad. Tell me what language to use.' It's all about behaviors to one another."

Clare Bayard, a trainer with the Catalyst Project in San Francisco, echoed Khan's experiences and offered some further analysis: "I think what has been happening is a very individualized way of thinking about anti-oppression, which, to oversimplify, is more about figuring out what's the right language and how do we interact with each other in a way that feels more responsible . . . . To some extent, [this] is about power relationships within an organization or between people, but [it] is not seen in connection to the institutional oppressions through which society is structured."

The tendency that Khan and Bayard described focuses narrowly on anti-oppression politics as a fixed set of behaviors and understandings that we can grasp individually, rather than as a dynamic set of politics, practices, and sensibilities that we develop and enact collectively as we struggle to change society. In its most reduced form, this tendency easily slips into an abstract list of "do's" and "don't's" for how individuals who experience a particular form of privilege should treat individuals who experience a related form of oppression. While these kinds of shifts in behavior are important, they don't, on their own, fundamentally challenge the foundations of exploitation and oppression in our society.[26]

At its worst, an individualized and "thingified" approach to prefigurative praxis can lead to dangerous kinds of absolutist thinking and acting. In these situations, particular prefigurative forms (such as conforming to certain behavior in consensus-based meetings or using specific anti-oppression terminology) become standards by which people are assessed as "in" or "out." Michelle O'Brien, a housing organizer in New York, characterized this as "a politics of purging," which she defined as "a politics of rigorously articulating what the right way of thinking is and punishing people who don't follow it." O'Brien continued, "The entire idea that we're going to put together the most radical, right-on, anti-oppressive subculture we possibly can and we're going to enforce its boundaries is an incredibly, incredibly dangerous one."

Still, this sort of absolutist idea can also be incredibly seductive. As activists and organizers, we feel—and often are—intensely embattled in the midst of systems that are perpetuating violence and misery of nearly unimaginable proportions. Meanwhile, we grapple with our complicity in these systems (some of us more than others) even as we struggle to protect ourselves from the ways that they hurt us. So, we frequently attempt to build spaces—through relationships, organizations, communities, and movements—that are apart from ruling relations. And we can get caught up in maintaining these spaces through what Montreal organizer Amy Miller called a "secular puritanism": scrutinizing one another's behavior, creating our own status hierarchies, and excluding those who don't live up to our righteous standards.

While perhaps comforting, this sort of absolutism prevents organizers from building the sort of broad and open movements we need. Among other problems, it is based on treating people badly and pushing them away. Tynan Jarrett, who did queer youth advocacy and political prisoner support in Montreal, discussed this self critically, in relation to his experience of trying to transform what was the Women's Centre at Concordia University into what is now the 2110 Centre for Gender Advocacy at Concordia:

> We used a lot of sort of heavy-handed tactics to make people feel guilty, to lecture them, to do all these things that ultimately may change people's behavior but won't change their minds and will only make them resent you and are not positive things at all in the end. We just pushed, pushed a lot of people away. What we would have argued was that the space is either going to be safe for some people and unsafe for others, so we have push away these middle-class white women who are racist and classist and ableist or else it's not going to be a safe space for other people. But I don't really think the world works like that, actually.

In short, pushing people away, while it may sometimes be required, is rarely a winning strategy. Absolutist ideas and practices aren't going to get us very far in the complicated world in which we live. More often than not, they'll end up making us isolated and insular.

Ultimately, there is one major danger underlying all of these debilitating tendencies: organizers may become so focused on our particular prefigurative activities that we lose sight of what we're trying to win in the big picture.[27] Prefigurative politics importantly links means and ends, but we can sometimes get transfixed on our means *as* ends.[28] As organizer Andréa Maria observed, "I have seen groups try to do effective immigration work, effective anti-war work, or effective anti-poverty work, who get so bogged down in their sense of process that it stops being political, first of all, and it certainly stops being effective because all their energy goes into those sets of concerns."

This inward-looking tendency is especially tempting when social transformation seems far away and internal group processes are close at hand. In this context, said Maria, "You can really fetishize prefigurative politics in a way that makes you very self-satisfied about how great your group is functioning and that really doesn't allow it to achieve [much of consequence]." So, for example, anti-authoritarians can become so obsessed with trying to create a perfect nonhierarchical process that we begin to forget what we hope to accomplish with that process—what we're attempting to build, with whom we're trying to connect, and what changes we seek to achieve. Or, as Stephanie Guilloud pointed out earlier in this chapter, activists can focus so intensely on "handling pain and internal process to heal" that we fail to build movements capable of changing the social structures that daily produce trauma and violence.

Activist work to transform power relations can also easily fall into this tendency. Joshua Kahn Russell and Brian Kelly, who were founding organizers with the new Students for a Democratic Society, described this in their experience: "For a period, SDS's approach to issues of accountability and oppression made members look exclusively inward and lose sight of our actual work combating oppression in society. Some chapters simply stopped organizing and became paralyzed by internal process, while others seemed more concerned with enforcing the 'correct' use of language than working together."[29] Many activists have similar stories to tell. For instance, Jill Chettiar, a former organizer with the Anti-Poverty Committee in Vancouver, highlighted the problem of people well versed in anti-oppression terminology using it to simply dismiss organizing efforts, rather than to propose solutions. In these sorts of situations, the tendency to look inward makes for lots of soul-searching, frequently unproductive internal conflict, and unfortunately little outwardly focused work. This is a dead end.

BEYOND

Although these dangers are persistent, they don't make reconstructive work any less necessary. Prefigurative praxis is a practical expression of the "beyond" essential to transformative organizing. As anti-authoritarians, we try to imagine another world organized on the basis of democracy, solidarity, and equality. Like many before us, we dare to dream of a liberatory society. At the same time, we attempt to put our aspirations into practice, to the greatest extent possible, in our lives, work, and organizations. We insist on realizing our visions through our processes of struggle. This is how we create compelling, sustainable movements that are able to pose radical alternatives.

The question is how to engage in prefigurative activities while avoiding the dangers that so often crop up. Fortunately, we can draw some helpful lessons from experiences within the anti-authoritarian current as well as previous movement efforts. One is about letting go of perfectionism. This requires grasping an uncomfortable truth: failure is an unavoidable part of trying to model and manifest a new world in our movements. Nonhierarchical decision-making processes go awry at times, attempts to develop more caring and collective ways of relating frequently falter, and more often than we'd like, anti-oppressive cultures break down. These failures are an inevitable result of working within the disjunction between what is and what we want.

Speaking about efforts to transform power relations, Helen Hudson, a member of the Montreal Anarchist Bookfair collective, framed this well. "At the same time as we're living in this movement," she said, "we're living in this unjust world and we continue to soak up the poison of that, however much we fight against our own tendencies to be oppressive. It's going to continue to seep in and we're going to continue to be oppressed, both by the oppressive tendencies of other people in the movement and by the rest of the world we live in." As much as we try, we are not going to be able to create completely democratic, liberatory, and healthy spaces while relations of exploitation and oppression are dominant in our society. There's no way around this.

This doesn't mean we should give up on prefigurative praxis. We do, however, have to take one foot out of the ideal world of what we want and place it squarely in the much more muddled world that actually exists. "If you want to build a movement," Toronto-based anti-poverty organizer Mike D argued, "then you have to deal with all the messiness and imperfections." This means working in less than ideal circumstances and often not fully succeeding in enacting our visions. But rather than being discouraged by our experiences of failure, we need to see that such experiences signal that we are approaching the limits imposed by existing social relations and the conditions they produce. These are limits that, through struggle, people can and do move. Prefigurative activities, including their inevitable failures, are an essential part of this process.

Another lesson is about experimentation. Rather than getting fixated on particular prefigurative forms, we need to think and act much more dynamically. For this, we can turn to a formulation from activists in the global justice movement. Naming an orientation of many successful struggles, they suggested that we understand our movements as "laboratories of resistance." Elaborating on this, longtime San Francisco organizer David Solnit writes, "When we shift our thinking to see our organizing and actions as a laboratory then we can see our actions as experiments. In keeping with this spirit, much of the value of the experiment is in the evaluation and discussion of what we learned."[30] At the heart of this experimental approach is a sequence of steps: trying, succeeding or failing (or, more commonly, a little of both), learning, and applying what we've learned to the next attempts. Using this sequence, organizers can grow and modify prefigurative activities.

There are plenty of examples of this. One is the development of nonhierarchical decision-making practices. In the early 2000s, some Earth First! groups in the northwestern United States changed their practice of consensus so that enacting a "block" required more than one person. This grew out of their experiences of dealing with police-affiliated infiltrators and other disruptive individuals. On the other side of the continent, Montreal anarchists in La Convergence des luttes anti-capitalistes/Anti-Capitalist Convergence developed a mode of making decisions in general assemblies that aimed for consensus but relied on a three-quarters majority vote if consensus couldn't be reached. This developed from a particular history of assemblies in Quebec, concerns about majority rule, and the practical challenges of working in assemblies with more than one hundred people regularly present. The general assemblies in the recent occupy movement created further opportunities for people to hone directly democratic decision-making practices.

The key point is that nothing should be set in stone. With an experimental approach, we can continually evaluate our prefigurative forms: How do these practices help us build and model the world that we want? And just as important, how do they help us move toward winning that vision on a broad scale? Through this kind of evaluation, we can learn what works and change what doesn't. As Solnit puts it, we can "infus[e] our political work with the humility and curiosity that comes with experimentation."[31] In this way, our prefigurative activities can become steps in an ongoing, movement-building learning process.

A final lesson is about holding together the "against" and the "beyond." On its own, prefigurative politics is not enough to fundamentally transform society. As many in the anti-authoritarian current are learning, we absolutely have to connect prefigurative praxis with struggles against exploitation and oppression. New York organizer and writer RJ Maccani discussed this in relation to the community of people with whom he works.

Prefigurative activity, he said, "is something that we think is a necessary part of movement-building *and* we gotta confront the oppressors too."

It can be tempting to just focus our efforts on building forms of a new society, however small. Whether general assemblies or liberatory communities of care, these initiatives help us tap into a sense of creative power that we otherwise mostly don't experience in our society as it is currently organized. But unless our prefigurative work is connected to efforts that directly challenge dominant institutions, it will remain disappointingly marginal and insignificant. The interlocking systems that rule our lives have an astounding capacity to accommodate—and, in many cases, profit from—rebellious subcultures and alternative communities so long as these living experiments don't blossom into oppositional movements that threaten the large-scale organization of power and profit-making. We sell ourselves short if we settle for—or worse, aim for—creating momentary or isolated prefigurative activities detached from struggles.[32]

Prefigurative praxis, in short, is genuinely transformative only as long as it is part of movements that are fighting to win a new world. As the Team Colors Collective writes, "The seed of the new society is not just created in the shell of the old (to use an old but still very true metaphor), *but seeks to organize toward the point of confrontation.*"[33] When we consciously link "against" and "beyond" in our organizing, we create possibilities for collective action that fundamentally challenges what is while practically building what we want. This dyad, the two aspects intentionally fused together, is the core political promise of another politics.

PART TWO

Strategy

4. "Do you want to have a chance at winning something?"

Developing Strategy

> Our activism is not simply a matter of "fighting the good fight," or some jaded push toward insularity or purism, but is instead grounded in the day-to-day reality of what it takes to build a movement that can win concrete objectives and ultimately transform society.
>
> Madeline Gardner and Joshua Kahn Russell

Members of the Coalition of Immokalee Workers perform street theater during the March for Rights, Respect, and Fair Food in March 2013 in Florida. (Courtesy of JJ Tiziou Photography, www.jjtiziou.net)

"WHAT'S THE CONNECTION between concrete activities and vision?" This is a provocative question longtime New York housing and HIV/AIDS organizer Michelle O'Brien posed in my interview with her. Chapter 3 offers one way to answer this question: we can attempt to manifest our vision in how we carry out our activities. This is vital. But as much of a proponent of prefigurative praxis as she is, O'Brien was getting at something else. She was expressing a concern that increasingly preoccupies anti-authoritarian organizers: How can our activities tangibly build toward future revolutionary transformation on a large scale? This, fundamentally, is a question of strategy.

What exactly is strategy? Rahula Janowski, who worked with the anti-imperialist collective Heads Up in San Francisco, summed it up well: "What's your goal? What can you do to get there? What are your plans to get there? That's your strategy." In this sense, strategy is something we can develop on many different timelines—from days to decades—and many different scales—from small groups to global movements. In all cases, however, a strategy is a plan or series of plans for moving us from where we are to where we'd like to be.

A major problem in left movements in North America is that we tend to do this sort of planning so infrequently. James Tracy, a housing organizer and writer also in San Francisco, argued that this lack of strategy often results in activists achieving very little. Using a metaphor from a friend, he explained, "Organizing without a strategy is like watching pee-wee soccer, where you throw a ball out and a bunch of little four-year-olds come. They kick the ball, they put everything into it, sometimes they just go crazy with it, with all their energy . . . and occasionally somebody gets the goal, but you can't figure out how it happened and you can't replicate it and you can't do it better in a more efficient manner." This, unfortunately, is what a lot of left political activity looks like. As we struggle, Tracy emphasized, there are no guarantees, but we can improve our chances of getting what we want if we're intentional about what we're doing. It comes down to a question, he said: "Do you want to have a chance at winning something?"

Those of us developing another politics generally say "yes." Although what "winning" ultimately means is still fairly vague in this current, most anti-authoritarians would like to do more than spin our wheels. We aim to change the world. But if we want to have a chance at winning, then we have to talk about strategy. That's what this chapter is about. I begin by looking at some activist habits that consistently prevent us from discussing strategy. Fortunately, anti-authoritarians are increasingly wrestling with these habits and developing new pathways, many of which follow what I see as a "movement-building" orientation. By this, I mean an approach to political work that is about moving beyond insular activist spaces, connecting with popular struggles, and building movements capable of engaging many, many people. With this movement-building orientation, we can bring much more intentionality into our efforts. In some ways, we are already doing this.

OBSTACLES TO DEVELOPING STRATEGY

Strategy is a consistent challenge in the anti-authoritarian current. As activists and organizers, we often talk abstractly about how crucial strategy is, but much of the time we recognize its importance mainly through its absence in our activities. If we're serious about social transformation and honest with ourselves, we eventually begin to realize that we can't simply do the same things week after week, month after month, with no clear plans for how these activities will help us build movements, achieve interim gains, pick up momentum, and move toward winning the world we want. Revolutionary change needs more than good intentions, commitment, and effort; it also requires conscious strategies and a movement culture that supports strategic discussion and planning.

Many in the anti-authoritarian current yearn for this. As Toronto-based youth organizer Pauline Hwang put it, "To have some level of dialogue at which these questions are being raised—the questions of long-term direction, the questions of how does our work fit into building the society we want to have after the so-called revolution—having that kind of dialogue is important to me." This yearning is something I've encountered again and again in conversations and workshops with activists across the continent. So why do we have such tremendous difficulty sustaining this kind of dialogue and developing strategy? In my view, there are three major obstacles that trip us up again and again.

The first of these obstacles is a tendency to focus on principles over plans. This focus, which comes out of some sectors of North American anarchism in particular, is based on a legitimate concern that radicals may sacrifice our core values and beliefs in order to win.[1] But focusing exclusively on principles slips into a kind of magical thinking: if we have the right ideas and values, so this goes, everything else will more or less follow. Brooke Lehman, an experienced activist and educator who was involved with Occupy Wall Street, characterized this tendency as "Well, I'm gonna do what I believe in and what feels right to me and just be a piece of this larger whole."

There is a certain prefigurative logic to this tendency—a sense that, if we announce our convictions loudly enough and do everything in the way that we think is most righteously radical, our activities will achieve what we want. But this is a prefigurative politics detached from calculated consequential action.[2] As Lehman said, "If I can't articulate what that larger whole is and where that larger whole is going or where it could potentially go, then I'm participating on blind hope, and I think there are a lot of us doing that. And I don't think you can operate on principles alone. We have to have a strategy, and it has to be a viable one—not just based on an idea of how it could possibly work but we don't know how to get from here to there."

One result of this fixation on principles over plans is that activists often spend a lot of time and energy debating whether particular individuals, activities, or organizations are sufficiently "radical" without asking basic questions about how they seek to move us toward actually winning. A focus on political ideas and rhetoric, in this way, eclipses strategic thinking. It also creates a context in which some activists are quick to dismiss any effort—often sloppily using the terms "liberal" and "reformist"—that doesn't lead directly to the complete destruction of the existing social order. San Francisco direct action organizer David Solnit didn't mince words about this: "A lot of radicals talk shit about anything short of smashing the state, but they don't have any idea of how to take necessary steps in that direction."

If we genuinely do want to fundamentally reorganize power in our society, then we have to think long-term about what we're doing and give up on all-or-nothing answers. This doesn't mean that we can't be firm in our politics and principled in our actions, but as many in the anti-authoritarian current are discovering, we have to combine this with actual planning based on what we want to achieve. Francesca Fiorentini, a longtime activist and former *Left Turn* editor now based in Argentina, emphasized this: "We need to somehow hold this space for our political principles, but also be strategic." We have to embrace both principles and plans without one trumping the other, and we need to foster movement cultures that enable this.

The second obstacle to developing strategy in the anti-authoritarian current is a tendency to fetishize particular tactics. By tactics, I mean specific forms of collective action such as lobbying politicians, occupying public spaces, engaging in armed struggle, going on strike, holding educational events, establishing boycotts, organizing consciousness-raising groups, using mass delegations to pressure power holders, marching in protests, street-fighting with cops, and running electoral campaigns.

Anti-authoritarians tend to prioritize direct action tactics. In general terms, these are tactics aimed at directly preventing something from happening (such as stopping an eviction by physically blockading attempts to move people out of a house) or directly making something happen regardless of whether or not it is legal (such as opening up a vacant building so that houseless people can live in it). We value direct action tactics because they involve people collectively recognizing and using their own power rather than appealing to those in power. In practice, this is more complicated, as these tactics are rarely completely "direct"; after all, even the most militant forms of direct action often rely on creating spectacles (mass arrests, major disruptions, damaged property) in order to raise public awareness and/or pressure power holders.[3] Nevertheless, the orientation here is positive: direct action tactics are based on not the goodwill of rich people and politicians, but the strength and determination of ordinary people.[4]

There are many different kinds of direct action. But since the late 1990s, a narrow understanding of this tactical approach has gained some popularity among radicals. This mainly involves street protests and confrontations with police, often including black bloc tactics (wearing masks and all-black clothing, staying together in a bloc formation, targeted property destruction).[5] Some activists have come to exclusively associate this particular conception of direct action with militancy, effectiveness, and righteously radical politics. More recently in the occupy movement, another narrow way of understanding direct action emerged at times. Some activists lifted up the tactic of occupying central public spaces as the most important form of direct action, to be defended, sustained, and replicated no matter what.

There is nothing wrong, in principle, with any of these tactics. Understood expansively, direct action is vital for any organizing that is aimed at fundamentally challenging dominant institutions and building popular power. The problem arises when activists come to think that any particular tactic or bundle of tactics should be used in any and all situations regardless of the circumstances. As David Solnit argued, "It's like we're trying to rebuild an engine and we're ignoring the repair manuals, we're ignoring the folks down the block who have actually rebuilt twenty or thirty engines. We're using the same wrenches and ignoring the toolbox—the many tactics and tools of movement-building and campaigns. We get stuck: we see a form, like a mass march, a black bloc, or a civil disobedience, and grab onto it—usually on an emotional basis, whatever form feels more powerful to us—without any clue of how are we going to get from here to there or [any] analysis of how power works." This is fetishism—fixation on particular forms without regard for context.[6]

One of the most troubling outcomes of this is that, as activists and organizers, we end up focusing most of our attention on debating the validity of certain tactics rather than on considering how those tactics fit into overall plans to achieve something. This was a consistent challenge in the global justice movement and has continued to be so in more recent movements, such as occupy. This is understandable: it's much easier to argue about whether particular tactics are valid or effective than it is to create plans to motivate our tactical choices. But the truth is, we can't evaluate tactics without having a more developed sense of where they are located in a bigger picture, which includes longer-term planning as well as analysis of our social and historical context. This is the role of strategy.

The third obstacle to developing strategy in the anti-authoritarian current is a tendency toward crisis mode organizing. In Montreal, several people I interviewed self critically described this as the "Montreal organizing cycle." Tatiana Gomez, who worked with Solidarity Across Borders, explained that "a lot of our organizing happens in response to emergencies. And so people will do a sprint of organizing over a few months, culminating in a giant action, and then, after the action, there's little energy left because everyone is burnt."[7]

While this organizing cycle has a specific character in Montreal, it's actually a widespread dynamic. Indeed, people in other cities described it again and again in their own circumstances. "It's hard to get strategy because there's so much stuff going on all the time that you have to react to," said Mike D, who was an organizer with the Ontario Coalition Against Poverty in Toronto. "Every crisis that erupts seems like the all-consuming crisis, and it's hard to look at what the next crisis will be and how you can better prepare for that." In New Orleans, organizers described the reactive stance their work has often taken in the wake of Hurricane Katrina. Rosana Cruz, who worked with Safe Streets / Strong Communities, observed that she sees this across a lot of organizing: "I think, collectively, we feel a deep and overwhelming sense of urgency because of what we've been through and we think, 'Aaaahhhhh, everything's falling apart, people are dying, there's terrible things happening, and oh my god!' Because . . . they have, but we also can't function effectively, can't do effective work with a long term impact when we are in that constant state of emergency."

Activists and organizers legitimately feel a continual sense of crisis. The ways in which power is organized and administered in our society require that many people experience pervasive insecurity so that a much smaller set of very rich people will experience nearly constant security. As I described in chapter 2, the last few decades have seen an all-out assault on movement gains from the last century. Since the onset of the worldwide economic crisis in 2008, this assault has only accelerated, now often under the banner of "austerity." The crises we experience, then, are generally quite real. And as Tatiana Gomez pointed out, "Planning follow-up in the context of a crisis or reflecting on how the organizing fits into a longer-term strategy is not always possible in times of emergencies." This is true.

The problem arises when we become so absorbed in crisis mode organizing that we constantly postpone any long-term or proactive planning. As activists and organizers, we usually feel compelled to focus on the emergencies sitting in front of us. But if we don't make space for strategic planning—putting our day-to-day fights into broader, conscious frameworks—we end up "running on a treadmill," in the words of Montreal anti-war and migrant justice organizer Mary Foster. Persistent crisis mode organizing is a good recipe for lots of frenzied activity linked, at times, to broader struggles. However, it's a poor recipe for achieving long-term transformative goals. While acknowledging the crises around us, then, we have to allow ourselves to pause, reflect, and become more intentional and visionary.[8] We need strategy.

These three obstacles—principles over plans, fetishizing particular tactics, and crisis mode organizing—shape a way of doing radical politics that is mostly oriented toward, on the one hand, immediate activities and, on the other hand, aspirations for a (hopefully not too) distant future. As a result, those of us in the anti-authoritarian current tend to be strong in talking about the ins and outs of our groups and projects as well as the big ideas that influence our visions for a better world. Yet we tend to be not so good at discussing what longtime activist Max Elbaum calls "a politics that is 'in between'"—the frequently difficult strategic questions that lie between our immediate activities and our long-term hopes.[9] We rarely talk in any detail about how we intend to make our aspirations into large-scale realities in the days, months, and years to come. This is a significant weakness.

All of this is compounded by a remarkably underdeveloped culture of strategic discussion and planning in most left movements in the United States and Canada. The anti-authoritarian current, situated across many of these movements, definitely suffers from this problem. In these circumstances, as activist and writer Scott Neigh points out, dialogue about strategy runs the very real risk of fueling disengagement and conflict. He observes, "Often we are just plain not very good at having such discussions in ways that don't alienate—radical posturing, masculinist tendencies, vestiges of 'correct line' approaches even in spaces not organized around them, that sort of thing. As well, different levels of experience, and our limited skills at talking effectively across them in ways that are productive and empower the less experienced people, can make discussions of strategy divisive in ways that make activists shy away from them."[10] Not only do we need strategy, then, but we also need better ways of collectively engaging it.[11]

A MOVEMENT-BUILDING ORIENTATION

Thankfully, these obstacles and their accompanying problems aren't insurmountable. Another politics partly grows out of the efforts of anti-authoritarians to move past them. In doing this, we are increasingly following what

I see as a "movement-building" orientation. Although this is an idea that circulates widely on the left, I came to appreciate it more deeply through my conversation with Rayan El-Amine, a former leading organizer with Direct Action to Stop the War and one of the co-founders of the Arab Resource and Organizing Center in San Francisco. El-Amine used this formulation as a way to talk about how we, as activists and organizers, direct our attention. Especially in the global justice, anti-war, and occupy movements, activists have tended to concentrate on big mobilizations. But rather than focusing primarily on specific events like these, argued El-Amine, we have to move into a larger framework of creating and sustaining movements. While certainly not the only way to grapple with strategic questions, this orientation offers a particularly promising set of navigational tools for moving forward.

One of these tools is a grounded critique of how we, as radicals, tend to sequester ourselves. A movement-building orientation challenges us to move outside the confines of what organizers frequently call "the activist ghetto"—the interlinked networks of scenes, communities, groups, and publications through which radical activists of various political stripes circulate in North America. For sure, this characterization can be too dismissive at times.[12] Activist social networks definitely help sustain people in struggle, generate and practice new ways of being and doing, share knowledge and resources, withstand state repression, and hold onto collective memory. But if we're not careful, they can also create thorny problems.

On the one hand, such networks can be spaces through which we become all too comfortable with being marginal. In carving out communities of resistance, we can craft self-conceptions as outsiders with righteous but always minority views. That is, we can come to identify with being perpetual critics who rarely appeal to anyone outside our own circles and hardly ever win anything. Brooke Lehman, herself a longtime participant in U.S. anarchist politics, saw this kind of self-marginalization among anarchists especially: "I feel like a lot of people within the anarchist movement don't truly have a desire to build a popular movement on some subconscious level, are not interested in being anything other than fringe."[13]

On the other hand, activist social networks can drift into a kind of insular and inflated self-importance. Because these communities are relatively small and yet linked up across the continent, those of us participating in them can develop an exaggerated sense of the significance of our efforts and the weight of our ideas. Within their boundaries, we can come to feel that revolutionary change hinges on us even while we're actually very disconnected from most other parts of society. Montreal-based organizer Tatiana Gomez, who had one foot in anarchist circles and another in broader migrant justice organizing, was very direct in challenging this tendency and the implicit ideas behind it: "I don't think we're going to build a movement with about a hundred anarchists in every major city."[14]

These problems of activist scenes are familiar to many in the anti-authoritarian current.[15] Whether making us comfortable with our irrelevance or inflating our significance, they leave us stuck in our customary spaces and all too focused on our own limited activities. But if we want to move out of the margins and we know we can't launch a revolution with small clusters of activists, what are we to do?

We need to engage with ordinary people and popular struggles. This is another crucial navigational tool that a movement-building orientation offers. It means recognizing the antagonisms built into current relations of exploitation and oppression, and connecting with the forms of resistance and collective action developing out of these antagonisms. In this way, it directs our attention toward the many sectors of society already in motion as well as those with enormous potential for carrying out transformative fights. With care and commitment, such engagement has the potential to ground our ideas and breathe life into our political activities.

Doing this calls for some humility. As San Francisco-based Catalyst Project organizer Clare Bayard pointed out, "We have a tendency on the left to focus so much on the visible apathy of people that we then really ignore the amount of daily resistance that's there." As activists and organizers, we have to work against this tendency and put ourselves in perspective as we strive to comprehend the landscape upon which we act. Leila Pourtavaf, who was active with the Anti-Capitalist Ass Pirates and No One is Illegal in Montreal, described this as "taking yourself out of the picture and seeing what's really happening outside of what you're organizing." She used the example of people moving across borders, frequently illegally:

> When I think of migration patterns and how those are unfolding right now—even as more restrictive measures are being put in place—I think that the ways that people, totally non-activist people who don't identify with "radical politics," are navigating these systems is amazing. That's a source of inspiration to me—how despite the restrictive and dehumanizing structures that are set up, people find ways to fuck with them—out of necessity but also out of a desire to not put up with bullshit and to seek a better life. People find ways to take down or go around all barriers. For me, those moments illustrate really amazing examples of resistance to the oppressive systems we live under.[16]

Migration is just one of the many ways that people evade, undermine, and fight dominant institutions every day in order to have better lives.

While self-identified activists often focus on big and highly confrontational instances of resistance (demonstrations, riots, direct actions), there are in fact much deeper—and frequently less visible—layers of social struggle happening all the time. Examples include workers stealing from their employers to supplement their inadequate wages, queers creating transgressive community spaces for socializing and sex, and youth of color developing and using art (graffiti, hip hop, dance) to seize urban space, among many other social forms and practices. These everyday activities frequently lay the foundations on which more public mobilizations and movements build, such as the historic protests against police raids on gay bathhouses in Toronto in 1981 or the unprecedented immigrant rights demonstrations in the United States in 2006. When we, as activists and organizers, "take ourselves out of the picture" and examine the world around us, we see that nothing is as it seems: where there is oppression and exploitation, there is frequently resistance, often hidden.[17]

A movement-building orientation means engaging with these everyday forms of struggle and the community-based initiatives that sometimes grow out of them. Vancouver-based No One Is Illegal organizer Harjap Grewal called this "being grounded in the struggle of people." As I describe in the next chapter, NOII-Vancouver offers direct support to migrants resisting deportations while building community-based campaigns to challenge the Canadian border regime altogether. Building on fights around particular cases, these sorts of struggles, Grewal argued, are not "just ideological" but rather about "people's day-to-day lives." He continued, "That's actually what the struggle's about. That's where movements get their capacity . . . . People are being affected by something in their day-to-day lives and they're going to struggle against it. And most of those people may not consider themselves to be political or activists." If we're serious about building large-scale movements to change the world, Grewal stressed, there really isn't any other option than engaging these struggles: "How do you organize around issues without [experiencing] the issues? How do you support people's mobilizations without being in contact with them?"

Becoming grounded in popular struggles is only a beginning. Just as important is the activity of *building:* helping struggles become more connected, coherent, sustained, and far-reaching; developing people's capacities to think critically and imaginatively, take initiative, and act collaboratively; constructing organizations and institutions through which people can deliberate together, care for one another, and fight injustice; and encouraging and participating in collective efforts to formulate audacious visions and strategies. This constructive emphasis is another navigational tool offered by a movement-building orientation. It directs our attention toward the future, calling on us to see our current efforts as laying groundwork for what we intend to be.

This is particularly reflected in how a growing number of anti-authoritarian organizers talk about our work. Paula Ximena Rojas-Urrutia captured this sentiment well. Reflecting on her organizing with young working-class women of color in Sista II Sista in Brooklyn, she characterized herself as an "ant worker," which she described as "working on the ground with people day-to-day." With this evocative term, I also understood Rojas-Urrutia to be gesturing to an approach of intention and persistence, based on creating something much bigger than any individual effort. As she put it, "I see myself as someone who is digging the dirt for something that's gonna come way later, but someone's gotta dig the dirt." Others echo this. In a widely read article drawing lessons from the civil rights movement, longtime organizer and writer Chris Crass discusses Ella Baker's important notion of organizing as "spade work." This, explains Crass, is "when you prepare the soil for seeds for the next season. It is backbreaking . . . and it is what makes it possible for the garden to grow."[18] Whether diligent ants or dedicated gardeners, these images get to the core of this orientation: consciously working to build movements, rooted in people's lives, on a scale and with capacities beyond what most of us can yet imagine.

This emphasis on building is also reflected in how many anti-authoritarian organizers are thinking about time. If much of organizing is tilling soil and planting seeds, movement-building is necessarily a long-term process and we thus have to cultivate a certain kind of patience. Oakland-based Critical Resistance organizer Rachel Herzing was especially clear on this point. "I definitely respect a healthy impatience because I think stuff is really screwed," she said, "*and* to be patient and not merely reactive, I think, is strategic. To see where things are going to head or let things settle a little bit before jumping into the fray can be really useful . . . . I don't think work that is mass and long-term can move quickly enough to be super responsive, so you need to be more thoughtful about how you're gonna engage." What Herzing emphasized is, in a sense, the urgent patience at the heart of this orientation: no patience for injustice, but abundant patience for the process of building movements that are capable of overturning injustice.[19]

This crucial long view, some anti-authoritarian organizers increasingly assert, has to be tempered with healthy attention to rapidly changing circumstances and unexpected upsurges. Otherwise, as Toronto activist and journalist Mick Sweetman pointed out, we run the danger of developing a mindset that "the revolution will never happen, we just gotta be here and keep plugging away, and maybe future generations will build off of that." This mindset, said Sweetman, is "unduly pessimistic. I just don't think social explosions are predictable. One could very well be right around the corner, and we just have no way of knowing that." The events of recent years have born this out. Whether the occupation of the Wisconsin capitol, the Arab Spring, major prisoner hunger strikes in the United States, the occupy movement, or the 2012 Quebec student strike, we've seen astonishingly fast-moving mobilizations emerge. Effective and strategic movement-building, Sweetman and others stress, requires engaging with these kinds of social explosions while maintaining a long-term constructive perspective.[20]

Movement-building, as it is developing in the anti-authoritarian current, thus names a set of aspirations. Toronto-based organizer Pauline Hwang vividly expressed them:

> I ideally want to be part of something that has a long-term vision and is building toward that vision. . . . I feel it's not enough to make changes as just small numbers of people doing cool things. Let's do cool things, but let's do them in a way that is constantly bringing more and more people together to do those things and building our strength. . . . I'm talking numbers, I'm talking movement-building. Most activist groups I've been involved in don't think about building. They think about a certain fight, a certain short-term goal. . . . To me, the fight is about putting ourselves in better and better positions to fight those battles as they come along—because it's a war; it's not a battle.

Moving beyond the efforts of small numbers of activists, bringing more and more people together, building collective strength and capacity, and looking ahead to a long-term struggle—these aims increasingly orient how many in the anti-authoritarian current are thinking about strategy.

GETTING SERIOUS

Part of what is promising about this emerging orientation is that it indicates a growing seriousness. People who want to change the world sometimes see seriousness as an attitude to emulate—a willingness to take risks, make sacrifices, criticize ruthlessly, and maintain single-minded focus. While this attitude has important aspects, it is frequently far too centered on the traits of idealized (and often masculinized) heroic individuals. It also tends to emphasize how activists are *acting* rather than what we're *achieving*. In order to foster combative and transformative movements, we need a seriousness that is collective, reflective, ambitious, and rooted in practical work—something that people in struggle feel and enact together. This is the kind of seriousness that I see as promising, if still underdeveloped, in a movement-building orientation.

As activists and organizers, we will have to deepen and extend this seriousness if we want to develop effective strategies for social transformation. How, concretely, can we do this? To start, we should be much more intentional in our activities. Among other things, this involves, as San Francisco organizer Clare Bayard stressed, "having clear goals, having clear plans, being honest and clear about who's our constituency, who's not at the table but should be, not getting defensive about it, and then evaluating instead of running onto the next thing, and prioritizing." Rahula Janowski, another San Francisco activist, emphasized the aspect of intentionality that is perhaps most crucial for organizations: creating a strategic plan. As she argued, "I think it's worth doing—really articulating it that way—because then we can relate back to it and be like, 'Our goal is this, this is our strategy, does this piece of work fit into it and, if so, how?'"

The core insight I take from these suggestions is that we should articulate our aims and how we intend to accomplish them. A common way that organizations carry this out is by developing campaigns—focused fights using alliances and escalating tactics to win specific demands from power holders, be they corporate CEOs, government officials, or others. The Coalition of Immokalee Workers (CIW) in southern Florida, which I mentioned in chapter 2, has run one of the most successful movement-based campaigns in the United States in the last decade. With a membership of Latino/a immigrant farmworkers, the CIW has used a series of focused and increasingly aggressive tactics—including alliance-building, "truth tours," marches, consumer boycotts, and hunger and labor strikes—to pressure the most powerful fast food companies in the world to agree to its demands for improved wages and working conditions.[21] A campaign, in this way, is a container that can bring often disconnected movement activities—such as educational events, direct action, and coalitional work—into a coherent plan with explicit aims. Even if we don't always use this model, there is much to learn from it.[22]

Becoming more intentional, as I touched on earlier, is also significantly about fostering a movement culture that enables collective and constructive strategic reflection. Crisis mode organizing—compounded by a toxic mix of devastating attacks by ruling elites and absolutist habits on the left—has produced chaotic and sometimes caustic movement cultures. In the blur of embattled activity, it's difficult to prioritize time for longer-term collective planning and it's easy to fall into either self-congratulatory or hypercritical patterns of talking about our efforts. Our movements can and must do better than this. "In order for us to discuss strategy," as Chris Crass suggests, "we need to believe in the worth of our ideas, develop a culture of supporting one another to explore our ideas, reflect on our experiments of practice, and generate an empowering culture that encourages people to share and engage in positive discussion that pushes beyond the limitations of our current thinking."[23] As part of this, we should especially invite deep, generous, and ongoing conversations about our theories of social change—how we see transformation happening and how we see ourselves playing a role.

As activists and organizers, we can bring such practices of collective exploration, support, sharing, and reflection into our work. And fortunately, there are models on which we can draw as we do this. For instance, many organizations—from Rising Tide to Iraq Veterans Against the War—have incorporated regular longer-term planning sessions into their organizing calendars. These sessions, often structured as retreats or daylong special meetings, allow for more open-ended brainstorming and in-depth discussions, as well as relationship-building and political education. With solid preparation, structured agendas, and attentive facilitation, such sessions can enable reflection and planning that is less overwhelmed by pressing tasks and emergency responses.[24]

Beyond special strategy sessions, however, generating a healthy movement culture involves incorporating more of this type of discussion into all ongoing political work. A key part of this is developing regular, collective practices for assessing how what we're doing measures against our intentions. This is how I understand Clare Bayard's recommendation the we spend time "evaluating instead of running onto the next thing." While organizing in crisis mode, it's quite compelling to jump from one activity to the next without much assessment of our efforts. And even when we do evaluate, it's tempting to gauge the effectiveness of our activities with metrics that are easy to see but actually not very useful: social recognition (how many other activists have noticed what we're doing), frenzy and exhaustion (how busy and tired we are because of what we're doing), or, sometimes, state repression (how much effort the police are putting into stopping what we're doing).

Moving out of the margins challenges us to use measures of effectiveness based on explicit goals. In general terms, we might ask: How are our activities winning tangible gains that demonstrate the power of collective action by ordinary people? In what ways is our work bringing more people together and creating new kinds of connections? How is what we're doing building new confidence and capacities in people, particularly those who are structurally excluded and oppressed in our society? In what ways are our efforts communicating a transformative vision, not just rhetorically but also through how they are organized and what they create? And how are our activities laying the basis for future successful struggles? These and other questions like them can serve as starting-points for crafting more fine-tuned evaluation routines appropriate to our specific circumstances of struggle.

This kind of assessment is one important way that we can hold ourselves accountable to our stated goals. Some groups already do this quite well. In 2009, for example, Project South offered an impressive example of evaluation with its collaborative report assessing its experience as the anchor organization for the first U.S. Social Forum. As the authors wrote, "We offer critical analysis and recommendations so that we as converging movements, so necessary in this time, can learn from mistakes and adjust our practices so that we move forward together and more powerfully than any of us have imagined."[25] In this spirit, they review their efforts, acknowledging specific successes and limitations and making concrete suggestions for future convergence organizing. This blend of celebrating, learning, and adjusting, grounded in practical activities, is something we can and should make a consistent part of all of our efforts—after events and actions, and regularly within our organizations and campaigns. Used consciously, it can nourish and sharpen our organizing work.

Ultimately, the point of striving for greater intentionality is to become more effective and pliable as we struggle in dynamic circumstances.[26] It's not to come up with infallible formulas. This is important to emphasize. Because of the perfectionism I mentioned in the last chapter, those of us committed to social transformation have a tendency to hold out for certainty and purity in our efforts. We sometimes act as if we have to figure everything out perfectly before engaging in any action. This is a recipe for paralysis and insularity. Atlanta-based organizer and educator Stephanie Guilloud, like many experienced people with whom I spoke, was insistent about this: "If we paused—and people do—at every contradiction, we'd be still. We'd be straight up, just completely stagnant. And that's just not interesting or what's needed."

Developing plans that can somehow guide us past all contradictions, uncertainties, and errors is simply impossible. It's also not desirable. A movement-building orientation helps us to see that successful fights for fundamental social change develop from long-term engagements with the lives and struggles of ordinary people. Such engagements, like anything worth doing in this beautiful and unpredictable world, are complicated and messy. People in struggle are never saints, we frequently have to make demands on institutions we despise, and very rarely do we win everything we want. At the same time, people fighting for justice and dignity have incredible capacities for courage and creativity, dominant systems are seldom as stable as they seem, and history sometimes takes wonderfully unexpected turns. In these circumstances, purity and certainty are for those who are content to sit on the sidelines. The rest of us have to get our hands dirty, grappling with contradictions and complexities—some of which we can resolve and some of which we can't.

This embrace of messiness is central to another politics. In refusing correct lines, those of us in the anti-authoritarian current are trying to generate forms of political action that come from popular self-activity and imagination, not the pristine ideas of a select few activists or revolutionaries. This, in part, means humbly acknowledging that our ways of thinking and acting are presently inadequate; they have to change and grow as we build movements involving more and more people with their own experiences, ideas, and priorities. Grappling with complexity and mistakes is key to this process of growth. With intentionality—collective discussion, planning, and evaluation—we can turn challenges and missteps into opportunities to learn lessons, strengthen our efforts, and stay nimble. Messiness and all, this is the only way to build movements rooted in the lives of millions of people and genuinely capable of taking on ruling relations and institutions. In other words, this how to have a chance at winning something.

5. "In the world but not of it"

An Emerging Strategic Framework

> It is a tremendous challenge to both hold long-term revolutionary
> vision for our world, and to be daily present within that world.
>
> Jeremy Lazaou

Members of Critical Resistance and allied organizations protest the
construction of a jail in San Mateo County, California, on April 22, 2013.
(Courtesy of Critical Resistance)

AS I SPOKE WITH HIM, Ashanti Alston had a lot of clarity to offer around
conceptions of strategy. This isn't surprising. Known for his wisdom and
commitment to complexity, Alston is a former member of the Black Panther
Party and the Black Liberation Army who spent more than a decade in
prison for revolutionary activities. Now a widely respected anarchist elder,
he has significantly influenced many younger radicals through his organizing, public speaking, and mentorship. When I asked him about vision
and strategy, he offered one of his characteristic gems: "It's like the biblical
thing: we can be in this world, but not necessarily of it. So, we're here.

The concrete is that we're here. But we don't have to live as if we're trapped in it." With this, Alston put words to something that I think many in the anti-authoritarian current are struggling to express—and to enact.

As I discussed in the previous chapter, most anti-authoritarians haven't been so good at discussing strategy explicitly and collectively. But this doesn't mean that we haven't been grappling with strategic questions in our work. If we look carefully at the practical choices that many activists and organizers are making as we figure out where and how to organize and fight, I think we can actually see the broad outlines of a shared strategic framework guided by a movement-building orientation. While it's not fully developed and it's rarely talked about in a focused way, it has much potential. The main way I understand this framework is through the formulation that Alston referenced: "in the world but not of it."

While Alston didn't create this formulation, the way he brings it into strategic thinking is tremendously useful.[1] "In the world but not of it" emphasizes both the circumstances in which we struggle and our capacity to collectively imagine and push beyond them. In this way, it gets at a promising emerging approach for strategy in another politics: building movements in the world as it is—engaging with where and how people are struggling—while orienting toward the world we want—the "new world in our hearts," as the Spanish anarchist Buenaventura Durruti famously put it.[2] This strategic framework, in many ways, develops from the "disjunction between what is and what you want" that Andréa Maria named in the chapter 3. What Alston identifies, it seems to me, is the way that anti-authoritarians are trying to work in this disjunction as we organize, struggle, and build.

This chapter explores "in the world but not of it" as a strategic framework that brings together the "against" and the "beyond" of another politics.[3] I examine two primary ways that activists and organizers are putting this into practice. To begin, I look at our engagements with reform struggles. The complicated ways that anti-authoritarians are thinking and acting in relation to these fights offer important lessons about staying grounded in day-to-day realities while pushing at and pointing beyond what is considered "possible." I then turn to our efforts to construct the infrastructure of a new society—what is sometimes called building "dual power" or "counterpower." These efforts, mostly tentative and experimental at this point, suggest crucial ways of relating to people's immediate needs while generating new social relations and new forms of social organization.

ENGAGING REFORM STRUGGLES

At the core of a movement-building orientation is its strategic emphasis on popular struggles. This opens up challenging questions because frequently such struggles are centered on winning reforms, defending past reforms, or fighting new right-wing initiatives. In general terms, reforms are measures that change policies and practices of dominant social, economic, and political institutions. Examples include minimum wage laws, amnesty measures for undocumented immigrants, anti-discrimination clauses for historically marginalized groups, and legal protections for endangered species. While few reforms fundamentally change how power is organized and administered in our society, many create tangible improvements in people's lives, such as raising unemployment benefits, banning toxic chemicals, or expanding voting access. In the current political climate of austerity, many previous reforms—from laws protecting union bargaining rights to programs providing for social welfare—are under assault, and ruling elites are pursuing new repressive efforts—from expanding imprisonment to aggressive clampdowns on immigration. As a result, many of the most dynamic struggles at present are defensive ones.

The challenge here is that organizers in the anti-authoritarian current aren't content with small changes in the existing structure of society or with defending previous gains; we want large-scale social transformation. This means that we aren't reformists: we don't believe that the major social problems we face can be solved by gradual reform with the state as the main instrument of change. Instead, we see our society as structured by systems of domination, and we believe that only revolutionary change can go to the roots of these systems. And yet those of us developing another politics also see many fights for reforms and defensive struggles as vital, if often partial, expressions of the "against" central to any liberatory transformation; much of the time, they are attempts to put limits on the worst effects of ruling institutions, and sometimes they create openings for more far-reaching fights. How, then, to reconcile a commitment to engaging such popular struggles with a commitment to revolution?[4]

For some radicals, there can be no reconciliation. In this way of seeing things, there is a fairly rigid dichotomy between "reform" and "revolution": reform work seeks to win hopelessly limited concessions from dominant institutions while revolutionary work seeks to directly confront and destabilize these institutions.[5] In North America, this view gained some popularity during the 2008–2010 cycle of campus occupations in California and New York and also influenced parts of the occupy movement.[6] Those who hold this perspective raise significant concerns about the ways in which states tend to grant reforms in order to co-opt and demobilize movements. They also ask crucial questions about the ways in which reform-oriented struggles often adopt and reinforce oppressive logics in order to win. One example is the state-based logic that encourages movements to orient their political action toward lobbying, legal battles, and electoral campaigns.[7]

While recognizing these concerns, those of us developing another politics tend to take a different view. Indeed, part of what distinguishes us is our shared uneasiness with a strict reform/revolution dichotomy. Often we simply refuse it. And in many cases, we try to create more complicated ideas and practices that link popular fights and revolutionary visions. There is a lot of diversity within—and many real disagreements about—how we are doing this, but across our various efforts, I see indications of "in the world but not of it."

Crucial Contributions

Anti-authoritarian organizers are developing a framework of "in the world but not of it" experimentally, in many different areas of work and through a variety of organizations. Here, I want to highlight two formations in particular that have made and are making crucial contributions to it. The first is No One Is Illegal (NOII). As I previously mentioned, NOII collectives across Canada participate in and initiate anti-deportation campaigns and also do "casework" or "direct support work," helping individual migrants as they struggle with the Canadian government for residency status. At the same time, NOII collectives maintain a focus on organizing to build power in migrant communities and horizontal relations among oppressed groups, such as migrants and Indigenous peoples.[8] Over ten years, NOII has kept up consistent support work while organizing mass disruptions of deportations, long-term campaigns against repressive government measures, support committees for people targeted by police violence, and solidarity initiatives with Indigenous communities, among many other initiatives.

NOII organizers frequently describe their efforts as an ongoing balancing act between casework and campaign work. They strive to bring collective self-organization and anti-colonial, anti-border politics into an arena of work that is usually guided by state logics, which relate to people as individual "cases" within legal frameworks. This is rarely easy. As Vancouver-based NOII organizer Harsha Walia explained,

> All the No One Is Illegal groups across the country currently have a majority of organizers of color who identify as radicals, anti-capitalists, anarchists, anti-authoritarians, anti-imperialists, and/or socialists. It is a

challenge then to, on the one hand, have demands and visions that call for the abolition of border controls, and on the other hand, on a daily basis to be embroiled within the legal and bureaucratic system in order to gain concrete victories for those facing detention or deportation. We are very conscious that individual casework can become apolitical and depoliticizing, but not if it is an inherent part of the other mobilizing that we do, such as organizing occupations, rallies, marches, and public forums.

In bringing these politics and community-based fights together, NOII is "dealing with day-to-day survival struggles while putting forward a larger vision of fighting for no borders," in the words of NOII-Montreal organizer Jaggi Singh.

Another formation making crucial contributions to our emerging strategic framework is Critical Resistance (CR), which I introduced in chapter 1. For more than a decade, local CR chapters and affiliated groups across the United States have supported prisoner organizing efforts, fought new policing initiatives, organized campaigns to shrink prison spending, developed community-based alternatives to cops and courts, and participated in working alliances with a variety of other organizations struggling against the criminal justice system.[9] In doing this work, CR takes a specific stance toward reform: "We understand that the prison industrial complex is not a broken system to be fixed. The system, rather, works precisely as it is designed to—to contain, control, and kill those people representing the greatest threats to state power."[10] CR's perspective here grows out of a critical understanding of "prison reform" efforts that, historically, have tended to further legitimize and expand institutions of incarceration.[11]

This orientation toward reform makes for an important ongoing tension in CR and among prison abolitionists more generally. Those involved in CR engage with some reform efforts, such as developing programs to assist people coming out of prison and campaigning to stop prison construction projects. But while they seek to improve the conditions of current and former prisoners, abolitionists explicitly try to avoid anything that furthers the growth of the prison industrial complex (PIC). This sets important bounds on the kinds of work and coalitional efforts in which CR engages. The developing approach to strategy in CR is thus grounded in the lives of those affected by the PIC while also intentionally directed toward a transformative vision of abolition.

As formations linked with the anti-authoritarian current, both NOII and CR work to abolish repressive systems—specifically, border/immigration regimes and the PIC—while also trying to support and facilitate communities surviving and struggling against them. Their efforts and experiences offer us important resources for understanding and further developing a strategic framework of "in the world but not of it."

Being in the Room

We can best understand this framework by looking at its two aspects. The first—"in the world"—means connecting with popular struggles, including around reforms. Drawing on his experience as a CR organizer, Alston called this "being in the room." As he said, "We can't sit outside. We can't be purists." This is a point that many anti-authoritarian organizers make: we can't flinch from the constantly imperfect circumstances in which we struggle and the consistently difficult choices we have to make. As I stressed in the last chapter, there are no easy answers—no ways to avoid getting our hands dirty in the messiness of the world. Trying to maintain some sort of radical purity, as New York abolitionist organizer Rafael Mutis observed, "is a ridiculous, impossible game to be into." Indeed, it's a strategy for irrelevance. So, argued Alston, "the reality is that we're gonna have to figure out how to use reform as a tactic."

This way of being "in the world," for many in the anti-authoritarian current, grows out of a shared ethical concern: if we care about people, then we can't ignore immediate conditions of suffering and injustice. Jill Chettiar, a former anti-poverty organizer in Vancouver's economically devastated Downtown Eastside, was emphatic about this: "As organizers, you can't, in good faith, work in a community or with a community and not be addressing the needs of that community." This is also about ethical consistency— following through on our political commitments by taking action in the complex realities of actually existing society. In talking about her previous work as an organizer with NOII-Montreal, Andréa Maria said, "There's just not much point in decrying the racism of the state if you're not going to support someone in their fight against deportation, and that inevitably means that you have to acknowledge that there's a state and there's a bureaucracy, and you have to talk to them." For many anti-authoritarian organizers, then, our ethical concern for people requires us to participate in reform struggles and make demands on dominant institutions.

This way of being "in the world" is also about strategy. We rarely fight ruling systems as abstractions. Instead, we have to take on such systems through the specific ways—such as poverty, criminalization, debt, sexual violence, and workplace exploitation—in which they manifest themselves in people's day-to-day lives. Tatiana Gomez, another former NOII-Montreal organizer, argued that "if you're going to say that you're actually in solidarity with people, then you have to meet them where they're at." She used the example of Solidarity Across Borders, a Montreal-based migrant justice coalition. One of the central campaigns in Solidarity Across Borders, Gomez explained, is for a regularization program—a comprehensive state-sanctioned process for undocumented immigrants to gain legal status.[12] She continued,

> That's going to make a big difference in people's lives. But we'll still have borders. Something like regularization is more immediately winnable than bringing down borders, but that doesn't mean that, as part of our organizing for regularization, we don't include the anti-borders analysis. And so, I think if we're going to start thinking long-term, how do we build the analysis or the power or the consciousness to get a place where you're going to bring down borders? You have to create steps along the way. And steps along the way would include reform campaigns because, if you have this elusive goal, people get tired, people get demoralized, and people leave. And if I'm a migrant and I come to Solidarity Across Borders, I'm not going to ask, "When are we going to smash borders?" I'm going to say, "What can you do for me right now? I might get deported." So, I think if we're not going to confine ourselves to the activist ghetto, then we can't subscribe to the dichotomy [of "reform work" versus "revolutionary work"]. I think you have to think about the relationship between the two and how reform can be used—not as an end in itself but as a means for our larger ends.

Being "in the world" thus anchors anti-authoritarian organizing efforts. It forces us, as activists and organizers, to relate to the actual conditions of people's lives, the needs in our communities, and, when present, the popular struggles and organizations.[13] It opens up opportunities for us to develop humility and love for people in all of their beauty, brokenness, and complexity. This puts us squarely on the terrain of reform fights. Being "in the world," as Gomez argued, also enables us to think about goals as "steps along the way" within broader strategies. Longtime organizer David Solnit emphasized this too: "One of the things that takes the winds out of our movements' sails is if you've got your eyes focused on an island two thousand miles away, but there's no interim, achievable milestone goals. If you look at any successful movement—like the CIW [Coalition of Immokalee Workers], like the civil rights movement—they had victories all along the way because they set stepping stone goals." In this sense, "a strategy is a series of reforms," as Oakland-based organizer Joshua Kahn Russell described it. It's something that builds, one win after another, toward a transformative vision.

Pushing at the Bounds of the "Possible"

The tricky part is that a series of reforms, no matter how ambitious, doesn't automatically lead to revolutionary social transformation. In fact, if we're not careful, reform efforts can keep us running in circles within the world as it is—making things better or preserving past gains, but not fundamentally changing dominant institutions and relations. So, while being "in the world" in this way crucially anchors organizing work, we need something else to direct our efforts strategically. This is where the second aspect of "in the world but not of it" is important. Being "not of it" means developing strategies based on a radical vision of another world, one that we can bring into being through large-scale collective action.

Alston described this second aspect as a practice of avoiding confinement to what seems "possible." This is a critical point. Much contemporary labor and community organizing in the United States and Canada focuses on "winnable" victories—things that organizers decide are possible to achieve given current conditions.[14] These might include successfully pressuring an employer to recognize a union, getting a landlord to take responsibility for repairing dilapidated rental housing, or forcing a police department to fire a particularly racist and violent cop. Wins like these are crucial. They help sustain people in struggle and demonstrate in practical terms what we can achieve when we fight together for what we want. As revolutionaries, however, our ultimate goals are rarely "winnable" in any immediate sense. Indeed, they're far outside what most people currently consider "possible." A core challenge of being "not of it," then, is how to fight for reforms in ways that bust out of the confines of the world as it is. As New York organizer Michelle O'Brien framed the question, "How can we actually do this work in a way that opens up the imaginative terrain?"

Prison abolitionists have made some progress toward addressing this challenge. Abolitionism, as I've explained, aims not for "better" or more "humane" prisons, but for something seemingly unimaginable: eliminating the PIC and generating community practices for reducing harm and creating safety. This, truly, is a vision "not of the world," but those in CR use it to guide their work "in the world." Rachel Herzing, a longtime CR organizer, offered some useful reflections for navigating this terrain. "For me," she said, "what that looks like in practice is acknowledging that we need to be engaged with the world around us today. We spend a lot of time [in abolitionist organizing] trying to convince people that we're not utopians—that we're not living in some fantasy world—but that what we want is good for people *today*. . . . So, we're always struggling to figure out which battles to fight, like any other organization is. The main thing for us, though, is: Is this going to create some obstacle that we're just gonna have to tear down later?"

This question is central for CR. To illustrate it, Herzing used the example of juvenile detention facilities. While some criminal justice reform organizations in California have called for constructing smaller, more "home-like" facilities, CR has opposed any new construction and argued instead for community-based alternatives to youth detention. "That's a pretty major political battle for us," said Herzing. "And it's not . . . about not taking seriously how bad the conditions are that young people are locked in currently. In fact, we take it so seriously that we say no one should be living there, period. And if we can't figure out how to keep young people out of jails and prisons, it's going to be much harder to keep adults out."

This principle of avoiding the creation of obstacles is one of the most precious gifts of abolitionism. With implications that reach far beyond struggles against prisons, it is a crucial tool for being "not of it." In particular, it helps us to think carefully about *what we're currently doing* in relation to *what we're trying to achieve* in the long-term: How does what we're fighting for right now limit and/or expand the possibilities of winning what we ultimately want? Answering this is hardly ever straightforward, especially given the messy conditions in which we struggle. This principle calls on us to articulate what we want as well as to gauge the effects of our actions, always within dynamic circumstances. Still, it can help us move away from simplistic rejections or uncritical embraces of reform-based work.[15]

In practical terms, this abolitionist principle offers two key priorities for reform-oriented organizing. One is struggling for gains that limit the power and scope of ruling institutions and relations. "[With] everything you do," as New York CR organizer Pilar Maschi stressed, "you have to ask yourself the question: Is this shrinking the system?" The other priority is fighting for victories that, as Michelle O'Brien put it, "invoke other solutions" beyond ruling systems. These wins press at the bounds of what seems "possible" and highlight more democratic, egalitarian, and cooperative ways of organizing society. Together, these priorities are vital for being "not of it." Using them, we can collectively discuss and evaluate *which* reform struggles to engage in, based on vision, not what seems "possible."

We can look to recent organizing initiatives for examples of how to use these kinds of priorities. Take the Repeal Coalition in Arizona. Formed in 2008, Repeal has been an important part of the surging immigrant rights movement fighting draconian anti-immigrant laws. Repeal organizers have tapped into a large reservoir of popular anger in Latino/a communities as they've gone door-to-door in immigrant neighborhoods, held mass meetings, and helped to generate enormous protests. And they've done all of this work with the explicit aim of *ending* all state measures that target undocumented immigrants. As Repeal activist and radical scholar Joel Olson writes, "Most immigrant rights groups here call for 'comprehensive immigration reform,' a law that would create a long, arduous path to citizenship for only some undocumented people, while leaving many in legal limbo. The Repeal Coalition, however, argues for the repeal of all anti-immigrant laws."[16] While firmly grounded in day-to-day struggles, Repeal's approach pushes against the current immigration regime and toward justice and mobility for all.[17] This is a powerful strategic combination.

Fighting in Ways That Point Beyond

The other relevant question here is *how* we engage in reform struggles. Being "not of it" suggests not only ways of orienting toward reforms, but also ways of fighting for them. Solnit presented this as a question: "How can we struggle for the reform in a way that gives people power, gives people experience in asserting their power, rather than reinforcing existing institutions or reinforcing existing power-holders?" Helen Hudson, a member of the Certain Days Political Prisoner Calendar collective in Montreal, put it a little differently: "If you're struggling around a single-issue reform, but you organize yourself in such a way that the process is transformative for the people involved, then I think that's what can make it nonreformist." The central point here is that the ways in which we struggle for reforms can point beyond them. Many in the anti-authoritarian current seek to enact this principle in their work.

Those involved in migrant justice work associated with NOII have crafted some especially helpful ways of fighting for reforms in transformative ways. In Montreal, Jaggi Singh concretely discussed this in relation to casework. "You gotta be wary of getting into the logic of reinforcing the system," he emphasized.

> In Solidarity Across Borders, we're fighting removals all the time. And this is why I prefer the term "support work" and not "casework," although I'm not against casework per se. You can do casework: you go all out for a given case, you do all the things that you need to do (lobbying, direct action), and you can win. But you know, you're not really winning because, for all that effort, there's all the other things that you can't do, like all the other "cases" of people you don't hear from or can't respond to. So, the system still functions: it still churns people out, and it will give you a couple of crumbs in order to give the impression of responding when it's not really responding to fundamental injustices, and is actually making things worse—a lot

worse. . . . So we developed this idea of "support work." Support work means that while we still work on cases—that is, we're still tangibly fighting removals—we're also trying to create a context where we generalize the solidarity, and build a network of mutual aid, so it's sustainable. Support work acknowledges all the different ways we can contribute to building a network of solidarity around a given case.[18]

To generalize the solidarity, said Singh, is to "create a culture whereby that support is shared within the entire network instead of thinking about a case in isolation and almost having a quasi-client, service relationship. Instead, we're walking together and fighting together." This gets at one crucial way of fighting for reforms that also points beyond them: building solidarity through struggle. In the face of systemic logics that encourage us to act as isolated individuals and to view our circumstances as ours alone, we can organize in ways that bring people together, demonstrate commonalities, and develop collectivity and mutual support. When we engage in reform struggles in this way, we can push at the bounds of "what is."

Another crucial way of fighting for reforms so as to point beyond them is prioritizing approaches through which people see and use their own power. In Vancouver, NOII organizer Harjap Grewal talked about "facilitating the efforts of people trying to do things on their own." As he said, "One of the biggest things, I think, in a struggle is that people should be able to struggle for themselves, right? I think that's amazing. It empowers people. Concrete change. Their own goals are accomplished. They can do things." Often what this means in practice is using tactics in which people, together, disruptively confront those who make decisions about their lives—whether bosses, cops, university administrators, or government officials—and win concessions. Frequently this involves some form of direct action, but not always or necessarily.

Mike D, who worked with the Ontario Coalition Against Poverty (OCAP) in Toronto, highlighted this in relation to OCAP's work with welfare recipients. "The issue," he said, "isn't whether you're flying at the government and trying to knock them over every single time. The issue is whether you're trying to build that movement. Every time you get somebody to challenge the government, you're doing that. People go onto welfare and they're treated like shit, they're told that they're shit, and the whole experience is incredibly depressing, incredibly demoralizing." As he explained, one of OCAP's campaigns in recent years has been to raise the welfare rates in Ontario. While they haven't achieved this yet, he said, "there has been created among a not insubstantial population of assistance recipients a sense of entitlement, a sense of 'Fuck you! I deserve this, and if you say no, I'm gonna get OCAP!' That kind of sense that you can stand up to them, even if it's just standing up to your welfare office, your welfare worker. That's a really positive thing."

What's most vital in this way of fighting is people experiencing themselves as capable of challenging and changing power relations. Harsha Walia described this as "a framework of political empowerment": "When people who are directly experiencing or impacted by systemic oppression are able to overcome their sense of marginalization, victimization, and hopelessness and come together to create their own self-determined culture of resistance, that process itself of consciousness-raising and community-building is a significant victory in shifting the terrain of political struggle. In that sense, individual casework is a concrete means of broadening the base of resistance." Reform-oriented work along these lines moves beyond the confines of how people are supposed to relate to the powerful institutions and decision-makers that so often determine the conditions of our lives. In this way, it points beyond how our society is organized and toward how it can and should be.[19]

At their best, these ways of fighting for reform—building solidarity and asserting people's power—offer an important kind of political education through practical experience. Mac Scott, active with both NOII and OCAP in Toronto, laid this out very clearly:

> When you're doing an action or a campaign, you have to look at what at the end is the lesson that's gonna be taught. For example, if you gain an increase in welfare through constantly organizing welfare recipient communities and collective actions, even if it's not a period where you can pull direct action—it's a period where you're doing forums or you're doing symbolic actions, but they're collective—and you get that win, the lesson at the end of the day is that a bunch of people coming together, even people who are shit-ass poor, can create change and even claw back something that they deserve. . . . If you win through collective direct action or collective action of any sort in the absence of collective direct action, I think [that] sends a lot different message than if you win through media work and legal lawsuits. And certainly those things can and should be part of it. . . . But if, at the end of the day, the people who are right there on the ground feel that it's their victory, that—even if it's a reformist goal—is a revolutionary win because the message we always have to be working on is, number one, you can win, number two, you can win through working together amongst large groups of people, diverse groups of people, and you can win without having to be a talented, privileged, university-trained professional.

Very practically, then, these ways of fighting for reform point beyond. They help establish and develop a sense of "not of it" within popular struggles.

Goals and Visions

Viable revolutionary strategies, many anti-authoritarians increasingly suggest, must build from popular struggles, which are often reform-based. When so many resources and so much repression are organized through dominant institutions, especially through the state, we can't simply ignore them; we have to make demands on them. And in the current moment, the struggles for these demands are mostly defensive—they seek to protect people and ecosystems from the worst effects of systems of exploitation and oppression. This is one important way that we enact the "against" at the heart of another politics. As activists and organizers attempt to connect these largely defensive fights to transformative aspirations, we are also building the "beyond."

Through all of this, we're learning about the importance of goals and visions. On the one hand, we have to set goals "in the world" as steps along the way. These should have outcomes that will be visible and that we can credibly imagine achieving soon. Anti-authoritarians are already involved in fighting for many short-term goals, such as stopping deportations, preventing evictions, and halting construction of resource extraction projects. More medium-term goals might include substantially raising welfare rates, abolishing some forms of incarceration, and complete military withdrawals. Collectively establishing these sorts of goals is essential for developing strategies on any scale.

On the other hand, we have to generate visions "not of the world" that mark out the features of the society that we ultimately wish to see. Many in the anti-authoritarian current are very good at talking about visions in general terms: "smashing capitalism," "abolishing prisons," "destroying borders," and "uprooting racism." We also emphasize egalitarianism, democracy, self-determination, solidarity, sustainability, and peace. While these name vital aspirations, they remain very abstract. Collectively fashioning more elaborated visions is essential for developing strategies that are genuinely revolutionary.

Goals keep us relevant; they build on our ethical commitments and ground us in popular struggles. Visions keep us focused; they guide us in choosing which reform fights to take up and how. As Joshua Kahn Russell said, "Goals have to build towards visions or else we are just pursuing reform for its own sake. But if we keep our heads in the clouds by only thinking about vision, we will never accomplish concrete wins."[20] Together, these two priorities can help us craft strategies, based in immediate struggles, that are at once practical and transformative.

BUILDING COUNTERPOWER

"In the world but not of it" isn't only about defensive struggles. Just as much, it involves developing the infrastructure of a liberatory society in ways that undermine, contest, and ultimately replace ruling relations and institutions. This is the broad strategy that most clearly expresses the "beyond" central to another politics. From an abolitionist perspective, Rachel Herzing evocatively captured the sensibility underlying it. "This is theoretical 'cause I don't think we've seen it yet," she clarified. "But I have in my head somewhere that creating situations in which the state becomes superfluous needs to be the goal. That's essentially my take on abolition. We stop using them. We stop legitimating them. We stop giving to them. We stop going to them to ask for things. And they become superfluous. And it does put a certain burden on us to be responsive to each other, to be responsible to each other. But I also think we're up to that, especially if we're consciously disengaging from the state."

Some anti-authoritarians, referencing a concept from Marxist and anarchist traditions, call this a strategy of building "dual power" or "counterpower."[21] In basic terms, this means creating popular institutions and organizations that can struggle with dominant institutions, particularly the state, for legitimacy. Activists Pat Korte and Brian Kelly usefully describe the aims of dual power: "By building and strengthening self-managing institutions that prefigure a participatory society and compete with oppressive institutions for power and support of the people, we arouse radical consciousness among the public, encourage people to want still more changes in society, and demonstrate the viability of alternatives to present systems of domination."[22] Developing such institutions is also an important defensive measure. As we've seen recently from Cairo to Montreal, when movements begin to pose a significant challenge to ruling institutions, the state often responds with repression. Having movement-based infrastructure to provide for people's basic needs (such as food, medical care, and safety) is crucial for weathering such situations.

Building counterpower holds the promise of combining prefigurative praxis with a strategic orientation toward revolution. On the one hand, it's about creating in our current circumstances, to the greatest extent possible, the liberatory capacities and institutions of the world that we wish to achieve. On the other hand, it's about developing forms of self-organization with such deep roots and to such levels of scale and coordination that they come to represent a new popular power in confrontation with state power. The face-off between these two powers would be a "dual power situation"—an essential step toward large-scale revolutionary transformation.

Anti-authoritarians are beginning to craft ambitious approaches for developing counterpower, although we don't all use that term for them. Some build on anarchist ideas and experiences, others grow out of abolitionist politics and practices, and many draw on examples of collective self-help from the global South and oppressed communities in North America. In developing them, organizers are grappling with how to be responsive to concrete realities while building liberatory alternatives—how to be "in the world but not of it."

Beyond Subcultures and Service Providers

One way to understand approaches to building counterpower in another politics is as attempts to move beyond two limited models: do-it-yourself activities largely rooted in anarchist subcultural scenes and nonprofit organizations or agencies engaged in service provision. The first of these has revolutionary aims. Many anarchist-oriented activists in the United States and Canada understand their efforts as building dual power in some way. For instance, this is an important aspiration underlying Food Not Bombs, an international network of local groups that collect and prepare discarded food to feed people for free while advocating radical politics. Activists also draw on this aspiration in running infoshops, political spaces that serve as hubs for anarchist projects, events, and literature distribution. In fact, we can see a dual power aspiration in most of the do-it-yourself activities of contemporary anarchists in North America, such as bike co-ops that help people learn to repair their bicycles, free schools that offer no-cost community classes, and "really, really free markets" that create public settings for people to give stuff away.[23]

It's crucial to recognize the work that goes into all of these efforts and to understand that they can be vital gateways into radical politics. We should also honor the aspiration that animates them. But at the same time, we do have to be honest about their limitations. One problem is that many of these sorts of activities remain largely sequestered in subcultural scenes, as I discussed in the last chapter. Although there are exceptions, these efforts primarily serve people who self-identify as activists and/or feel comfortable in communities based around this identity. Another problem is that "dual power," in many of these initiatives, translates into "autonomous from the state and capitalism." What's largely missing is the aim of not just *being autonomous from*, but also *competing with* dominant institutions. For this, a movement-building orientation is absolutely crucial.[24]

Clare Bayard, a longtime anarchist organizer in San Francisco, was frank in discussing these problems. "If it's all about building our alternative institutions," she said, "then that's cool, but you need to do it on a scale that's not just about your anarchist community. . . . You're gonna have to fuckin' go for it in a really major, large-scope way that I don't ever see anyone going for because of the discomfort that it would involve in really opening themselves up to what a community that's not theirs wants. 'Cause people don't always want to hear the answer of what the community wants, which is not always an infoshop."[25] While contemporary anarchist attempts to build counterpower in North America have got the "not of it" part down— developing and, in small ways, enacting liberatory visions—most are faltering at being "in the world"—rooting and growing these visions in broad sections of society. For this reason, they remain profoundly limited.

The second model that many in the anti-authoritarian current are trying to move beyond is one that has humanitarian aims. Most people who volunteer or work for nonprofit organizations and agencies, also known as nongovernmental organizations (NGOs), understand their efforts as directly responding to urgent community needs. This, indeed, is the central motivation behind food banks, sexual assault centers, literacy programs, health clinics, homeless shelters, and many other NGOs that provide services. Especially as governments have gutted social programs over the last three decades, such NGOs have often been the ones to fill in the gaps.[26] In this way, nonprofits and agencies do respond to essential needs. As well, there are many well-intentioned people who are finding ways to use these organizations and their resources to further left movements.

Still, anti-authoritarians are critical of what is called the "nonprofit sector" in the United States and the "social service sector" in Canada. As I mentioned in chapter 1, INCITE! has played an important role in developing and circulating a critique of what many have come to call the "nonprofit industrial complex."[27] This critique points to some crucial limitations of nonprofit organizations in the United States, limitations that are also relevant to agencies in the Canadian context.[28]

One problem has to do with money. Funding for NGOs tends to come from state programs run by bureaucrats and private foundations run by rich people. Organizations applying for these funds have to orient themselves around the grant cycles, cultures, and priorities of governments or foundations, rather than the needs and aims of movements.[29] Another problem has to do with an organizational form that mimics dominant institutions. NGOs are based on a model that centers on paid staff, usually in a hierarchical structure overseen by a board of directors. No matter how well-intentioned, these individuals fill positions in organizations that are competing for funds and prestige. And though staff members may be deeply committed to the caring aspects of their work, the structural logic of these organizations encourages them to understand themselves as "professionals" pursuing "careers." The NGO model thus tends, in the words of INCITE! cofounder Andrea Smith, to "redirect activist energies into career-based modes of organizing instead of mass-based organizing capable of actually transforming society."[30]

These two problems shape the specific limitations of NGOs engaged in what is known as "service provision." This set of activities involves providing things such as training, food, and shelter to generally poor and working-class people. The vast majority of NGOs that provide services work within a model that relates to people individually as "clients." At the core of this model is a power relationship between those who provide services and those who receive them. As a result, there isn't much space for people to organize collectively to meet their own needs. As well, this model of service provision is largely oriented toward helping people survive within society as it is currently organized, rather than helping them challenge and change the systems that force them to need services in the first place.[31] So, while the service provision efforts of NGOs are solidly "in the world"— responding to community needs—most are unable to be "not of it"—pushing at the bounds of dominant institutions and logics.

There are certainly good reasons for moving beyond these two limited models. But rather than wholly discarding these initiatives, we ought to learn from both their strengths and their weaknesses. These experiences pose crucial questions for any efforts to develop counterpower: How can we build truly popular institutions rather than projects in mostly marginal activist scenes? And how can we build institutions that provide for people's often pressing needs without becoming trapped in client/service models?

Reinventing "Serving the People"

The last decade has seen activists and organizers striving to develop workable answers to these questions. In these efforts, building counterpower has become closely connected, though not always explicitly so, to discussions about responding to community needs. In the anti-authoritarian current, the model that comes up most consistently in such conversations is the Black Panther Party's "survival programs pending revolution." As I described in chapter 1, these included free breakfast programs for children, clothing giveaway initiatives, and no-cost health clinics, all connected to the BPP's organizing and revolutionary vision. Like many others, Montreal-based migrant justice organizer Tatiana Gomez discussed her admiration for this model: "These programs were part and parcel of something bigger and radical." So, she asked, "How do we reproduce that in a way that is right for today? Because I do think that this will get worse and people are going to have immediate needs that need to be responded to."

Some organizers have tried to recreate aspects of this model through radical base-building NGOs that innovatively combine service provision and community organizing. Rayan El-Amine, a founding organizer of the Arab Resource and Organizing Center (AROC) in San Francisco, highlighted one such organization, Mujeres Unidas Y Activas, which organizes and supports Latina immigrants in San Francisco and Oakland:

> They not only have legal services to set living wages and protect [immigrant women workers] from people who aren't going to pay them or other abuses; but there's also a space for the women to talk about their own lives, their own politics, and their own struggles, and that becomes an organic part of this service-oriented group. So at AROC, we look at groups like Mujeres Unidas in order to think about how to get people who are facing discrimination in the Arab community right now to get help from a lawyer and fight discrimination at the workplace or [in] housing. But we also want people to feel it's a community organization to work with collectively that is going to help defend them personally and defend their family and community.

Mujeres Unidas Y Activas is one in a relatively small set of such organizations in North America.[32] Although there is a lot of diversity among them, these groups share an ability to bring together needs-based work and struggles for justice while moving away from the client/service model. At their best, they offer genuinely useful things, such as advocacy and resources, and lead campaigns that win tangible victories, such as the groundbreaking Domestic Workers Bill of Rights that Domestic Workers United won in New York in 2010.[33] This combination is essential to these organizations' recipe for building power among oppressed and exploited people. Outside this small cohort, no other groups on the left in North America are doing this work on this scale.

Many smart and committed radicals, including a fair number of anti-authoritarians, have dedicated themselves to building these organizations. Others in the anti-authoritarian current are more suspicious, seeing the base-building NGOs as too compromised and professionalized.[34] People in both camps tend to be quite clear that the critique of the nonprofit industrial complex applies to these organizations: NGOs face funding constraints and restrictive organizational logics even when they're staffed by radicals and engaged in radical organizing.[35] The disagreement has more to do with the question of whether, while recognizing these realities, there is any transformative work that can be done through such organizations. Still, people on both sides of that question agree that more organizational models are needed. Paula Ximena Rojas-Urrutia, a community organizer and former NGO worker who helped develop the INCITE! critique, voiced this need in her call for a proliferation of forms beyond nonprofits. "If we want to build powerful movements here," she writes, "we need a spectrum of approaches and we need to figure out ways to organize without paid staff and without funding. We need to take risks, and then compare strategies. In addition, we need to think of strategic ways to involve people of all sectors in the movement—be they unwaged mothers, nonprofit workers, teachers, or grocery store workers."[36]

The popularity of these radical NGOs shows that solid needs-based work is not only crucial but also possible. However, we have to be very intentional about how and why we do it, and ensure that meeting needs is consistently connected to radical organizing. Rafael Mutis, an experienced abolitionist organizer in New York, talked about this as trying "to meet people's immediate needs, not in a servicey kind of way. . . . Some service can be helpful in meeting the needs, as long as you know that's not your goal, as long as you know what your goal is—transforming society together with people." In San Francisco, longtime housing organizer James Tracy echoed this: "It's always about meeting people's basic survival needs, but trying to take it one step further." Referencing a Maoist slogan popular in the 1960s and 1970s, he argued that we need to "reinvent 'serving the people.'" The base-building NGOs are undeniably one attempt to do this.

The encampments of the occupy movement, in perhaps a less intentional way, were another attempt along these lines. Indeed, the occupy movement was an intense, if brief, crash course for thousands of activists in reinventing "serving the people." As encampments sprang up across the continent in fall 2011, occupiers immediately began developing infrastructure to feed, shelter, and otherwise care for themselves. Some encampments also created libraries, clinics, and other institutions. These efforts were incredibly ambitious and, in many cases, difficult to sustain. As encampments began hosting sizeable houseless populations, occupiers struggled with how to balance responding to immediate needs with ongoing organizing activities.[37] Because the encampments were so short-lived, this tension was never resolved. Nevertheless, many people learned new skills and experienced for the first time their capacities to build responsive forms of social organization, even if temporarily. These experiences also made clear to relatively privileged activists the profound magnitude of human need in society as it is currently organized and the power of movements that respond to this need.[38]

The occupy encampments built on and in turn laid the basis for more sustained radical responses to popular needs. Grassroots disaster relief efforts in recent years have been the most prominent of these; through such experiences, organizers have worked to reinvent "serving the people" and grappled with issues related to building dual power, sometimes explicitly. The aftermath of Hurricane Katrina on the Gulf Coast, particularly in New Orleans, opened this up in a big way in 2005.[39]

As I mentioned in chapter 1, post-Katrina New Orleans saw various grassroots relief and reconstruction efforts, including several connected to the anti-authoritarian current. The local chapter of Critical Resistance, in collaboration with other groups, publicized the plight of the thousands of prisoners left locked up in rising waters during the storm, and spearheaded an amnesty campaign for people arrested for "looting" (in other words, attempting to meet their material needs) in the immediate wake of Katrina.[40] The local INCITE! group launched a number of initiatives, including the New Orleans Women's Health Clinic, aimed at furthering health and reproductive justice for women of color and low-income women, an effort that was all the more pressing given the substantially damaged medical infrastructure of the city. They also assisted out-of-town volunteers who came to New Orleans through radical women of color networks to support ongoing organizing.[41] The CR and INCITE! groups were part of a local network of community-based organizations, mostly led by radicals of color, that existed before Katrina and generated important new organizational efforts after the storm, some of which have continued into the present.[42]

The anti-authoritarian relief initiative that garnered the most attention was the Common Ground (CG) collective, an organization started just days after Katrina through the collaboration of a community organizer and former Black Panther and a small crew of white anarchists. Drawing on networks primarily based in the global justice movement, CG was able to rapidly bring resources and volunteers to New Orleans and initiate an array of relief activities under the slogan "Solidarity, Not Charity." These included distributing supplies, cleaning up houses, and eventually establishing the Common Ground Health Clinic. In the few years following Katrina, thousands of predominantly young and white activists traveled to New Orleans and volunteered in these efforts, contributing vital skills and labor. However, the large influx of these volunteers, combined with an overwhelming sense of urgency, longstanding patterns shaped by racism and sexism, and an FBI informant in a prominent leadership role, also produced significant challenges. In particular, CG struggled with navigating race, responding to sexual assault within the organization, and developing accountable relationships with the people they were assisting.[43]

The more recent relief experience in the wake of Superstorm Sandy has some important continuity with post-Katrina efforts. After Sandy battered the East Coast in 2012, millions in New York were without power and transportation, and some were left with destroyed homes and neighborhoods. As in New Orleans, this devastation was the product of structural inequality together with a vicious storm. While state agencies and large NGOs were unable to cope with the scope of need, a network of Occupy Wall Street activists stepped into the void, launching Occupy Sandy with the slogan "We Got This." Partnering with dozens of community organizations, they set up central collection hubs for donations and established distribution lines to nodes throughout the greater New York area. Occupy Sandy also created an impressive network of relief centers, complete with a sophisticated communications infrastructure, through which thousands of people were able easily to volunteer, matching their skills and talents with specific needs.[44]

These recent radical relief initiatives show the power of movements to respond to popular needs. It's clear that there are many skilled people and untapped resources that organizers can draw upon, especially during dire circumstances. It also seems clear that, with practice, we can get better at "filling the shoes of a government that's gone AWOL," as some leading CG organizers put it in 2007.[45] The occupy encampments, particularly in New York, trained a whole layer of activists in doing needs-based work without—and often against—ruling institutions. They were thus well prepared for working in the post-Sandy situation. As Occupy Sandy organizer Michael Premo observes, "It's amazing how organized we are, it's amazing how much so many people involved with the social movement have learned about themselves, about each other, about all of how—how to put these values into practice."[46]

As inspiring as such activities are, we also have to keep them in perspective. Writing about the post-Katrina experience, organizer and journalist Jordan Flaherty points out that "volunteer efforts cannot replace the damaged infrastructure of an entire city. At best, volunteers can contribute by reinforcing a safety net and by supporting local projects that bring a systemic analysis. The problems are structural, and any solution must address this larger context."[47] This is a crucial reminder about the limited capacities of actually existing movements and the importance of ongoing struggles for justice and dignity. In the long run, as New Orleans organizer Lydia

Pelot-Hobbs argues, "the political work needed to confront disasters in many ways isn't about disasters at all."[48] Rather, it's about building powerful movements that can change the structural conditions that make disasters so consistently disastrous. In other words, the "beyond" of another politics—building the infrastructure of a more sustainable and egalitarian society—is insufficient without the "against"—challenging and transforming the systems that create misery and destruction.

Radical relief initiatives have also opened up the question of institution-building. Yotam Marom, another Occupy Sandy organizer, lays this out well: "Flexible networks like Occupy Sandy are incredible machines—more fluid than big organizations, more dynamic than government agencies. But they rely on having people or strong communities to network. Networks connect dots, but you still need the dots themselves to be ready." The often fast-paced ad hoc organizing that happens in response to disasters can thus be effective, but it's not enough on its own. It's certainly not sufficient for supporting the broad, enduring, and combative movements that we need. As Marom writes, "We have to build infrastructure and create the institutional frameworks that can sustain a struggle over the long haul."[49]

Creating Counterinstitutions

Part of the way to build this long-haul infrastructure is by creating institutions through which people can self-organize to meet popular needs and undermine dominant systems. As I explained in chapter 3, these are counterinstitutions. They can be physical spaces, such as clinics and cooperatives, as well as new forms of social organization, such as childcare collectives and community-based conflict resolution networks. Regardless of what they offer—housing, health care, or other things—what they have in common is that they develop social relations of cooperation, self-management, and equality in opposition to ruling institutions and relations. Counterinstitutions—grounded in the lives of ordinary people and yet pointing to a more liberatory society—are perhaps the most explicit approach in another politics for developing counterpower.

Counterinstitutions have been central to the success of movements across the globe, from Brazil's Landless Workers' Movement to the German autonomous movement. In the United States and Canada, however, these kinds of institutions are currently small in number and scale. They include health care initiatives such as the Rock Dove Collective in New York and the New Orleans Women's Health and Justice Initiative, community education efforts such as the Purple Thistle Centre in Vancouver and the Experimental Community Education of the Twin Cities, and community spaces such as the AKA Autonomous Social Center in Kingston, El Kilombo Intergaláctico social center in Durham, and the 2640 space in Baltimore. For the most part, the anti-authoritarian current is still figuring out how to successfully create and sustain counterinstitutions. In doing this, we can learn a lot from efforts already underway.

The San Francisco Community Land Trust (SFCLT) offers one particularly rich experience. The SFCLT establishes inexpensive, resident-controlled housing for poor and working-class people on community-owned land. With skyrocketing housing prices in the Bay Area, low-income people, particularly in communities of color, are being rapidly displaced from their homes and neighborhoods. Fighting this, the SFCLT "pursues the collectivization of residential buildings as an anti-displacement strategy," in cofounder James Tracy's words.[50] The SFCLT won its first victory in late 2005, when it acquired an apartment building in Chinatown. The working-class Chinese American tenants had been fighting for seven years to protect the building from demolition, and the SFCLT was able to facilitate them taking over cooperative ownership. In its continuing work to develop housing co-ops in San Francisco, the SFCLT is part of a broader wave of community land trusts across the United States.[51]

What's powerful about the SFCLT and other effective counterinstitutions is that they bring together prefigurative praxis and fights for concrete gains. Reflecting on his work with the SFCLT, Tracy helpfully described this combined orientation:

> I really want to embody feasible solutions in the here and now because, if you're able to unlearn capitalist social relations, that's great. When people actually learn how to share a social, vital resource like housing, they can learn to share a city and they can learn to share a world eventually. . . . But it's also not just like, "Oh, we're going to go plant a garden and learn how to be nice to each other"; it's actually a tangible economic reform when it's done correctly. That's just embodying the world I would like to fight for in the here and now. 'Cause . . . I get really sick of always doing a defensive battle. . . . I really wanted to build something [about which] we could say, "this is what we want."

One lesson we can take from this is that building counterinstitutions has to be about *both* responding to survival needs and creating new social relations. The first without the second too often leads to service provision, and the second without the first too often leads to activist insularity. But together, they can lay an important basis for building dual power.

Still, counterinstitutions face a common challenge. This is the understandable tendency for those involved to become so immersed in their work that they lose sight of the bigger picture. In other words, the day-to-day activities necessary for keeping counterinstitutions going can end up isolating institution-builders from movements. As Tracy observed, "You saw in the seventies people making a lot of co-ops and stuff like that. They were trying to embody their sixties values, their revolutionary values, their leftist values in the here and now, but they checked out of the fight for social justice because the whole making your own cooperative dairy farm or making your own housing co-op took up all your time." Similarly, he said, "when you look at the growth of nonprofit housing providers, almost all of them have radical pedigree, all the original fathers and mothers of the movement. It just becomes really hard to manage housing and deal with all the paperwork and the grants and the funders and still stay in the fight."

In all of these cases, Tracy stressed, "it was a good idea to embody cooperative, communitarian values in the here and now." However, he emphasized, we have to guard against the tendency to become disconnected from popular struggles. "I think that one way of doing that is creating new counterinstitutions that don't check out of the political climate, that actually do ask people to come out and oppose war and oppose empire." For instance, Tracy said, "You've got your housing, you live in this co-op, but why can't your neighbor get housing? Well, it could be because of this thing called imperialism that feels directed at your neighborhood."

This is another crucial lesson: counterinstitutions have to be intentionally embedded in transformative movements. In all of their activities, such institutions must navigate the treacherous tides of capitalism and other ruling systems. Without movements to hold and orient them, counterinstitutions are much more susceptible to pressures to become either more subcultural or more professional. The solution, never easy, is to consistently link these institutions with organizing campaigns. Speaking about the New Orleans Women's Health Clinic, INCITE! organizer Shana Griffin articulately outlined this aim: "It's more than providing health care services; it's also about challenging the conditions that limit our access and our opportunities, such as poverty, racism, gender-based violence, imperialism, and war. We see it as more than just a clinic—we want it to also be an organizing center that can meet immediate needs while also working for racial, gender, economic, and environmental justice."[52] If we don't forge such links between counterinstitutions and organizing campaigns, there is no hope for building counterpower in any meaningful way.[53]

Developing Alternative Formations

Abolitionist and anti-racist feminist organizing has generated another approach to building counterinstitutions. Based largely in heavily policed communities of color, this increasingly popular approach involves building community-based alternatives to police and prisons that respond to conflict and violence while fostering genuine safety and security. It grows out of what INCITE! organizer Andrea Smith calls "prison abolition as a positive rather than a negative project." As she explains, "It's not simply about tearing down prison walls, but it's about building alternative formations that actually protect people from violence, that crowd out the criminalization regime."[54]

While these alternative formations don't have stationary physical infrastructures like housing co-ops or radical clinics, they are crucial new forms of social organization. What they're developing, argued New York organizer Michelle O'Brien, "are real, concrete projects that build actual substantive alternative infrastructure to state violence." Building this infrastructure—responsive to the realities of people's lives while putting forward a radical vision—is presently one of the clearest modes of developing counterpower. The central question for this work is one that former New York CR organizer Pilar Maschi poses: "[How do we] stop hurting each other in a way that is loving, community-led, and community-driven, not state-driven?"[55]

Sista II Sista (SIIS), a community-based organization of working-class Black and Latina women in Brooklyn, developed one promising answer through their Sista's Liberated Ground (SLG) project. Initiated in 2004, SLG grew out of SIIS's sustained organizing around police violence in their neighborhood, Bushwick. As founding member Paula Ximena Rojas-Urrutia described, "We were doing a particular campaign against a [police] precinct where there was tons of sexual harassment and violence against young women of color. It was very concrete and neat—the way that U.S. community organizing likes it. But you get to a point where you're like, what would be a demand that would make us happy? Is there one, other than we don't want the police anymore?" She continued, "When we hit that wall, [we were] thinking, okay, even if, let's say, the precinct shuts down tomorrow, there's still all these incidences of violence happening in the neighborhood—interpersonal stuff that happens." This was particularly the case for young women, who were regularly experiencing all sorts of gender-based violence and harassment from men in the community.

SLG was what SIIS developed to deal with these twin problems of police violence and gendered interpersonal violence. SLG sought to create, in the words of SIIS, "a space where violence against sistas is not tolerated, and where women turn to each other instead of the police to address the violence in their lives."[56] Organizers used posters, T-shirts, stickers, and murals to physically create this territory, and they deepened it through workshops aimed at young women in their neighborhood. SIIS also developed what they called "Sista Circles," small groups of young women collectively supporting one another and, when necessary, intervening in circumstances of harassment or violence. For instance, Rojas-Urrutia said, "When somebody is getting stalked, the whole group would go to the [stalker's] workplace and embarrass him in front of the boss and call attention and make some direct demands of what he needed to do. And it would work actually—more than calling the cops—and [it would] heighten the profile publicly of this question of violence in the neighborhood. . . . And we would bring in the fathers too; it wasn't just all women but other people in the neighborhood too."[57]

SLG created a context for women in Bushwick to tangibly improve the conditions of their lives without relying on the cops. This project thus offers a useful recent example of an alternative formation developing real safety for people while actively disengaging from the state. Impressively, it managed to be "in the world"—relating to everyday problems of violence—and yet "not of it"—pointing beyond policing and prisons to a new society. And SIIS was able to pull this off while staying deeply connected to broader movements.

SLG is one of several attempts to build alternative formations in North America. Community-based groups are currently engaged in this kind of work in Atlanta, Chicago, Durham, Madison, Oakland, Philadelphia, San Francisco, Seattle, and other places. In recent years, many of the most dynamic of these efforts have focused on intimate violence.[58] Often influenced by abolitionism and women of color feminism, these initiatives frequently draw on nonstate models of community accountability and violence prevention from other parts of the world, especially in the global South.[59] As well, significant efforts in Indigenous communities across North America are working to preserve and/or recover traditional practices of conflict resolution and justice without involving state-affiliated institutions.[60]

Among these initiatives, the Harm Free Zone (HFZ) project in New York City was particularly groundbreaking. This project developed in the early 2000s out of La Escuela Popular Norteña, a popular education collective, with participation from the New York CR chapter. The basic idea of the HFZ was, as organizer Rafael Mutis explained, "creating community structures and institutions to deal with conflict instead of relying on prisons and police." "To me," he said, "it's a very significant thing in New York City, given the long history of the NYPD and how it acts in communities of color." As in many places, this history is one of intense police violence and the regular presence of the criminal justice system in the lives of racialized people, especially in poor and working-class communities. Because of this history, organizers in New York have spent a lot of time fighting for various forms of police accountability.

Those involved in the HFZ took a different approach. While recognizing the importance of police accountability campaigns, they focused instead on the ways in which systemic violence is reproduced within oppressed communities. In trying to protect themselves from this violence, people often turn to the police and, from there, the jails, courts, and prisons. But as HFZ organizers point out, "The PIC is based on punishment and economics, and not on repairing the interpersonal and state harms which are a reality in our communities." They argue, then, for "refocusing our energies and our efforts on addressing and repairing harms in our communities ourselves. We call this process creating Harm Free Zones."[61]

The HFZ project was able to put these ideas into practice only on a small scale, mainly through mediation, popular education, and de-escalation work. Nevertheless, HFZ organizers managed to engage unusual cross-sections of their communities, bridging ages and experiences. As well, they developed a very thoughtful framework for building alternative formations, one that continues to be quite relevant. In particular, they stressed the centrality of generating processes for community accountability—ways that people can be responsive and responsible to one another and to the broader community in which they live.[62]

At the core of this approach is a radical orientation toward community-building. This means working against the ways in which dominant power relations tend to divide people and make the notion of "community"—whether based on where we live, what we do, or what identities we share—increasingly meaningless. In Mutis's words, "What we're working on in the Harm Free Zone is kind of knitting back the fabric of our communities and being responsible and accountable to each other. But in order to do that, we have to see ourselves—at some level, it doesn't have to be this perfect level—as responsible for each other, as a community in this together." We should thus understand this abolitionist approach as both *rebuilding* communities and *creating* new communities through struggle against state forms of punishment and control.[63] This is how it "crowds out the criminalization regime" and develops dual power.

While this approach is promising, it's also hard. Community-building along these lines is a tremendous challenge in the U.S. and Canadian contexts, where most communities are deeply fragmented; effective organizing efforts have to resist structural forces that pull people apart and encourage us to see ourselves as isolated individuals. Another significant challenge is the time and energy required to keep these efforts going. Speaking about

SLG, Paula Ximena Rojas-Urrutia stressed that "the woman-power that it takes to sustain something like that compared to a little, tight campaign is much more intensive. It's kind of like a whole-way-of-life type of organizing; it isn't just like this little thing." Indeed, this is a consistent feature of most initiatives to build counterinstitutions. Facing and working with these challenges, as some anti-authoritarians are beginning to do, is essential for moving forward.

Scaling Up

The anti-authoritarian current is experimenting, tentatively, in developing (and sometimes recovering or reinventing) "an alternative set of social practices, relations and institutions to the oppressive ones," as HFZ organizers put it.[64] The promise of these initiatives comes from the possibilities that they suggest for much broader and more ambitious work. CR organizer Rachel Herzing discussed this in terms of community accountability efforts that disengage from the state:

> If you don't call the cops and you figure out—over time and with support and in a smart way—how to respond to conflict, and they don't have any calls to respond to—even if they're doing beat drives or beat walks [and still] nobody's engaging with them—then we start to understand our own power and we're able to actively reject state power, which I don't think we can do when we're in a collusion with them. I imagine that's possible at all levels. . . . I think about it on a neighborhood level, that you could do this. . . . But it seems to me possible, at some level, to do that at a larger scale as well.

The same could be said for the full range of institutions and formations that anti-authoritarian organizers are building. There is tremendous potential— and pressing need—for generating these initiatives in more far-reaching ways.

Even with the bigger possibilities opened by post-disaster relief efforts, most of these initiatives are currently small and sparse, sometimes dishearteningly so. This is one of the most consistent criticisms of actually existing counterpower initiatives: they don't measure up to the size and complexity of the society in which we live. I think anti-authoritarians should take this seriously. It's true that, when it comes to movements, innovative efforts generally start small and then, in certain kinds of circumstances, rapidly spread. It's also true that almost everyone currently working to develop counterinstitutions and alternative formations aspires for these efforts to grow. But aspirations are one thing and reality is another. While genuinely celebrating our achievements, we have to carefully guard against the temptation to become satisfied with them at their present scale.

We have our work cut out for us. An initial task, as the Team Colors Collective argues, is "amplifying and replicating" existing counterpower efforts and, I would add, generating new ones that are ever more deeply rooted in the lives and struggles of ordinary people.[65] This will require continuously evaluating and reshaping the institutions and formations that we are building; what works on a small scale may well be impractical on a larger one.[66] In time, we will also need to consider how we can actually take over substantial pieces of state infrastructure, such as schools and health services, and incorporate them into our movements. All the while, we have to keep our efforts squarely rooted in on-the-ground realities while also introducing new realities and possibilities.

SEEING WITH DOUBLE VISION

Being "in the world but not of it," as I've suggested, means firmly planting our feet in existing social conditions and struggles while also imagining and acting beyond them. I see the anti-authoritarian current elaborating this strategic framework through two essential approaches. The first is engaging popular fights around immediate issues. While these help keep us anchored in the world, they're also opportunities for us to challenge what's considered "possible" and to struggle in ways that advance more visionary possibilities. The second approach is building forms of counterpower. While these help keep us oriented toward the world that we are trying to bring into being, they're also vital for meeting popular needs and creating long-term movement infrastructure. We might think of these against-and-beyond approaches, together, as "fight power, build counterpower."[67]

This strategic framework offers us a way to work within the disjunction that Andréa Maria described in chapter 3. As she pointed out, all of us fighting for social transformation must live and struggle, uncomfortably, in the tension between "what is" and "what we want." Being "in the world but not of it" is a way to cultivate a double vision through which we can clearly see both ends of this tension at the same time. From one end, we focus on what is: a world structured by systems of domination in which people nevertheless use their power to live better, create beauty, and, sometimes, fight injustice. From the other end, we focus on what we are trying to build: a world based on cooperation, self-management, equality, and sustainability in which people use their power to run society and live well. In this way of seeing, everything has two simultaneous incarnations: *what has been made* and *what we could make.*

This double vision is the basis for developing the more specific strategies our movements need. On the one hand, it guards against disconnected dreaming: we're forced to ground our aspirations in the real circumstances in which we struggle and craft plans that relate to these circumstances. On the other hand, it prevents pure practicality: we're forced to articulate what we want and, at every step, critically assess the extent to which our efforts reflect and help us move toward our larger aspirations. In this way, "in the world but not of it" isn't a formula with a ready-made order of activities. It's a framework to construct and continually modify as we work in the space between the realities we confront and our hopes for what will be. It's how we connect day-to-day efforts with vision for social transformation.

PART THREE

Organizing

6. "Bringing people together to build their power"

Anti-authoritarian Organizing

While innovative tactics are important tools for movements, direct action without base-building is ephemeral; it may exert power in a given moment, but it does not build or accumulate the capacity to use it. . . . The ability to mobilize constituencies around social conditions and political issues is built through the hard, long-term work of face-to-face conversations between neighbors, workers, family members, organizers, and communities.

Rose Bookbinder and Michael Belt

The Ontario Coalition Against Poverty marches against government bailouts for the rich on November 5, 2009, in Toronto, Ontario. (Photo by Edward Hon-Sing Wong)

WHEN I SPOKE WITH HER in San Francisco, Sonya Z. Mehta highlighted one fundamental implication of the "in the world but not of it" framework. Drawing on her extensive experience in anarchist politics and labor organizing with Young Workers United, she asserted:

> I have a very clear vision of what I would like to see, and I also understand now that there's no way to do it besides a mass movement. Without really mass support of the people, we're not going to change anything. And even say, amazingly enough, we had a revolution. To really sustain that kind of democracy and equality, we [would] need to have built that within individuals and in the mass of people. So, my political commitment is to organizing. I think that we need to build people's confidence to a point where they actually feel they can do these things, where they feel like they engage democratically with each other, where they feel that they can take power.

Aiming in this way for large-scale social transformation and movement-building leads to organizing. How exactly to define "organizing" is, as I explain below, a topic of intense discussion. In general, however, anti-authoritarians tend to use it to describe bringing wider and wider circles of people together through collective struggles.

A political commitment to organizing is a distinguishing feature of another politics. Vancouver-based Justicia for Migrant Workers organizer Adriana Paz, for example, discussed what she consciously called her "organizing practice"—her day-to-day work of developing relationships with migrant workers, contributing to their self-organization, and assisting them in struggle. "In terms of organizing approaches and strategies, I seek to be oriented and guided by my own practice along with the workers I organize with. Our praxis will tell us what is the most efficient way to organize and to win concrete battles," she said. This focus on practice "grounded in the struggle of people," as NOII-Vancouver organizer Harjap Grewal put it in chapter 4, is widespread in the anti-authoritarian current.

But our organizing is never divorced from our politics. Harsha Walia, also active with NOII-Vancouver, was blunt about this: "What does it mean to organize? Like we're cattle? That doesn't make any sense." Our organizing, in other words, isn't about herding people; it's about building collective power and capacity so that people can engage in self-determined fights for structural transformation. This necessarily means, as Walia argued, "organizing along certain principles." Like many of us developing another politics, she pointed to "anti's"—our "against"—as foundational to organizing. Adriana Paz named the other side: "Organizing in the social struggle is not only to overthrow the imperialist system and . . . the capitalist system; it's also to propose a new society based on equal rights, based on new and different values coming from love, solidarity, and respect for every human being and mother earth." Organizing, then, is also about our "beyond"—about proposing a new society by means of the way in which we collectively struggle.

Organizing in another politics is very much a work in progress. Over the last two decades, anti-authoritarians have taken up ideas and practices associated with organizing and grappled with them in frequently productive ways. Like many aspects of another politics, this process has moved in multiple directions. Labor and community organizing models contribute ways of engaging in sustained movement-building, prioritizing relationships and accountability, and connecting strategy and action. Bearing influences I described in chapter 1, anti-authoritarians contribute politics and practices that lift up dimensions of organizing that are often sidelined, such as deeply democratic decision-making, affective organizing, and noninstrumental relationship-building. Anti-authoritarians are thus being transformed by and transforming organizing. Through this process, many of us have started to consciously see ourselves as organizers.

In this chapter, I look at the shift toward organizing in the anti-authoritarian current and what this synthesis has created so far. I critically examine the widely used distinction between "activism" and "organizing," and how this has influenced another politics. I explore what I think we should understand as "anti-authoritarian organizing"—a wide range of efforts to bring together another politics and organizing work. I describe both the broad features and the concrete practices of these efforts, emphasizing the ways in which anti-authoritarian organizing challenges some core aspects of more conventional models.

ACTIVISM AND ORGANIZING

The convergence of radical strands in another politics is fueled in part by a shared frustration with prevailing activist approaches. Although circumstances vary among strands, people in this current have commonly come to grapple with the reality, as I discussed in chapter 4, that winning fundamental social change will require cultivating mass movements much broader and deeper than current activist networks. This realization has been catalyzed in significant ways by the successes of movements in the last two decades. To take one example, the global justice movement, by bringing people together and making longstanding struggles more visible and connected, created opportunities for activists to better see the limitations of their customary activities as well as new possibilities for more broad-based action. As a result, some activists became more ambitious. There have been similar dynamics in other recent upsurges, such as the immigrant rights movement and the occupy movement.

Another politics has grown out of these illuminating experiences, as anti-authoritarians have attempted to shift from expressing periodic outrage to building power strategically. We have primarily come to describe this shift as a move from "activism" to "organizing," which many see as two distinct kinds of activities.[1] Because this distinction is so widespread, we should look at it more closely. There is much we can learn from it, and it also has some problems.

Activism, following this distinction, is mobilizing people around particular issues based on morality or politics. Rosana Cruz, an organizer working against the criminal justice system in New Orleans, laid this out very clearly. Individuals engage in activism, she explained, "because they've got an intellectual or an emotional—maybe a spiritual—commitment, but [what they're fighting] is not something that necessarily impacts them directly." In general, activists are only responsible to themselves; though some may develop relationships with directly affected people, activist work isn't necessarily oriented toward this. Activism is thus associated with people who are relatively privileged—those who can choose to be concerned about something or not. As well, activist work frequently involves educational events, such as conferences, lectures, and film-screenings. It is aimed at expressing opposition to specific policies or institutions, whether through holding vigils, marching, occupying, street fighting, or some other form of action. There are plenty of examples of this, including activism against war, economic inequality, and environmental destruction, as well as activism to promote specific politics.

Organizing, following this same distinction, is building the capacity of a group of people directly impacted by injustice so that they can struggle to transform their situation. For Toronto-based abolitionist organizer Marika Warner, this means that "you're (a) challenging power structures, you're (b) working to build power structures, and you're (c) dealing with a problem that you share collectively with the people that you're organizing with." Organizers are accountable to the groups with whom they're organizing; developing trust through sustained relationships is the essential basis for this work. Fundamentally, organizing is aimed at supporting people in asserting their power through collective action, as individuals standing up for one another, mass delegations to pressure power holders, or direct actions. Organizing, then, is understood as something that happens with people who are immediately affected by systems of exploitation and oppression. As Rosana Cruz said, "You're building power with people who, even if they don't at first understand the extent of the struggles, their investment is so deep that they'll learn in the process." Examples of this include organizing related to environmental justice, labor, housing, and police accountability.

The distinction between activism and organizing is useful. It brings up questions of motivation and accountability: Why are we, individually, engaged in political work? To whom are we responsible in what we're doing? It highlights the importance of people who are directly affected by ruling relations and institutions being at the center of struggles for justice; it turns our attention to people who are dealing with immediate issues in their lives and who often aren't already self-identified activists. This distinction also opens up questions of approach and orientation: Why are we engaged in particular forms of political work? And in Marika Warner's words, "What is this work *building* for?" This points to the significance of being strategic in our efforts and building relationships rooted in communities as a foundation for developing collective power.

Used well, the distinction between activism and organizing can help us think and act more deliberately. It can provoke us to reflect on what, if anything, our efforts are constructing in the long term, and it can encourage us to be outwardly focused—always pushing beyond activist scenes and networks. Most importantly, it can guide us toward more powerful, strategic, and grounded forms of political activity.

But this distinction isn't always used well. Sometimes people on the left, including anti-authoritarians, use it to broadly dismiss certain kinds of political work and glorify others. In the most caricatured version, "activism" is negatively associated with supposedly rootless white middle-class people mobilizing for protests around one faraway cause or another, while "organizing" is positively associated with locally based work in working-class communities of color aimed at winning tangible gains. At its worst, this perspective basically suggests that activism is bad and organizing is good. This is unfortunately simplistic.

Political activity in real life is much more complicated and messy. Thankfully, it's full of possibilities that exceed easy dichotomies. As Vancouver organizer Harsha Walia pointed out, there are always activists within exploited and oppressed communities—"people who speak out and take action on a wide variety of global justice issues, not just the issues within their so-called 'community.' Their work is critical in building alliances and analysis between and across movements and communities."

Successful organizing, in many cases, builds on the frequently underappreciated efforts of such activists. At the same time, using ideas and practices associated with organizing doesn't necessarily insure accountable or transformative work. People can and do organize in ways that mainly benefit individuals or organizations rather than build collective power. As well, some kinds of essential political work nearly always require activism. This is true for most solidarity initiatives, which involve mobilizing and demonstrating support for other people's struggles, whether they are in another workplace, another community, or another country.

Activism and organizing, in fact, are dynamically related and not so easily separable. Sarita Ahooja, long involved in a wide range of political activity in Montreal, told a compelling story about the grassroots migrant justice coalition Solidarity Across Borders to make this point: "How did Solidarity Across Borders get off the ground? Well, it began with the encounter between the Palestinian, Algerian, Indian, and Colombian people fighting against their deportation[s]. And who facilitated that? Activists. We're the ones that saw that there were these anti-deportation campaigns going on in different communities and we said, 'You guys should talk to each other and share tips about such and such.' These meetings generated a formal organization a year later."[2] Activists, in other words, can play crucial roles in sparking and then sustaining broader movement initiatives. Organizing efforts, meanwhile, can provide strategic anchor points for activists. And at times, we can't completely distinguish between the two.

ORGANIZING AS AN ORIENTATION

Those of us in the anti-authoritarian current have diverse views on the distinction between activism and organizing. This is healthy. What's important—and what I see many of us trying to do through another politics—is to use the helpful aspects of this distinction without falling into debilitating caricatures.[3] I think we can see the beginnings of this through the ways in which we are increasingly using organizing as an *orientation* for a whole range of political activities. In one sense, an organizing orientation is a way of taking up the ideas and practices of more conventional organizing models. More profoundly, it's a way of relating to organizing as a constructive guide for action.

Mike D, who worked with the Ontario Coalition Against Poverty in Toronto, vividly captured the spirit of this orientation:

> What I'm trying to do and what I think a lot of other people are trying to do is to actually create the type of thing where it's not just a

campaign, it's not just a little piece of activism around an issue; it's actually trying to bring this type of culture of resistance, with taking ownership over our environment, our surroundings, our lives—bringing an idea of resistance and building something better into our actual day-to-day. . . . I think what we have to try to do is . . . not just have the demonstration and then go home and that's it—but to actually build up relationships on a neighborhood level, on every level.

These aspirations—"not just a campaign," "taking ownership over our environment," and "building up relationships"—strongly resonate with how other anti-authoritarian organizers describe their aims.

In New Orleans, Rosana Cruz summed these up in a compelling formulation. Organizing, she said, is "bringing people together in ways that link them in a long-term struggle and build their power." Cruz's formulation gets to the heart of the organizing orientation in another politics, which is about widening participation, creating collectivity, fighting strategically, and building power. This orientation moves us away from questions about what counts as organizing or who can rightfully engage in it and instead challenges us to bring organizing practices and priorities into all of what we do. An organizing orientation, in this way, has very useful implications. I'll mention three here.

The first has to do with *why* we engage in particular kinds of political work. In other words, what are we aiming to achieve with our efforts? Much of the time, left political activity is oriented toward either "educating the public" (about an issue, a politics, a system) or "demonstrating opposition" (to a policy, an institution, a system). These are crucial aims, but limited on their own. As many in the anti-authoritarian current are starting to discover, such aims make the most sense within a broader framework of movement-building. An organizing orientation offers this framework. Joshua Kahn Russell, a social and ecological justice organizer based in Oakland, was explicit about it. "Activism," he said, "is about raising your voice, but organizing is about getting a lot more people to raise their voices *together*."

Organizing, in this sense, is a set of practices for creating more activists and organizers. This is much deeper than getting more individuals involved in one campaign or another. Fundamentally, it means helping people to develop the analysis, confidence, and skills to engage in struggles on their own behalf, move others, and thus lay the basis for large, visionary, and combative movements. We can see this approach in the most innovative organizing initiatives coming out of the anti-authoritarian current. For instance, it's at the center of the efforts of NOII collectives to build power in migrant communities. It's also a major feature of INCITE! groups in their work with women of color. Some anti-authoritarians, borrowing an idea from more conventional organizing models, call it "leadership development," something I discuss in more detail in the next chapter.

The second implication has to do with *where* we engage in political work. The sites most closely associated with organizing tend to be neighborhoods and workplaces. These are indeed key for movement-building, but we also need to think critically and creatively about them. As veteran New York activist Brooke Lehman pointed out, we especially need to be careful about "the romanticization of 'community.'"[4] I understood Lehman, in this way, to be questioning the idea that "community" is necessarily just about where we live or work. More generally, she was inviting us to look beyond hardened ideas about what a "community" is. People have all kinds of social ties in their lives. While such ties are shaped by ruling relations, this doesn't mean that we can't draw on them as we struggle. In fact, we must.

An organizing orientation encourages us to recognize the many communities in which people live, work, study, play, resist, and make meaning as potential spaces for organizing. Some of the most crucial of these are communities built through shared experiences of exploitation, oppression, and marginalization. However, there are also vital communities that people develop through schools, subcultural scenes, recreational groups, kinship ties (chosen and not), friendship circles, faith-based institutions, and work-related associations. As organizers are learning, there are opportunities in many of these communities to work with ordinary, nonactivist people in identifying and struggling against injustice, building alliances, and developing collective capacities.[5] We can see examples of this sort of work in Queers for Economic Justice in New York, which organized from 2002 to 2014 in queer communities to fight against systems that produce poverty and exploitation, and the efforts of the Catalyst Project in San Francisco to support anti-racist education and organizing through Unitarian Universalist youth organizations. Recent mobilizations, such as occupy and Idle No More, have been able to grow with astounding speed partly because they have been so successful at tapping into all sorts of communities.

The third implication has to do with *what* organizing is. Stephanie Guilloud, an Atlanta-based organizer with experience in a lot of movements, pointed to perhaps the most widely used understanding: "You were hired as an 'organizer' and you are, as an 'organizer,' gathering members to launch a 'campaign.'" This definition characterizes much labor and community organizing, whether gathering together workers to start a union drive or neighbors to fight discriminatory lending practices. But, as Guilloud noted, this definition leaves out many other ways that people come together to struggle, whether in prisons, Indigenous communities, schools, environmental defense campaigns, or, indeed, workplaces and neighborhoods. Feminist and queer movements, for instance, have crafted forms of organizing based on shared intimacy, collective consciousness-raising, and community-building.[6]

With an organizing orientation, we can take a more open-ended approach. Conventional organizing models highlight key aspects of successful movement work, such as fostering a sense of community through sustained relationship-building, creating collective accountability and trust through intentional group process, and developing long-term strategy grounded in shared circumstances. But at the same time, we have to relate to the realities of specific contexts. This means growing and nourishing forms of organizing in struggle rather than applying models in rigid ways. Prison abolitionists, to take one notable example, are significantly reinventing organizing in order to work in and across the overlapping communities impacted by the PIC; among other things, this involves innovative approaches to consciousness-raising and alliance-building.[7] Likewise, groups such as Iraq Veterans Against the War are developing new models of organizing, foregrounding political education and collective healing, in order to build a broad U.S. GI resistance movement.[8]

ANTI-AUTHORITARIAN ORGANIZING

Anti-authoritarians involved in grassroots work firmly believe that organizing approaches are not only *methods* of politics but also *manifestations* of politics. We're organizing in order to achieve concrete, day-to-day victories in people's lives and to fundamentally transform ruling institutions and relations. But how we bring people together in struggle and build collective power—how we organize—is closely related to the society that we're trying to create. To take one of the most frequently used examples, if we want a genuinely democratic society, then we have to create movements through which people can develop and practice the skills and capacities necessary for governing their communities and institutions at every level. Anti-authoritarian organizers are thus trying to manifest and build, as much as possible, ways of being, relating, and doing "not of the world" through our organizing "in the world."

What fundamentally defines the practical activity of another politics is the combination of an organizing orientation with this commitment to prefigurative praxis. Anti-authoritarians have been working across a chain of movements for more than a decade to put this combination into practice.

What we've been doing is experimental and thus uneven, messy, and at times contradictory. There has rarely been enough continuity between successive efforts, collective learning has frequently been slow, and there are still many unresolved questions. Nevertheless, I think it is now possible to use the term "anti-authoritarian organizing," without exaggeration, to describe a wide range of connected efforts that blend our political aspirations with practical organizing methods, all in pursuit of tangible victories on the way to large-scale social transformation.

These efforts share a number of distinguishing features. One is what anti-authoritarians tend to call "nonhierarchical" or "horizontal" organizing. These expressions name what is perhaps the most visible characteristic of organizing influenced by the anti-authoritarian current: our use of nonhierarchical decision-making processes. As I explained in chapter 3, these processes include consensus models, assembly structures, and other forms of highly participatory democratic decision-making. Those of us who use such forms face persistent questions: How do we develop people's capacities to fully and equitably participate in these sorts of structures? How do we value these processes without becoming so focused on them that we fail to pursue larger goals? And how do we make use of them in ways that are oriented outward?[9]

The best efforts in the anti-authoritarian current are actively working with these challenges and against dogmatic attachments to particular forms. Many are successfully bringing nonhierarchical decision-making processes into broader movement spaces and/or strengthening the democratic practices that already exist in such spaces. The 2012 Quebec student strike offered one impressive example of this as tens of thousands of students regularly used general assemblies at departmental and university levels to determine the course of their movement.[10] Another example is Critical Resistance, which consistently uses consensus in local chapters and at the national level. In these and many other cases, anti-authoritarians are working to create situations in which ordinary people are, in the words of San Francisco organizer Clare Bayard, "making decisions together in a way that is less about decisions where someone has to lose and more about how to have decisions that really represent the fullest involvement possible of all the people who are going to be affected by them." This is a key practice in our organizing work.

Anti-authoritarian organizing is distinguished by more than just nonhierarchical decision-making, although we're only beginning to adequately articulate its other aspects. In chapter 3, I explored two important emerging features. One is a mode, sometimes called "affective organizing," that prioritizes care and how we treat one another as essential to building movements. The other, often called "anti-oppression organizing," is an approach that works, in the process of struggle, to create equalitarian ways of being, doing, and relating. Neither of these aspects is completely coherent or fully developed, and each has its own specific limitations, especially when used in absolutist or insular ways. Still, we should understand both as live—and mostly very positive—anti-authoritarian contributions to organizing.

But in order to fully understand anti-authoritarian organizing, we need to turn to the feature that I think most clearly brings together an organizing orientation and prefigurative praxis. This is what I call "noninstrumental organizing," by which I mean an organizing approach that aims to build relationships with people as collaborators in struggle rather than as instruments to achieve already determined ends. This approach is about relating to people as dignified subjects who are capable of critically analyzing the world, crafting sophisticated strategies for fighting against injustice, taking courageous risks in struggle, and envisioning a better society. It's also about understanding organizing as a collective process through which we develop new ideas, new relations, new practices, and new questions.

Noninstrumental organizing is a reaction against a central characteristic of prevailing organizing approaches. In many labor, electoral, student, and community organizing models, organizing tends to be about building relationships with people mostly to get them to do something that someone else has decided is in their "best interest." These models frequently involve popular consultation and participation, and many achieve gains that improve people's lives, whether that's obtaining labor contracts, passing ballot measures to better fund public education, or getting commitments from city officials to build low-income housing. In the midst of struggles, people also often grow and push beyond the bounds of these models, making use of them to organize more democratically and with more radical aspirations. But fundamentally, such models are structured in one direction—using people to achieve aims that have already been largely determined.[11]

Michelle O'Brien, a veteran organizer around housing and HIV/AIDS struggles in New York, was blunt in her criticisms of this feature of so many organizing models. Speaking about one particularly influential community organizing approach, she said that "when it comes right down to it, it relates to people in profoundly manipulative ways. It relates to people as these chips on a board." A striking example of this attitude can be found in organizing methods, popular in some unions, that routinely use targeted personal shaming to motivate people to assume responsibilities or take risks.[12] A more mundane but no less important example is the highly centralized structures and processes that many organizing initiatives use for developing goals and campaigns. Members of these groups frequently don't have meaningful ways to participate in making such decisions, but they're nonetheless expected to carry them out.[13] We can see a different (but related) kind of example in the organizational practices of many Leninist formations, as I discussed in chapter 2.

Activists and organizers in the anti-authoritarian current tend to feel very strongly that what Michelle O'Brien called "manipulative instrumentalization" isn't consistent with our political aspirations. Founding *Upping the Anti* editor Sharmeen Khan made this argument as she discussed her experiences with a community organizing initiative in Vancouver. "If you're wanting to organize to raise people's consciousness and to build solidarity," she concluded, "you have to give up the mindset that they're our minions and tools that we're using—even if the agenda is very noble." RJ Maccani, an organizer with the Challenging Male Supremacy Project in New York, took this even further. The point at which we "instrumentalize people," he said, "is where we start to lose even as we win." It's where our means for fighting for another world significantly undercut our ability to bring that world into being—or just as bad, where they leave us so individually and collectively damaged that we can't effectively fight.

Noninstrumental organizing is an approach that anti-authoritarians are developing through our attempts to steer away from this sort of instrumentalization. It focuses on the analysis, strategies, and actions that people can create when we come together in dialogue and struggle.[14] Crucially, the basis for this is not a set of predetermined answers, but a shared inquiry. The key question for this approach is, as O'Brien argued, "What do *you* think? And that's not really about getting everyone to a fixed point. That's about opening up the imagination." With so many organizing approaches, she elaborated, "There's this incredible arrogance. . . . And the arrogance is thinking that we know what it's going to take to overthrow global capitalism, and we don't! Sure, we want to overthrow it, and sure, we can talk about that, and sure, we can do revolutionary work right now, but we don't know what it's going to take. So 'what do *you* think?' is about opening up the conversation of trying to envision that."

Noninstrumental organizing uses our shared "not knowing" as a starting point for creating answers together and building our collective capacities. To be clear, this is not about concealing our politics or pretending that we don't have analysis or proposals for action. Rather, it is a mode of engagement with people that calls for collaboration and emphasizes, in the words of anarchist scholar-activist Andrew Cornell, "people developing the capacities to define their own goals and shape their own campaigns."[15] In this way, it resonates with the approach Atlanta-based Project South organizer Stephanie Guilloud described in chapter 2 as "revelatory." This approach, as I understand it, sees organizing as a collective process through which we come to encounter one another as dignified subjects and to learn new things about our world, our movements, and ourselves. This is organizing as *revelation*—a process through which all involved are transformed as we fight to transform society—and it is at the core of another politics.

While there are many effective initiatives along these lines, some of the most instructive come out of direct action anti-poverty organizing. For the last two decades, the Ontario Coalition Against Poverty (OCAP) has organized poor people in Toronto and, at times, in other parts of Ontario to defend themselves against attacks on their living and working conditions. Drawing on a direct action approach from the U.S. welfare rights movement, OCAP has made a name for itself through the successful use of mass delegations to pressure welfare caseworkers to grant benefits, landlords to halt evictions, and employers to pay back-wages owed.[16] In more recent years, the Seattle Solidarity Network has developed a narrower model based on this approach, consistently winning victories against bosses and landlords and inspiring the growth of similar networks in cities across North America.[17] And with the occupy movement, this approach has become even more widespread, particularly in the anti-eviction campaigns of Occupy Our Homes groups across the United States, which also build on longer-term housing reclamation initiatives such as Take Back the Land.[18]

Although structured in different ways, all of these efforts share a combative organizing approach that puts the collective ideas, demands, and power of poor and working-class people at the center. As longtime OCAP organizer John Clarke writes, "Our tactics and campaigns have been selected on the basis of transforming the latent discontent that exists in poor communities into disruptive action so as to challenge attacks or obtain concessions from the state."[19] At its best, this is noninstrumental organizing: engaging people in a collaborative process of using their power and directing their own struggles for justice and dignity.

ORGANIZING PRACTICES

Shaped by these broad features and priorities, anti-authoritarian organizing is based in a fairly common set of practices that organizers use in day-to-day work. Many of these practices are consistent across a wide range of organizing models: bringing people together in groups, helping to identify shared concerns, supporting reflection and planning, seeking out allies, facilitating decision-making, taking collective action, and encouraging evaluation and further reflection. Writing from their experience in the climate justice movement, Hilary Moore and Joshua Kahn Russell sum these up well: "Organizers identify where groups of people are at, meet them there, and work with them in a way that compels them to action."[20] These practices are fundamental for any successful organizing effort.

Intertwined with these common practices, anti-authoritarians have also been crafting organizing practices that are more specifically rooted in another politics. Here I'll highlight a handful that came up consistently in my interviews and have wide resonance in the anti-authoritarian current. While none of these are new or completely unique to this current, each expands on core commitments of another politics. In particular, all grow from a noninstrumental understanding, articulated pointedly by Stephanie Guilloud: "We're not moving parts around a table; we're moving people with real lives and hearts and souls and bodies."

One of the most foundational anti-authoritarian organizing practices is what RJ Maccani called "building relationships first." Lydia Pelot-Hobbs, who was involved in housing and prison abolition struggles in New Orleans, framed the question underlying this practice: "How do we build relationships with people that are really authentically grounded?" The kind of relationship-building often used in more conventional organizing models focuses on getting to know people in order to move them to do something. Pelot-Hobbs critically described this approach as: "'I want to have a relationship with you because I want you to have better politics, and if you have better politics, maybe you'll do this and that'—in this creepy agenda-type way." Against this, she offered the approach that she tries to use: "'Your humanity's at stake and my humanity's at stake. . . . And we're all gonna benefit from this [particular effort], and you have the potential to do really exciting things.'" "Building relationships first" is more than a matter of emphasis. Drawing particularly on women of color feminism, it involves cultivating trust, sharing stories, and engaging in dialogue, all as a basis for collective decisions and action.

But to do this effectively, organizers have to struggle to assert the importance of relationship building against a culture in which it's often dismissed as "touchy-feely" and insignificant. Pelot-Hobbs brought this up while discussing her experience with anti-racist organizing in New Orleans. Relationship-building activities, she observed, "have been really hard for us to justify as work. A lot of the men who used to be involved left . . . and, at times, have de-legitimized our stuff . . . because it isn't seen as traditional work. Relationship-building organizing is often this really feminized thing—it's not 'really' activism." This unfortunately common dismissal, as I discussed in chapter 3, is rooted in patriarchal relations that construct relationship building as "women's work" that isn't serious and significant. But this work should not be discounted: it is vital for creating and sustaining resilient movements. "Building relationships first" is an attempt, through another politics, to make affective organizing more central and explicitly prefigurative.

Two practical ingredients for this are humility and appreciation of people. Rafael Mutis, a longtime abolitionist organizer in New York, laid these out clearly: "You've gotta check your arrogance. . . . If you're going to do any kind of work in community, you've gotta step back." This "stepping back" reflects an underlying attitude of respect in interacting with others. As Mutis put it, "You just have to value people, honor people, wherever they are—not assume that you know what's going on versus what they know." This doesn't mean romanticizing people—treating them as if they're always right or can do no wrong—or concealing the knowledge and ongoing work we bring, as activists and organizers. But it does mean understanding people as experts about their own lives and circumstances, and as capable of developing critical analysis about the structures that shape these. It also means valuing people holistically—with all of their quirks, gifts, and flaws.

These practices lay the foundation for building more grounded kinds of relationships. They make it more possible for us to encounter one another "face-to-face," in the words of veteran organizer and former political prisoner Ashanti Alston. "The value of face-to-face," he explained, "not only allows you to see each others' faces, but it means that there's dignity there, there's respect there. You have to listen."

Indeed, listening is another crucial organizing practice. As Mutis argued, "being willing to step back and listen is, to me, really what anti-authoritarian organizing is." Organizers are using listening in an effort to move away from pronouncing politically rigid "lines" and toward opening generative spaces. Mutis elaborated on this: "For me, the important part about organizing isn't about getting out the correct information, but creating spaces with people to think together and to develop relationships, and to provide back up for people in making of sense, given all the propaganda. . . . You can grandstand, you can preach, you do all that stuff, but that's not useful. What's more useful is helping people have spaces where they can talk with each other and make connections." This isn't talking and listening simply for its own sake, however. The point is to convene situations in which people share their experiences and ideas as a basis for developing shared aims and strategies and taking collective action.[21]

A key practice for convening such situations is popular education. People on the left use this term in various ways, some of which, simplistically, mean "getting out the correct information," as Mutis mentioned. Growing out of a chain of movement experiences and radical educational experiments, this term also has a much more precise meaning—one with growing significance for anti-authoritarians. Ora Wise, a longtime Palestine solidarity organizer and educator in New York, usefully captured much of this definition. Popular education, she said, is "the practice and process of oppressed communities coming together to have a facilitated process of . . . analyzing the problems in their own lives and then, through that analysis, articulating their vision for change, and then practicing and processing how they can make that change happen."

Experienced popular educators have important disagreements about this practice. These relate to issues such as which forms of popular education are best, when to bring in other educational practices, and whether popular education is effective with people who don't have firsthand experiences of oppression and exploitation. But most would agree on what constitutes popular education: it is an approach and a set of methods for helping groups of people to develop critical analysis from their lived experience—linking individual understandings in a broader context—and to use that shared analysis as a basis for planning and action.[22] As an approach, popular education focuses on getting people actively engaged in reflecting and learning together rather than passively receiving information. As a set of methods, popular education includes different kinds of brainstorming and discussion, a mix of small- and large-group activities, participatory modes of presentation, and, in some cases, theater and other art-making.

It makes sense that those of us developing another politics are drawn to popular education. As San Francisco housing organizer James Tracy said, "Popular education's strength is that it tries to reconcile an alternative path between vanguardism and flaky (and often manipulative) 'let the people decide.'" It starts with people's lives, experiences, and critical reflections rather than with already determined answers. But at the same time, as Tracy pointed out, effective popular education for social transformation doesn't deny its political priorities: "Once the popular educator basically starts trying to bullshit people and say that 'we don't actually care what the conclusions are that the students [reach]'—no, you want students to connect their individuals miseries and contexts and how things work. And if you're honest about that, you're a good popular educator. But if you're just trying to manipulate people to be in your organization, it's stupid." Used well, then, popular education turns the facilitated process of dialogue, listening, and reflection into a political weapon.

Organizers coming out of the anti-authoritarian current use these practices in a wide variety of circumstances. Sometimes we use them in generating new organizing efforts, as they are tremendously valuable for developing common purpose, analysis, and plans. Much of the time, though, we use such practices in preexisting initiatives with already developed goals, strategies, and commitments. In these circumstances, they are excellent tools for bringing more people into our organizing efforts, sustaining healthy group process, facilitating alliance-building, and encouraging regular discussion and reflection. In all cases, these practices help us to make our struggles more deeply rooted and to take our fights further.[23]

ORGANIZING IN THE DISJUNCTION

The organizing efforts that activists and organizers are developing through another politics sit uneasily in the disjunction between "what is" and "what we want." On the one hand, we're organizing amid the realities of the world as it is. This is world in which people are separated and contorted by social relations of domination, and the vast majority of us have very little control over the institutions that affect and direct our lives. We organize, then, in order to bring people together, build links among our experiences, articulate our desires, develop our capacities to fight, craft shared strategies, enact our collective power, and force powerholders to accede to our demands. To do this effectively, we have to keep our eyes not only on the big picture, but also on everyday realities. As Montreal migrant justice organizer Sarita Ahooja argued, "We have to look at ways to organize that relate to the way people are already living their lives: a lot of work, a lot of debt, domestic problems, and commitments for families with children." These pressing day-to-day realities, shaped by enormous structural forces, are the ground on which we must build.

On the other hand, we're organizing toward the world that we want. Growing from our prefigurative praxis, this partly means working to practice our vision through our means of struggle. This conflicts at times with more instrumental forms of organizing, but such forms ultimately won't get us to where we want to go. "Reducing organizing to numbers of people, numbers of actions, and numbers of campaigns and potential wins," as Atlanta organizer Stephanie Guilloud put it, "is not effective in a context where reform is rolled back so quickly and where the nation-state becomes more and more irrelevant and where life sustainability is in deep question." Instead, we need to organize in ways that point beyond what is—that create new capacities, new relations, new forms of social organization, and new possibilities for what our world could be. We need organizing that fosters self-management, cultivates care and collectivity, undermines oppressive power relations, and helps people recognize one another as creators, as cata-lysts.

Those of us with a "political commitment to organizing" are dancing between these practical realities and visionary possibilities. This isn't easy. Anti-authoritarian organizing has come a long way in the last decade espe-cially, but we still face big challenges and difficult questions. For one, while it has become much more common to call ourselves "organizers" and our activities "organizing," this change in terms doesn't always match up with actually integrating organizing frameworks and practices into what we're doing. If we want to build broad transformative movements, we need to go further than simply renaming our customary activities, which are largely sequestered within activist scenes.[24] More generally, as experienced direct action organizer Rayan El-Amine pointed out, "There are also some real limitations around leadership, sustainability, continuity within nonhierar-chical organizing, and we've got to figure out how to do those things bet-ter." Dealing with these kinds of limitations, as I suggest in the next two chapters, requires honest discussion and imaginative experimentation.

The best organizing initiatives in the anti-authoritarian current are wrestling with these and other challenges. Like all serious people on the left, we're trying to figure out what relevant and effective organizing looks like today in circumstances of intense social fragmentation, massive con-centration of wealth and power, and accelerating crises. We still have a long way to go. But judging from the widespread use of our approaches in recent movements, we're making some headway. Although unfinished and imper-fect, these approaches have something profound to offer: the possibility of modes of struggle through which ordinary people can fundamentally change the world while also recovering and recreating their own humanity. This is the promise of anti-authoritarian organizing.

7. "Leadership from below"

Taking Initiative and Building Capacities

> It would be wise to stop articulating that this is a leaderless movement; it might be more honest to suggest that We Are All Leaders. Denying that leadership exists deflects accountability, obscures potential hierarchies, and absolves us of actively creating structures within which to build collective leadership.
>
> Harsha Walia

Members of Iraq Veterans Against the War participate in a collective liberation workshop at their 2011 national convention in Portland, Oregon. (Photo by Clare Bayard)

WHEN I INTERVIEWED Jill Chettiar, a veteran anti-poverty organizer in Vancouver, she was bursting with useful ideas and stories. One was about her struggle with political designations and organizing realities. With characteristic bluntness, she told me that her biggest hesitation about identifying as an anarchist has to do with "the leadership issue." As she put it, "I really think [leadership] is important and needs to be acknowledged." But anarchist politics, she argued, frequently falls down in this regard.

Chettiar makes a crucial point. Leadership is a big unresolved issue not just for anarchism but for anti-authoritarian organizing more generally. Developing out of the movement experiences that I traced in chapter 1, anti-authoritarians of various stripes have come to be deeply suspicious of leaders and leadership. The very word "leadership" is nearly unmentionable in some radical circles. There are some good reasons for this stance, based on concerns about "power-over" forms of organizing and on desires for more participatory structures. However, a knee-jerk rejection of leadership—and silence about it—has created some significant problems for anti-authoritarian organizing, particularly in relation to questions of how to be accountable and develop people's capacities as activists and organizers.

More and more anti-authoritarians are discussing these problems. They came up frequently in my interviews, a few people have written about them, and many are attempting to work through them in practice.[1] While leadership continues to be a contentious topic, I think we can see the beginnings of an alternative form of leadership—what I call "another leadership"—coming from these discussions and experiments. Organizers are creating another leadership through new ways of understanding, enacting, and building leadership in grassroots groups. In a sense, we're turning the conventional idea of leadership on its head: rather than an exclusive form of power and command, this is leadership as a set of collective practices interwoven with individual capacities.

This chapter examines leadership in the anti-authoritarian current. I review the main anti-authoritarian critiques of leadership, emphasizing the insights these offer. I look at the problems that result from a complete rejection of leaders and leadership, focusing on troubling assumptions that make our efforts less effective and transformative. I follow this by exploring how activists and organizers are approaching another leadership, as well as consciously working to develop the leadership capacities of other people. These efforts, I suggest, hold significant potential for more substantially fostering solidarity and accountability, undermining oppressive power relations, and sustaining democracy and participation in our movements.

ANTI-AUTHORITARIAN CRITICISMS OF LEADERSHIP

At the core of the "anti" of anti-authoritarianism, as I discussed in chapter 2, is a desire to refuse hierarchy and domination. This "anti" is a foundational "no" to social relations and institutions based on power-over, as they rely on coercion. This shared "no" profoundly influences how many in the anti-authoritarian current relate to leaders and leadership. And this critical stance has a solid basis: the prevailing model of leadership in our society is in fact infused with power-over, whether in workplaces, governments, military institutions, schools, or families.

Mick Sweetman, a journalist and longtime anarchist organizer in Toronto, laid out a key part of this anti-authoritarian critique. The prevailing model of leadership, he argued, is based on a "hierarchical command structure where somebody is ultimately in charge and they're called 'leaders.'" Like most forms of organization in our society, this leadership model flows from the top downward: people who are "leaders" make decisions (business plans, laws, strategies) and everyone else is expected to follow them. Sometimes those of us who aren't leaders have ways to offer our input on such decisions, but leaders ultimately make the final determinations. Most positions of leadership also have the power to punish, physically or materially, in socially and legally sanctioned ways. The conventional form of leadership, in short, is closely tied to the centralized, hierarchical ways that power is organized and administered in our society.

This model of leadership also tends to be linked to specific individual characteristics, including assertiveness, enthusiasm for taking initiative, analytical skills, aggressiveness, ease with public speaking, self-confidence, and facility with telling other people what to do. We also hear frequently about a special leadership quality called "charisma"—the ability to inspire and motivate people. Not coincidentally, these are all characteristics usually taught to and encouraged in men, and thus the dominant model of leadership in our society is a masculinized one. Qualities taught to and encouraged in women—such as caretaking, sustaining relationships, listening, resolving conflict, building community, and supporting others emotionally—largely don't fit into this model of leadership. What many of us understand as "leadership," then, is deeply shaped by patriarchal relations.[2]

This model of leadership, despite its problems, circulates widely in movements. When we look at labor, immigrant rights, environmental, or anti-war movements, we can see examples of highly visible top-down leadership that involve individual, often charismatic leaders. At the same time, however, people active in these and other movements have consistently pointed to the problems of this leadership model. In the civil rights movement, the visionary organizer Ella Baker criticized the individual charismatic leadership of figures such as Martin Luther King, Jr. "Strong people don't need strong leaders," she famously asserted.[3] As I described in chapter 1, the Student Nonviolent Coordinating Committee took up this view and influenced how many other radicals related to leadership.

The radical wing of the women's liberation movement built on this critique as it challenged the prevailing masculinized leadership in the New Left. This radical feminist perspective tended toward a general rejection of leaders and leadership as inherently oppressive.[4] From the 1970s into the present, this stance against leadership has become linked with anti-authoritarian politics through the nonviolent direct action movement, radical queer organizing, direct action environmentalism, the global justice movement, and, most recently, the occupy movement.[5] Anarchists, in particular, have come to identify with this understanding of leadership as basically a thinly veiled form of manipulation and domination.[6] Today, many anti-authoritarians take this stance for granted.

THE "NO LEADERS" SLEIGHT OF HAND

There are some significant problems with a complete rejection of leaders and leadership. These most often arise when we try to put well-intentioned but significantly flawed conceptions about leadership into practice. Thankfully, though, growing numbers of anti-authoritarian organizers are critically examining these ideas and measuring them against our actual experiences of political work. With the help of these developing critical reflections, I think we can identify two conceptions that are especially influential and troubling. Both, by concealing crucial realities, interfere with our aims of creating stronger, more deeply democratic, and highly participatory forms of organizing and organization.

The first of these flawed conceptions is that we have no leaders. The core idea here is that nonhierarchical groups don't—and, indeed, shouldn't—have any set of people designated as leaders. Instead, everyone in an organization should be equally involved in making decisions and equally responsible for carrying out plans. Given how many anti-authoritarians think about leadership as a form of domination, this is understandable. If we see the conventional model of top-down, individualized leadership as the *only* model of leadership, then developing horizontal organization necessarily means avoiding leaders.

The trouble is that saying "we have no leaders"—and even using nonhierarchical practices—doesn't make leaders and leadership vanish. "Whether we're anti-authoritarian or not," observed Montreal migrant justice organizer Tatiana Gomez, "there are definitely people in organizations who, for one reason or another, are perceived as more credible or have a more powerful or persuasive voice." Mike D, who worked with the Ontario Coalition Against Poverty in Toronto, was more emphatic: "Maybe there are groups that don't [have leaders], but I've never been in one. . . . There are people who are really incredibly sharp with their analysis, their strategy, their tactics—their politics are solid, they're very confident in them, and they're the leadership." And these people frequently play important roles: they take care of tasks that few others consider, initiate new ideas, figure out logistics, articulate shared visions, mediate conflicts, follow up with people who are newly involved, forge links with other organizations, and much more. Although they may not define themselves as such, these people are leaders.

While the "we have no leaders" approach can't get rid of leadership, it does make actual leaders and leadership practices much harder to notice and name. It creates situations in which, as Mick Sweetman noted, leadership "isn't talked about. Or if it is talked about, it's [treated as either] good or not. . . . It's not talked about to develop it and bring it into the structure of the organization, where people who display [leadership] are both recognized and accountable." This "no leaders" conception produces a sleight of hand: it makes leadership seem as though it has vanished when it is really still present. This disappearing act makes leadership harder to evaluate, appreciate, and share.[7]

One unfortunate effect of this, as Sweetman mentioned, is a lack of clearly defined accountability and responsibility. Jill Chettiar highlighted the difficulty of holding leaders accountable when we have no intentional leadership structures. "What happens," she asked, "if you transition from a 'vote-based' leadership to a more organic, collectively recognized and sanctioned leadership? You de facto move into a realm that [is] more emotional: it's trust-based, it's psychosocial. So, [it's] much more complicated if you're feeling uncomfortable with a leader." When there are clear procedures for determining leadership, she said, "you can impeach somebody or elect a new leader or whatever. There's process around that kind of stuff." But when a group doesn't explicitly acknowledge and designate leadership, this is much more difficult. There are no clear procedures or structures for holding leaders accountable, other than simply criticizing them for acting as leaders.

This lack of explicit accountability is even more challenging when unacknowledged leaders steer organizing efforts in ways that aren't collectively determined. This can happen in all sorts of ways, from setting broad political priorities to making immediate tactical decisions. Tatiana Gomez stressed this problem:

> I think there is something to be said for the power that particular individuals wield, and I don't know if we want to call them "leaders"—I

don't know what we want to call them. But whether they consider themselves leaders or not, or whether they act as leaders or not, they have a lot of power, whether they know it or not, and it affects how things occur. They definitely set the tone or the pace for how things are going to go down. And so I think that until those particular individuals are ready to reflect or do things differently, it's hard for others to do so too.

This influence of unacknowledged leaders is incredibly difficult to discuss when activists and organizers have no clear way of talking about leadership. Indeed, without acknowledging leadership, we can barely name what is happening, much less explore better alternatives. It should be no surprise, then, that groups that don't acknowledge leadership frequently find themselves embroiled in conflicts that focus on individuals, rather than deeper political or organizational questions. In the absence of tools to identify how power and influence are working in groups, it's easy to blame particular people rather than practices or politics when difficulties arise.

A lack of discussion about leadership all too often also creates a vacuum of responsibility. Francesca Fiorentini, an experienced anti-war organizer and member of the *War Times* collective, emphasized this: "When it's everyone's space, it's no one's space. When it's everyone's project, it's no one's project. Which I think is unfortunately really true in how things work out. If we all are supposed to be equally responsible, we all are supposed to have equal leadership, then who's the one following up with people? Who's the one who is tasked with certain things?" In most anti-authoritarian groups, specific people do take on particular tasks, both tasks that are explicitly recognized by the group and those that are not. We step into all sorts of leadership roles with accompanying sets of responsibilities. But the "no leaders" sleight of hand makes it challenging to identify clearly what these roles and responsibilities are and, just as crucial, to hold anyone accountable for carrying them out.

The "no leaders" sleight of hand affects not only how leadership work is recognized, but also who does it. When we don't intentionally designate leadership, it's organized in less explicit ways. In one common scenario, Fiorentini said, people in anti-authoritarian groups "end up, by default, following and talking to the people who have the most power, either because they're the oldest, because they're the most experienced, [or] because they're perhaps more rooted in the communities that we're talking about." In other words, people often gravitate into leadership roles because of important qualities that they have to offer, such as experience, skills, knowledge, initiative, connections, and dedication. But without intentional discussion, this process of people becoming leaders is mostly haphazard; it's definitely, as Fiorentini noted, "not transparent." And without transparency, it is difficult for anyone else to learn how to become credible leaders themselves.

Leadership in anti-authoritarian groups can be organized along the lines of friendship as well. Activist and researcher Jo Freeman examined this tendency as it appeared in the women's liberation movement. Much of her analysis remains relevant for the anti-authoritarian current today, and this at least partly explains why her 1972 article "The Tyranny of Structurelessness" continues to be popular. Freeman points to the kinds of friendship networks that develop among activists who are working together. "These friendship groups," she argues, "function as networks of communication outside any regular channels for such communication that may have been set up by [an activist] group. . . . Because people are friends, because they usually share the same values and orientations, because they talk to each other socially and consult with each other when common decisions have to be made, the people involved in these networks have more power in the group than those who don't."[8] This is just as true for contemporary groups as it was for those Freeman analyzed. In the absence of clear structure (and sometimes even with it), friendships can create an unacknowledged circuit for leadership, as activists quite naturally hang out together, discuss ideas, and develop shared priorities and plans.

All of these less visible kinds of leadership are also deeply enmeshed with dominant forms of social organization. Indeed, the "we have no leaders" approach significantly contributes to this tangle. "To pretend that there's no leadership," NOII-Vancouver organizer Harsha Walia pointed out, "will ignore that leadership will exist based on all the social hierarchies that exist—race, class, gender, sexuality—and often other ones in terms of length of experience, those who are most familiar with the issues, dominant personalities, people with educational backgrounds or language that allow them to read and write and do public speaking." Without conscious structures that push in other directions, the people who take on leadership responsibilities will often be those who are socialized to feel confident and who already have skills associated in the dominant culture with leadership. Such people are overwhelmingly likely to be relatively privileged within relations of exploitation and oppression. Labor organizer Sonya Z. Mehta laid this out plainly: "What's so clear and obvious is that, when you don't have democratic structures, the power just goes to men, white men, whoever is going to be the most vocal, whoever is going to take it, and that deprives all of us of benefiting from the greatness that each of us brings." This is how, in the absence of intentionality, the rarely acknowledged leadership of anti-authoritarian groups so regularly replicates existing social hierarchies.[9]

THE "ALL THE SAME" FALLACY

The second flawed conception around leadership is that we're all the same. The central idea here is that people come into nonhierarchical groups with more or less the same skills, kinds of knowledge, and levels of confidence. Anti-authoritarians share an aspiration that everyone should be able to participate equally in making decisions and carrying out plans, and we frequently assume that the way to put this into practice is to proceed as though everyone is already pretty much capable of doing everything or will quickly figure it out. For the most part, activists and organizers correctly understand that skills, knowledge, and confidence are forms of power. But we don't have clear ways to acknowledge or appreciate these kinds of power and how they affect which leadership roles—if any—an individual takes on. In denying leadership, then, we frequently pretend that everyone in our projects and organizations is similar in terms of what they can do, what they know, and how they feel about their abilities—or at least, similar enough that we don't need to devote much energy to developing these capacities.

Sharmeen Khan, a longtime organizer and editor of *Upping the Anti* in Toronto, talked about this conception as "the assumption that we're walking into this equal." But, she argued, this doesn't reflect what's actually happening. In fact, people come into movement spaces with vast differences between them. Clare Bayard, an organizer in San Francisco with the Catalyst Project, elaborated on this point: "People not only have different life experiences in terms of what they bring in organizing experiences and their perspectives and their understanding, but [they] also have had different amounts of mentoring, of study, of really thinking things through, of doing their own visioning or strategizing." Rahula Janowski, another San Francisco organizer, offered the specific example of political experience: "How can someone who's been in the movement for ten years and been in the organization for three years operate on the same level as someone who's been in the movement for two years and the organization for two months? It just is completely unrealistic." The reality is that, as Bayard concluded, "We all actually are bringing different things to the table."

The notion that "we're all the same" is a fallacy. In accepting and sustaining it, we confuse *acknowledging* differences in skills, knowledge, and confidence with *justifying* such differences and the power bound up in them. In some cases, anti-authoritarians see even the act of identifying differences in ability as inherently oppressive, as if naming power relations somehow creates or maintains them. In this way, the "all the same" fallacy feeds on our silence: when we don't talk about differences, we don't have to confront their crucial implications and the challenges they pose for our organizing. But ignoring them doesn't make them go away. On the contrary, the conception that "we're all the same" creates persistent problems.

Joshua Kahn Russell, reflecting on his experiences as a founding organizer with the new SDS, talked helpfully about some of these problems as they arise in anti-authoritarian groups:

> One of the reasons that so few people are drawn to anti-authoritarian movements, I think, is that there's an assumption that everyone comes with the same level of background and experience—or *should*. And so, you go to your first meeting somewhere and you say, "What can I do? I'm new." They say, "Well, you can do anything you want. We're not going to assign you a role." And you're like, "I don't even know what there is to do! What are my options? I don't know *how* to plug in." It's not just an allergy to acknowledging differences in skill or experience; there is a blindness to differing levels of capacity and interest. It should be self-evident that not everyone is able to contribute the same amount of time, but anti-authoritarians tend to act like there is some correlation between *capacity* and *commitment*. Like if you can't give *everything* then you must not care enough, and you might as well not come back, because there isn't a medium or low-commitment option. That's one reason why membership is so often limited to such a small, self-selecting group of people.
>
> By contrast, other groups across the progressive spectrum welcome new members by *asking* them what they like to do, *asking* them what they're good at, and *offering* tasks that fit and have meaningful mentorship. They suggest, "You could flier here and table with these people to get more of a sense of what we do, and you'll have a buddy that will help you do it, and you'll learn the ropes from that. And after that, we have A, B, and C that you can plug into, and there'll be a buddy that can help you do that stuff too." They really give people support, and anti-authoritarians deny each other mentorship or even peership because of the notion that support, in and of itself, is authoritarian or something, which is why so many people leave after the first meeting—because there's no way to plug in. With an aversion to building meaningful doorways, anti-authoritarian groups often make themselves inaccessible by design.

Russell's comments get at the core problems created by the "all the same" fallacy. Believing that everyone should be equally ready and able to contribute makes it incredibly difficult to bring new people into anti-authoritarian groups, help them get oriented, assist them in determining what they can contribute, and support them in developing as activists and organizers. And Russell is not alone in observing that a distinct strength of some other left groups is the welcoming, support, and education that they provide for new members.

When anti-authoritarians do recognize these sorts of problems, we have only a few readily available models for contending with them. One such model, especially popular in anarchist circles, is the "skillshare." This involves one or more people showing others how to do a particular activity, such as designing posters, fixing bicycles, or writing press releases. Skillshares tend to happen through informal sharing and discussion. Another model, common across the anti-authoritarian current, is the "training," also known as the "workshop." In this, one or more people guide a group through learning a combination of information and skills, such as how to use consensus decision-making, how to engage in specific forms of direct action, or how to incorporate anti-oppression principles into collective work. Trainings are generally more structured than skillshares, and often make use of popular education methods.

Both of these models create important opportunities for sharing skills, knowledge, and experiences. They make it possible to have more explicit discussions about the capacities that some of us have and how we can share them. Still, these models can only get us so far. Sporadic skillshares and trainings, on their own, can only partly make up for significant differences in our capacities. What's more, these models can only indirectly help people to develop the confidence and experience necessary for taking on roles involving more initiative and responsibility—taking on what are, in fact, leadership roles. Although they point in helpful directions, skillshares and trainings aren't sufficient.

The "all the same" fallacy ultimately prevents anti-authoritarians from creating the models that we urgently need. First and foremost, it makes it harder for us to talk openly about our differences. As a result, we have trouble identifying areas in which people can use support in growing and learning. We also have trouble seeing the special things that we each have to contribute. Clare Bayard emphasized this: "I think that our reluctance sometimes, as anti-authoritarians, to acknowledge that people aren't all in the same place means that we actually totally invisibilize whatever gifts people *are* bringing, which is stupid." Secondly, this fallacy makes it harder for us to experiment with structures for intentionally sharing skills and knowledge, and for helping people to develop confidence and experience.

While activists and organizers make use of some models with which we're comfortable, we often steer away from more ambitious efforts that would require us to work directly with the uncomfortable reality that we're not all the same.

ANOTHER LEADERSHIP

Both of these flawed conceptions rest on a basic confusion about what leadership is. Rahula Janowski described this confusion as "not being able to tell the difference between leadership and domination."[10] This, as I've argued, is completely understandable since, in our society, the prevailing model of leadership is closely connected to domination. The mistake is in thinking that the patriarchal, top-down form of leadership is the *only* form. Against this, more and more of us in the anti-authoritarian current are working to recover, imagine, and craft another form of leadership. In creating another politics, we're trying to actively acknowledge, as activist and journalist Andréa Maria maintained, "that leadership is necessary—not just that it happens, but [that] it's important." We're also wrestling with the vital question that Janowski posed: "How do you develop a responsible leadership model that is not a domination model?"

The Another Politics Is Possible (APP) study group in New York has been confronting this question head on. APP is the effort of a group of organizers influenced by various anti-authoritarian politics who have been studying and reflecting together. Leadership has been a core theme for them. "Coming together for our initial round of study," they write, "many of us shared critiques concerning the patriarchal nature of the 'charismatic' and individualized styles of leadership that have dominated many traditional forms of left organizing. As we grew, the need for a pro-active definition of leadership became increasingly clear. One of our current goals is to articulate an alternative leadership that emphasizes deep listening, actively nurturing a culture of participation in which everyone feels that their voice is valuable, and being cognizant of how power dynamics impact participation and emotional well-being."[11]

This desire to "articulate an alternative leadership" resonates among many in the anti-authoritarian current. In the U.S. context especially, some have looked to the experience of the civil rights movement for help, particularly to the ideas and work of Ella Baker, who argued for what she called "group-centered leadership."[12] "Instead of the leader as a person who was supposed to be a magic man," she proposed, "you could develop individuals who were bound together by a concept that benefited the larger number of individuals and provided an opportunity for them to grow into being responsible for carrying out a program."[13] Baker put forward a model that sees leadership as a set of capacities and activities—skills, knowledge, confidence, and responsibility—that we should develop and share in order to deepen democracy and widen participation.

Baker's model—or at least an interpretation of it—has importantly influenced those of us developing another politics. In New York, for instance, Palestine solidarity organizer Ora Wise reflected: "In a lot of ways, I'm very inspired by Ella Baker's model of leadership. . . . It's the model of facilitative leadership and actually it's a mentor model, it's an educator model—it's about helping introduce certain concepts, principles, and processes into larger structures and organizing." Chris Crass, a cofounder of the Catalyst Project in San Francisco, maintains that there is much we can learn from Baker: "A leader or organizer in the spirit of Ella Baker is one who actively encourages other people's participation, who works with others to develop skills, confidence, analysis, and ability to take action for the long haul. . . . Although [Baker and SNCC] were not anarchists, the theory and practice they developed for egalitarian organizing was far more sophisticated than what most anarchists are working with."[14]

Using this model, activists and organizers are redefining the antiauthoritarian understanding and practice of leadership. Vancouver migrant justice organizer Harsha Walia thoughtfully summed this up: "To me, the idea of anti-authoritarian politics isn't that there are no leaders; it is the idea that there is no arbitrary leadership and that leadership is shifting. Leadership is actually encouraged to the degree that you have group-centered leadership or collective leadership, or even individual leadership based on specific roles and responsibilities and experiences rather than an arbitrary and stagnant leadership." These are sentiments that many share. Some, like Walia, talk about "alternative," "group-centered," or "collective" leadership, and others don't yet have terms to express what they want. Nonetheless, I think many anti-authoritarian organizers are in the process of envisioning and building a new form of leadership—another leadership.

What is another leadership exactly? I think we can best understand it as a growing attempt to be *clear, conscious,* and *collective* about leadership. Being clear involves identifying actually existing leadership roles and practices: Who speaks to the media? Who mediates internal conflict? Who maintains continuity between meetings? Who initiates new plans? Who provides childcare? Who is thinking about the overall health of the group and of the individuals involved? Who is developing strategic priorities? As we answer these and similar questions, we can become more explicit about how things happen in our organizations and movements. We can name roles, identify which individuals take on what responsibilities, and discuss how this work is organized in visible and not-so-visible ways.

Being clear also involves looking more closely at leadership. Rather than seeing it as something that some people "naturally" have (or don't), we can understand leadership, in the words of Atlanta-based organizer Stephanie Guilloud, "as a set of work, a set of choices." We can begin, she suggested, by simply asking, "What is it? What are the qualities? What are the activities involved in leadership?" Although answers to these questions may vary based on context, we can make some generalizations. Chris Crass, drawing again on Ella Baker, lists three types of leadership and associated activities: "as facilitator, creating processes and methods for others to express themselves and make decisions; as coordinator, creating events, situations, and dynamics that build and strengthen collective efforts; and as teacher/educator, working with others to develop their own sense of power, capacity to organize and analyze, visions of liberation, and ability to act in the world for justice."[15] To these, we might add at least one other type of leadership: the leader as nurturer, caring for people, sustaining relationships, and keeping our groups and movements healthy and functional. As we identify these kinds of roles and activities, we can begin to demystify leadership and discuss it more clearly.

With this kind of clarity in place, we can be conscious in designating who will fill leadership roles. Instead of defaulting to the less explicit ways through which leadership is so often organized—experience, friendship, and social hierarchies—we can make intentional group decisions about who does what and why. This involves using democratic processes to delegate responsibilities to particular people or sets of people. It also involves, as Toronto prison abolitionist organizer Marika Warner noted, being clear about the factors that influence such decisions: "I do think it's really important to identify, like, 'Leaders need to have a, b, and c,' whether they should be young people or they should be people of color or should be whatever, or they should be the person who knows the most or has a particular skill. But it just needs to be made explicit." With this kind of consciousness, we can start to move out of habitual patterns and begin to set our own priorities around how responsibilities are organized.

Being conscious also involves transforming how we act as leaders. Whether it takes the form of serving as an organizational representative, facilitating a meeting, or taking care of logistics for a protest, stepping into a leadership role means assuming special obligations to others. Harsha Walia stressed this: "Rather than ignoring that leadership exists—which is frustrating when you

pretend it does not exist—you take ownership over it and are very accountable and transparent for your words, actions, expectations, and responsibilities." In this discussion, Walia pointed to the Zapatista formulation *mandar
obedeciendo* ("leading we obey" or "leading, obeying"), which has had wide
influence in the anti-authoritarian current. As the Zapatistas use it, *mandar
obedeciendo* indicates a relationship of direct accountability between dele-
gated leaders and communities, in which leaders always answer to those who
empower them.[16] For organizers in the United States and Canada, this formulation offers a way to be more intentional about accountable leadership. It
can help us enact a form of leadership that is, as Toronto anti-poverty organizer Mac Scott described, "below" those who delegate it.[17]

Given clarity and consciousness about leadership roles, we can reorganize
responsibilities in our groups to be much more collective, dynamic, and effective. There are many ways to do this. Some responsibilities that are usually
held by one or two people can be more widely distributed. Nonhierarchical
decision-making processes, for instance, make it possible for groups to collectively discuss and determine strategic plans, media messaging, and logistical
details, among other things. Even when it comes to the many responsibilities
that can't be easily shared, there are options for working more collectively. Jill
Chettiar highlighted one especially popular one, which the Vancouver Anti-
Poverty Committee used. "I'm very, very much all about clear definition of
roles and assigning people into those roles," she said. "If you do that, then you
can rotate those responsibilities and it becomes a power-sharing and a knowl-
edge-sharing experience." Systems of rotation, in other words, can ensure that
particular individuals don't always have the same leadership roles. Instead,
different people can take turns holding specific responsibilities. NOII-
Vancouver uses this practice, for example, to rotate public speaking duties
among different members of the collective. We can do this with many other
leadership roles, including coordinating outreach efforts, facilitating educational sessions, and checking in with people emotionally.[18]

ANOTHER LEADERSHIP DEVELOPMENT

There is another crucial dimension to making leadership responsibilities
more collective, and it too requires a redefining of leadership. San Francisco
housing organizer James Tracy called it "the Ella Baker thing—'the role of
the leader is to make more leaders.'"[19] This formulation—leaders train more
leaders—comes up again and again among those of us developing another
politics. Rahula Janowski talked about it in her experience working with the
anti-imperialist Heads Up Collective. "We think of leadership as helping

people figure out what to do and how to do it," she explained. This means "supporting people and helping them—instead of being on top of them, being below them." The core idea here is that, if we're going to challenge the ways that leadership is conventionally organized, then we need to create structures for training and supporting people. Systems of rotation and other collective practices won't do this on their own. Indeed, without confronting the "all the same" fallacy, such practices will mainly just mask differences and set people up for stress and failure. Instead, we have to actively and explicitly work to help people to develop capacities and confidence.[20] Another leadership requires a collective process for creating leaders.

Organizers in the anti-authoritarian current have various ways of discussing this process. Some, as I mentioned, primarily talk about skills-sharing or training. Others speak more generally about "leadership development," a term commonly used in labor and community organizing. Toronto-based organizer Pauline Hwang argued for this second term. Drawing on her experience with community-based organizing in Montreal, San Francisco, and Toronto, she described leadership development as a process that makes organizations more open, equitable, and participatory. Leadership development, in Hwang's view, involves encouraging and supporting people in moving past the barriers—based on skills, knowledge, confidence, and experience—that prevent them from taking on leadership roles. She contended that, using this understanding, there is no contradiction between horizontal politics and explicit leadership development. In fact, one leads to the other. "I'm still an anti-authoritarian," Hwang said, "and I think it makes me more concerned about leadership development than if I wasn't."

Still, some anti-authoritarian organizers are uneasy with this term. There are definitely good reasons for their discomfort, given the range of meanings associated with it. In corporate, nonprofit, and agency sectors, "leadership development" frequently refers to training programs aimed at helping people to advance within workplace hierarchies. Although they are sometimes couched in the language of individual fulfillment, such programs are not about political empowerment for collective action. Even in social justice organizing, this term has some troubling connotations. LA COIL (formerly known as the LA Crew), a collective of people involved in organizing work in the garment industry, public schools, and the health care sector in Los Angeles, is sharply critical of how leadership development has looked in some movement contexts. "In many community organizations and unions," they write, "leadership development is often understood as [training] someone who is 'naturally' a good speaker to be better. These individuals are then used to inspire the base as well as generate public sympathy (or pity, according to some of our garment worker compañer@s)."[21] This form of leadership development, though based in good intentions, is far too limited if our goal is to help people actually step into collective leadership for social transformation.

But these models aren't the only ones, even if they are more common and visible. Organizers are beginning to create and use another form of leadership development that mixes some aspects of prevailing models with more horizontal practices. This is what Pauline Hwang was talking about—an anti-authoritarian way to develop leaders. LA COIL proposes something similar and suggests that it should be oriented toward "throwing power back." This, they explain, means "a different culture of leadership and consciousness that has the development of political analytical skills, technical skills, and leadership skills and the sharing of power at its core."[22] "When we 'throw power back,'" they continue, "we commit to being 'leaders' that inspire others to see themselves as agents capable of making social change, and to see their most important role as developing others to participate in making that change."[23]

Although some of these terms are specific to LA COIL, the orientation that they name broadly resonates among those of us developing another politics. This form of leadership development aims to build people's skills, knowledge, confidence, and experience so that they can act with initiative and responsibility in struggles for justice and dignity. It responds to "what is"—a world where so many of us are excluded from meaningful decision-making roles—with an eye toward "what we want"—a world where all people can fully and collectively participate in the decisions that affect our lives. For shorthand, I call this emerging form "another leadership development."

Anti-authoritarian organizers are, in many ways, still crafting this approach to building people's capacities. We're really just getting started. But looking carefully at shared ideas and practices that organizers are using, we can identify some crucial pieces of another leadership development. These, it seems to me, are the beginnings of the intentional structures that we need but don't yet fully have.

One key piece of this is creating spaces in which people can learn skills. Coming to understand how to do particular activities is essential not only for getting things done, but also for fostering shared confidence, competence, and effectiveness. Drawing on her experience with the migrant justice coalition Solidarity Across Borders in Montreal, Tatiana Gomez stressed the value of such learning:

> One of the things we've been talking about . . . is . . . skills-sharing and developing an orientation program because, in the last year, a lot of younger people have come in who [have] neither the relationships with

some of the communities that some of us had, nor the skills. This way, when we establish priorities such as outreach, everyone can feel comfortable and confident undertaking the tasks. Movement-building has to include such a building of skills—that includes sharing the lessons learned and learning from past mistakes. I think this would make our organizing more sustainable because you have this constant process of building the capacity. It's very easy to think about this in terms of leadership development and investing in human capital. But the truth is, we need more people to be able to do more things. When there's only one or two people in Solidarity Across Borders who know how to do media work and those two people are not available, you get stuck. So we need to do that skill-sharing and sharing of information. I also think this should be part of any organization that considers itself anti-authoritarian if we espouse [beliefs] in "mutual aid" and "participatory work" and "rotation of tasks."

Although Gomez was uncomfortable with the notion of leadership development, her comments get at something crucial: to create deeper democracy, wider participation, and more sustainable organizing, "we need more people to be able to do more things."[24]

But developing people's skills isn't just about participation and sustainability. This process is also vital for challenging power relations as they manifest in our organizations and movements. "It's very easy," Gomez explained, "for people to fall into what they know, to do what's easiest for them because there's no skill-sharing. And one result of this is that it's pretty predictable who ends up doing things like childcare or the dishes after a community dinner and who does the media work. This is one reason why I think it's important to do these skillshares and rotation of tasks. I think it builds capacity and I think it can be part of our anti-oppression practice in terms of affecting the dynamics of who does what and what work is valued."

This is critical. The "dynamics of who does what and what work is valued" tend to be shaped by which kinds of labor are seen as "men's work" or "women's work." As I discussed earlier, the skills involved in visible leadership roles (such as speaking publicly, delegating responsibilities, and guiding organizational planning) are generally associated with men—often able-bodied, straight, white men with class privilege. We have to be clear about this reality as we support people in developing their capacities. Former NOII-Montreal organizer Andréa Maria put it well: "Obviously, there's something messed up about fetishizing these different skills, but I do think it's important to identify what those skills are that make you a leader and try to make sure that people are given a chance to learn them." Even as we redefine leadership, then, we also need to create structures that enable people traditionally excluded from visible leadership roles to develop more conventional leadership capacities. Likewise, we need to create structures that enable relatively privileged people to develop their capacities to do things like dishes and childcare.

So, how should we encourage the growth of new skills? Skillshares and trainings, as I've discussed, are currently two of the most common forms of skills development in the anti-authoritarian current. Both of these draw on the legacy of the nonviolent direct action movement. In that context, radical organizers intentionally built a culture of training as a way to foster more egalitarian, cooperative, and democratic spaces of struggle.[25] San Francisco organizer David Solnit, who was radicalized in this movement in the 1980s, remembered this very clearly. "When I came into the anti-nuke movement, there was a huge emphasis on skills training and development," he recounted. "Even the nonviolent direct action trainings we did—we had tens of thousands of people in early '80s in the United States taking eight-hour training sessions about theory, practice, and process, and about the issue."

In discussing this, Solnit called for revitalizing a culture of training in which organizations and movements regularly dedicate significant time to skills development. At present, we can see pockets of this revitalization, but we have to broaden it much further. Partly, this means working to make learning a bigger priority in movement spaces. It also means experimenting with a variety of modes of building people's competencies. The orientation program that Tatiana Gomez described is one good example. Another example, on a bigger scale, are the periodic PowerShift conferences within the climate justice movement, which offer extensive training for hundreds of activists at a time.[26] We can explore many more such possibilities.

Skills, meanwhile, are only one part of what we need to foster. Political knowledge and analysis are just as important for cultivating confident and competent people. Based on this, a second piece of another leadership development is what many increasingly describe as "political education." This generally involves building spaces in which people can learn about ideas, history, and politics, and develop analytical frameworks for critically understanding the world around them. Reflecting on her training work with the Catalyst Project, Clare Bayard emphasized the importance of development along these lines. "I'm starting to think that maybe all organizations should have some kind of political education," she said. Among other things, Bayard stressed, solid political development can help us, as activists and organizers, to situate our struggles in broader social and historical contexts, understand what we're up against as systemic, see links between our fights and those of others, and think in a long-term way about what we're trying to do. Political education thus offers crucial resources for people in building sustained movements, carrying out leadership responsibilities, and engaging in the kinds of strategic planning I discussed in chapters 4 and 5.

Anti-authoritarian organizers are currently practicing many forms of political education. Some groups based around shared politics have focused on internal political education—collective study to reflect on ideas and practices. A number of collectives and other organizations have developed deliberate models for such study. For several years, the Heads Up collective in San Francisco held bimonthly "Homeskools" for group members and close allies to read and discuss materials around chosen themes. In Vancouver, the NOII collective has used the writing of organizational statements as an occasion for group reflection and discussion of specific issues.[27] Some organizers have also started study groups, such as Another Politics Is Possible and LA COIL, as intentional spaces for political development.[28] Through these mostly small-scale activities, we're modestly fostering what Toronto-based anarchist organizer Mick Sweetman called a "political culture"—a shared context of ideas, discussion, and analysis.

Anti-authoritarians working in organizations that are based in specific struggles and constituencies have also been crafting broader forms of political education. In one increasingly popular approach, organizers are incorporating political training into development programs aimed at members. This approach significantly overlaps with the practice of popular education that I discussed in the previous chapter.

In other cases, anti-authoritarians are using more eclectic approaches. Critical Resistance offers a particularly rich example, as veteran organizer Rachel Herzing described:

> One of things I really value about CR is we spend a lot of time on political education, internally and externally. When we set ourselves up, one of the purposes we set for ourselves in going from a network to an actual organization was an interventionist role—so, to intervene in the movement against the prison industrial complex in order to make abolition commonsensical, to focus on the entirety of the PIC and not just prisons, to show some of the connections to other movements, and essentially to educate ourselves and everybody else around us about what those connections were, where we had shared interest. . . . And we've done that in a number of different ways. We've done it through these conferences that we hold. And there are tons of different workshops and different kinds of settings where people can learn stuff in. So, people can go to a panel and listen very passively and hear something or people can go to a workshop that's really interactive, go to a cultural event—there are all kinds of avenues. . . . We have film festivals that do that stuff. We

are workshop-rageous—we're holding workshops all the time for our partner organizations and schools, churches, all kinds of places. And we produce a lot of media. So, we produce videos, and we produce a radio show, and we produce a newspaper, we produce books, pamphlets, and that kind of stuff. It's a combination of all those different things. So, we have certain super-heady intellectual stuff that you can dig into if that's your thing. And if you want to sit and hear someone else talk or you want to watch a video or you want to tune in [for] twenty minutes on the radio, you can do that. But all of that, when it's integrated well, provides a really good foundation for our members and the people who work with us to understand the base politic.

By bringing together "all kinds of avenues" of political education, CR suggests a range of possible models. And with its "interventionist" approach, CR also pushes us to think more ambitiously about developing the political knowledge and critical analysis of people outside our organizations and movements. This approach is about building radical political culture on a much larger scale.

Skill-building and political education, while important, are insufficient without a third piece of another leadership development—what some organizers call "empowerment." This is the process of helping people to experience and understand "that they have the power and the ability to affect change and take ownership," in the words of labor organizer Sonya Z. Mehta. As New Orleans organizer Lydia Pelot-Hobbs pointed out, we live "in a world that is telling people that they can't do things and that they don't have agency a lot of the time and that they can't make change." The lower our status in dominant social hierarchies, the more frequently and intensively we get these messages. Empowerment aims to challenge this dynamic, supporting people in claiming and asserting their own agency— their power to struggle on their own behalf and create change. Crucially, empowerment also involves people coming to see themselves as linked to others in *collective* struggles for dignity and justice.

Empowerment is perhaps the most challenging and critical piece of leadership development. But what does it mean in practice? Chris Crass emphasizes "treat[ing] different levels of responsibility as stepping stones to help people get concrete things done, to build their involvement, to increase their sense of capacity, and to develop the skills necessary for the job." This approach connects skill-building and political education with opportunities to accomplish things, gain experience, become more competent, and feel more confident. Empowerment involves intentionally providing not only training but also access to responsibility. An essential part of this approach is encouraging people to step forward into new and challenging roles while offering consistent support—following up, giving advice, creating space for evaluation, and recognizing accomplishments.[29]

One crucial form for facilitating this kind of development is mentorship, in which more experienced, often older activists and organizers work directly with less experienced ones. Done well, mentorship blends empowerment with skills-training and political education, all while helping people to root themselves in the politics, strategy, and organizing approach of a group or campaign. Montreal migrant justice organizer Sarita Ahooja argued that this practice is key for helping people to learn and grow politically. "You need mentors," she stressed. "That's how it happens." David Solnit agreed: "That's the core of how I've learned stuff and how I try and work with other people: Do something and then a person who's done it before helps them and then they can do it themselves." In one-on-one relationships, mentors can share skills and analysis while also supporting ongoing reflection. In the anti-authoritarian current, however, mentorship mostly happens in informal ways. (The main exception is the "buddy system," which links older and newer activists around particular tasks.) Many anti-authoritarian organizers with whom I spoke see a pressing need for us to become much more explicit in encouraging and coordinating mentorship.[30]

Some anti-authoritarian organizers, particularly those influenced by women of color feminism, also see an important healing dimension in empowerment. Along these lines, founding Sista II Sista organizer Paula Ximena Rojas-Urrutia proposed what she called "holistic leadership development." In describing it, she focused on the example of Sista II Sista's Freedom School for Young Women of Color—a political and personal development program.[31] She explained,

> Oppression in the world doesn't just affect us just in our material conditions, but has also affected us and damaged us in other ways, emotionally and psychologically and spiritually and physically—in our bodies and in our health. Therefore the way to fight and change would also have to be in all those areas. So, I think about leadership development or political development in a way where I've usually seen it of focusing on helping someone build their consciousness and intellectual knowledge and skills for transformational work. . . . [That] seems like one dimension, and doesn't even seem like the most important one, actually. I know part of what makes me have the energy and the ability to contribute on a day-to-day is dealing with all those areas of myself and finding strength in myself to be my whole self as an organizer.
>
> So, in our Freedom Schools for Young Women of Color . . . it's holistic leadership development where part of [the] time is focused on the intellectual, consciousness-raising stuff in a popular ed[ucation] kind of

style, but there's equal parts given to looking at how society and oppression has affected us emotionally and what we can do, individually and collectively, to heal from that or transform from that, to also create some kind of sacred space or connection that we do together but also help people figure out what they need at home or want to do at home or practice—some way to contemplate in some way. And also physical work—so we do a lot of self-defense, Afro-Caribbean dance, b-girling— just physical manifestations of power, something physical that really feels like you're manifesting power in a way that helps you. And then a creative element as well—so, we have these projects called "herstory" where everyone tells their own life story and then they get woven into a collective herstory at every Freedom School.

This notion of "holistic leadership development" is very promising. In particular, we can see that many of the activities that Sista II Sista used in their Freedom School were geared toward the people with whom they organized—young, working-class women of color living in Brooklyn. This example can provoke us, as activists and organizers, to create and practice forms of empowering leadership development that connect with the many parts of people's lives—minds, bodies, hearts, and spirits—in ways that speak to their situations and struggles.

These three pieces—skill-building, political education, and empowerment—convey the emerging shape of leadership development in the anti-authoritarian current. The most promising efforts aimed at another leadership development combine them. Project South in Atlanta, for instance, brings them together in its Building A Movement workshops and its eight-month organizing institutes with various community organizing projects in the southern United States. In San Francisco, the Catalyst Project combines these aspects in its workshops and its four-month Anne Braden Anti-Racist Training Programs aimed at white activists.[32] Outside these sorts of movement-building programs, however, another leadership development is mostly happening in small and fragmented ways. To move beyond isolated practices and programs, we have to be much more systematic in our efforts. This means working to bring skill-building, political education, and empowerment into all of our movement spaces, always with careful attention to what's appropriate and useful. Collective leadership doesn't just magically happen; we have to build it through sustained and deliberate work.

BUILDING LEADERFUL MOVEMENTS

The issue of leadership brings us back to the central challenge facing another politics: How can we struggle in ways that are grounded in the existing world and yet oriented toward transformation? Anti-authoritarian politics highlight the ways in which "power-over" relations shape much of our society, including the dominant form of leadership. Our politics also point to the liberatory relations that people can create based on equality, cooperation, and self-management. If we aren't careful, though, we can become so transfixed by our values and visions that we lose sight of the complexities sitting in front of us. The "we have no leaders" sleight of hand and the "we're all the same" fallacy are examples of this. Both are attempts to wish our hopes into being while ignoring the realities of how leadership actually happens. This is a dead end.

Another politics grows out of our attempts to do better. Through efforts to create anti-authoritarian leadership, we're working to be both practical and visionary in our approach to one of the most vital aspects of organizing. The pull to be more practical leads many anti-authoritarian organizers to an increasingly sober understanding about how leadership roles tend to be organized and distributed, even in supposedly nonhierarchical groups. It's visible as well in the various ways in which organizers are intentionally building people's skills, knowledge, confidence, and experience. We can see the visionary pull in the insistence of many organizers on *another* leadership—an explicit alternative to the top-down, patriarchal form—and an corresponding new approach to leadership development. Even as we're beginning to recognize the concrete capacities and responsibilities of leadership, then, we're also proposing more collective and horizontal ways of organizing, designating, and cultivating them. Some activists in the occupy movement described this as a shift from "leaderless" to "leaderful" movements.[33]

Despite some promising efforts, another leadership is still mostly unformed. We have much further to go in fully developing it, and there are some hard, even contradictory, questions that we have yet to adequately answer. One has to do with effectiveness. Paula Ximena Rojas-Urrutia brought this up in discussing how some social justice organizers respond to an alternative leadership model. "No one in U.S. grassroots organizing work is saying that individual charismatic top-down leadership is *better*," she explained. "People are saying, 'But we just need to get shit done. It's more efficient.'" So, how do we think about another leadership and efficiency, particularly when we're often organizing in response to urgent crises? Another challenging question has to do with hierarchy and leadership. Although we often call ourselves nonhierarchical, do leadership roles—facilitation, coordination, education, and others—necessarily involve some kind of hierarchy? And if so, can there be such a thing as anti-authoritarian hierarchy? These are thorny issues, but ones we may well have to resolve if we truly want to be clear, conscious, and collective about leadership.

The best way to approach these and other questions is with a spirit of openness and reflection. "A theory and practice of anti-authoritarian leadership," as Chris Crass writes, "are full of contradictions, tensions, questions, discomforts, confusion, and uncertainties . . . and that's what I like about it. Being honest about contradictions opens up possibilities for understanding in a way that denial does not. Furthermore, tensions . . . can be a creative force to develop something new, something uncharted."[34] By thoughtfully embracing productive tensions, we can begin building consciously leaderful movements capable of unleashing people's capacities to self-organize and remake the world.

8. "Vehicles for movement-building"
Creating Organizations

> We need to grow our collective knowledge, analysis, experience, and
> strength—and numbers. We don't expect any one organization to
> have all the answers, have the right plan or strategy, or have
> everything figured out. We don't think there is only one
> organization that all revolutionaries should be a part of, and can see
> the destructive effects of this type of functioning in multiple
> historical moments. We also know that the form of organization will
> be different at different moments of movement activity.
>
> Another Politics Is Possible and LA COIL

No One Is Illegal-Vancouver members and other activists participate in an Idle
No More march on January 11, 2013, in Vancouver, British Columbia. (Photo
by Caelie Frampton)

AS I SPOKE WITH Andréa Maria, I was struck by her clear-eyed view of the
anti-authoritarian current. Her clarity comes in part from her extensive
movement experience, which includes deep involvement in La Convergence
des luttes anti-capitalistes / Anti-Capitalist Convergence in the mobilization against the 2001 Summit of the Americas in Quebec City and then
years as an organizer with NOII-Montreal before moving into work as a
radical journalist. As she and I discussed strategy, she introduced the piece

so often missing from such conversations: organization. "Wrestling with organization- and institution-building," she stressed, "is part of a strategy that needs to happen."

Maria's use of the word *wrestling* is apt. The topic of organization is a complicated one for another politics. Most anti-authoritarians, after all, work in organizations—organized groups of people with shared goals and activities. These include collectives and affinity groups, community-based organizations, ad hoc activist groups, advocacy organizations, trade unions, student groups, coalitions, and networks. Some of these organizations are based in shared politics, others are oriented around particular struggles and constituencies, and some attempt to bridge these approaches. Some are volunteer run and others have paid staff. These organizations come in many sizes—from less than a dozen people to thousands—and work at many different scales—local, regional, national, and international.

Yet for all of this experience with individual organizations, many anti-authoritarian ways of relating to organization are surprisingly limited. For one, there is a tendency among some activists to reject intentional, long-term organizations altogether, or at least to be deeply suspicious of them.[1] There is also a tendency, somewhat related, to see any organization larger than a small group as inherently hierarchical and therefore suspect.[2] Both of these stances contribute to activist insularity and undercut our ability to build sustained and broad-based movements. More significantly, anti-authoritarians have a tendency, like others on the left, to get stuck in organizational ruts. As I explain below, this often happens when we focus on idealized organizational models rather than specific contexts of struggle. This tendency makes for an unfortunately narrow organizational approach, preventing the openness, experimentation, and ambition that we need.

There is, however, another approach to organization—what I call a "movement-building approach"—that organizers are developing through another politics. This emerging approach grows out of a shared sense that the question of organization requires serious attention, as Maria expressed, and that there is no perfect organizational answer. Clare Bayard, an organizer with the Catalyst Project in San Francisco, laid this out well: "What is important right now is not so much the form—like the general category of the organization—but how it's being done. . . . This is clearly a time period—and this is probably always true—where we need multiple forms. But I think the question is how self-conscious these organizations are about what they're trying to do and who they're trying to work with. What are the ways that their form helps or hinders that?" Instead of idealizing particular models, then, this approach is concerned with fostering organizations through which people can build movements and struggle effectively for social transformation.

This chapter examines how anti-authoritarian organizers are wrestling with questions of organization and organization-building. I consider the main forms of left organization in the United States and Canada, fore-grounding both their limitations and their lessons. I then lay out a move-ment-building approach to organization, describing its key components and offering some concrete examples of how organizers are nourishing anti-authoritarian organizational features in a variety of circumstances. In these examples and in conversation with those of us developing another politics, I see a trio of unfulfilled organizational longings; I suggest that each of these opens up important questions for anti-authoritarian organizational practices.

MINDING THE RUTS

As activists and organizers, we make our way through a political landscape crisscrossed by ruts left by various organizations. Some of these ruts are heavily used but veer dramatically away from our liberatory aspirations. Others are more faint and seem to head in the general direction we'd like to travel. And some ruts just go in circles. If we examine this landscape care-fully, we can see that there is no already constructed track to take us pre-cisely where we want to go. Instead, "we make the road by walking," as the radical educator Paulo Freire famously put it.[3] This is a core lesson for another politics: we have to experiment, learn from our successes and fail-ures, and try again as we go. And as we travel, we have to mind the ruts: there are some that we should avoid entirely, others that we can use strate-gically, and some that we can incorporate into roads of our own making. The key is to avoid getting stuck in any of them.

Perhaps the deepest rut is the political party. Ranging from the neocon-servative U.S. Republican Party to the nominally social democratic Canadian New Democratic Party, electoral parties are the officially sanc-tioned forms for engaging in politics in North America. Elections and polit-ical representation, we are repeatedly told, are essential mechanisms for democratic governance in our society, and parties are the primary organiza-tional vehicles for maneuvering in that arena. It should be no surprise, then, that some on the left focus tremendous energy on trying to influence existing parties—or to launch new ones. Likewise, it should be no surprise that parties frequently try to make use of movements to further their own electoral or legislative agendas. In broad terms, this back-and-forth between movements and parties—in a social context in which "politics" all too often means electoral politics—is how the political party has become such a heavily used track for left organizations.

Anti-authoritarians have significant hesitations about the electoral party as an organizational form. These are based in our critical stance toward the state and state-based social change approaches, which I described in chapter 2. Many activists and organizers reject parties altogether, seeing them as mostly indistinguishable and, at best, politically irrelevant. Too often, though, these kinds of dismissals are harmfully simplistic. For one thing, not all political parties are the same. They have real differences in composition, allegiance, and political orientation, and these differences have tangible effects on people's lives.[4] And whether we like it or not, engaging with electoral parties—even if just by voting for them—continues to be the main way that most people in the United States and Canada deliberately involve themselves in politics and seek to create change.[5] Grappling with these realities is a key challenge for the anti-authoritarian current. If we want to have a genuine impact on our society, we can't afford to ignore political parties.

But even as we face these realities, we should stay critical of the political party as an organizational form. A crucial insight in anti-authoritarian critiques is that, organizationally, electoral parties tend to closely mirror the structure of the state: centralized, hierarchical, and instrumental. This makes sense. Parties are organized for winning and holding political office—in other words, for gaining and exercising state power within the existing system. To be successful, they have to be prepared to subordinate any other concerns—internal democracy, popular accountability, and even political principles—to this goal. Understanding this, we can at times make strategic use of parties to further movement goals.[6] As organizations, though, electoral parties are poor tools for building combative, bottom-up movements aimed at social transformation.

Recognizing some of these limitations, some radicals propose an alternative form—the revolutionary party. This is another deep organizational rut on the left. Based in the Marxist tradition and significantly shaped by Leninism, it has a long history. All over the world, the first half of the twentieth century saw a flowering of socialist and communist parties that were, in many cases, closely connected to mass working-class and peasant movements. In colonized and formerly colonized parts of the world, such parties played important roles in anti-colonial and anti-imperialist struggles, particularly during the post-WWII period.[7] Taking inspiration from these struggles, radicals in the United States and Canada launched a new round of party-building in the late 1960s and 1970s.[8] Although many of these efforts eventually collapsed, a few are still around today. And over the last decade, some activists and organizers have once again begun talking seriously about building revolutionary parties or political formations leading to parties.[9]

Those of us in the anti-authoritarian current tend to be wary of such party-building efforts. In part, this wariness overlaps with our hesitations about electoral parties. In North America, however, revolutionary parties and party-building organizations generally don't confine themselves to the electoral arena in the same way that political parties do. This allows them to articulate more radical politics and to have different relationships with movements. But this party model is nonetheless oriented toward winning state power, a task that requires revolutionary parties to take on many of the features of states. As anti-authoritarian writer and organizer Elliott Liu notes, such parties "usually function by building hierarchical power and prefiguring the governing structures they hope one day to manage."[10] In doing this, revolutionary parties and party-building organizations tend to understand themselves as vanguards or future vanguards—bringing political consciousness to the working class. This, in turn, slips all too easily into the "correct line" politics I described in chapter 2 and, in the worst cases, into sectarian conflicts and power abuses. Anti-authoritarians see this kind of organizational practice as fracturing, not furthering, emancipatory movements.[11]

Anti-authoritarians are justified in feeling wariness about revolutionary parties. But some of our criticisms rely on caricatures that paint anyone involved in party-building as either an authoritarian or dupe. These smug simplifications prevent us from appreciating *why* people choose to build or join revolutionary parties, and thus learning from such efforts. In fact, many dedicated radical organizers turn to party-building because they want to get more serious about social change: they want to develop intentional spaces, structures, and strategies for planning and carrying out long-term, coordinated revolutionary activity that can potentially involve millions of people.[12] These are desires that many anti-authoritarian organizers share. We should acknowledge that we're still trying to figure out how to fulfill these desires on our own terms. As Liu writes, the "anti-authoritarian movement in the U.S. has a long way to go before it can demonstrate that building struggle from below is more effective than strategies that rely on parties and the state."[13] Even as we recognize the rut of the revolutionary party, then, we have to honestly face the challenge of building nonparty forms with similar seriousness and ambition.

Steering away from revolutionary party-building, activists and organizers of various political stripes have been exploring other kinds of organizations. At present, the most common form is probably the nonprofit or nongovernmental organization (NGO).[14] This is another organizational rut on the left, one that's been developing over the last three decades. While there are plenty of NGOs that aren't connected to left movements, there are also many that do have such connections. They provide services, spearhead advocacy efforts, and, in some cases, engage in organizing. These sorts of NGOs include women's centers, popular education and training organizations, workers centers, and various movement-based advocacy groups. As I discussed in chapter 5, radicals have also been developing base-building NGOs that combine service provision and campaign-based organizing with the explicit aim of building power among oppressed and exploited people.

There are anti-authoritarians working—and, at times, playing leadership roles—in some of these left-leaning NGOs. Even so, those of us developing another politics have critical questions about the NGO form, as I also highlighted in chapter 5. The best of these critiques come from people with firsthand experience of NGOs and make valuable contributions to developing another politics. When not so grounded in direct experience, though, these critiques can sometimes slide into simplistic thinking. Atlanta-based Project South organizer Stephanie Guilloud, who has contributed to critiques of the nonprofit industrial complex, warned about what she called "501c3 bashing"—blanket dismissals of NGOs rather than clear-headed conversations about their uses and contradictions.[15] While herself being explicit about the limitations of this organizational form, Guilloud urged activists and organizers to think about how and under what circumstances it can be used effectively. Given the current dominance of NGOs in so many movements, I think this is smart advice. If we're truly serious in our criticisms, we also have to wrestle with the question of what sorts of resilient alternatives we can construct to meet the needs that NGOs currently fill—and go further.

Besides NGOs, the other main body of alternatives to the party form is nonhierarchical organizations. Coming out of the histories I described in chapter 1, various nonhierarchical forms have become quite widespread in recent decades. These forms include affinity groups, collectives, and organizations more ad hoc in nature. We can see examples of all of them on the radical edges of a variety of movements across North America. Together, they constitute another organizational rut on the left.

The affinity group, composed of three to fifteen people who make decisions using consensus process, is primarily a model that activists use for organizing and carrying out direct actions. Affinity groups can operate independently or federate together as "clusters" that allow for thousands of people to direct and participate in mass actions, such as the 1999 Seattle protests against the World Trade Organization or the 2003 shutdown of the San Francisco financial district in response to the U.S. ground invasion of Iraq.[16] Another form, the collective, brings a small-group, consensus-based format into more sustained work, whether that's running a project or coordinating a campaign. For instance, No One Is Illegal groups are structured as collectives, as are many of the crews that produce activist publications and run radical spaces.[17] In practice, activists and organizers use a lot of variations on these and other models, many of which are less defined. Indeed, perhaps the most widespread nonhierarchical form is the ad hoc group, which is usually founded on some loosely shared politics, a connection to a movement, a commitment to directly democratic practices, and common work on particular efforts. Many radical environmental and campus-based activist groups function this way. The encampments of the occupy movement were another, more expansive, example of this.[18]

These nonhierarchical forms have much to offer. Organizations using face-to-face democratic practices are vital participatory spaces, and they can also be generative structures for developing new kinds of social relations. When effectively connected through networks, assemblies, federations, and other structures, such groups can be building blocks for combative, bottom-up movements. David Solnit, a longtime direct action organizer in Oakland, talked about them as "incubators"—structures through which people can develop capacities for struggle and self-management. "Having tens of thousands of people experience working in affinity groups and coordinating between affinity groups seems like a model of practice for running society," he argued. "It's the same skills you need to coordinate between worker co-ops or neighborhood assemblies or forms like that." The occupy movement and the 2012 Quebec student strike, in their own messy ways, put this argument into practice on much bigger scales, involving tens of thousands of people in general assemblies linked to direct action.

Anti-authoritarians have a tendency to idealize these nonhierarchical organizational forms. This is a mistake. Although such forms have many positive features, they also have some significant limitations. Solnit was frank about this: "I think anti-authoritarian/radical organizations . . . have trouble organizing themselves well. They have trouble sustaining themselves and building capacity. There's something to be said for not having cumbersome organizations that suck resources and don't do anything and stick around long after they're useful, on the one hand. But on the other hand, anti-authoritarians in the United States . . . have very little functional networks, very little infrastructure … and yet we have [a] large number of folks engaged in those movements." Solnit is not alone in voicing these frustrations. Many activists identify problems of sustainability, consistency, and resilient infrastructure when talking about nonhierarchical organization.

Some organizers with whom I spoke in Montreal were particularly self-critical about these issues. Drawing on her experience in a wide range of anti-authoritarian formations, Sarita Ahooja pointed out that "the fluidity and flexibility that has given us a higher capacity to challenge power … also has its weaknesses—where every three years or so, people are in and out, or transforming from an anti-war collective to another anti-this collective, and [so on]." Andréa Maria was even more critical: "We've trapped ourselves in this cycle where we're so scared of being co-opted or becoming agency-like that we're just gonna replicate the same seven-person collective or eighteen-person campaigns over and over and over again."

This dynamic is all too common among nonhierarchical groups across North America. On the positive side, as Ahooja mentioned, this organizational "fluidity" can produce moments of astonishing energy and possibility. But on the downside, it frequently makes for organizations that have limited capacity for building and working over the long haul. Nonhierarchical structures, in other words, have an unfortunate tendency to burn brightly and then burn out.[19] This tendency can contribute in turn to activist insularity, as people who stick around mostly sustain their political work through friendship circles, rather than enduring connections to movement-based organizations. Those of us in the anti-authoritarian current would do well to discuss these issues more openly and directly, and think seriously about how to address them in practice.

ORGANIZATIONS FOR MOVEMENT-BUILDING

Minding the ruts makes one thing quite clear: there are many readily available examples of organizations that co-opt, fragment, or weaken movements. At times, anti-authoritarians criticize such organizations and, at other times, we idealize them. The movement-building orientation in another politics, which I discussed in chapter 4, pushes us to strive for something more, something better than these familiar forms. It challenges us to move beyond insular political spaces, ground ourselves in popular struggles, and build toward the future. Joined together, a practice of minding the ruts and a movement-building orientation open up a fundamental question for the anti-authoritarian current: How can we create and support resilient organizations that nurture broad, combative, strategic, and bottom-up movements?

For better or worse, we don't have easy formulas already in front of us and we don't seem to be drafting any. By and large, anti-authoritarian organizers grappling with this question are not looking to establish new ruts—and that's promising. Clare Bayard's comments at the beginning of this chapter, about form not being as important as self-conscious activity, articulate this desire to move forward without rigid formulas. New Orleans organizer Jennifer Whitney talked in similar terms. "I don't think there is a perfect organizational structure," she said. "I think that it's about, how does participation in that organization develop leadership and develop analysis and political education through the process of the meeting, through the process of the debate, the discussion, the project, whatever it is?"

In New York, housing organizer Michelle O'Brien also emphasized not fixating on any one structure. When it comes to organization, she observed, "there are a lot of very different models." Many of these can be used in ways that transform power relations, facilitate self-management, foster collectivity, and help people to be more effective in struggles for justice and dignity. As O'Brien put it, "Organizations need to challenge internal violence and oppression, and that means being accountable and democratic. But it's also crucial to be flexible, to recognize the value of a lot of very different kinds of structures and models."

Bayard, Whitney, and O'Brien, it seems to me, get at something central about the relationship between another politics and organization. Most organizers have opinions about what works best in particular circumstances, and some certainly have strong allegiances to specific kinds of organization. For the most part, however, we're not interested in elevating particular forms as somehow always "correct." We aspire to something else: we want to nourish organizational practices that make for stronger, healthier, and more democratic movements—and we recognize that such practices may take a variety of forms. In this way, many anti-authoritarians are creating something that another politics doesn't yet fully have—a way to be critical, conscious, creative, and constructive in how we approach organizational structures. We're doing this in different ways and in a variety of circumstances. Still, I think this emerging shared approach to organization underlies many efforts in the anti-authoritarian current. Since it grows from the movement-building orientation in another politics, I call it a "movement-building approach" to organization.

This approach has a few central components. One foundational piece is a shared desire for intentional, long-term, and evolving structure. In part, this desire is a response to the problems of sustainability, consistency, and resilience that plague so many of our efforts. Anti-authoritarians, as

Montreal organizer Sarita Ahooja argued, "need more formalized, permanent structures." We can use these to move away from the "burn bright, burn out" cycle. This desire also comes out of a commitment to anti-oppression politics. Paula Ximena Rojas-Urrutia, an organizer associated with INCITE!, emphasized that "open" or intentionally unstructured forms of organization are susceptible to reinforcing dominant social hierarchies. In such organizations, she said, "those that already have more power, more privilege than others just tend to rise up and take up too much space." For this reason, Rojas-Urrutia maintained, we need structure:

> Even though I'm very committed to collective organizations and nonhierarchical organizations, I've been part of creating models and practices that are very highly structured—with coordination roles that rotate every six months [and] that include help with accountability and follow-through of work as well as emotional support and the overall well-being of the whole collective. It actually takes tons of structure, tons of really thought-out roles and responsibilities, to make sure that everyone is encouraged to participate. There is some power in certain roles, but those structures make sure that that power doesn't cement and that it's constantly having to shift.[20]

A second foundational piece of this movement-building approach is being attentive to context. This means paying close attention to the circumstances in which we build new organizations and work with existing ones. As Michelle O'Brien pointed out, "No one forms organizations in a vacuum. We form organizations in usually highly specific institutional contexts—either, in my case, a subset of a big nonprofit, or within a particular neighborhood facing a particular crisis with systems of authority already in place, or in a nonprofit terrain where there's particular funding available at particular times." There are many other contexts as well, including campaign-oriented organizations in issue-based movements, trade unions in workplaces, student organizations on campuses, and formal and informal groups in a wide variety of communities. With sensitivity to the specificities of these organizational contexts, we can figure out relevant ways to carry our commitments into them. As O'Brien said, "We have to bring anti-authoritarian and revolutionary values to our organizing, but that can't mean identifying with one narrow model and thinking it will always work."

This also brings up the question of aims. A third foundational piece of a movement-building approach is a grounded practicality about what we're trying to *do* with organizations. My conversation with Stephanie Guilloud in Atlanta was especially helpful in highlighting this. Guilloud suggested that we have to be "very honest about what organizations are and aren't." We should, she said, "treat them exactly as they are, which is a vehicle."

> It's a vehicle that will run out of gas, and we have to decide how long we are going to fill it with gas. We decide what we are inside the car— inside that thing that's moving. . . . But as a vehicle, it can look many different ways. You've got an eighteen-wheeler to pull this and a little sports car to move fast. You've got something to go up the hill. You have these different functions, and you make different choices about what vehicle you need to get where. So, the vehicle works in a certain way. But the variations in vehicles don't change the map, they don't change the road, they don't change the need for people to drive and people in the back or the people moving it. We will always have and need the people who can push it and the people that can work on the insides, the people who can never get a ride, et cetera.

This evocative metaphor of organizations as vehicles comes out of Guilloud's work with Project South and, as far as I know, is otherwise not widely used. Still, I think it's a wonderfully clear way of talking about something that many organizers feel but have trouble expressing: a desire to make conscious choices about organization based on what we're trying to accomplish, rather than on ideal models.

Building on this foundational desire, anti-authoritarian organizers are redefining how we think about what organizations do. Specifically, we're trying to prioritize both strategic aims *and* prefigurative praxis. The metaphor of organizations as vehicles is useful for seeing this. It directs our attention to the journey—the road that we're traveling in our vehicle. We can understand this journey in both a strategic and a prefigurative sense. The strategic aspect is about *moving toward* specific victories and goals, whether they are gaining union recognition in a workplace, winning amnesty for undocumented immigrants, launching counterinstitutions, or overthrowing capitalism. This involves creating organizations that will bring people together to struggle against dominant institutions and relations, and to fight for more liberatory possibilities. The prefigurative sense, meanwhile, is about *moving through* a process that creates new ways of being, relating, and doing. This involves creating organizations that facilitate self-management, foster collectivity and care, and undermine oppressive relations. As Jennifer Whitney stressed, it also involves working to develop people's capacities and their confidence so that they can struggle on their own behalf.

The challenging part is bringing these two priorities together in actual organizations. This is tricky because it requires us to plan and organize in both ways at once. In the strategic sense, we have to identify what qualities in a vehicle can help us move *from where we are to where we'd like to be.* What mechanisms can ensure continuity and sustainability? Do we need an organization that can involve a broad base, a small group, or some other constellation of people? And what structure will be most effective at mobilizing the resources (labor, money, skills) that we need in order to do what we want? In the prefigurative sense, we have to consider what qualities can help us move *from who we are to who we'd like to be.* What structures will help people gain skills and knowledge, and support them in taking on new responsibilities? How can our organizations enable collective deliberation and deeply democratic decision-making? And what mechanisms can ensure that people from oppressed and exploited groups are able to meaningfully participate? These are just a handful of the questions that we face, but they reveal the complexity—and potential—of this two-sided practice.

FEATURES, NOT FORMS

When it comes to organization, anti-authoritarians tend to get stuck when we confuse the specific forms we use with our broader transformative aspirations. We can come to see organizational forms such as the affinity group or general assembly as unique carriers of our dreams of a self-managed society, and we can easily get locked in trying to create these forms over and over again without paying enough attention to context. In some circumstances, these forms make a lot of sense, but in others, they are very limited. General assemblies, for instance, can be amazing structures in the midst of a growing movement, but they are much less effective when there isn't an already existing collective fight bringing people together.

If we idealize certain forms, it becomes very difficult to assess soberly when they're appropriate and when they're not. With our eyes on what seem to be (and often are) powerfully transformative organizational models, we can lose sight of the contexts in which we struggle. A movement-building approach to organization—a way of relating to organizations in ways that are "in the world but not of it"—helps us focus more carefully. Depending on the context, a movement-building approach to organization can involve work in already established organizations, work to start new ones, or some of both. The key point is what we're trying to accomplish via these organizations: some progress in our particular circumstances, as Michelle O'Brien argued, "towards some positive anti-authoritarian, revolutionary values." In this way, a movement-building approach moves our focus from *forms* to *features* of organization. Rather than vigilantly guarding our ideal models, we can nourish the values and practices we want in diverse organizational settings.

We can see anti-authoritarians using this approach in a wide range of organizations. Take, for example, the Association pour une solidarité syndicale étudiante (Association for Student Union Solidarity, known as ASSÉ), a radical Quebec student union federation with more than forty thousand members. With strong participation from anti-authoritarians, ASSÉ was built over the course of a decade and, in 2011, launched a bigger student coalition known as CLASSE (the *"coalition large"* of ASSÉ) that effectively led the successful 2012 student strike. One feature of CLASSE's structure that significantly contributed to this success was direct democracy.[21] As organizer and researcher Marianne Garneau describes, "CLASSE met regularly, [in meetings] composed of elected, recallable delegates from each member student group, who voted (according to the mandate assigned by their assembly) upon strategy and strike actions, as well as responses to government offers during the course of the strike. Thus, CLASSE was able to disseminate the model of direct, democratic decision-making by stipulating that its member student associations implement the assembly system, and [that they] allow that body to be the supreme decision-making entity concerning the strike and negotiations, even above the local union executive."[22]

In CLASSE, direct democracy through general assemblies was not always easy. Speaking in an *Upping the Anti* roundtable in the midst of the strike, student organizer Nastassia Williams pointed out that "sometimes our meetings are long and difficult, sometimes questions or resolutions or proposals do not get resolved in one day. We have to spend a lot of time discussing and sometimes, in the end, we have to abstain from a vote."[23] Nevertheless, this directly democratic structure made many other things possible. For one, it provided a clear framework for organizing—bringing students together in assemblies at departmental and other levels to deliberate and, in the process, build a visible sense of collectivity. Procedurally, it also involved tens of thousands of students in assessing their circumstances, establishing goals, weighing options for action, and making plans—the necessary work of building movement-wide strategies. And combined with the combative orientation of CLASSE, this directly democratic structure enabled students to develop and sustain an astounding breadth of committed participation in mass direct action, even in the face of terrible police violence. Taken together, ASSÉ and its work in CLASSE demonstrate some of the possibilities of building anti-authoritarian organizational features on a very large scale.

Another example from a very different context is the Sylvia Rivera Law Project (SRLP) in New York City. Founded in 2002, SRLP is a nonprofit organization that works for gender self-determination as part of broader struggles for justice and dignity. With a commitment to putting those affected by multiple systems of oppression at the center, the organization focuses on raising, in its words, "the political voice and visibility of low-income people and people of color who are transgender, intersex, or gender non-conforming."[24] SRLP offers free legal assistance, advocates for changes to laws and policies, conducts trainings and public education, and engages in community organizing. In doing this work, it consciously fights against the institutions that consistently create misery and violence in the lives of trans people of color and poor people, such as immigration authorities and prisons. And SRLP is remarkably effective in these fights, providing for the legal needs of those it supports, lifting the profile of trans and gender non-conforming struggles, and building a wider community.

Part of what makes SRLP so effective is its innovative nonhierarchical structure, which is especially unique among nonprofits. Six work-based teams, including both paid staff and volunteers, run the organization as a large consensus-based collective. With clearly defined structure, responsibilities, and decision-making procedures, the organization is able to use this collective structure to be more responsive and productive. As longtime queer organizer Rickke Mananzala and SRLP founder Dean Spade write, "SRLP's structure maximizes efficiency by using teams and committees to delegate decision-making power and implementation powers to small groups and individuals while employing annual work plans and other accountability measures to make sure that the broad strokes of programming are approved by the entire organization."[25]

SRLP's structure also enables strong leadership development and anti-oppression praxis. All volunteers go through an extensive orientation and those who aspire to be collective members have access to a clear application process. Once invited to join, each new member is paired up with a "buddy" who offers further orientation and ongoing support.[26] While Mananzala and Spade observe that leadership development is an ongoing challenge given the workload of the organization, SRLP's experience is still quite instructive.[27] This is especially the case in relation to anti-oppression praxis in the organization. SLRP has a stated aim that "the majority of the collective should be comprised of people of color, people of trans, intersex and gender nonconforming experience, and low-income people."[28] Its approach to leadership development, combined with internal educational initiatives and explicit diversity goals, has made it possible to meet and exceed this aim over the last decade.[29] In this and other ways, SRLP offers a helpful model for bringing anti-authoritarian organizational features into NGOs and other midsize organizations, particularly those engaged in a mix of service provision and organizing.

Another useful example is the Heads Up Collective, an all-volunteer white anti-racist, anti-imperialist group that was active in the San Francisco Bay Area from 2001 to 2008. Launched in response to the post-September 11 "war on terror," Heads Up initially focused on bringing lessons and energy from the global justice movement into the nascent anti-war movement; it played an important role during the mass direct action in San Francisco against the 2003 U.S. ground invasion of Iraq. A central goal of Heads Up was to help unite the predominantly white sections of the anti-war movement with radical efforts led by people of color that emphasized economic and racial justice at home and abroad. The group worked toward this primarily through Palestine solidarity and immigrant rights organizing, in close partnership with Palestinian and immigrant organizations. Heads Up provided its partners with ongoing support—such as childcare, fundraising, and security for marches—and organized white people to speak out and participate in collective actions with its partner organizations.

Over the years, Heads Up developed an organizational structure that combined aspects of more typical consensus-based collectives with customized features designed to strengthen the group's work. For one, it functioned as a closed collective, only admitting new members once or twice a year after group deliberation, a timeline that allowed for more intentional orientation and integration. Heads Up also used regular study sessions and annual retreats to develop shared analysis, vision, and organizational strategy. As well, the collective used a shared leadership model with defined (and shifting) responsibilities for all members, both in relation to partner organizations and in running Heads Up. Some responsibilities were formalized into what was called the "Internal Planning Group," composed of a rotating set of members. Speaking in a 2006 group interview, former member Rahula Janowski described this body as "entrusted with keeping track of our internal process, mapping out when we have certain discussions, following decision-making processes through several meetings, making sure things don't fall through the cracks."[30] Marc Mascarenhas-Swan, another former member, added: "It's easy to get caught up in the moment and lose track of priorities, so I find it helpful to have folks bottom lining, rooting our day-to-day work in the bigger picture that we have collectively decided upon."[31] With these sorts of innovations, the example of Heads Up suggests a more intentional and exploratory way of refining anti-authoritarian organizational features.

These are just a handful of examples of anti-authoritarians usefully experimenting. There are many others, including democratic membership organizations such as the Ontario Coalition Against Poverty in Toronto and the Coalition of Immokalee Workers in South Florida, staff collectives within membership organizations such as Young Workers United in San Francisco, activist collectives that join organizers from multiple sectors such as LA COIL in Los Angeles and the Black Orchid Collective in Seattle, networks of movement-based collectives such as No One Is Illegal, national organizations with collectively-run chapters and affiliates such as Critical Resistance and INCITE!, and unions such as the Canadian Union of Postal Workers and the Industrial Workers of the World. In these and other settings, anti-authoritarian organizers are working to develop features consistent with our principles and structures that further our aims. Fundamentally, we're fixing up and assembling vehicles for movement-building—organizations that widen, deepen, and strengthen liberatory movements. While we need to do this more expansively and self-consciously, we actually have more established models than we often realize.

ORGANIZATIONAL LONGINGS

Even as anti-authoritarians bring our values and practices into many organizations, some of the features we seek to create are still largely aspirational. These are structures for which many of us feel a strong need, but which we have not yet been able to develop concretely or completely. I understand them as organizational longings, and I think it's crucial to discuss them even though they may seem abstract. Each of these longings points to critical unresolved issues in anti-authoritarian organizational practices; they get at questions that we should be—and, in some cases, are—trying to answer. Here, I want to highlight three such longings and the questions they raise.

The first of these has to do with accountability. Problems of accountability come up when we aren't conscious about leadership, as I mentioned in the previous chapter, but accountability concerns more than leadership. In organizations, it involves people acknowledging that what they do affects others, acting out of a sense of collective responsibility, and following through on what they say they will do. Too often, though, anti-authoritarians treat accountability as if it were a form of domination. Oakland CR organizer Rachel Herzing was especially blunt about this: "The main thing I struggle with in anti-authoritarian spaces is a lack of accountability and a lack of a willingness to be held accountable." Harjit Singh Gill, a longtime anarchist also based in Oakland, echoed Herzing. Accountability, he said, is "almost like another word that's kind of dirty, like we don't want to have obligations to each other. And yet, if we're going to work together collectively, we have to."

What I hear in these and other conversations is a longing for accountability mechanisms that are based in a vision of shared power. In Herzing's words, "To hold you accountable doesn't mean I'm trying to have power over you, it doesn't mean I'm trying to control you, it doesn't mean I'll necessarily even stop you from what you're doing; it means I want you to know that you're being seen and that, if we are in this space together and we're sharing this work, you impact it." This resonates with the sentiments of other activists and organizers I've spoken with and encountered. Many in the anti-authoritarian current yearn for nonhierarchical but nonetheless explicit organizational practices for naming and navigating individual and collective obligations. This is significant, and it leads to difficult questions: Without being cult-like or dictatorial, what kinds of structures can we develop to foster and sustain accountability among people working together in organizations and movements? What does anti-authoritarian accountability look like in practice?

The second organizational longing that I've encountered has to do with cultivating many points of engagement. Mac Scott, who worked with the Ontario Coalition Against Poverty in Toronto, usefully discussed this: "I think people need to be able to come into an organization without already having figured everything out, already knowing the language, already having twenty demonstrations under their belt—especially if you're gonna have people who work and have families, and [people who] don't necessarily have the subculture that activists sometimes foster." Scott's own response to this challenge is to argue for building membership organizations. But even for those who organize in or favor other forms, I think he raises a crucial point: If organizations truly are going to function as vehicles for movement-building, then they have to create spaces in which people can participate with varying levels of commitment and experience. We need organizational practices and structures that create openings, rather than barriers, for involvement.

Founding Sista II Sista organizer Paula Ximena Rojas-Urrutia talked about this too, emphasizing the importance of developing "really creative structures that have a lot of points of participation." Some people, Rojas-Urrutia maintained, "want and have the time to step up into working more hands on, more day to day, taking on responsibility," while others "want to stay active but in a lower-frequency way." She continued:

> And that can change over time. It's not a linear progression of the more time you give equals the more committed you are. And people's time and commitment levels can ebb and flow over the years. This is where we have to bring in the lens of valuing the caretaking work that people

are doing, not just within our political organizations but also within our families and communities. So, if we always carry that lens, we can see how important it is to create different options or entry points for commitment and responsibility. And it's not just about assessing people's commitment based on how much time they can give, but about creating an organization that works to support each person's meaningful participation, regardless of how much or how little time they can give, and where the political participation somehow overlaps or connects to their daily life as opposed to asking that they give up parts of their life.

Instead of explicitly or implicitly requiring that people take on heavy commitments in order to participate in organizational work, we should develop more possibilities for involvement and affiliation. This means creating structures that sustain a range of ways that people can take on responsibilities.[32] Based on my experiences and conversations, I gather that many anti-authoritarian organizers long for such structures and practices. The key questions here are: How do we build organizations and movements that can offer many "entry points" and levels of commitment? How do we develop open organizational cultures that invite and sustain such participation?

The third organizational longing that I've consistently come across has to do with finding a "political home." This is a term that Toronto-based youth organizer Pauline Hwang used and others echoed. Hwang talked about a political home in a couple of senses. One was about having, in her words, a kind of "support group"—a space for discussion about life choices among organizers involved in different areas of work but with shared politics and commitments to lives in struggle. The other sense was about having a space through which, as she explained, "we can strategically make our projects complement each other and work toward a common political goal at some points, when that seems appropriate."

In New York, housing organizer Michelle O'Brien proposed something similar. It's important, she said, to have "people that you're in dialogue with over the long-term and that you're in a relation with over the long-term, where there's a level of investment in each other that isn't easily lost." Reflecting on her own organizing experience, she continued, "I think that's particularly valuable for people with a high level of political analysis who find themselves in different kinds of institutional circumstances, particularly non-profit professionals, to have another space of dialogue according to revolutionary values not often included in our nonprofit settings." It's just as valuable, I would add, for those who are not full-time organizers, those trying to bring their politics into their workplaces and schools, and those working as lone radicals in neighborhood associations and other civic organizations.[33]

I don't think it's surprising that many in the anti-authoritarian current are looking for these intentional, long-term political spaces. They fill needs that Hwang and O'Brien both mentioned: sustaining radical community, enabling discussion and reflection, and facilitating multi-sector strategic planning, all with the long-haul perspective that is so often missing from day-to-day organizing work. People on the left have long wrestled with how best to create such spaces. In revolutionary traditions influenced by Leninism, radicals have tended to build or find their political homes in parties or party-building organizations. These organizations have usually been organized as cadre groups in which dedicated militants come together around highly defined politics and strategic programs.[34]

Anti-authoritarians, especially anarchists, have tended to be critical of the vanguardist aspirations and centralized structures of cadre groups. But within the anarchist tradition, there is a tendency that focuses on developing nonvanguardist, democratic political organizations based in a closely shared politics and program.[35] Some in the anti-authoritarian current today find political homes in such organizations, including Common Cause in Ontario, Common Struggle in the northeastern United States, the First of May Anarchist Alliance, Miami Autonomy and Solidarity, Solidarity and Defense in Detroit, and the Workers Solidarity Alliance. Others find political homes in collectives and other groups that, in some ways, resemble cadre organizations, such as the Black Orchid Collective mentioned above and Organization for a Free Society, which has branches in a few U.S. cities.[36] There are also organizers who are suspicious of anything that smacks of cadre organizing and focus, instead, on finding political homes in activist networks and movement-based organizations.

Most of us developing another politics haven't found political homes. To varying degrees, our friendship circles offer spaces for discussing politics and strategy. Some of us partly meet our needs through close-knit efforts in study groups and publications.[37] Like Hwang and O'Brien, however, many yearn for something more. This opens challenging questions: How can we build organizations to serve as sustained political homes without getting stuck in the ruts of insularity and sectarianism that so often plague such projects? What kinds of structures can facilitate mutual care and support while also enabling political development and big-picture strategic planning?

ORGANIZATIONS AND MOVEMENTS

There are big questions around organization facing another politics. In working toward social transformation, how do we develop organizations and organizational practices that are adequate to the vast range of communities, sectors, and struggles across North America? And what does "revolutionary organization" even mean in our present circumstances? No one, as far as I can tell, has great answers to these questions. The anti-authoritarian current certainly doesn't. But in a sense, I think we can understand the emerging movement-building approach to organization as a way that anti-authoritarian organizers are trying to explore possible answers—or perhaps to hone more useable questions.

In our explorations, some things are getting clearer. One is that we have to mind the ruts of left organization, no matter how attractive they may be. We have to pay close attention to the circumstances in which we work, and think very intentionally about what we're trying to do with our organizations. With mindfulness of our contexts and aims, we can begin to put a movement-building approach into practice. Like so much else in another politics, this approach is an attempt to navigate between actual circumstances and transformative aspirations. It starts with what is—a world in which people use all sorts of organizations in order to fight for dignity and justice—while staying oriented toward what we want—a world based on values of equality, cooperation, and self-management. Concretely, this approach involves cultivating the transformative features of actually existing organizations as well as building new kinds of organizations based on liberatory principles.

All of this begs another big question. One defining aspect of a movement-building approach is a focus on organizations that *further* movements. This is not a rhetorical point. Left organizations have a long and unflattering track record of trying, in various ways, to subordinate popular upsurges and movements to their own (often self-serving) aims. This is how organization-building and movement-building can come into conflict. Through another politics, activists and organizers are attempting to establish a fundamentally different relationship between organizations and movements. I think this is positive but still needs more clarification. Recent fast-moving upsurges such as the occupy movement have been propelled by ad hoc forms of organization that, in large part, faded fairly quickly. More enduring forms of organization can potentially help to turn such episodes into more resilient radical movements. The big question is, how? "How," as the editors of *Upping the Anti* write, "can organizations provide a structure to spontaneity without dampening it or appearing on the scene too late?"[38] How can organizations help movements to grow into a sustained challenge to ruling institutions?

If we're going to assemble effective vehicles for movement-building, we'll ultimately have to tackle these sorts of questions. Fortunately, our movements have rich organizational experiences to draw upon and, as I've indicated, organizers are currently creating a promising set of organizational forms—diverse experiments and structures, connected by a shared approach. With collective reflection, we can distill lessons and principles from these experiences. With further work, we may well be able to develop some compelling answers to the big questions we face. We may, in other words, be able to talk seriously about revolutionary organization in the United States and Canada.

Conclusion

"Imagining ourselves outside of what we know"

When we think about change, we think about change within the constraints of what we already know. And what gets really scary is to think about it without having a blueprint. So, taking some risks, experimenting. We don't have a fixed notion of what . . . the world should look like, but we're putting forth some ideas and engaging people in dialogue about those ideas.

Kai Barrow

In the largest street mobilization in Quebec's history, students and allies march in Montreal on May 22, 2012, as part of the student strike. (Photo by Thiên V.)

WHAT I'VE WRITTEN in this book doesn't fit together smoothly and may well be contradictory in places. I've made some big claims, and yet what I've offered is stubbornly open ended. This is deliberate. It reflects the various—and not always compatible—ways I've come to see another politics based on my interviews and experiences. I group these ways of seeing into two main understandings: one sees another politics as a political pole and the other, as an open political space. As far as I can tell, these understandings broadly resonate with how many anti-authoritarian organizers think about our developing politics. I begin with them here because I think engaging them is key to moving forward.

As a *political pole*, another politics is an effort to assert a way of understanding and acting in the world. This pole is centered in a broad political tendency that, for shorthand, I call the anti-authoritarian current. Across a wide range of movements, anti-authoritarians are staking out this political pole through work based in the principles I've highlighted throughout this book: opposing exploitation and oppression, developing new social relations and forms of social organization, linking day-to-day struggles with transformative visions, and engaging in grassroots, bottom-up organizing. Built with these principles and their related practices, this pole draws many activists and organizers who are looking to get more organized and strategic but who are ambivalent about the NGO world, critical of the various forms of party-oriented organizing, and not satisfied with radical subcultural scenes. In this understanding, another politics is the set of shared politics, practices, and sensibilities that anti-authoritarians are in the process of forging, as a still not fully coherent political pole. It's a politics to be elaborated and refined.

As an *open political space*, another politics is an effort to generate new conversations and possibilities across movements. This, in my view, grows out of a general feeling among many people engaged in struggle that we don't yet know how to make revolution in the twenty-first century, and that we need useable alternatives to correct line politics. In this sense, another politics is based not so much on certainties as on common questions: What strategies can we use both to struggle more effectively and to create meaningful alternatives? How can we organize in ways that foster liberatory modes of being, doing, and relating? What structures can we develop to tap into ongoing antagonisms, bring people together, and cultivate collective power? And fundamentally, how can we build movements broad, deep, and radical enough to displace ruling systems? Another politics, in this understanding, names a space in which people are grappling with pressing questions through experimentation and discussion. It's a politics in motion—something that is growing and can never be fully captured by words on paper.

These two understanding don't necessarily sit together easily. They call for different projects: while the first is about defining shared principles and approaches, the second is about holding space for shared political uncertainty and questions. Still, I think that to fully comprehend another politics, we have to embrace both definitions. On the one hand, anti-authoritarians could really use more a defined and outward-oriented politics. San

Francisco-based direct action organizer David Solnit put this well: "We need to develop a new politics and popularize it—build organizations and movements that can carry it and have it carry new stories and new identities. . . . We desperately need some new language." This is a project of building a political pole that can attract and animate people who get involved in movements and left politics.

On the other hand, anti-authoritarians could really use more developed ways of avoiding rigidity in theory and practice. Left political currents, despite their best intentions, are a treasure trove of ideological dogmas, idealized models, fetishized practices, and sectarian conflicts, and the anti-authoritarian current has its fair share of these problems. Given this, I'm convinced that skepticism about certainties can be healthy. We need to cultivate fresh thinking that begins not with rigid formulas but rather with hard questions grounded in the dynamic, complicated circumstances in which we struggle. We also need synthetic political approaches that draw on the best of many radical traditions and legacies of resistance. This is a project of creating an open space for a new kind of question-based politics.

Some anti-authoritarian organizers are consciously engaged in one or both of these projects of another politics. This is crucial work, and we need more of it. Time will probably tell whether the two projects are at odds with one another. I don't believe they have to be. In fact, I think that the uneasiness between them is useful, at least for the moment. On the one side, it keeps the project of building a political pole from becoming too rigid, and on the other side, it prevents the project of creating an open political space from floating away. This uneasiness, in other words, can generate—and, to some extent, is generating—more dynamism, self-consciousness, and intentionality in the anti-authoritarian current.

Ultimately, the power of these projects lies in the demands they put on us. Whether we envision it as a political pole or an open political space, another politics is something that does not yet fully exist. It has to be built. In this sense, another politics calls on us to acknowledge soberly where we're at and to think and act in bigger, more ambitious ways. This, it seems to me, is an exciting challenge, usefully summed up in the words of Atlanta-based organizer Stephanie Guilloud: "We have to imagine ourselves outside of what we know." Guilloud made this comment while talking about cultivating vision in organizing. I understood her mainly to be gesturing toward the importance of thinking beyond what we take for granted—"beyond our assumptions of the way we are organized," as she said. This "thinking beyond" applies not only to our society, but also to our movements and ideas, to our visions of how to create another politics.

GETTING REAL, GOING FOR IT

Imagining ourselves outside of what we know might seem mostly to involve dreaming about the future. Certainly, imagining where we'd like our movements to be—and what we'd like our world to look like—in one, ten, or even one hundred years is worthwhile. As I've argued, developing vision is particularly important for grounding our day-to-day organizing and orienting our efforts strategically. However, I want to propose that thinking outside of what we know requires us, first, to get real: we have to look lovingly and critically at what the anti-authoritarian current is at present and what it can presently do. This means examining our collective efforts without belittling or exaggerating them, focusing on what we're actually accomplishing rather than what we hope to achieve.

When we undertake this kind of examination, what do we see? Viewed in the best light, the anti-authoritarian current is a large set of projects and groups that play a leading role in many ongoing struggles and periodically kick off wider mobilizations. But viewed in the worst light, this current is a set of fairly transient and insular activist enclaves engaged in frenetic activity that only occasionally connects to broader movements in any significant way. The reality, substantially shaped by specific circumstances, is probably somewhere between these two depictions. What is clear is that the anti-authoritarian current, as it is, *is not enough.* In its present form and size, it's not capable of winning large-scale structural change. Montreal migrant justice organizer Tatiana Gomez was refreshingly frank about this: "I don't think we're going to build a movement with about a hundred anarchists in every major city." This is something that many activists and organizers recognize but have an understandably difficult time talking about.

The good news is that the anti-authoritarian current is well positioned to help grow the movements that we need. But in order to do that, those of us in this current will have to push beyond where we are right now. In part, this means imagining how we can contribute to social transformation on a scale and with a depth that we've barely experienced. In New York, long-time organizer RJ Maccani offered a helpful way to think about this. His "biggest fear," he said, is "that we'll do everything right, according to us, and it'll matter—it'll matter to us, it'll matter to some people in certain places in some ways, things will carry on, it might be a seed for something else in the future." But we can't settle for this, Maccani argued: "I want us to really go for it. And I don't just mean 'go for it' like we all rise up on this or that day, but 'go for it' in the sense of moving our vision and connecting with a lot of people." The promise of another politics—the promise I've tried to develop through this book—is precisely in this desire, shared by many organizers, to "go for it," to bring our vision and values into broader struggles and movements in a process that transforms everyone involved, including us. We've seen some of the ways in which anti-authoritarians are beginning to do this, and we need to take these efforts much further.

Occupy and other recent movement experiences have convinced me that a central aspect of pushing beyond where we are right now is tapping into an expansive understanding of anti-capitalism and class struggle. Let me be clear here: I'm not advocating for seeing capitalism as the primary system of domination or for subsuming all relations of exploitation and oppression into class. The integrated analysis developed through anti-racist feminism, as far as I'm concerned, has fundamentally reframed how we should think about ruling systems. But while another politics has made some progress in advancing anti-oppression politics, it has been less successful in highlighting how interlocking systems contribute to the wider dynamic through which a relatively small number of rich people wield power over a deeply divided majority. The need for this kind of anti-capitalist analysis, deepened by anti-oppression and anti-imperialist insights, has become all the more pressing in recent years, as ruling elites have used the global economic crisis to further their assault on the rest of us while propelling the whole planet into profound ecological crisis.

Although "the 99 percent" slogan of the occupy movement sometimes simplistically assumed commonality, it also worked as an invitation to come together against a common enemy, "the 1 percent." Developed further, this kind of approach can be useful. A few years before activists set up tents in Zuccotti Park, INCITE! co-founder Andrea Smith discussed it in terms of the 95 percent and the 5 percent. "In my teaching," she said,

> I find that when I talk about issues of racism—which are the most difficult to address—it is easier to talk about capitalism first. When everyone begins to see that they are not part of the 5 percent, it gives them the investment to start addressing the other privileges. They realize that addressing issues of class entails their own liberation too. This realization enables everyone to see that the reason they need to deal with racism is not so that they can be nice to people of color, but so that they can dismantle the larger system that oppresses them too.[1]

None of this is straightforward in practice. I think the crucial step here is developing a distinction between those who *gain privileges* (by race, gender, sexuality, ability, and class status) through the current systemic arrangement versus those who *gain immense profit and power.* In order to build successfully transformative movements, we must prioritize the struggles of those most disadvantaged by ruling systems and bring more and more of the first category of people onto our side by giving them investment to address their privileges—all while consistently targeting the second category of people and the structures that sustain their power and profit-making. This is true whether we're organizing around border regimes, the prison industrial complex, neoliberal austerity, wars of occupation, or the climate crisis.

This nonreductive class politics has many implications for movement-building. I'll mention two here. First, this politics calls for seriously engaging with the material realities of people's daily and nightly lives. In chapter 6, Montreal migrant justice organizer Sarita Ahooja stressed this: "We have to look at ways to organize that relate to the way people are already living their lives: a lot of work, a lot of debt, domestic problems, and commitments for families with children." I agree with Ahooja's initial emphasis on work. With some crucial exceptions, the anti-authoritarian current has been surprisingly absent from labor organizing. Now is a time to reengage this, especially since promising efforts are taking shape with workers' centers, solidarity networks, and some militant organizing in the service sector. But notice that Ahooja also mentions other, equally important material realities: debt, interpersonal conflict and violence, and responsibilities for children. We could add more, including housing evictions, entanglements with the criminal justice system, precarious immigration status, health crises, and cuts to public services and entitlement programs. While there are some radical initiatives working to address these realities, we need many more. Organizing that relates to these, I believe, is the basis for movements capable of winning fundamental social change.

Secondly, this kind of class politics asks us to rediscover how to work in mass movements. On this, I tend to agree with anarchist musician and organizer Ryan Harvey when he writes, "I have long believed that if a radical movement for economic and social justice of any sort was to emerge in this country, it had to somehow find a balance, or a recognized alliance of cooperative differences, with folks from a large segment of the population."[2] The trouble is, many of us in the anti-authoritarian current—and the left more broadly—have become accustomed to *not* working in such contexts. So much left political work happens in bubbles, among activists who share very similar backgrounds and vocabulary and are largely disconnected from broader layers of working-class people in all of their diversity. This creates big problems. Some of these were visible in the occupy movement, for instance, as more experienced organizers struggled to relate with large numbers of people who had similar concerns and brought energy and ideas, but who often didn't have the skillsets and analysis that frequently get taken for granted in small activist communities. As the occupy experience demonstrated, people coming into movements bring with them contradictions—alongside liberatory aspirations, we carry destructive views and behaviors that we learn by living in this society. Working in mass movements requires patience and humility, and also a willingness to struggle with these inevitable challenges. It calls on us to listen and share rather than tell and assume.

REFLECTING ON EXPERIENCES, DRAWING LESSONS

Imagining ourselves outside of what we know also means learning from collective experience. This isn't as simple as it may first appear. It can be tempting to use our experiences, as activists and organizers, to validate what we believe. As much as we can though, we have to struggle against this tendency and instead use our experiences as resources to bring out difficult questions and generate new ways of thinking and acting. This involves an ongoing process of evaluation and action—critically reflecting on what we've done, drawing lessons, and applying these lessons through political practice. Many of us in the anti-authoritarian current are already working hard to create this sort of process in our work. Thanks to these efforts, we can access a lot of hard-earned lessons from experienced organizers. These lessons are, in many ways, the basis for this book. And many of them can help us not only to imagine but also to act outside of what we know. I'll highlight the most important ones here.

Let me begin with the two lessons I have tried to convey through the core themes of this book. The first is "against-and-beyond": in order to transform our society, we have to fight ruling systems and institutions *and* cultivate liberatory relations and forms of social organization. Generally, this means engaging in oppositional organizing campaigns, nourishing visionary ideas and practices through them, and building counterinstitutions that remain closely connected to them. But as we attempt to combine these elements in our movements, we frequently find ourselves in an uncomfortable disjunction. This, as activist and journalist Andréa Maria described in chapter 3, is the tension between "what is"—actually existing social realities—and "what we want"—the liberatory possibilities that we seek to manifest. We can choose to ignore this tension—to exclusively focus on one end or the other—but if we're serious about social transformation, we have to figure out how to work from *within* it. This is the second lesson: being "in the world but not of it," that is, staying grounded in daily and nightly realities while also pushing and pointing beyond them toward a vision of another world.

While sometimes difficult, none of this is impossible. The key part is sustaining dynamic tensions that ensure that our work stays relevant and radical. As anarchist scholar and activist Andrew Cornell explains, "Being rooted in organizing for change helps keep those focused on institution-building from inadvertently constructing insular projects for the radical minority (such as some infoshops, pirate radio stations, and other projects), or alternative institutions that are either ignored or recuperated by the state and capital (such as some domestic violence shelters across the United States and food co-ops in gentrifying neighborhoods). Running organizing campaigns *in combination with* building counterinstitutions, and with a view toward paralyzing and toppling the system, also works to prevent such campaigns from becoming solely reformist."[3] Using prison abolition-ist terms, this is how we can "dismantle and build" from within actual cir-cumstances without being completely constrained by them.[4]

But to work within such dynamic tensions, anti-authoritarians need to create alternatives to purity-based politics. Francesca Fiorentini, an experi-enced anti-war organizer, expressed this third lesson bluntly: "purism has got to go." There is a tendency on the radical left to hold onto a "pure" politics—as if "staying true" to particular ideas can guide us unwaveringly toward revolution and keep us from having to engage in messiness and contradictions along the way. At times, radicals combine this tendency with a specific kind of elitism—a sense that those who hold onto the "pure" politics are the "righteous few." The trouble, as I've maintained throughout this book, is that messiness and contradictions are an inescapable part of being in a world structured by social relations of domination. As abolition-ist organizer Alexis Pauline Gumbs writes, "We are in the messy everyday of each other, we cannot remain clean, but we can hold each other account-able to learn from our mistakes, to hold ourselves to ever more intentional levels of engagement."[5] Although she is discussing transformative justice efforts, Gumbs offers an insight relevant for all organizing work: to act in this world, we have to jump in, get our hands dirty, and learn. This is the necessary starting place for doing almost anything that matters.

Gumbs hits on another important insight as well: while we can't be "pure," we can be deliberate. This leads to the fourth lesson: anti-authoritarians need to cultivate intentionality in all of our political work. For one, we should con-sciously create spaces to talk about vision. These conversations can offer us essential guidance as we make decisions about how to fight and what to fight for. Additionally, we need to bring intentionality into strategic planning in our campaigns and groups. Being intentional as we set goals and lay plans allows us to connect "what is" and "what we want" through deliberate efforts, and to assess our progress. We should also be intentional in our organizations themselves. These are the main contexts in which people take on responsibilities, develop new capacities, make decisions, navigate power relations, and carry out collective work. And through all of this, both making plans and building structures, we need greater intentionality about prefigurative praxis. Refusing absolutism and fetishism, we have to be conscious about both the importance and the limitations of our work to develop new ways of being, doing, and relating. Ultimately, cultivating this kind of intentionality is how we can begin to approach what we're doing with the seriousness that it deserves.

Being intentional also involves adopting a particular orientation to practices, structures, and approaches. As I've emphasized in this book, anti-authoritarians should see all of these as *experiments* rather than as forms that are somehow universally correct. This is the fifth lesson. No single organizing mode, type of organization, or strategic model works across all circumstances. Treating any practice, structure, or approach as infallible is thus a dead end; it shuts down our abilities, as people engaged in movements, to think and act innovatively. Instead, we have to act without any pretense of complete certainty, and with a genuine eagerness to learn from our attempts, whether they be successes, failures, or, more often, something in between. New York occupy organizer Shyam Khanna aptly calls this "a try-and-let's-see style of organizing, open to experiments and learning from experience."[6] To practice this, we need to develop regular systems of evaluation through which we can figure out how to adjust our current attempts and launch new ones. In this way, an experimental orientation can usefully shift how we understand what we're doing: perhaps we can begin to see our efforts as part of an ongoing creative process, rather than attempts to hammer out perfected forms.

The sixth lesson has to do with how we treat one another in movements. Most of us in this society know all too well how to relate to people with contempt, rivalry, objectification, and exclusion. That is, we know how to treat people like shit. At their high points, movements manage to create spaces in which people can partially manifest a different relational vision, one based in respect, generosity, collaboration, and openness. Much of the time though, those of us in movements and left circles are no better than anyone else in how we treat one another. And sadly, there is no way to transform this reality quickly. These ways of relating are deeply ingrained in how power works in this society, and it's not surprising that they seep into our movements. Still, anti-authoritarians have a responsibility to reach toward other ways of being and acting. "Struggle," as Montreal anti-prison organizer Helen Hudson pointed out, "can be a really humanizing experience." When people come together to fight collectively, we can experience our own humanity and the humanity of others in profound ways. We need to build movements whose appeal comes, in part, from the opportunities they offer for people to experience their best selves. This is vital for imagining ourselves outside of what we know.

GETTING SMARTER, DOING IT BETTER

One final lesson is worth discussing here: we have to preserve and transmit knowledge across cycles of struggle. This lesson is implicated in all of the others since, in the end, what we collectively learn is worth little to our movements unless we are able to share it more widely and use it to become more effective. But this kind of preservation and transmission is actually quite difficult in the anti-authoritarian current. Reflecting on the occupy movement with which he was intimately involved, anarchist scholar and activist David Graeber notes, "In the U.S. at least, there was a real problem with passing on the wisdom of past generations."[7] Many have observed this about anti-authoritarian-influenced movements. The unfortunate outcome of this problem is, as Helen Hudson put it, "a reinvention of the wheel, where people continue to repeat the same mistakes because they are not aware that something has already been tried and failed (or that it succeeded before because of a particular circumstance that is no longer in place)." Without access to previous experiences, anti-authoritarians tend to come back to the same issues over and over again. Many of the topics featured in this book (prefigurative praxis, strategy, organizing, leadership) are examples of this.

So, what causes this problem? Without a doubt, the biggest cause is ruling relations and institutions that systematically cut us off from movement histories. This happens in many ways, including "the social organization of forgetting" I discussed in chapter 1 and, as Oakland-based Critical Resistance organizer Rachel Herzing argued, the imprisonment or murder of many of the most dedicated revolutionaries of previous generations. Moreover, the neoliberal assault of the last few decades has created a political climate in which movements are on the defensive, reacting to attacks and often losing. This, numerous organizers pointed out to me, strongly conditions a rhythm of crisis in which it is very challenging to distill and hold onto lessons, much less pass them on.

Those of us in the anti-authoritarian current also bear some responsibility for this problem. As I suggested in chapter 4, we frequently allow ourselves to get absorbed in crisis mode organizing with all of its accompanying difficulties. We also still have a long way to go toward creating a movement culture in which people can stick around as they grow older and, particularly, as they have children. In anarchist-influenced activist scenes especially, people tend to "age out" by their thirties, if not earlier. Our difficulty with leadership compounds these dynamics, as Vancouver migrant justice organizer Harsha Walia highlighted: "Since leadership is a divisive concept within much of the anti-authoritarian left, there tends to be an unspoken consensus that each generation of activists has to make their own mistakes. This usually manifests as older activists not wanting to intervene and younger activists not wanting to be talked at." Sometimes this is justified, particularly given the tendency for those who are older to use their experience to push their own agendas. Often, though, it's unnecessary and counterproductive.

In the face of this problem, San Francisco organizer David Solnit posed the important question: "How do we get smarter and do it better?" How can we accumulate and share knowledge in ways that build from one movement experience to the next? One helpful answer Solnit offered is developing "humble continuity"—a practice of carrying lessons and challenges between movements. This, he said, "requires some gracefulness of those of us . . . who've been around for a while to figure out how to work with newer movements—sometimes it's younger people, but sometimes it's just newer activists—and do it gracefully—where you're not dictating, you're respecting, you're leaving space for innovation." While individuals can take up this approach, it can also be built into training and political education programs in which older organizers are invited to share history and reflections, and learn from the experiences and ideas of younger people. In addition, Solnit emphasized, "We need to be militant about skills-, experience-, and information-sharing." This leads toward the leadership development practices I discussed in chapter 7. When we explicitly identify leadership activities and acknowledge differences in people's capacities (including those based on organizing experience), we can begin to develop structures to collect and pass on knowledge as part of growing more leaders.

All of this is much easier to do within movement-oriented organizations and institutions that have some longevity. Michelle O'Brien, an HIV/AIDS and housing organizer in New York, stressed this point: "We need mechanisms for collectively sorting through lessons when we learn them; making collective changes in our practice that go beyond individual, voluntary shifts; and then having a reasonable level of discipline to hold each other to those shifts." We also need mechanisms for preserving knowledge beyond the inherent limitations of individual memories, small-circulation activist magazines, and short-lived blogs. Informal groups and networks, for the most part, can't provide these kinds of mechanisms; they're too fleeting and fragmented. This is why we need more enduring structures, both within and between movements, that can enable us to sort through lessons and transmit them across cycles of struggle. Building such organizations and institutions will take time and work, but there is no reason that even more modest organizational efforts can't start generating useable resources—for instance, handbooks and training curricula—that can circulate knowledge much more widely. With these kinds of concrete activities and others that we have yet to imagine, we can get smarter and do it better.

ASKING QUESTIONS, MOVING FORWARD

At the beginning of this book, I introduced a Zapatista notion, "walking we ask questions." This formulation, central to another politics, names an approach that values acting and reflecting together in the process of fighting for another world. It is especially significant that this approach focuses on asking questions. This focus, in my understanding, comes out of an aspiration to avoid dogmatism—rigidity and righteousness in theory and practice. Asking questions unsettles: it provokes us to reconsider things we've taken for granted, face uncertainty and complexity in what we're doing, and grapple with questions for which we don't have easy—or perhaps any—answers. Helping us imagine outside of what we know, "walking we ask questions" is aimed at strengthening struggles for justice and dignity. Its method is inquiring, learning, and trying to improve. This is the approach I have attempted to take in writing this book. In this spirit, I conclude with six questions for those of us in the anti-authoritarian current to consider as we journey together:

1. How can anti-authoritarians foreground the interconnections among multiple forms of oppression while also making strategic choices about which fights we take up?[8] Resisting what is sometimes called a "hierarchy of oppressions" is central to the anti-racist feminist analysis that has so deeply influenced this current. But how should we develop priorities in on-the-ground struggle? Are there hierarchies in specific circumstances or do we need to take up completely new understandings of fights for liberation?

2. How can prefigurative praxis be intentional and yet avoid reinforcing insular activist communities?[9] It frequently feels much easier to "live the world we want" in self-selected subcultural

scenes than in broader communities that aren't built around shared values. But all the while, people outside movement circles are developing new ways of being, doing, and relating as they fight injustice, though they might not call this activity "prefigurative" or identify themselves as "activists." In what ways, then, can organizers root the development of new social relations organically in the world as it is and cultivate the already existing reconstructive dimensions of popular struggles?

3. How should the anti-authoritarian current relate to electoral politics? In general, our critical stance toward the state has meant that we steer clear of electoral campaigns. But is a complete disengagement from the voting booth viable when millions of people are energized through such campaigns, and when a denial of the vote has been a key means to sustain oppression and marginalization, particularly of prisoners, people of color, Indigenous people, and immigrants?[10] And if anti-authoritarians do participate in electoral fights, in what ways can we do this with integrity?

4. How can another politics foster visionary organizing approaches that are useful and meaningful to ordinary, nonactivist people? Many of the tools of anti-authoritarian organizing—egalitarian relationship-building, horizontal decision-making structures, popular education models, specific direct action tactics—are not immediately familiar to most people. How can we work with this challenge in a way that doesn't impose priorities and models but rather opens spaces for collectively creating new practices and visions grounded in people's day-to-day lives?

5. What kinds of organizations and institutions should the anti-authoritarian current build in order to further movements, consolidate gains, and lay infrastructure for a new society? Too often activists and organizers shy away from this question by relying on the models to which we're already accustomed. But while we can certainly draw on existing models, they aren't enough. So, what sorts of structures make sense in our present circumstances? What new forms can and should we develop? And how can we construct them to be resilient, self-managed, and self-funding?

6. How should anti-authoritarians relate to liberal, social democratic, Leninist, and other left political currents? We have important—

and, in many cases, longstanding—differences that can't be simply wished away. At the same time, sectarianism has been disastrous for the left, and has significantly contributed to its current weakness. How, then, can anti-authoritarians best avoid the often tempting sectarian impulse while also being clear about differences? And in what ways can another politics contribute to creating a lively, multi-tendency left that has a broad appeal and real power?

I think these are some of the most difficult questions that the anti-authoritarian current presently faces. And although I'd be happy to learn otherwise, I don't think anyone has well developed answers. I certainly don't. While there are some resources for formulating responses within another politics, these questions remain sites for ongoing work and call for fresh, nondogmatic thinking and practice. In order to resolve them, we will most certainly have to imagine ourselves outside of what we know.

We'll see if the anti-authoritarian current is up for this. I'm hopeful. Part of what distinguishes those of us developing another politics is our commitment to winning, not just expressing dissent or continually resisting. This is key. A commitment to winning forces activists and organizers to wrestle with hard questions even when no easy solutions or easy victories are within reach, to look beyond comfortable and customary political frameworks, and to avoid self-satisfied answers. Any prospects for viable revolutionary politics in the United States and Canada will require just this sort of relentless, open-ended reflection and practical experimentation.

What I've written in this book is one contribution, partial and tentative, to this collective project. It's not a final word, but a beginning.

Resources for Movement-Building

STARTING POINTS

Alfred, Taiaiake. *Wasáse: Indigenous Pathways of Action and Freedom.* Peterborough, ON: Broadview Press, 2005.

Davis, Angela. *Are Prisons Obsolete?* New York: Seven Stories Press, 2003.

Federici, Silvia. *Caliban and the Witch: Women, the Body, and Primitive Accumulation.* Brooklyn: Autonomedia, 2004.

hooks, bell. *Feminism Is for Everybody: Passionate Politics.* Cambridge, MA: South End Press, 2000.

Kaufman, Cynthia. *Ideas for Action: Relevant Theory for Radical Change.* Cambridge, MA: South End Press, 2003.

Kivel, Paul. *Uprooting Racism: How White People Can Work for Racial Justice.* Philadelphia: New Society Publishers, 1995.

Leondar-Wright, Betsy. *Class Matters: Cross-Class Alliance Building for Middle-Class Activists.* Gabriola Island, BC: New Society Publishers, 2005.

McNally, David. *Another World Is Possible: Globalization and Anti-Capitalism,* 2nd ed. Winnipeg: Arbeiter Ring, 2006.

———. *Global Slump: The Economics and Politics of Crisis and Resistance.* Oakland: PM Press, 2010.

Smith, Andrea. *Conquest: Sexual Violence and American Indian Genocide.* Cambridge, MA: South End Press, 2005.

Spade, Dean. *Normal Life: Administrative Violence, Critical Trans Politics, and the Limits of Law.* Brooklyn: South End Press, 2011.

Walia, Harsha. *Undoing Border Imperialism.* Oakland: AK Press, 2013.

Withers, A. J. *Disability Politics and Theory.* Halifax: Fernwood, 2012.

HANDBOOKS AND MANUALS

Bobo, Kim, Jackie Kendall, and Steve Max. *Organizing for Social Change: Midwest Academy Manual for Activists,* 3rd ed. Santa Ana, CA: Seven Locks Press, 2001.

Boyd, Andrew, and Dave Oswald Mitchell, eds. *Beautiful Trouble: A Toolbox for Revolution.* New York: OR Books, 2012.

Coover, Virginia, Ellen Deacon, Charles Esser, and Christopher Moore. *Resource Manual for a Living Revolution: A Handbook of Skills and Tools for Social Change Activists,* 4th ed. Philadelphia: New Society Publishers, 1985.

Prison Research Education Action Project and Critical Resistance. *Instead of Prisons: A Handbook for Abolitionists.* Oakland: AK Press, 2005.

Project South. *Popular Education for Movement Building: A Project South Resource Guide.* Atlanta: Project South, 2001.

Shields, Katrina. *In the Tiger's Mouth: An Empowerment Guide for Social Action.* Gabriola Island, BC: New Society Publishers, 1994.

Slaughter, Jane, ed. *A Troublemaker's Handbook 2: How to Fight Back Where You Work and Win!* Detroit: Labor Notes, 2005.

Starhawk, *The Empowerment Manual.* Gabriola Island, BC: New Society Publishers, 2011.

LEADERSHIP AND GROUP PROCESS

Butler, C.T., and Amy Rothstein. *On Conflict and Consensus: A Handbook on Formal Consensus Decisionmaking,* 2nd ed. Portland, ME: Food Not Bombs, 1991.

Freeman, Jo. "The Tyranny of Structurelessness." Available at www.jofreeman.com/joreen/tyranny.htm.

Kokopeli, Bruce, and George Lakey. *Leadership for Change: Toward a Feminist Model.* Philadelphia: New Society Publishers, 1984.

Polleta, Francesca. *Freedom is an Endless Meeting: Democracy in American Social Movements.* Chicago: University of Chicago Press, 2002.

Ransby, Barbara. *Ella Baker and the Black Freedom Movement: A Radical Vision.* Chapel Hill: University of North Carolina Press, 2003.

ORGANIZING AND ORGANIZATION

Choudry, Aziz, Jill Hanley, and Eric Shragge, eds. *Organize! Building from the Local for Global Justice.* Oakland: PM Press, 2012.

Cold B and T Barnacle. *Building a Solidarity Network Guide.* Available at http://libcom.org/library/you-say-you-want-build-solidarity-network.

Crass, Chris. *Towards Collective Liberation: Anti-Racist Organizing, Feminist Praxis, and Movement Building Strategy.* Oakland: PM Press, 2013.

Fisher, Robert. *Let the People Decide: Neighborhood Organizing in America,* 2nd ed. New York: Twayne Publishers, 1994.

Glick, Brian. *War at Home: Covert Action Against U.S. Activists and What We Can Do About It.* Boston: South End Press, 1989.

Horton, Myles, and Paulo Freire. *We Make the Road by Walking: Conversations on Education and Social Change.* Philadelphia: Temple University Press, 1990.

INCITE! Women of Color Against Violence, ed. *The Revolution Will Not Be Funded: Beyond the Non-Profit Industrial Complex.* Cambridge, MA: South End Press, 2007.

Mann, Eric. *Playbook for Progressives: 16 Qualities of the Successful Organizer.* Boston: Beacon Press, 2011.

Moore, Hilary, and Joshua Kahn Russell. *Organizing Cools the Planet: Tools and Reflections to Navigate the Climate Crisis.* Oakland: PM Press, 2011.

Payne, Charles. *I've Got the Light of Freedom: The Organizing Tradition and the Mississippi Freedom Struggle.* Berkeley: University of California Press, 1996.

We Are Oregon. *Economic Emergency Kit: Building Power and Winning Change in Your Community.* Available at http://economicemergencykit.com.

PREFIGURATIVE PRAXIS AND COUNTERPOWER

Another Politics Is Possible and Communities Organizing Liberation. *So That We May Soar: Horizontalism, Intersectionality, and Prefigurative Politics.* Available at http://zinelibrary.info/so-we-may-soar-horizontalism-intersectionality-and-prefigurative-politics.

Chen, Ching-In, Jai Dulani, and Leah Lakshmi Piepzna-Samarasinha, eds. *The Revolution Starts at Home: Confronting Intimate Violence within Activist Communities.* Brooklyn: South End Press, 2011.

Cornell, Andrew. *Oppose and Propose! Lessons from Movement for a New Society.* Oakland: AK Press, 2011.

Creative Interventions. *Creative Interventions Toolkit: A Practical Guide to Stop Interpersonal Violence.* Available at www.creative-interventions.org/tools/toolkit.

Generation Five. *Towards Transformative Justice.* Available at www.generation-five.org/resources/transformative-justice-documents.

Law, Victoria, and China Martens, eds. *Don't Leave Your Friends Behind: Concrete Ways to Support Families in Social Justice Movements and Communities.* Oakland: PM Press, 2012.

Rose City Copwatch. *Alternatives to Police.* Available at http://rosecitycopwatch.wordpress.com/alternatives-to-police.

Sitrin, Marina. *Everyday Revolutions: Horizontalism and Autonomy in Argentina.* London: Zed Books, 2012.

STRATEGY AND VISION

Albert, Michael. *The Trajectory of Change.* Cambridge, MA: South End Press, 2002.

Allison, Aimee, and David Solnit. *Army of None: Strategies to Counter Military Recruitment, End War, and Build a Better World.* New York: Seven Stories Press, 2007.

Kelley, Robin. *Freedom Dreams: The Black Radical Imagination.* Boston: Beacon Press, 2002.

Lakey, George. "Strategizing for a Living Revolution." In *Globalize Liberation: How to Uproot the System and Build a Better World,* edited by David Solnit, 135–160. San Francisco: City Lights Books, 2004.

Reinsborough, Patrick, and Doyle Canning. *Re:Imagining Change—How to Use Story-based Strategy to Win Campaigns, Build Movements, and Change the World.* Oakland: PM Press, 2010.

WEBSITES

Beyond the Choir: www.beyondthechoir.org

Buildthewheel.org: www.buildthewheel.org

Center for Story-Based Strategy: www.storybasedstrategy.org

Joshua Kahn Russell's Resources for Organizers: http://joshuakahnrussell.wordpress.com/resources-for-activists-and-organizers

Ruckus Society: www.ruckus.org

School of Unity and Liberation: www.schoolofunityandliberation.org

Training for Change: www.trainingforchange.org

Organizations and Projects Mentioned

The Abolitionist: https://abolitionistpaper.wordpress.com
Al-Awda, the Palestine Right to Return Coalition: http://al-awda.org
Anarchists Against the Wall: http://awalls.org
Arab Resource and Organizing Center: http://araborganizing.org
Association pour une solidarité syndicale étudiante: http://www.asse-solidarite.
    qc.ca
Black Orchid Collective: http://blackorchidcollective.wordpress.com
Bloquez l'empire / Block the Empire: http://blocktheempire.blogspot.ca
Boycotts, Divestment, Sanctions: www.bdsmovement.net
Bring the Ruckus: http://bringtheruckus.org
Californians United for a Responsible Budget: http://curbprisonspending.org
Canadian Union of Postal Workers: www.cupw.ca
Catalyst Project: http://collectiveliberation.org
Coalition Against Israeli Apartheid: www.caiaweb.org
Coalition of Immokalee Workers: www.ciw-online.org
Colours of Resistance: www.coloursofresistance.org
Common Cause: www.linchpin.ca
Common Ground Collective: www.commongroundrelief.org
Common Struggle: commonstruggle.org
Courage to Resist: www.couragetoresist.org
Critical Resistance: http://criticalresistance.org
Decarcerate PA: http://decarceratepa.info
Direct Action to Stop the War: https://bayareadirectaction.wordpress.com
El Kilombo Intergaláctico: www.elkilombo.org
End the Prison Industrial Complex: http://epic.noblogs.org
Experimental Community Education of the Twin Cities: www.excotc.org
First of May Anarchist Alliance: http://m1aa.org
Food Not Bombs: www.foodnotbombs.net
Heads Up Collective: http://collectiveliberation.org/resources/heads-up-
    collective

Idle No More: http://idlenomore.ca

INCITE! Women of Color Against Violence: http://incite-national.org

Indigenous Peoples Solidarity Movement: http://ipsm.ca

Industrial Workers of the World: www.iww.org

Institute for Anarchist Studies: www.anarchist-studies.org

International Jewish Anti-Zionist Network: www.ijsn.net

International Solidarity Movement: http://palsolidarity.org

Iraq Veterans Against the War: www.ivaw.org

LA Garment Workers Center: http://garmentworkercenter.org

Left Turn: www.leftturn.org

Make/Shift: www.makeshiftmag.com

Miami Autonomy and Solidarity: http://miamiautonomyandsolidarity.word-press.com

Montréal-Nord Républik: http://montrealnordrepublik.blogspot.ca

Mujeres Unidas Y Activas: www.mujeresunidas.net

No One Is Illegal: www.nooneisillegal.org

Occupy Our Homes: http://occupyourhomes.org

Occupy Sandy: www.occupysandy.org

Ontario Coalition Against Poverty: www.ocap.ca

Organization for a Free Society: www.afreesociety.org

Peoples' Global Action: www.nadir.org/nadir/initiativ/agp

Pittsburgh Organizing Group: www.steelcityrevolt.org

Project South: www.projectsouth.org

Public Interest Research Groups (Canada): www.pirg.ca

Purple Thistle Centre: www.purplethistle.ca

Queers for Economic Justice: www.q4ej.org

Queers Undermining Israeli Terrorism: http://quitpalestine.org

Regeneración Childcare: http://childcarenyc.org

Repeal Coalition: www.repealcoalition.org

Rising Tide North America: www.risingtidenorthamerica.org

Rock Dove Collective: www.rockdovecollective.org

San Francisco Community Land Trust: www.sfclt.org

Seattle Solidarity Network: www.seattlesolidarity.net

Solidarity Across Borders: www.solidarityacrossborders.org

Solidarity and Defense: http://solidarityanddefense.blogspot.com

Strike Debt: http://strikedebt.org

Students for a Democratic Society (new): www.newsds.org

Student/Farmworker Alliance: www.sfalliance.org

Sudbury Coalition Against Poverty: http://sudburycap.com

Sylvia Rivera Law Project: http://srlp.org

Tadamon!: www.tadamon.ca

Take Back the Land: www.takebacktheland.org

2640: www.redemmas.org/2640

United Students Against Sweatshops: http://usas.org

Upping the Anti: http://uppingtheanti.org
War Resisters Support Campaign: www.resisters.ca
Women's Health and Justice Initiative: www.whji.org
Workers Solidarity Alliance: http://workersolidarity.org
Young Workers United: www.youngworkersunited.org

Biographies of Interviewees

Sarita Ahooja is a grassroots anti-capitalist organizer in Montreal. Over the past two decades she has been active in self-determination liberation struggles including Indigenous solidarity, anti-police brutality, and migrant justice movements. She is a founding member of La convergence des luttes anti-capitalistes, No One is Illegal-Montreal, and Solidarity Across Borders.

Ashanti Alston is an anarchist activist, speaker, writer, former member of the Black Panther Party (BPP) and the Black Liberation Army (BLA), and former political prisoner. He joined the BPP while still in high school, starting a chapter in Plainfield, New Jersey, and later going underground with the BLA. In 1974, he was involved in a Connecticut "bank expropriation," and was captured and imprisoned for more than twelve years. Ashanti has worked as an organizer with Estacion Libre to support the Zapatistas, Critical Resistance, and the Malcolm X Grassroots Movement. Today, he is active in the National Jericho Movement and Anarchist People of Color organizing. He lives with his wife Viviane Saleh-Hanna and two children, Biko and Yasmeen, in Providence, Rhode Island.

Clare Bayard was raised in a military family and came up in queer and feminist activism as a teenager. Clare got involved in anarchist organizing in the late 1990s, working locally on issues of homelessness and displacement, and internationally against war and global capitalism. Through the Catalyst Project, the War Resisters League, and the War Resisters International network, Clare organizes for demilitarization and racial justice, with a particular focus on migrant justice, Palestine self-determination, and G.I. resistance.

Jill Chettiar spent many of her formative years working as an organizer in Vancouver. She is currently working in public health research, parenting two young daughters, and going to school full time.

Rosana Cruz is the associate director of V.O.T.E., a grassroots membership-based organization of formerly incarcerated persons that builds political and economic power with the people most impacted by the criminal justice system in New Orleans. Previously, Rosana worked for a diverse range of community organizations, including Safe Streets/Strong Communities, the National Immigration Law Center, the New Orleans Worker Center for Racial Justice, Hispanic Apostolate, the Lesbian and Gay Community Center of New Orleans, People's Youth Freedom School, and the Southern Regional Office of Amnesty International in Atlanta.

MIKE D is an organizer with the Ontario Coalition Against Poverty in Toronto.

RAYAN EL-AMINE is a former editor and founding member of *Left Turn Magazine* and a former San Francisco Bay Area Arab community organizer. He currently resides in Lebanon, where he works at American University of Beirut and teaches at Lebanese American University.

FRANCESCA FIORENTINI is an independent journalist and comedian based in Argentina. A former coeditor of *Left Turn Magazine* and *WIN*, the magazine of the War Resisters League, she is presently a regular contributor and member of the online anti-militarist publication *War Times*. She is also the creator of the YouTube comedy vlog *Laugh to Not Cry*.

MARY FOSTER is a community organizer in Montreal who has worked with initiatives such as Block the Empire, Iraq Solidarity Project, Solidarity Across Borders, Tadamon!, and the People's Commission Network.

HARJIT SINGH GILL is a South Asian American activist living in Oakland and a board member of the Institute for Anarchist Studies. He holds advanced degrees in humanities and social work. His work focuses on providing clinical support for low-income people in the Bay Area and is informed by a commitment to anti-imperialist, feminist, and queer-positive perspectives toward collective liberation. Harjit is a Unitarian Universalist, and is deeply committed to a vegan and straight-edge lifestyle.

TATIANA GOMEZ has been active on labor and migration issues for over ten years. Currently, she is a community-based lawyer in Montreal.

HARJAP GREWAL organizes in Vancouver, Coast Salish Territories, working within movements against immigration controls, in solidarity with Indigenous struggles, for environmental justice, and to promote anti-capitalist resistance. While he has been a part of various spaces and communities, his work has predominantly been with the No One Is Illegal-Vancouver collective.

STEPHANIE GUILLOUD is the codirector at Project South: Institute for the Elimination of Poverty and Genocide, based in Atlanta, Georgia. An organizer with over seventeen years of experience, Stephanie was a lead local organizer in the Seattle World Trade Organization shutdown in 1999 and edited and designed *Voices from the WTO*, an anthology of first-hand narratives from the participants in the historic demonstrations. Her essays have been published in *Letters from Young Activists* (Nation Books) and *The Revolution Will Not be Funded* (South End Press). Since 2005, she has served on the board of Southerners On

New Ground (SONG), a multiracial queer organization building power for racial and economic justice.

RACHEL HERZING is a member of Critical Resistance, a national grassroots organization dedicated to abolishing the prison industrial complex.

HELEN HUDSON is a queer Black anti-authoritarian organizer living in Montreal. For close to two decades, she has been actively involved in immigration struggles; prisoner justice; queer, trans, and feminist struggles; and student organizing. She spent four years working as the coordinator of QPIRG Concordia, an activist resource center at Concordia University that serves as a central hub for student and community activists in Montreal. A former board member of the Institute for Anarchist Studies, Helen currently is a member of the Montreal Anarchist Bookfair collective and the Certain Days: Freedom for Political Prisoner Calendar collective. She is also a mother and a nurse.

PAULINE HWANG was active in youth, immigrant, worker, tenant, and Indigenous solidarity organizing for many years. She has more recently focused on meditation, traditional Chinese medicine, and creativity. Pauline intends to bridge radical organizing with personal and community healing, and be part of a revolution that connects us back to our bodies, our ancestors, the Earth, and each other.

RAHULA JANOWSKI grew up white and working class in a rural New England community. She came of age politically in the 1990s in the West Coast anarchist community/movement. She lives in queer, radical left community in San Francisco, where she engages in political work including taking arrest at direct actions against war, supporting the development of younger white anti-racist activists and organizers, Palestine solidarity work, and organizing with other parents (most of whom know she is an anarchist) in her child's school.

TYNAN JARRETT is a Montreal-based community organizer and activist. His work has revolved primarily around queer and trans youth, and political prisoners. Some projects he has been involved in include the Trans Health Network, a coalition of groups working for better access to health care services for transgender, transsexual, and gender-variant people in Montreal and Quebec, and the Certain Days: Freedom for Political Prisoners Calendar.

SHARMEEN KHAN became an activist with socialist and activist media organizations in Regina, Saskatchewan. She has organized in women's centers, transit justice organizations, and community radio stations in Victoria and Vancouver. She moved to Toronto in 2005 where she finished a masters degree in communication and culture and worked in community radio and the PIRG circuit. She currently works at CUPE 3903, is on the board of the Media Co-op, and edits *Upping the Anti: A Journal of Theory and Action.*

BROOKE LEHMAN has been active as an educator and organizer in New York City since the mid-1980s. She was a founding member of the Direct Action Network and of Bluestockings Bookstore. Brooke is currently the codirector of

246 / Biographies of Interviewees

the Watershed Center, an educational center in upstate New York, where she leads seminars and retreats on designing healthy democratic organizations. She also serves as a faculty member of the Institute for Social Ecology, and as a board member for smartMeme and the Yansa Foundation.

RJ MACCANI, based in New York City, has played many different roles in the struggle for a better world over the past fifteen years. As a cofounder and organizer with the Challenging Male Supremacy Project and a leadership team member for generationFIVE, his work focuses on building transformative justice responses to violence against women, queer and trans people, and children. RJ is a generative somatics practitioner and pays the bills as coleader and community programs producer for the Foundry Theatre.

ANDRÉA MARIA began organizing with Montreal's Anti-Capitalist Convergence more than a decade ago, then worked as an ally to migrant justice struggles with No One Is Illegal-Montreal. Since then, she has worked with a range of anti-authoritarian collectives, international solidarity projects, and anti-poverty organizations in both Montreal and Toronto. Now a journalist, she continues to be student of resistance movements, learning about politics, strategy, and tactics from many angles and many sides.

PILAR MASCHI is a survivor, former prisoner, mother, anarchist, and prison industrial complex abolitionist. Formerly the national membership and leadership development director of Critical Resistance, Pilar is currently a member of All of Us or None and Anarchist People of Color. She is also an alumna of the New Voices fellowship program and a founding member of Community in Unity. She lives in New York City.

SONYA Z. MEHTA is a recent graduate of the City University of New York School of Law. She was first an organizer, then codirector, at Young Workers United San Francisco, a workers' center of young and immigrant service-sector workers and students. YWU passed the first paid sick leave law in the country, improved conditions at work, won $4.5 million in backpay for employment law violations, and built community solidarity and leadership.

AMY MILLER is a media maker and social justice organizer based in Montreal. She directed the featurette documentary *Myths for Profit: Canada's Role in Industries of War and Peace,* which was screened extensively across Canada and at festivals. She has worked with *The Dominion* and the Media Co-op as both a writer and editor. She continues to focus on developing critical documentaries for transformative social change.

RAFAEL A. MUTIS GARCIA is an immigrant from Colombia living in the United States. He has worked in community and academic settings across the United States in defense of poor communities of color, immigrant communities, women, and LGBTQ folks, as well as in Nicaragua, Mexico, Colombia, the Dominican Republic, and Haiti. A popular educator between 1994–2006 in the Escuela Popular Norteña, an organizer with Critical Resistance NYC between

2003–2008, and with Anarchist People of Color since 2003, currently Rafael does food justice work through the Morning Glory Garden in the Bronx. He is completing a doctorate in earth and environmental sciences focusing on geography at the CUNY Graduate Center. His research is an ethnobotany project with Afro and Indigenous communities in Colombia.

MICHELLE O'BRIEN is an organizer and scholar living in Brooklyn. Much of her fifteen years of social justice activism has been within the U.S. communities hardest hit by HIV and AIDS. She writes on revolutionary strategy, the politics of social services, and the nonprofit industrial complex. Currently, Michelle organizes with Power for Rank and File Employees in the Social Services, a project to support union struggles at New York City's nonprofit social service agencies. She is a graduate student in sociology at New York University.

ADRIANA PAZ is a Bolivian born and raised community organizer, social researcher and popular educator with over ten years of experience working on social justice, labor and (im)migrant rights. She has a background as a community radio broadcaster, columnist for Latin American newspapers, and contributor to online magazines in Canada. Adriana is founding member and organizer of Justicia for Migrant Workers in B.C., a grassroots national organization advocating for migrant farm workers' social, economic, and labor rights. She has participated in research studies and written about migrant farmworkers on the borders of Bolivia/Argentina, Mexico, and Canada. She just completed her masters degree at the University of British Columbia, focusing on transnational labor migration and transnational organizing models for migrant farmworkers in North America.

LYDIA PELOT-HOBBS is a facilitator, organizer, writer, and activist-scholar living between New York City and New Orleans. She was originally politicized through the Unitarian Universalist youth movement as a teenager. Over the past ten years, Lydia has been involved in organizing against prisons and policing, supporting affordable housing struggles in New Orleans, and strengthening solidarity economies. She is also a cofounder of the Anti-Oppression Resource and Training Alliance (AORTA).

LEILA POURTAVAF has organized with a number of Montreal-based migrant justice and radical queer groups including No One Is Illegal, Solidarity Across Borders, the Anti-Capitalist Asspirates, and Qteam. She is currently pursuing a doctorate in history at the University of Toronto.

PAULA XIMENA ROJAS-URRUTIA has twenty-one years of experience working as a community organizer. Born in Chile and raised in Houston, she spent thirteen years as an organizer in Brooklyn. Her experiences working for social justice nonprofit organizations led her to cofound various community organizations focused on issues affecting young and adult women of color, including Sista II Sista, Pachamama, and Community Birthing Project. Paula's organizing work and life experience have drawn her to work at the intersections of welfare injustice and women of color, midwifery and local grassroots organizing. In addition, she has supported and amplified local work, as a national board member and trainer for INCITE! She is currently living in Austin, Tejas, continuing to work collectively with other women of color to model a more just and loving world. She is a doula, apprentice midwife, self-defense teacher, mother of two, and an advisor to Mamas of Color Rising.

JOSHUA KAHN RUSSELL is an organizer working to bridge movements for ecological balance and racial justice. He is a strategy, organizing, and nonviolent direct action trainer with the Ruckus Society, and coauthor of *Organizing Cools the Planet* (PM Press). You can keep up with him at www.praxismakesperfect.org.

SOPHIE SCHOEN is a community organizer based in Montreal. She was an active member of Association pour une solidarité syndicale étudiante from 2003 to 2008.

MAC SCOTT is an anarchist who does legal work in Toronto (go figure). He is also a member of the Ontario Coalition Against Poverty and No One Is Illegal-Toronto. When he's not fighting against the man, he enjoys his collective house, his family, beer, and bad suits, not necessarily in that order.

JAGGI SINGH is a community organizer and anarchist based in Montreal whose work focuses on indigenous solidarity, migrant justice and anti-capitalist struggles, as well as community-based popular education. He has helped to initiate and continues to be active with several local campaigns, initiatives, and groups, including the Anti-Capitalist Convergence, No One Is Illegal, Solidarity Across Borders, the Indigenous Solidarity Committee, and the Montreal Anarchist Bookfair.

DAVID SOLNIT has been a mass direct action organizer for over three decades in global justice, anti-war, environmental justice, climate justice, and solidarity movements in North America, including the mass direct action shutdowns of the Seattle WTO in 1999 and the San Francisco Financial District on March 30, 2003, the day after the United States invaded Iraq. He is a trainer, an arts organizer, a puppeteer, and editor/coauthor of *Globalize Liberation* (City Lights), *Army of None* (Seven Stories), and *The Battle of the Story of the Battle of Seattle* (AK Press). He lives in San Francisco.

MICK SWEETMAN is the managing editor of *The Dialog* newspaper at George Brown College and a labor and community journalist. His articles and photos have also been published in Alternet, *Basics, Canadian Dimension, Clamor, Industrial Worker, Linchpin,* Media Co-op, rabble.ca, and ZNet. He calls Toronto home and is unabashedly a supporter of Toronto FC.

JAMES TRACY is the coauthor of *Hillbilly Nationalists, Urban Race Rebels, and Black Power: Community Organizing in Radical Times* (Melville House Publishers). Based in San Francisco, he is a longtime organizer active in housing and economic justice work.

HARSHA WALIA is a South Asian activist and writer currently based in Vancouver, Coast Salish Territories. For the past decade she has been active in migrant justice, anti-racist, feminist, Palestine solidarity, Indigenous sovereignty, anti-capitalist, anti-imperialist, and anti-poverty movements. She is involved in No One Is Illegal, Radical Desis, Defenders of the Land, Women's Committee for Missing and Murdered Women, and works as a frontline anti-violence worker and legal advocate in Vancouver's Downtown Eastside. She is also a writer, with work in numerous publications and anthologies. Her most recent book is *Undoing Border Imperialism* (AK Press).

MARIKA WARNER is a black/mixed race actor, writer, and anarchist based in Toronto. She has been active with anti-capitalist, anti-racist, and anti-poverty organizations in Winnipeg, Edmonton, and Toronto. Most of her organizing work has focused on violence against women and prison abolition.

JENNIFER WHITNEY has been a healthcare worker and organizer in New Orleans, since the levees broke and flooded the city in 2005. Prior to that, she worked with global justice coalitions in Seattle, Prague, Quebec City, Cancun, Edinburgh, Mexico City, and elsewhere to disrupt summit meetings of transnational power brokers, and also to help bring about effective, creative alternatives. She is a coauthor of *We Are Everywhere*, has published extensively on Latin American social movements, and continues to write about and work at the intersection of health, justice, art, dignity, ecology, and liberation.

ORA WISE cofounded the Palestine Education Project and coproduced *Slingshot Hip Hop*, a grassroots documentary about hip-hop in Palestine which premiered at the Sundance Film Festival in January 2008. Ora is the youth education director at an independent synagogue in Brooklyn and is the curriculum specialist for Detroit Future Media, an intensive program that trains people to use media for a more just, creative, and collaborative city. Ora maintains thebigceci.wordpress.com, a space dedicated to elevating our consciousness about what we eat by sharing stories and resources, supporting the creation of alternatives to the industrial food system, and indulging in the sensuality and wisdom of the culinary arts.

Notes

Epigraph: Max Uhlenbeck, "A Light Within," *Left Turn*, August 2007, 10.

1. To be clear, I don't believe this is primarily a matter of people in the anti-authoritarian current coming up with terms that are perfectly descriptive. Rather, it's one of clarifying shared politics and developing a common vocabulary to describe them.

2. The delegation brought more than one hundred New York-based organizers, and the workshop track pulled together fifteen organizations from across the United States, around shared political principles. The participating organizations were Catalyst Project, Center for Immigrant Families, Coalition of Immokalee Workers, Harm Free Zone, INCITE!, Kitchen Table Collective, LA Garment Workers Center, *Left Turn* magazine, Pachamama, Refugio, Regeneración Childcare, Sista II Sista, Sisterfire, and Student/Farmworker Alliance. For descriptions of the delegation and track, see Jeffrey Juris, "Spaces of Intentionality: Race, Class, and Horizontality at the United States Social Forum," in *Insurgent Encounters: Transnational Activism, Ethnography, and the Political*, ed. Jeffrey Juris and Alex Khasnabish (Durham: Duke University Press, 2013), 58–59; and RJ Maccani, "Another Politics Is Possible!" *Zapagringo* (blog), June 25, 2007. These initiatives were also connected to a study group in New York City. For some writing from this group, see Another Politics is Possible and Communities Organizing Liberation, *So That We May Soar: Horizontalism, Intersectionality, and Prefigurative Politics* (zine, New York and Los Angeles, 2010); Dan Berger and Chris Dixon, eds. "Navigating the Crisis: A Study Groups Roundtable," *Upping the Anti* 8 (2009): 159–77.

3. For more on the Other Campaign, see Zapatista Army of National Liberation, "Sixth Declaration of the Selva Lacandona." *Enlace Zapatista*, June 2005. For an excellent introduction, see RJ Maccani, "From Below and to the Left: Zapatistas and the Other Campaign." *Left Turn*, June 2006.

4. In large part, these themes come out of ongoing discussions within the anti-authoritarian current. The shared principles formulated by the APP

delegation and workshop track have especially influenced my thinking. For these, see Maccani, "Another Politics Is Possible!"

5. See John Holloway, *Change the World Without Taking Power*, 2nd ed. (London: Pluto, 2005), 216–245.

6. Stephanie Guilloud, "Spark, Fire, and Burning Coals: An Organizer's History of Seattle," in *The Battle of Seattle: The New Challenge to Capitalist Globalization*, ed. Eddie Yuen, George Katsiaficas, and Daniel Burton Rose (New York: Soft Skull Press, 2001), 228.

7. Elizabeth Martinez, "Where Was the Color in Seattle? Looking for Reasons Why the Great Battle Was so White," *ColorLines* 3, no. 1 (2000): 11–12.

8. The materials that COR collected and generated are available at www.coloursofresistance.org.

9. Robin Kelley, *Freedom Dreams: The Black Radical Imagination* (Boston: Beacon Press, 2002), 8.

10. Barbara Epstein, *Political Protest and Cultural Revolution: Nonviolent Direct Action in the 1970s and 1980s* (Berkeley: University of California Press, 1991), 20.

11. I have learned especially from Dan Berger, *Outlaws of America: The Weather Underground and the Politics of Solidarity* (Oakland: AK Press, 2006); Andrew Cornell, *Oppose and Propose! Lessons from Movement for a New Society* (Oakland: AK Press, 2011); Chris Crass, *Towards Collective Liberation: Anti-Racist Organizing, Feminist Praxis, and Movement Building Strategy* (Oakland: PM Press, 2013); Alice Echols, *Daring to Be Bad: Radical Feminism in America 1967–1975* (Minneapolis: University of Minnesota Press, 1989); Max Elbaum, *Revolution in the Air: Sixties Radicals Turn to Lenin, Mao and Che* (London: Verso, 2002); Epstein, *Political Protest and Cultural Revolution;* Caelie Frampton, Gary Kinsman, AK Thompson, and Kate Tilleczek, eds., *Sociology for Changing the World: Social Movements/Social Research* (Halifax: Fernwood Publishing, 2006); James Green, *Taking History to Heart: The Power of the Past in Building Social Movements* (Amherst: University of Massachusetts Press, 2000); George Katsiaficas, *The Subversion of Politics: European Autonomous Social Movements and the Decolonization of Everyday Life* (New Jersey: Humanities Press, 1997); Robin Kelley, *Hammer and Hoe: Alabama Communists During the Great Depression* (Chapel Hill: University of North Carolina Press, 1990); Alex Khasnabish, *Zapatismo Beyond Borders: New Imaginations of Political Possibility* (Toronto: University of Toronto Press, 2008); George Lipsitz, *A Life in the Struggle: Ivory Perry and the Culture of Opposition*, 2nd ed. (Philadelphia: Temple University Press, 1995); Ian McKay, *Rebels, Red, Radicals: Rethinking Canada's Left History* (Toronto: Between the Lines, 2005); Scott Neigh, *Gender and Sexuality: Canadian History Through the Stories of Activists* (Black Point, NS: Fernwood Publishing, 2012); Frances Fox Piven and Richard Cloward, *Poor People's Movements: Why They Succeed, How They Fail* (New York: Vintage Books, 1977); Francesca Polletta, *Freedom Is an Endless Meeting: Democracy in American Social*

Movements (Chicago: University of Chicago Press, 2002); Judy Rebick, *Ten Thousand Roses: The Making of a Feminist Revolution* (Toronto: Penguin, 2005); Stevphen Shukaitis, David Graeber, and Erika Biddle, eds., *Constituent Imagination: Militant Investigations, Collective Theorization* (Oakland: AK Press, 2007); Marina Sitrin, *Horizontalism: Voices of Popular Power in Argentina* (Oakland: AK Press, 2006); Michael Staudenmaier, *Truth and Revolution: A History of the Sojourner Truth Organization, 1969–1986* (Oakland: AK Press, 2012); Team Colors Collective, *Wind(s) from Below: Radical Community Organizing to Make a Revolution Possible* (Portland, OR: Eberhardt Press, 2010); Becky Thompson, *A Promise and a Way of Life: White Antiracist Activism* (Minneapolis: University of Minnesota Press, 2001); Emily Thuma, "'Not a Wedge, But a Bridge': Prisons, Feminist Activism, and the Politics of Gendered Violence, 1968–1987" (PhD dissertation, New York University, 2010).

12. For more on movement-generated theory, see Douglas Bevington and Chris Dixon, "Movement-Relevant Theory: Rethinking Social Movement Scholarship and Activism," *Social Movement Studies* 4, no. 3 (2005): 193–97. See also Aziz Choudry and Dip Kapoor, eds., *Learning From the Ground Up: Global Perspectives on Social Movements and Knowledge Production* (New York: Palgrave Macmillan, 2010).

13. This notion comes from Michel Foucault, *Discipline and Punish: The Birth of the Prison*, trans. Alan Sheridan (New York: Vintage Books, 1977), 31.

14. See, in particular, the work of the Research Group on Collective Autonomy / Collectif de recherche sur l'autonomie collective, some of which is available online at www.crac-kebec.org. For one of their articles in English, see Émilie Breton, Sandra Jeppesen, Anna Kruzynski, and Rachel Sarrasin, "Prefigurative Self-Governance and Self-Organization: The Influence of Antiauthoritarian (Pro)Feminist, Radical Queer, and Antiracist Networks in Quebec," in *Organize! Building from the Local for Global Justice*, ed. Aziz Choudry, Jill Hanley, and Eric Shragge (Oakland: PM Press, 2012), 156–73.

15. Charles Payne, *I've Got the Light of Freedom: The Organizing Tradition and the Mississippi Freedom Struggle* (Berkeley: University of California Press, 1996), 68.

1. "FIGHTING AGAINST AMNESIA"

Epigraph: Gary Kinsman and Patrizia Gentile, *The Canadian War on Queers: National Security as Sexual Regulation* (Vancouver: UBC Press, 2010), 21.

1. See, for instance, David Graeber, "The New Anarchists," *New Left Review* 13 (2002): 61–73; David Solnit, "The New Radicalism: Uprooting the System and Building a Better World," in *Globalize Liberation: How to Uproot the System and Build a Better World*, ed. David Solnit (San Francisco: City Lights, 2004), xi–xxiv.

2. My approach here is influenced by Luke Cole and Sheila Foster, *From the Ground Up: Environmental Racism and the Rise of the Environmental Justice Movement* (New York: New York University Press, 2001), 19.

3. For introductory histories of Indigenous struggles in North America, see Gord Hill, *500 Years of Indigenous Resistance* (Oakland: PM Press, 2009); Peter Kulchyski, *The Red Indians: An Episodic, Informal Collection of Tales from the History of Aboriginal People's Struggles in Canada* (Winnipeg: Arbeiter Ring, 2007).

4. On contemporary forms of Indigenous social organization in opposition to the state, see Taiaiake Alfred, *Wasáse: Indigenous Pathways of Action and Freedom* (Peterborough, ON: Broadview Press, 2005); Ward Churchill, "Indigenism, Anarchism, and the State," *Upping the Anti* 1, no. 1 (2005): 30–40; Glen Coulthard, "Beyond Recognition: Indigenous Self-Determination as Prefigurative Practice," in *Lighting the Eighth Fire: The Liberation, Resurgence, and Protection of Indigenous Nations,* ed Leanne Simpson (Winnipeg: Arbeiter Ring, 2008), 187–203; Andrea Smith, "Against the Law: Indigenous Feminism and the Nation-State," *Affinities: A Journal of Radical Theory, Culture, and Action* 5, no. 1 (2011): 56–69.

5. For histories of the abolitionist movement, see Herbert Aptheker, *Abolitionism: A Revolutionary Movement* (Boston: Twayne Publishers, 1989); Fergus Bordewich, *Bound for Canaan: The Underground Railroad and the War for the Soul of America* (New York: Amistad, 2005).

6. On this, see Nikhil Pal Singh, *Black Is a Country: Race and the Unfinished Struggle For Democracy* (Cambridge, MA: Harvard University Press, 2004).

7. Mikhail Bakunin, "Statism and Anarchy," in *No Gods, No Masters: An Anthology of Anarchism*, ed. Daniel Guérin (San Francisco: AK Press, 1998), 165–66.

8. For instructive perspectives on how these questions played out historically in the Marxist tradition, see Angela Davis, *Women, Race and Class* (New York: Vintage Books, 1981); Robin Kelley, *Freedom Dreams: The Black Radical Imagination* (Boston: Beacon Press, 2002), chapter 2; Maria Mies, *Patriarchy and Accumulation on a World Scale: Women in the International Division of Labor,* 2nd ed. (London: Zed Books, 1998); Cedric Robinson, *Black Marxism: The Making of the Black Radical Tradition* (London: Zed Books, 1983). For some examination of them within the historic anarchist tradition, see Michael Schmidt and Lucien van der Walt, *Black Flame: The Revolutionary Class Politics of Anarchism and Syndicalism* (Oakland: AK Press, 2009), chapter 10.

9. For a global history of the anarchist tradition, see Schmidt and van der Walt, *Black Flame.* See also Peter Marshall, *Demanding the Impossible: A History of Anarchism* (London: Fontana Press, 1993); George Woodcock, *Anarchism: A History of Libertarian Ideas and Movements* (Cleveland: Meridian Books, 1962).

10. My account of the IWW is based on Donald Avery, *"Dangerous Foreigners": European Immigrant Workers and Labour Radicalism in Canada*

1896–1932 (Toronto: McClelland and Stewart Limited, 1979); Stewart Bird, Dan Georgakas, and Deborah Shaffer, eds., *Solidarity Forever: An Oral History of the IWW* (Chicago: Lake View Press, 1985); Paul Buhle and Nicole Schulman, eds., *Wobblies! A Graphic History of the Industrial Workers of the World* (London: Verso, 2005); Melvin Dubofsky, *We Shall Be All: A History of the Industrial Workers of the World* (New York: Quadrangle, 1969); Joyce Kornbluh, ed., *Rebel Voices: An I.W.W. Anthology* (Ann Arbor: University of Michigan Press, 1964); Mark Leier, *Where the Fraser River Flows: The Industrial Workers of the World in British Columbia* (Vancouver: New Star Books, 1990); A. Ross McCormack, *Reformers, Rebels, and Revolutionaries: The Western Canadian Radical Movement 1899–1919* (Toronto: University of Toronto Press, 1977); Franklin Rosemont, *Joe Hill: The IWW & the Making of a Revolutionary Workingclass Counterculture* (Chicago: Charles H. Kerr Publishing Company, 2003); Salvatore Salerno, *Red November, Black November: Culture and Community in the Industrial Workers of the World* (Albany: State University of New York Press, 1989); Fred Thompson and Jon Bekken, *The I.W.W.: Its First One Hundred Years, 1905–2005* (Cincinnati: Industrial Workers of the World, 2006).

11. Industrial Workers of the World, "Preamble of the Industrial Workers of the World," in *Rebel Voices: An I.W.W. Anthology*, ed. Joyce Kornbluh (Ann Arbor: University of Michigan Press, 1964), 13.

12. This paragraph and the previous one draw on Barbara Epstein, *Political Protest and Cultural Revolution: Nonviolent Direct Action in the 1970s and 1980s* (Berkeley: University of California Press, 1991), 27–33; James J. Farrell, *The Spirit of the Sixties: Making Postwar Radicalism* (New York: Routledge, 1997); Scott Neigh, *Resisting the State: Canadian History Through the Stories of Activists* (Black Point, NS: Fernwood Publishing, 2012), chapter 1; Francesca Polletta, *Freedom Is an Endless Meeting: Democracy in American Social Movements* (Chicago: University of Chicago Press, 2002), chapter 2.

13. Ella Baker, "Bigger Than a Hamburger," in *The Eyes on the Prize Civil Rights Reader: Documents, Speeches, and Firsthand Accounts from the Black Freedom Struggle*, ed. Clayborne Carson, David. J. Garrow, Gerald Gill, Vincent Harding, and Darlene Clark Hine (New York: Penguin Books, 1991), 121. Emphasis in original. Baker gently guided SNCC in this direction. To better understand the experiences and politics that shaped her in doing this, see Barbara Ransby, *Ella Baker and the Black Freedom Movement: A Radical Vision* (Chapel Hill: University of North Carolina Press, 2003), chapters 6–8.

14. This account of SNCC is based on Clayborne Carson, *In Struggle: SNCC and the Black Awakening of the 1960s*, 2nd ed (Cambridge, MA: Harvard University Press, 1995); Payne, *I've Got the Light of Freedom;* Polletta, *Freedom Is an Endless Meeting*, chapters 2–3; Ransby, *Ella Baker and the Black Freedom Movement*.

15. See, for instance, Benedict Anderson, *Under Three Flags: Anarchism and the Anti-Colonial Imagination* (London: Verso, 2005); Steven Hirsch and Lucien van der Walt, eds., *Anarchism and Syndicalism in the Colonial and Postcolonial World, 1870–1940: The Praxis of National Liberation,*

Internationalism, and Social Revolution (Leiden: Brill, 2010); Maia Ramnath, *Haj to Utopia: How the Ghadar Movement Charted Global Radicalism and Attempted to Overthrow the British Empire* (Berkeley: University of California Press, 2011).

16. See Vijay Prashad, *The Darker Nations: A People's History of the Third World* (New York: New Press, 2007), part 1.

17. Dan Berger, *Outlaws of America: The Weather Underground and the Politics of Solidarity* (Oakland: AK Press, 2006), 54–55; Max Elbaum, *Revolution in the Air: Sixties Radicals Turn to Lenin, Mao and Che* (London: Verso, 2002), chapters 2–3.

18. On state repression against the BPP, see Ward Churchill and Jim Vander Wall, *Agents of Repression: The FBI's Secret Wars Against the Black Panther Party and the American Indian Movement* (Boston: South End Press, 1988), chapter 3.

19. For histories of the BPP, see Mumia Abu-Jamal, *We Want Freedom: A Life in the Black Panther Party* (Cambridge, MA: South End Press, 2004); Joshua Bloom and Waldo Martin Jr., *Black Against Empire: The History and Politics of the Black Panther Party* (Berkeley: University of California Press, 2013); Elaine Brown, *A Taste of Power: A Black Woman's Story* (New York: Pantheon Books, 1992); Kathleen Cleaver and George Katsiaficas, eds., *Liberation, Imagination, and the Black Panther Party: A New Look at the Panthers and Their Legacy* (New York: Routledge, 2001); Charles E. Jones, ed., *The Black Panther Party (Reconsidered)* (Baltimore: Black Classic Press, 1998); Huey P. Newton, *Revolutionary Suicide* (New York: Harcourt Brace Jovanovich, 1973); Bobby Seale, *Seize the Time: The Story of the Black Panther Party and Huey P. Newton* (New York: Random House, 1970).

20. For accounts of these programs, see David Hilliard and The Dr. Huey P. Newton Foundation, *The Black Panther Party: Service to the People Programs* (Albuquerque: University of New Mexico Press, 2008); Alondra Nelson, *Body and Soul: The Black Panther Party and the Fight Against Medical Discrimination* (Minneapolis: University of Minnesota Press, 2011).

21. For a glimpse into this, see Abu-Jamal, *We Want Freedom*, 185–94. On gender relations within the BPP, see Abu-Jamal, *We Want Freedom*, chapter 7; Brown, *A Taste of Power*; Kathleen Cleaver, "Women, Power, and Revolution," in *Liberation, Imagination, and the Black Panther Party: A New Look at the Panthers and Their Legacy*, ed. Kathleen Cleaver and George Katsiaficas (New York: Routledge, 2001), 123–127.

22. On these movements, see David Austin, *Fear of a Black Nation: Race, Sex and Security in Sixties Montreal* (Toronto: Between the Lines, 2013); Dick Fidler, *Red Power in Canada* (Toronto: Vanguard, 1970); Fred Ho, *Legacy to Liberation: Politics & Culture of Revolutionary Asian/Pacific America* (Oakland: AK Press, 2000); Myrna Kostash, *Long Way From Home: The Story of the Sixties Generation in Canada* (Toronto: James Lorimer & Company, 1980); Steve Louie and Glenn Omatsu, *Asian Americans: The Movement and the Moment* (Los Angeles: UCLA Asian American Studies Center Press, 2001);

Peter Matthiessen, *In the Spirit of Crazy Horse* (New York: Viking Press, 1983); Miguel Melendez, *We Took the Streets: Fighting for Latino Rights with the Young Lords* (New York: St. Martin's Press, 2003); Sean Mills, *The Empire Within: Postcolonial Thought and Political Activism in Sixties Montreal* (Montreal and Kingston: McGill-Queens University Press, 2010); Carlos Muñoz, *Youth, Identity, Power: The Chicano Movement*, 2nd ed. (London: Verso, 2007); Laura Pulido, *Black, Brown, Yellow, and Left: Radical Activism in Los Angeles* (Berkeley: University of California Press, 2006); Paul Chaat Smith and Robert Allen Warrior, *Like a Hurricane: The Indian Movement from Alcatraz to Wounded Knee* (New York: New Press, 1996); Amy Sonnie and James Tracy, *Hillbilly Nationalists, Urban Race Rebels, and Black Power: Community Organizing in Radical Times* (Brooklyn: Melville House, 2011); Andrés Torres and José Velázquez, *The Puerto Rican Movement: Voices from the Diaspora* (Philadelphia: Temple University Press, 1998); William Wei, *The Asian American Movement* (Philadelphia: Temple University Press, 1993).

23. Activist-scholar Jason Ferreira's work has helped me think through this: Jason Ferreira, "Medicine of Memory: Third World Radicalism in 1960s San Francisco and the Politics of Multiracial Unity," presentation at University of California, Santa Cruz, February 23, 2005. See also Berger, *Outlaws of America*, chapter 2.

24. In this way, they played a similar role to abolitionism more than a century earlier. Carson, *In Struggle*, 147.

25. Greg Calvert, "A Left Wing Alternative," in *The Movement Toward A New America*, ed. Mitchell Goodman (Philadelphia: Pilgrim Press, 1970), 588.

26. This discussion of the New Left draws on Epstein, *Political Protest and Cultural Revolution*, 38–50; George Katsiaficas, *The Imagination of the New Left: A Global Analysis of 1968* (Boston: South End Press, 1987), 17–27, 117–73; Kostash, *Long Way From Home*; Polletta, *Freedom Is an Endless Meeting*, chap. 5; Kirkpatrick Sale, *SDS* (New York: Random House, 1973).

27. "Leninist" refers to people and organizations who, in significant ways, follow the ideas of the Russian revolutionary Vladimir Ilyich Lenin, a leader of the Bolshevik revolution.

28. On this current in the United States, see Elbaum, *Revolution in the Air*; Michael Staudenmaier, *Truth and Revolution: A History of the Sojourner Truth Organization, 1969–1986* (Oakland: AK Press, 2012). For some materials related to this current in English-speaking Canada (primarily Trotskyist) and Quebec (primarily Maoist), see the Socialist History Project's collection, available at www.socialisthistory.ca.

29. On this current, see Berger, *Outlaws of America*; Ron Jacobs, *The Way the Wind Blew: A History of the Weather Underground* (London: Verso, 1997); Mills, *The Empire Within*; Jalil Muntaqim, *On the Black Liberation Army* (Paterson, NJ: NJ ABC-BG, 1998); Akinyele Omowale Umoja, "Repression Breeds Resistance: The Black Liberation Army and the Radical Legacy of the Black Panther Party," in *Liberation, Imagination, and the Black Panther Party: A New Look at the Panthers and Their Legacy*, ed. Kathleen Cleaver and George

Katsiaficas (New York: Routledge, 2001), 3–19; Jeremy Varon, *Bringing the War Home: The Weather Underground, the Red Army Faction, and Revolutionary Violence in the Sixties and Seventies* (Berkeley: University of California Press, 2004).

30. On the split in SDS, see Berger, *Outlaws of America,* chapter 4; Elbaum, *Revolution in the Air,* 69–73; Sale, *SDS,* chapters 23–25. On the split in the BPP, see Abu-Jamal, *We Want Freedom,* chapter 9; Brown, *A Taste of Power,* chapters 11–12; Donald Cox, "The Split in the Party," in *Repression Breeds Resistance: The Black Liberation Army and the Radical Legacy of the Black Panther Party,* ed. Kathleen Cleaver and George Katsiaficas (New York: Routledge, 2001), 118–22.

31. Sara Evans, *Personal Politics: The Roots of Women's Liberation in the Civil Rights Movement and the New Left* (New York: Vintage Books, 1980), chapters 6–8.

32. On this, see Jo Freeman, "The Tyranny of Structurelessness," in *Quiet Rumors: An Anarcha-Feminist Reader,* ed. Dark Star Collective (Edinburgh: AK Press, 2002), 54–61.

33. My account of the women's liberation movement draws on Alice Echols, *Daring to Be Bad: Radical Feminism in America 1967–1975* (Minneapolis: University of Minnesota Press, 1989); Kostash, *Long Way From Home,* 166–87; Judy Rebick, *Ten Thousand Roses: The Making of a Feminist Revolution* (Toronto: Penguin, 2005); Ruth Rosen, *The World Split Open: How the Modern Women's Movement Changed America* (New York: Penguin Books, 2007); Benita Roth, *Separate Roads to Feminism: Black, Chicana, and White Feminist Movements in America's Second Wave* (Cambridge: Cambridge University Press, 2004); Becky Thompson, *A Promise and a Way of Life: White Antiracist Activism* (Minneapolis: University of Minnesota Press, 2001), chapters 4–7. See also Roxanne Dunbar-Ortiz, *Outlaw Woman: A Memoir of the War Years, 1960–1975* (San Francisco: City Lights, 2001).

34. On these events, see Martin Duberman, *Stonewall* (New York: Plume, 1993).

35. Adrienne Rich, "Compulsory Heterosexuality and Lesbian Existence," in *Blood, Bread, and Poetry: Selected Prose 1979–1985* (New York: W.W. Norton and Co., 1986), 23–75. See also Audre Lorde, *Sister Outsider* (Freedom, CA: The Crossing Press, 1996); Suzanne Pharr, *Homophobia: A Weapon of Sexism* (Inverness, CA: Chardon Press, 1988).

36. For histories of the gay and lesbian movement of this period, see Tommi Avicolli Mecca. ed., *Smash the Church! Smash the State! The Early Years of Gay Liberation* (San Francisco: City Lights Press, 2009); Gary Kinsman, *The Regulation of Desire: Homo and Hetero Sexualities,* 2nd ed. (Montreal: Black Rose Books, 1996), chapter 9; Marc Stein, *Rethinking the Gay and Lesbian Movement* (New York: Routledge, 2012); Tom Warner, *Never Going Back: A History of Queer Activism in Canada* (Toronto: University of Toronto Press, 2002).

37. On the construction of this category, see Angela Davis and Elizabeth Martinez, "Coalition Building Among People of Color," in *The Angela Y. Davis*

Reader, ed. Joy James (Malden, MA: Blackwell Publishers, 1998), 300. For accounts of the development of women of color feminism, see Linda Carty, *And Still We Rise: Feminist Political Mobilizing in Contemporary Canada* (Toronto: Women's Press, 1993); Enakshi Dua, "Canadian Anti-Racist Feminist Thought: Scratching the Surface of Racism," in *Scratching the Surface: Canadian Anti-Racist Feminist Thought,* ed. Enakshi Dua and Angela Robertson (Toronto: Women's Press, 1999), 7–31; Kelley, *Freedom Dreams,* chapter 5; Rebick, *Ten Thousand Roses,* chapters 9–11 and 19; Roth, *Separate Roads to Feminism;* Kimberly Springer, *Living for the Revolution: Black Feminist Organizations, 1968–1980* (Durham: Duke University Press, 2005); Thompson, *A Promise and a Way of Life,* chapter 5.

38. Combahee River Collective, "The Combahee River Collective Statement," in *Home Girls: A Black Feminist Anthology,* ed. Barbara Smith (New York: Kitchen Table: Women of Color Press, 1983), 272.

39. Important publications that have helped to develop women of color feminist politics include Gloria Anzaldúa, *Borderlands/La Frontera: The New Mestiza* (San Francisco: Spinsters/Aunt Lute, 1987); Himani Bannerji, *Thinking Through: Essays on Feminism, Marxism and Anti-Racism* (Toronto: Women's Press, 1995); Patricia Hill Collins, *Black Feminist Thought: Knowledge, Consciousness, and the Politics of Empowerment* (New York: Routledge, 1991); Davis, *Women, Race and Class;* Enakshi Dua and Angela Robertson, eds., *Scratching the Surface: Canadian Anti-Racist Feminist Thought* (Toronto: Women's Press, 1999); Joyce Green, ed., *Making Space for Indigenous Feminism* (Black Point, NS: Fernwood, 2007); bell hooks, *Feminist Theory from Margin to Center* (Boston, MA: South End Press, 1984); June Jordan, *On Call: Political Essays* (Boston: South End Press, 1985); Joanna Kadi, ed., *Food for Our Grandmothers: Writings by Arab-American and Arab-Canadian Feminists* (Boston: South End Press, 1994); Lorde, *Sister Outsider;* Elizabeth Martinez, *De Colores Means All of Us: Latina Views for a Multi-Colored Century* (Cambridge, MA: South End Press, 1998); Cherríe Moraga, *Loving in the War Years: Lo Que Nunca Pasó Por Sus Labios* (Boston: South End Press, 1983); Cherríe Moraga and Gloria Anzaldúa, eds., *This Bridge Called My Back: Writings by Radical Women of Color* (New York: Kitchen Table, Women of Color Press, 1983); Sonia Shah, ed., *Dragon Ladies: Asian American Feminists Breathe Fire* (Boston: South End Press, 1997); Barbara Smith, ed., *Home Girls: A Black Feminist Anthology* (New York: Kitchen Table, Women of Color Press, 1983); Barbara Smith, *The Truth That Never Hurts: Writings on Race, Gender, and Freedom* (New Brunswick, NJ: Rutgers University Press, 1998).

40. Although the concept of intersectionality has roots in earlier women of color feminist work, it was first introduced in Kimberlé Crenshaw, "Mapping the Margins: Intersectionality, Identity Politics, and Violence Against Women of Color," *Stanford Law Review* 43, no. 6 (1991): 1241–99

41. We can see the significance of the "race, class, and gender" trio in university classes through a widely-used course text: Margaret L. Andersen and Patricia Hill Collins, eds., *Race, Class, and Gender: An Anthology,* 7th ed. (Belmont, CA: Wadsworth Publishing, 2009).

42. Combahee River Collective, "The Combahee River Collective Statement," 281.

43. See, for example, hooks, *Feminist Theory from Margin to Center*. See also Chela Sandoval, *Methodology of the Oppressed* (Minneapolis: University of Minnesota Press, 2000), chapter 6.

44. On this understanding of coalition, see Davis and Martinez, "Coalition Building Among People of Color"; Bernice Johnson Reagon, "Coalition Politics: Turning the Century," in *Home Girls: A Black Feminist Anthology,* ed. Barbara Smith (New York: Kitchen Table: Women of Color Press, 1983), 356–68

45. On the Coalition of Visible Minority Women, see Rebick, *Ten Thousand Roses,* chapter 11.

46. On these defense campaigns, see Emily Thuma, "'Not a Wedge, But a Bridge': Prisons, Feminist Activism, and the Politics of Gendered Violence, 1968–1987" (PhD dissertation, New York University, 2010), chapter 2.

47. For more on INCITE!, see INCITE! Women of Color Against Violence, ed., *Color of Violence: The INCITE! Anthology* (Cambridge, MA: South End Press, 2006); INCITE! Women of Color Against Violence, ed., *The Revolution Will Not Be Funded: Beyond the Non-Profit Industrial Complex* (Cambridge, MA: South End Press, 2007).

48. On this, see Sista II Sista, "Sistas Makin' Moves: Collective Leadership for Personal Transformation and Social Justice," in *Color of Violence: The INCITE! Anthology,* ed. INCITE! Women of Color Against Violence (Cambridge, MA: South End Press, 2006), 196–207.

49. In 2004, INCITE! helped to organize a groundbreaking conference in Santa Barbara, California, called "The Revolution Will Not Be Funded: Beyond the Non-Profit Industrial Complex." This event brought together a range of activists and organizers, many with experience working in nonprofits, to participate in collective critical reflection on this sector. Some of the contributions to this conference were later collected in a book by the same name, INCITE! Women of Color Against Violence, ed., *The Revolution Will Not Be Funded.*

50. For indications of the influence of women of color feminist politics, see Ching-In Chen, Jai Dulani, and Leah Lakshmi Piepzna-Samarasinha, eds., *The Revolution Starts at Home: Confronting Intimate Violence Within Activist Communities* (Brooklyn: South End Press, 2011); Harmony Goldberg, "Building Power in the City: Reflections on the Emergence of the Right to the City Alliance and the National Domestic Workers Alliance," in *Uses of A Whirlwind: Movement, Movements, and Contemporary Radical Currents in the United States* (Oakland: AK Press, 2010), 97–108; Kimiko Inouye, ed., "Home and a Hard Place: A Roundtable on Migrant Labour," *Upping the Anti* 7 (2008): 163–78; Manissa McCleave Maharawal, "Reflections from the People of Color Caucus at Occupy Wall Street," in *We Are Many: Reflections on Movement Strategy from Occupation to Liberation,* ed. Kate Khatib, Margaret Killjoy, and Mike McGuire (Oakland: AK Press, 2012), 177–83; Scott Neigh, *Gender and Sexuality: Canadian History Through the Stories of Activists* (Black Point, NS: Fernwood Publishing, 2012), chapter 4; Jael Miriam Silliman,

Marlene Gerber Fried, Loretta Ross, and Elena Gutiérrez, eds., *Undivided Rights: Women of Color Organize for Reproductive Justice* (Cambridge, MA: South End Press, 2004); Nat Smith and Eric A. Stanley, eds., *Captive Genders: Trans Embodiment and the Prison Industrial Complex* (Oakland: AK Press, 2011); Matt Bernstein Sycamore, ed., *That's Revolting: Queer Strategies for Resisting Assimilation* (Brooklyn: Soft Skull Press, 2004). See also the magazine *Make/Shift*.

51. INCITE! co-founder Andrea Smith has played an especially important role in developing these politics within the anti-authoritarian current. See, for instance, Andrea Smith, "Beyond Inclusion: Recentering Feminism," *Left Turn,* June 2006.

52. The classic text on post-abolitionist vision is W. E. B. Du Bois, *Black Reconstruction* (Millwood, N.Y: Kraus-Thomson Organization Ltd., 1976). For some recent reflections, see Angela Davis, *Abolition Democracy: Beyond Empire, Prisons, and Torture* (New York: Seven Stores Press, 2005); Joel Olson, *The Abolition of White Democracy* (Minneapolis: University of Minnesota Press, 2004). On the historic continuities between slavery and mass incarceration, see Mary Ellen Curtin, *Black Prisoners and Their World, Alabama, 1865–1900* (Charlottesville: University Press of Virginia, 2000); Angela Davis, *Are Prisons Obsolete?* (New York: Seven Stories Press, 2003), chapter 2; Alex Lichtenstein, *Twice the Work of Free Labor: The Political Economy of Convict Labor in the New South* (London: Verso, 1996).

53. See, for instance, Emma Goldman, "Prisons: A Social Crime and Failure," *Anarchism and Other Essays* (New York: Dover Publications, 1969), 109–26; Peter Kropotkin, "Prisons and Their Moral Influence on Prisoners," *Anarchist Archives,* 1927; Georg Rusche and Otto Kirchheimer, *Punishment and Social Structure* (New York: Russell and Russell, 1968).

54. This account of prison activism in the 1970s is based on Dan Berger, "'We Are the Revolutionaries': Visibility, Protest and Racial Formation in 1970s Radicalism" (PhD dissertation, University of Pennsylvania, 2010); Prisoners' Justice Day Committee, "History of Prisoners' Justice Day," *Prisonjustice.ca,* 2001; Liz Samuels, "Improvising on Reality: The Roots of Prison Abolition," in *The Hidden 1970s: Histories of Radicalism,* ed. Dan Berger (New Brunswick, NJ: Rutgers University Press, 2010), 21–38.

55. Prison Research Action Project, *Instead Of Prisons: A Handbook for Abolitionists* (Syracuse, NY: Prison Research Action Project, 1976), 16.

56. Prison Research Action Project, *Instead Of Prisons,* 20.

57. On this transformation in the United States, see Ruth Wilson Gilmore, *Golden Gulag: Prisons, Surplus, Crisis, and Opposition in Globalizing California* (Berkeley: University of California Press, 2007); Christian Parenti, *Lockdown America: Police and Prisons in the Age of Crisis* (London: Verso, 2000). On the parallel, if smaller-scale, transformation in Canada, see Wendy Chan and Kiran Mirchandani, eds., *Crimes of Colour: Racialization and the Criminal Justice System in Canada* (Toronto: University of Toronto Press, 2001); Dave Oswald Mitchell, "Killers in High Places: Drugs, Gangs, and

Harper's War on the Poor," *Briarpatch*, February 2013. For an international perspective, see Julia Sudbury, *Global Lockdown: Race, Gender, and the Prison-Industrial Complex* (New York: Routledge, 2005).

58. On *Bulldozer/Prison News Service,* see Jim Campbell, "Bulldozer/ Prison News Service," in *Only A Beginning: An Anarchist Anthology,* ed. Allan Antliff (Vancouver: Arsenal Pulp Press, 2004), 74–81. On *Prison Legal News,* see www.prisonlegalnews.org.

59. On these support campaigns, see Matt Meyer, ed., *Let Freedom Ring: A Collection of Documents from the Movements to Free U.S. Political Prisoners* (Oakland: PM Press, 2008).

60. On this prison activist work, see Thompson, *A Promise and a Way of Life,* chapter 9.

61. Writer and activist Mike Davis first coined this term in 1995. Mike Davis, "Hell Factories in the Field: A Prison-Industrial Complex," *The Nation,* February 20, 1995.

62. To get a sense of the histories, analyses, and political approaches that converged in this movement in the 1990s, see Elihu Rosenblatt, ed., *Criminal Injustice: Confronting the Prison Crisis* (Boston: South End Press, 1996).

63. On the first CR conference, see Dylan Rodriguez, Nancy Stoller, Rita Bo Brown, Terry Kupers, Andrea Smith, and Julia Sudbury, "Reflections on Critical Resistance," *Social Justice: A Journal of Crime, Conflict and World Order* 27, no. 3 (Fall 2000): 180–94.

64. For more about abolitionist organizing in the United States, see CR-10 Publications Collective, ed., *Abolition Now! Ten Years of Strategy and Struggle Against the Prison Industrial Complex* (Oakland: AK Press, 2008); Jenna Loyd, Matt Mitchelson, and Andrew Burridge, eds., *Beyond Walls and Cages: Prisons, Borders, and Global Crisis* (Athens, Georgia: University of Georgia Press, 2012); Smith and Stanley, *Captive Genders.* On abolitionist organizing in the Canadian context, see Caitlin Hewitt-White, ed., "Prison Abolition in Canada," *Upping the Anti* no. 4 (2007): 125–46; Kim Pate, "A Canadian Journey into Abolition," in *Abolition Now! Ten Years of Strategy and Struggle Against the Prison Industrial Complex,* ed. CR-10 Publications Collective (Oakland: AK Press, 2008), 77–85. See also the newspaper *The Abolitionist.*

65. On this, see Loyd, Mitchelson, and Burridge, *Beyond Walls and Cages.*

66. Critical Resistance, "Not So Common Language," *Critical Resistance,* accessed April 19, 2009, www.criticalresistance.org/article.php?id = 49,

67. Critical Resistance, "Mission and Vision," *Critical Resistance,* accessed November 2, 2012, http://criticalresistance.org/about/. For an introduction to abolitionist politics, see Davis, *Are Prisons Obsolete?*

68. On these and other abolitionist approaches, see Kai Barrow, "Swan Song Manifesto," *Organizing Upgrade,* July 1, 2012. www.organizingupgrade.com/ index.php/modules-menu/community-organizing/item/57-kai-barrow.

69. Critical Resistance, "Mission & Vision."

70. Victoria Law, "Protection Without Police: North American Community Responses to Violence in the 1970s and Today," *Upping the Anti* no. 12 (2011): 91.

71. For the statement that created a basis for collaboration, see Critical Resistance and INCITE! Women of Color Against Violence, "Gender Violence and the Prison-Industrial Complex," in *Color of Violence: The INCITE! Anthology,* ed. INCITE! Women of Color Against Violence (Cambridge, MA: South End Press, 2006), 223–26.

72. For influential elaborations of this critique, see Joy James, *Resisting State Violence: Radicalism, Gender, and Race in U.S. Culture* (Minneapolis: University of Minnesota Press, 1996) Andrea Smith, *Conquest: Sexual Violence and American Indian Genocide* (Cambridge, MA: South End Press, 2005).

73. See, for example, Alexis Pauline Gumbs, "Freedom Seeds: Growing Abolition in Durham, North Carolina," in *Abolition Now! Ten Years of Strategy and Struggle Against the Prison Industrial Complex,* ed. CR-10 Publications Collective (Oakland: AK Press, 2008), 145–55.

74. On the growing queer and feminist dimensions of this work, see INCITE! Women of Color Against Violence and FIERCE!, "Re-Thinking 'The Norm' In Police/Prison Violence & Gender Violence: Critical Lessons from the New Jersey 7," *Left Turn,* November 2008; Beth Richie, "Standing with Duanna Johnson Against Police Brutality: A Challenge for the Gay and Civil Rights Movements," *Left Turn,* May 2009; Smith and Stanley, *Captive Genders;* Jessica Stern, "Transforming Justice," *Left Turn,* February 2008.

75. My account of the nonviolent direct action movement draws on Andrew Cornell, *Oppose and Propose! Lessons from Movement for a New Society* (Oakland: AK Press, 2011); and Epstein, *Political Protest and Cultural Revolution.*

76. This discussion of direct action AIDS activism is based on Deborah Gould, *Moving Politics: Emotion and ACT UP's Fight Against AIDS* (Chicago: University of Chicago Press, 2009); Gary Kinsman, "AIDS Activism and the Politics of Emotion: An Interview with Deborah Gould," *Upping the Anti* 8 (2009): 65–80; Gary Kinsman, "Managing AIDS Organizing: 'Consultation,' 'Partnership,' and 'Responsibility' as Strategies of Regulation," in *Organizing Dissent: Contemporary Social Movements in Theory and Practice,* ed. William K. Carroll (Toronto: Garamond Press, 1997), 213–39; Benjamin Shepard, "DIY Politics and Queer Activism," in *Uses of A Whirlwind: Movement, Movements, and Contemporary Radical Currents in the United States,* ed. Team Colors Collective (Oakland: AK Press, 2010), 163–82; Benjamin Shepard and Ronald Hayduk, eds., *From ACT UP to the WTO: Urban Protest and Community Building in the Era of Globalization* (London: Verso, 2002). See also the ACT UP Oral History Project: www.actuporalhistory.org.

77. For more on Judi Bari's organizing, see Judi Bari, *Timber Wars* (Monroe, ME: Common Courage Press, 1994); Douglas Bevington, "Earth First! in Northern California: An Interview with Judi Bari," in *The Struggle for Ecological Democracy: Environmental Justice Movements in the United States,* ed. Daniel J. Faber (New York: Guilford Press, 1998), 248–71.

78. My account of 1990s Earth First! organizing draws on my own experience, conversations with EF! organizers, and Douglas Bevington, *The Rebirth of Environmentalism: Grassroots Activism from the Spotted Owl to the Polar*

Bear (Washington: Island Press, 2009), chapter 3; Douglas Bevington, "Strategic Experimentation and Stigmatization in Earth First!" in *Extreme Deviance*, ed. Erich Goode and D. Angus Vail (Los Angeles: Pine Forge Press, 2008), 189–96; L.A. Kauffman, "Who Are Those Masked Anarchists?" in *The Battle of Seattle: The New Challenge to Capitalist Globalization*, ed. Eddie Yuen, Daniel Burton Rose, and George Katsiaficas (New York: Soft Skull Press, 2001), 124–29.

79. Cornell, *Oppose and Propose!*, 55–56.

80. Food Not Bombs is an international network of autonomous local groups that collect and prepare discarded food to feed people for free while advocating against militarism and for social justice. Anti-nuclear activists in Cambridge, Massachusetts, started the first group in 1980. See C.T. Lawrence Butler and Keith McHenry, *Food Not Bombs: How to Feed the Hungry and Build Community* (Philadelphia: New Society Publishers, 1992); Chris Crass, *Towards Collective Liberation: Anti-Racist Organizing, Feminist Praxis, and Movement Building Strategy* (Oakland: PM Press, 2013), 37–105. For more on anarchism in this period, see Barbara Epstein and Chris Dixon, "A Politics and a Sensibility: The Anarchist Current on the U.S. Left," in *Toward a New Socialism*, ed. Anatole Anton and Richard Schmitt (Lanham, MD: Lexington Books, 2007), 452–53; Allan Antliff, ed., *Only A Beginning: An Anarchist Anthology* (Vancouver: Arsenal Pulp Press, 2004); Abby Scher, "Anarchism Faces the '90s," *Dollars and Sense*, April 1999. Activist researcher L.A. Kauffman has offered some of the best analysis tracing the anarchist and direct action politics that led into the North American global justice movement: L.A. Kauffman, "A Short History of Radical Renewal," in *From Act Up to the WTO: Urban Protest and Community Building in the Era of Globalization*, ed. Benjamin Shepard and Ronald Hayduk (London: Verso, 2002), 35–40; L.A. Kauffman, "A Short Personal History of the Global Justice Movement," in *Confronting Capitalism: Dispatches from a Global Movement*, ed. Eddie Yuen, George Katsiaficas, and Daniel Burton-Rose (New York: Soft Skull Press, 2004), 375–88; Kauffman, "Who Are Those Masked Anarchists?".

81. So far, there is very little written about these publications, formations, and events in the 1990s. On Love and Rage, see Roy San Filippo, ed., *A New World in Our Hearts: Eight Years of Writings from the Love and Rage Revolutionary Anarchist Federation* (Oakland: AK Press, 2003). On the Active Resistance conferences, see Antliff, *Only A Beginning*, 353–56; Solnit, "Active Resistance at the Democratic Convention: Planting Seeds for an Anarchist Movement," *Fifth Estate*, Fall 1996. One book that was particularly influential for many involved in these efforts was Lorenzo Kom'boa Ervin, *Anarchism and the Black Revolution* (Philadelphia: Monkeywrench Press, 1994).

82. On the emergence of this global revolt against neoliberalism, see George Caffentzis and Silvia Federici, "A Brief History of Resistance to Structural Adjustment," in *Democratizing the Global Economy: The Battle Against the World Bank and the International Monetary Fund*, ed. Kevin Danaher (Monroe, ME: Common Courage Press, 2001), 139–44; Thatcher Collins, "A Protestography," in *Confronting Capitalism: Dispatches from a Global Movement*, ed. Eddie Yuen,

George Katsiaficas, and Daniel Burton Rose (New York: Soft Skull Press, 2004), xxxiv–xlviii; James Davis and Paul Rowley, "Internationalism Against Globalization," in *Confronting Capitalism: Dispatches from a Global Movement*, ed. Eddie Yuen, George Katsiaficas, and Daniel Burton Rose (New York: Soft Skull Press, 2004), xxx–xxxiii; George Katsiaficas, "Seattle Was Not the Beginning," in *Confronting Capitalism: Dispatches from a Global Movement*, ed. Eddie Yuen, George Katsiaficas, and Daniel Burton Rose (New York: Soft Skull Press, 2004), 29–35; Jessica Woodroffe and Mark Ellis-Jones, *States of Unrest: Resistance to IMF Policies in Poor Countries* (report, World Development Movement, September 2000).

83. For histories of the Zapatistas, see Gloria Muñoz Ramírez, *The Fire and the Word: A History of the Zapatista Movement* (San Francisco: City Lights Books, 2008); John Ross, *The War Against Oblivion: Zapatista Chronicles, 1994–2000* (Monroe, ME: Common Courage Press, 2000). On their significance for the global justice movement, see Notes from Nowhere, "Emergence: An Irresistible Global Uprising," in *We Are Everywhere: The Irresistible Rise of Global Anticapitalism*, ed. Notes from Nowhere (London: Verso, 2003), 19–29. And on their ongoing importance for movements in the United States and Canada, see Alex Khasnabish, *Zapatismo Beyond Borders: New Imaginations of Political Possibility* (Toronto: University of Toronto Press, 2008); El Kilombo Intergaláctico, *Feliz Año Cabrones: On the Continued Centrality Of the Zapatista Movement After 14 Years* (Durham, NC: El Kilombo Intergaláctico, 2008); Maccani, "Enter the Intergalactic: The Zapatistas' Sixth Declaration in the US and the World," *Upping the Anti* 3 (2006): 105–21.

84. Peoples' Global Action, "Hallmarks of Peoples' Global Action," *Peoples' Global Action*, 2001, http://nadir.org/nadir/initiativ/agp/free/pga/hallm.htm. For more on the PGA, see Olivier de Marcellus, "Peoples' Global Action: The Grassroots Go Global," in *We Are Everywhere: The Irresistible Rise of Global Anticapitalism*, ed. Notes from Nowhere (London: Verso, 2003), 97–101; Sophie Style, "People's Global Action," *Z Magazine*, January 2002.

85. For grounded accounts of the combination of politics and practices around the Seattle protests, see Stephanie Guilloud, "Spark, Fire, and Burning Coals: An Organizer's History of Seattle," in *The Battle of Seattle: The New Challenge to Capitalist Globalization*, ed. Eddie Yuen, George Katsiaficas, and Daniel Burton Rose (New York: Soft Skull Press, 2001), 225–31; Starhawk, *Webs of Power: Notes from the Global Uprising* (Gabriola, B.C.: New Society Publishers, 2002), 16–20.

86. This history of the global justice movement is based on my own experiences as well as Jen Chang, Bethany Or, Eloginy Tharmendran, Emmie Tsumara, Steve Daniels, and Darryl Leroux, eds., *Resist! A Grassroots Collection of Stories, Poetry, Photos and Analyses from the Québec City FTAA Protests and Beyond* (Halifax: Fernwood Publishing, 2001); Dissent Editorial Collective, ed., *Days of Dissent: Reflections on Summit Mobilisations* (London: Dissent! Network, 2004); Stephanie Guilloud, ed., *Voices from the WTO: An Anthology of Writings from the People Who Shut Down the World*

Trade Organization (Olympia, WA: The Evergreen State College, 2000); Notes from Nowhere, ed., *We Are Everywhere: The Irresistible Rise of Global Anticapitalism* (London: Verso, 2003); Peoples Lenses Collective, ed., *Under the Lens of the People: Our Account of the Peoples' Resistance to the FTAA, Quebec City, April 2001* (Toronto: The Peoples Lenses Collective, 2003); Eddie Yuen, George Katsiaficas, and Daniel Burton Rose, eds., *The Battle of Seattle: The New Challenge to Capitalist Globalization* (New York: Soft Skull Press, 2001); Eddie Yuen, George Katsiaficas, and Daniel Burton Rose, eds., *Confronting Capitalism: Dispatches from a Global Movement* (New York: Soft Skull Press, 2004).

87. Martinez, "Where Was the Color in Seattle? Looking for Reasons Why the Great Battle Was so White," *ColorLines* 3, no. 1 (2000): 11–12.

88. Influential contributions included: Ingrid Chapman, "We Can Do This: Direct Action Against Global Capitalism and U.S. Imperialism: An Interview with Ingrid Chapman," *Clamor* 35 (December 2, 2003); Laura Close, "Organizer + Catalyst = Laura Close." *Clamor*, August 2003; Chris Crass, *Collective Liberation on My Mind: Essays by Chris Crass* (Montreal: Kersplebdeb, 2001); Chris Dixon, "Finding Hope After Seattle: Rethinking Radical Activism and Building a Movement," *Onward*, Spring 2001; Andrew Hsiao, "Color Blind: Activists of Color Bring the Economic War Home, But Is the Movement Missing the Message?" in *The Battle of Seattle: The New Challenge to Capitalist Globalization*, ed. Eddie Yuen, George Katsiaficas, and Daniel Burton Rose (New York: Soft Skull Press, 2001), 343–46; Pauline Sok Yin Hwang, "Anti-Racist Organizing: Reflecting On Lessons from Quebec City," in *Under the Lens of the People: Our Account of the Peoples' Resistance to the FTAA, Quebec City, April 2001*, ed. The Peoples Lenses Collective (Toronto: The Peoples Lenses Collective, 2003), 48–52; Nrinder Nindy Kaur Nann, "Grounding Power: An Interview with Nrinder Nindy Kaur Nann," Colours of Resistance Archive, December 2, 2003; Michelle O'Brien, "Whose Ally? Thinking Critically About Anti-oppression Ally Organizing," Colours of Resistance Archive, 2003; Colin Rajah, "Globalism and Race at A16 in D.C.," *ColorLines*, Fall 2000; Gabriel Sayegh, "Redefining Success: White Contradictions in the Anti-Globalization Movement," Colours of Resistance Archive, 2001; Jaggi Singh, "Resisting Global Capitalism in India," in *The Battle of Seattle: The New Challenge to Capitalist Globalization*, ed. Eddie Yuen, George Katsiaficas, and Daniel Burton Rose (New York: Soft Skull Press, 2001), 48–50; Sonja Sivesind, "Combating White Privilege in the Anti-Globalization Movement," *Clamor*, April 2002; Kristine Wong, "Shutting Us Out: Race, Class, and the Framing of a Movement," in *Confronting Capitalism: Dispatches from a Global Movement*, ed. Eddie Yuen, George Katsiaficas, and Daniel Burton Rose (New York: Soft Skull Press, 2004), 204–14. For a more comprehensive collection, see the Colours of Resistance Archive: www.coloursofresistance.org.

89. For a statement and synthesis of this direction as it was developing at the time, see Kim Fyke and Gabriel Sayegh, "Anarchism and the Struggle to Move Forward," *Perspectives on Anarchist Theory* 5, no. 2 (2001).

90. Lesley J. Wood, "Organizing Against the Occupation: U.S. and Canadian Anti-war Activists Speak Out," *Social Movement Studies* 3, no. 2 (2004): 249.

91. For some anti-authoritarian perspectives on this, see A.K. Gupta, "Moving Forward: UFPJ and the Anti-War Movement," *Left Turn*, March 2006; Max Uhlenbeck, "The Antiwar Movement and the 2008 Elections," *Left Turn*, February 2008; Upping the Anti Editorial Committee, "Growing Pains: The Anti-Globalization Movement, Anti-Imperialism and the Politics of the United Front," *Upping the Anti* 3 (2006): 27–44.

92. This account of the anti-war movement draws on Aimee Allison and David Solnit, *Army of None: Strategies to Counter Military Recruitment, End War, and Build a Better World* (New York: Seven Stories Press, 2007); Clare Bayard, "Demilitarization as Rehumanization," *Left Turn*, May 2011; Catalyst Project, "Justice and Survival: A Forum on Building Movements to Stop War," *Left Turn*, August 2007; Barbara Epstein, "Notes on the Antiwar Movement," *Monthly Review* 55, no. 3 (2003): 109–16; Francesca Fiorentini and Sasha Wright, "New Hope for the Anti-War Movement," *Left Turn*, November 2006; Beca Lafore, Helia Rasti, Jonathan Stribling-Uss, and Meddle Bolger, *Shutdown: The Rise and Fall of Direct Action to Stop the War* (AK Press, 2009); Steve Theberge, "Vibrant, Young, and Relevant: Reflections on the Counter Military Recruitment Movement," *Left Turn*, November 2005; Doug Viehmeyer, "Steppin' It Up: The New SDS," *Left Turn*, May 2007; Lesley J. Wood, ed., "Roundtable on Anti-War Organizing in Canada," *Upping the Anti* 2 (2005): 127–50; Sasha Wright, "The Second Superpower: Prospects for the Anti-War Movement," *Left Turn*, October 2004.

93. On this, see Jeff Monaghan and Kevin Walby, "The Green Scare Is Everywhere: The Importance of Cross-Movement Solidarity," *Upping the Anti* 6 (2008): 115–34; Will Potter, *Green Is the New Red: An Insider's Account of a Social Movement Under Siege* (San Francisco: City Lights Publishers, 2011).

94. Ingrid Chapman, "Hearts on Fire: The Struggle for Justice in New Orleans," *Znet*, September 8, 2007.

95. My discussion of Katrina and its aftermath is based on Scott Crow, *Black Flags and Windmills: Hope, Anarchy, and the Common Ground Collective* (Oakland: PM Press, 2011); Jordan Flaherty, *Floodlines: Community and Resistance from Katrina to the Jena Six* (Chicago: Haymarket Books, 2010); Rachel Luft, "Looking for Common Ground: Relief Work in Post-Katrina New Orleans as an American Parable of Race and Gender Violence," *NWSA Journal* 20, no. 3 (Fall 2008): 5–31; South End Press, ed., *What Lies Beneath: Katrina, Race, and the State of the Nation* (Cambridge, MA: South End Press, 2007); Clyde Woods, "The Politics of Reproductive Violence: An Interview with Shana Griffin by Clyde Woods, March 12, 2009." *American Quarterly* 61, no. 3 (September 2009): 583–91.

96. This account of the immigrant rights mobilizations draws on Clare Bayard, "Immigrant Justice Rising," *Left Turn*, September 2006; Subhash Kateel, "Immigrant Rights Movement at the Crossroads," *Left Turn*, June 2006; Alexis Mazón, "The U.S. Occupation of Border Communities," *Left Turn*,

September 2006; James Petras, "The Rise of the Migrant Workers Movement," *Left Turn*, September 2006.

97. For glimpses into this recent wave of organizing, see Luis Fernandez and Joel Olson, "To Live, Love and Work Anywhere You Please," *Contemporary Political Theory* 10, no. 3 (August 2011): 412–19; Marisa Franco, "How a Bus Full of Undocumented Families Could Change the Immigration Debate," *YES! Magazine*, November 30, 2012; Paulina Gonzalez, "The Strategy and Organizing Behind the Successful DREAM Act Movement," *Narco News*, July 10, 2012; B. Loewe, "Turning the Tide: Migrant Rights, Barrio Defense, and New Directions," *Left Turn*, February 2011.

98. On these organizing efforts, see Mostafah Henaway, Nandita Sharma, Jaggi Singh, Harsha Walia, and Rafeef Ziadah, "Organizing for Migrant Justice and Self-Determination," *Infoshop.org*, October 22, 2007; Thomas Nail, ed., "Building Sanctuary City: NOII-Toronto on Non-Status Migrant Justice Organizing," *Upping the Anti* 11 (2010): 147–60; Macdonald Scott, ed., "Fighting Borders: A Roundtable on Non-Status (Im)migrant Justice in Canada," *Upping the Anti* 2 (2005): 151–59; Harsha Walia, *Undoing Border Imperialism* (Oakland: AK Press, 2013).

99. On this, see Harsha Walia and Stefan Christoff, "Resistance Without Reservation!" *Znet*, August 5, 2004; Harsha Walia, "Resisting Displacement, North and South: Indigenous and Immigrant Struggles," *Znet*, August 12, 2003.

100. On these struggles, see Hazel Hill, "Sago from Grand River: Dispatches from the Six Nations Land Reclamation Struggle," *Left Turn*, August 2007; Keefer, "Declaring the Exception"; Tom Keefer, "The Politics of Solidarity: Six Nations, Leadership, and the Left," *Upping the Anti* 4 (2007): 107–23; Keefer, "The Six Nations Land Reclamation," *Upping the Anti* 3 (2006): 135–67; Jeff Shantz, "Reclamation: The Role of Solidarity in the Six Nations Struggle for Their Land," *The Northeastern Anarchist*, Winter 2007.

101. For accounts of these struggles, see Chris Arsenault, "Native Leader Serving Six Months for Opposing Mine: Supporters Call Algonquin Leader a 'Political Prisoner'," *The Dominion*, March 16, 2008; Henry Martin, "A Border Runs Through It: Mohawk Sovereignty and the Canadian State," *Briarpatch*, August 2010; Tim McSorley, "Reprieve in Barriere Lake Forestry Battle," *The Dominion*, October 2012; Shiri Pasternak, "'They're Clear-Cutting Our Way of Life': Algonquins Defend the Forest," *Upping the Anti* 8 (2009): 125–41; Justin Podur, "Canada's Newest Political Prisoners: Indigenous Leaders Jailed for Protesting Mining Exploration on Their Lands," *The Dominion*, October 23, 2008.

102. On this, see Julien Lalonde, Murray Bush, and Brett Rhyno, "Many Pipelines, More Resistance," *The Dominion*, December 2012; Tyler McCreary, "Oil and Water Don't Mix: Dakelh Communities Defend Their Land and Watercourses from Enbridge's Northern Gateway Pipeline Project," *Briarpatch*, April 2011; Toghestiy Wet'suwet'en, "A Wet'suwet'en Grassroots Alliance," *The Dominion*, May 2011.

103. On these mobilizations, see David Ball, "Idle No More Sweeps Canada and Beyond as Aboriginals Say Enough Is Enough," *Indian Country Today,* December 22, 2012; "Idle No More Across Turtle Island," *The Dominion,* April 2013; Martin Lukacs, "Canada's First Nations Protest Heralds a New Alliance," *The Guardian,* December 20, 2012.

104. See "Our Way or the Highway: Inside the Minnehaha Free State," in *The Struggle Is Our Inheritance: A Radical History of Minnesota* (zine, Minneapolis, 2008), 70–74; Austin Night, Emily Night, and David Night, "From Here to the Free State: Building the Bridge in Minneapolis," *Arsenal: A Magazine of Anarchist Strategy and Culture,* Spring 2001.

105. See Liza Minno Bloom, Hallie Boas, and Berkley Carnine, "Collective Liberation: Lesson Learned in Allyship with Indigenous Resistance at Black Mesa," *Left Turn,* August 2011.

106. On the anti-Olympics mobilization, see Maryann Abbs, Caelie Frampton, and Jessica Peart, eds., "Going for Gold on Stolen Land: A Roundtable on Anti-Olympic Organizing," *Upping the Anti* 9 (2009): 141–57; Jane Kirby, "Mass Protests and the Future of Convergence Activism: Is Summit-Hopping a Dying Tactic or the Next Olympic Sport?" *Briarpatch,* February 2010; Maya Rolbin-Ghanie, "'It's All About The Land': Native Resistance to the Olympics," *The Dominion,* March 1, 2008.

107. This account of the climate justice movement is based on Bryan Farrell, "The Eyes of Texas Are Upon You, Keystone XL," *Waging Nonviolence,* November 21, 2012; Bryan Farrell, "From the Tar Sands Action to Moving Planet," *Waging Nonviolence,* September 9, 2011; Cameron Fenton, "Changing the System," *The Dominion,* April 2011; Hilary Moore, "An Ethic of Care: A Relationship-Based Approach to Climate Justice Organizing in the Bay Area," MA thesis, Institute for Social Ecology, 2010; Hilary Moore and Joshua Kahn Russell, *Organizing Cools the Planet: Tools and Reflections to Navigate the Climate Crisis* (Oakland: PM Press, 2011); Clayton Thomas-Muller, "Tar Sands: The World's Largest Climate Crime," *Left Turn,* February 2010; Tricia Shapiro, *Mountain Justice: Homegrown Resistance to Mountaintop Removal, For the Future of Us All* (Oakland: AK Press, 2010); Brian Tokar, "Toward a Movement for Climate Justice," in *Uses of A Whirlwind: Movement, Movements, and Contemporary Radical Currents in the United States,* ed. Team Colors Collective (Oakland: AK Press, 2010), 135–48.

108. My discussion of recent organizing against prisons and policing draws on Abolitionist Editorial Collective, "Taking Stock of Critical Resistance," *The Abolitionist,* Summer 2011; Dan Berger, "Social Movements and Mass Incarceration: What Is to Be Done?" *Souls* 15, no. 1–2 (January 2013): 3–18; Niko Block, "Prison Farms on Death Row," *The Dominion,* October 2010; Rachel Herzing and Isaac Ontiveros, "Reflections from the Fight Against Policing," in *We Are Many: Reflections on Movement Strategy from Occupation to Liberation,* ed. Kate Khatib, Margaret Killjoy, and Mike McGuire (Oakland: AK Press, 2012), 217–27; Robyn Maynard, "Double Punishment for Villanueva," *The Dominion,* July 2010; Isaac Ontiveros and Rachel Herzing, "Repression Breeds

Resistance: Reflections on 10 Years of the Prison Industrial Complex," *Left Turn*, May 2011; Isaac Ontiveros and Rachel Herzing, "Resisting the War on Gangs (Inside and Out)." *The Abolitionist*, Summer 2012; Raider Nation Collective, ed., *From the January Rebellions to Lovelle Mixon and Beyond* (booklet, Oakland: Raider Nation, 2010); Ana Clarissa Rojas Durazo, Alisa Bierria, and Mimi Kim, eds., *Community Accountability: Emerging Movements to Transform Violence,* special issue of *Social Justice: A Journal of Crime, Conflict and World Order* 37, no. 4 (2011–2012).

109. On this movement wave, see Bassam Haddad, Rosie Bsheer, and Ziad Abu-Rish, eds., *The Dawn of the Arab Uprisings: End of an Old Order?* (London: Pluto Press, 2012); Paul Mason, *Why It's Kicking Off Everywhere: The New Global Revolutions* (London: Verso, 2012); Michael D. Yates, ed., *Wisconsin Uprising: Labor Fights Back* (New York: Monthly Review Press, 2012).

110. Manissa McCleave Maharawal, "Reflections from the People of Color Caucus at Occupy Wall Street," in *We Are Many: Reflections on Movement Strategy from Occupation to Liberation*, ed. Kate Khatib, Margaret Killjoy, and Mike McGuire (Oakland: AK Press, 2012), 178.

111. This description of the occupy movement is based on my own experiences as well as the documents, reports, and reflections collected in Carla Blumenkranz, Keith Gessen, Mark Greif, Sarah Leonard, Sarah Resnick, Nikil Saval, Eli Schmitt, and Astra Taylor, eds., *Occupy! Scenes from Occupied America* (London: Verso, 2011); Kate Khatib, Margaret Killjoy, and Mike McGuire, eds., *We Are Many: Reflections on Movement Strategy from Occupation to Liberation* (Oakland: AK Press, 2012); Amy Lang and Daniel Lang/Levitsky, eds., *Dreaming in Public: Building the Occupy Movement* (Oxford: New Internationalist Publications, 2012).

112. On the 2012 Quebec student strike, see Marianne Garneau, "Austerity and Resistance: Lessons from the 2012 Quebec Student Strike," *Insurgent Notes*, October 15, 2012; Anna Kruzynski, Rachel Sarrasin, and Sandra Jeppesen, "It Didn't Start with Occupy, and It Won't End with the Student Strike! The Persistence of Anti-authoritarian Politics in Quebec," *Wi Journal*, 2012; Jerome Raza, "The History of the Quebec Student Movement and Combative Unionism," *Anarkismo*, November 26, 2012; Elise Thorburn, ed., "Squarely in the Red: Dispatches from the 2012 Quebec Student Strike," *Upping the Anti* 14 (2012): 107–21.

2. "DEFINING OURSELVES IN OPPOSITION"

Epigraph: Maia Ramnath, *Decolonizing Anarchism* (Oakland: AK Press, 2011), 16.

1. No One Is Illegal-Montreal, "No One Is Illegal-Montreal's Basis of Unity," *No One Is Illegal-Montreal* (blog), December 27, 2006. http://nooneis-illegal-montreal.blogspot.com/2006/12/no-one-is-illegal-montreals-basis-of.html.

2. *Upping the Anti* lists three "anti's": anti-capitalism, anti-oppression, and anti-imperialism. Upping the Anti Editorial Committee, "Editorial," *Upping the Anti* 1 (2005): 7. To these, I've added anti-authoritarianism.

3. Mao Tsetung, *Five Essays on Philosophy* (Peking: Foreign Languages Press, 1977), 156.

4. Max Elbaum, *Revolution in the Air: Sixties Radicals Turn to Lenin, Mao and Che* (London: Verso, 2002), 157.

5. John Holloway, *Change the World without Taking Power*, 2nd ed. (London: Pluto, 2005), 121, 122.

6. For an analysis of this tendency in the anti-war movement, see Max Uhlenbeck, "The Antiwar Movement and the 2008 Elections," *Left Turn*, February 2008. Uhlenbeck's argument has strongly influenced my discussion here.

7. For commentary on this, see Marina Sitrin, "'Walking We Ask Questions': An Interview with John Holloway," *Perspectives on Anarchist Theory* 8, no. 2 (2004): 8–11; RJ Maccani, "Enter the Intergalactic: The Zapatistas' Sixth Declaration in the U.S. and the World," *Upping the Anti* 3 (2006): 105–21..

8. El Kilombo Intergaláctico, *Feliz Año Cabrones: On the Continued Centrality Of the Zapatista Movement After 14 Years* (Durham, NC: El Kilombo Intergaláctico, 2008), 37.

9. Starhawk, *Webs of Power: Notes from the Global Uprising* (Gabriola, B.C.: New Society Publishers, 2002), 170. See her original discussion of this concept in Starhawk, *Truth or Dare: Encounters with Power, Authority, and Mystery* (San Francisco: Harper and Row, 1987), 9–20. See also El Kilombo Intergaláctico, *Beyond Resistance: Everything* (Durham, NC: Paperboat Press, 2007), 9–11; Holloway, *Change the World*, chapter 3. Anarchist scholar-activist Uri Gordon has engaged this discussion of power in great detail, though I am unconvinced by the way he uses it to oppose formal organizational structures. See Uri Gordon, *Anarchy Alive! Anti-Authoritarian Politics from Practice to Theory* (London: Pluto Press, 2008), chapter 3.

10. The actual development of anarchist ideas and movements has a far richer and more complex history than is usually understood. Migration, expatriation, and exile—all fundamental to the world-historical experience of colonialism, capitalism, and imperialism—have long created conditions for the global circulation of anarchist ideas and activists. Historians of anarchism are only beginning to uncover this. For some contributions to a non-Eurocentric history of anarchism, see Jason Adams, "Nonwestern Anarchisms: Rethinking the Global Context," May 6, 2006. http://www.infoshop.org/texts/nonwestern.pdf; Steven Hirsch and Lucien van der Walt, eds., *Anarchism and Syndicalism in the Colonial and Postcolonial World, 1870–1940: The Praxis of National Liberation, Internationalism, and Social Revolution* (Leiden: Brill, 2010); Maia Ramnath, *Haj to Utopia: How the Ghadar Movement Charted Global Radicalism and Attempted to Overthrow the British Empire* (Berkeley: University of California Press, 2011); Michael Schmidt and Lucien van der Walt, *Black Flame: The Revolutionary Class Politics of Anarchism and Syndicalism* (Oakland: AK Press, 2009).

11. For further elaboration on this, see Ramnath, *Decolonizing Anarchism.*

12. Roger White, *Post Colonial Anarchism: Essays on Race, Repression and Culture in Communities of Color, 1999–2004* (Oakland: Jailbreak Press, 2004), 65. See also Otto Nomous, "Race, Anarchy, and Punk Rock: The Impact of Cultural Boundaries Within the Anarchist Movement," Colours of Resistance Archive, accessed August 31, 2012, http://www.coloursofresistance.org/575 /race-anarchy-and-punk-rock-the-impact-of-cultural-boundaries-within-the-anarchist-movement/.

13. Since 2000, two waves of the Anarchist People of Color (APOC) network have consistently raised these questions. For more on APOC, see the two APOC collections: Ernesto Aguilar, ed., *Our Culture, Our Resistance: People of Color Speak Out on Anarchism, Race, Class and Gender* (Houston: APOC, 2004); Ernesto Aguilar, ed., *Our Culture, Our Resistance: Further Conversations with People of Color on Anarchism, Race, Class and Gender* (Houston: APOC, 2004).

14. Paula X. Rojas, "Are the Cops in Our Heads and Hearts?" in *The Revolution Will Not Be Funded: Beyond the Non-Profit Industrial Complex,* ed. INCITE! Women of Color Against Violence (Cambridge, MA: South End Press, 2007), 200.

15. As Lenin put it, "Class political consciousness can be brought to the workers *only from without,* that is, only from outside the economic struggle, from outside the sphere of relations between workers and employers." Lenin, "What Is to Be Done? Burning Questions of Our Movement," in *The Lenin Anthology,* ed. Robert C. Tucker (New York: W.W. Norton and Company, 1975), 50.

16. It is worth noting that many experienced anti-authoritarian organizers explain that they understand the impulses behind vanguardism. Clare Bayard, an organizer with the Catalyst Project in San Francisco, acknowledged, "There's a lot of questions for me about the role of leadership in the sense that gets proposed by the vanguard. And I even mean that in the charitable sense of 'vanguard'—of people who think that there has to be this grouping of full-time people who are just giving themselves to the movement and that part of their job is to be getting the mandate from the people." In discussing this, Bayard referenced what she called "the Zapatistas' version" of vanguardism, *mandar obedeciendo,* which roughly translates as "leading we obey." She said, "It's very hard for me to dismiss that, given that we're in circumstances where some of us are full-time or part-time—whatever, some of us are devoted to the 'rev' [revolution]. And there's a lot of people who we know want to be connected to the movement, and what they need is non-full-time ways to do that because it's not what they want or are able to do currently. And then what's our relationship to them?" This is an important question. James Tracy, a writer and housing organizer also based in San Francisco, offered the beginning of an answer; he suggested "trying to figure out something that is really organized, has structure, but doesn't do that type of top-down, sectarian, dogmatic, uncreative, unjoyful, burn your ass out, cult-of-personality bullshit."

17. This paragraph and the previous one draw on Harry Cleaver, *Reading Capital Politically* (San Francisco: AK Press, 2000); Silvia Federici, *Caliban and*

the Witch: Women, the Body, and Primitive Accumulation (Brooklyn: Autonomedia, 2004); Rosa Luxemburg, *The Accumulation of Capital*, trans. Agnes Schwarzschild (London: Routledge, 2003); Karl Marx, *Capital: A Critique of Political Economy*, trans. Ben Fowkes, vol. 1 (London: Penguin Books, 1976); Karl Marx, *Early Writings*, trans. Gregor Benton and Rodney Livingstone (New York: Vintage Books, 1975); Vandana Shiva, *Staying Alive: Women, Ecology and Development* (London: Zed Books, 1988).

18. This account of neoliberalism is based upon Michel Chossudovsky, *The Globalization of Poverty: Impacts of IMF and World Bank Reforms* (Penang, Malaysia: Third World Network, 1997); Peter Gowan, *The Global Gamble: Washington's Faustian Bid for World Dominance* London: Verso, 1999); David Harvey, *A Brief History of Neoliberalism* (New York: Oxford University Press, 2005); Midnight Notes Collective, ed., *Auroras of the Zapatistas: Local and Global Struggles of the Fourth World War* (Brooklyn: Autonomedia, 2001); Midnight Notes Collective, ed., *Midnight Oil: Work, Energy, War, 1973–1992* (Brooklyn: Autonomedia, 1992); Vandana Shiva, *Stolen Harvest: The Hijacking of the Global Food Supply* (Cambridge, MA: South End Press, 2000).

19. On the economic crisis and the new round of neoliberal measures, see David McNally, *Global Slump: The Economics and Politics of Crisis and Resistance* (Oakland: PM Press, 2010); Midnight Notes and Friends, *Promissory Notes: From Crises to Commons* (Jamaica Plain, MA: Midnight Notes, 2009).

20. Cindy Milstein, *Anarchism and Its Aspirations* (Oakland: AK Press, 2010), 89.

21. Activist and writer Eddie Yuen argues this very convincingly. See Yuen, "Introduction," in *Confronting Capitalism: Dispatches from a Global Movement*, ed. Eddie Yuen, George Katsiaficas, and Daniel Burton Rose (New York: Soft Skull Press, 2004), vii–xxix.

22. See Holloway, *Change the World*, 114–117; John Holloway, *Crack Capitalism* (London: Pluto Press, 2010), 253–61.

23. For more on the CIW, see Coalition of Immokalee Workers, "Consciousness + Commitment = Change," in *Globalize Liberation: How to Uproot the System and Build a Better World*, ed. David Solnit (San Francisco: City Lights, 2004), 347–60; Elly Leary, "Immokalee Workers Take Down Taco Bell," *Monthly Review* 57, no. 5 (2005): 11–25; Marc Rodrigues, "Coalition of Immokalee Workers: McDonald's Campaign Escalates," *Left Turn*, February 2007; Marc Rodrigues, "Farmworker and Student Victory Over Burger King," *Left Turn*, November 2008; Marc Rodrigues, "Organizing After Victory: Immokalee Encuentro," *Left Turn*, November 2005; David Solnit, "The New Face of the Global Justice Movement: Taco Bell Victory—A Model of Strategic Organizing," *Left Turn*, September 2005.

24. This analysis of capitalism has principally developed from the "So-Called Primitive Accumulation" section in Marx, *Capital*, 1:871–940.

25. For some of the basis of this view, see Karl Marx and Friedrich Engels, "Manifesto of the Communist Party," in *The Marx-Engels Reader*, ed. Robert C. Tucker (New York: WW Norton & Company, 1978), 469–500.

26. Movement-oriented publications that have helped develop and circulate this analysis include Massimo De Angelis, *The Beginning of History: Value Struggles and Global Capital* (London: Pluto Press, 2006); Federici, *Caliban and the Witch;* Naomi Klein, *The Shock Doctrine: The Rise of Disaster Capitalism* (New York: Picador, 2008); Midnight Notes Collective, *Auroras of the Zapatistas;* Notes from Nowhere, ed., *We Are Everywhere: The Irresistible Rise of Global Anticapitalism* (London: Verso, 2003); Vandana Shiva, *Biopiracy: The Plunder of Nature and Knowledge* (Boston: South End Press, 1997).

27. This analysis has developed from many sources, some of which have crystallized in writing. See Mariarosa Dalla Costa and Selma James, *The Power of Women and the Subversion of the Community* (Bristol: Falling Wall Press, 1975); Angela Davis, *Are Prisons Obsolete?* (New York: Seven Stories Press, 2003); Silvia Federici, *Revolution at Point Zero: Housework, Reproduction, and Feminist Struggle* (Oakland: PM Press, 2012); Ellen Malos, ed., *The Politics of Housework* (London: Allison and Busby, 1980); Maria Mies, *Patriarchy and Accumulation on a World Scale: Women in the International Division of Labor,* 2nd ed. (London: Zed Books, 1998); Cedric Robinson, *Black Marxism: The Making of the Black Radical Tradition* (London: Zed Books, 1983); Shiva, *Staying Alive.*

28. On this, see Luxemburg, *The Accumulation of Capital.*

29. This section builds on Upping the Anti Editorial Committee, "Breaking the Impasse," *Upping the Anti* 2 (2006): 14–21.

30. This paragraph and the previous one draw on Michael Albert, Leslie Cagan, Noam Chomsky, Robin Hahnel, Mel King, Lydia Sargent, and Holly Sklar, *Liberating Theory* (Boston: South End Press, 1986); Himani Bannerji, *Thinking Through: Essays on Feminism, Marxism and Anti-Racism* (Toronto: Women's Press, 1995); Eli Clare, *Exile and Pride: Disability, Queerness and Liberation* (Cambridge, MA: South End Press, 2009); Angela Davis, *Women, Race and Class* (New York: Vintage Books, 1981); Leslie Feinberg, *Trans Liberation: Beyond Pink or Blue* (Boston: Beacon Press, 1998); bell hooks, *Feminist Theory from Margin to Center* (Boston, MA: South End Press, 1984); Joanna Kadi, *Thinking Class: Sketches from a Cultural Worker* (Boston: South End Press, 1996); Gary Kinsman, *The Regulation of Desire: Homo and Hetero Sexualities,* 2nd ed. (Montreal: Black Rose Books, 1996); Scott Neigh, *Gender and Sexuality: Canadian History Through the Stories of Activists* (Black Point, NS: Fernwood Publishing, 2012); Joel Olson, *The Abolition of White Democracy* (Minneapolis: University of Minnesota Press, 2004); Michael Omi and Howard Winant, *Racial Formation in the United States: From the 1960s to the 1990s,* 2nd ed. (New York: Routledge, 1994); David Roediger, *The Wages of Whiteness: Race and the Making of the American Working Class,* 2nd ed. (London: Verso, 1999).

31. Elizabeth (Betita) Martinez, "Where Was the Color in Seattle? Looking for Reasons Why the Great Battle Was so White," *ColorLines* 3, no. 1 (2000): 11.

32. For a list of important contributions to these conversations, see note 88 of the previous chapter.

33. The Anti-Racism for Global Justice project of Challenging White Supremacy Workshop became the Catalyst Project in 2004.

34. One of the first efforts to develop anti-oppression principles of this sort was in the Los Angeles Direct Action Network in its organizing against the 2000 Democratic National Convention in Los Angeles. These principles have remained influential, particularly as they were integrated with other principles by direct action organizer and trainer Lisa Fithian. See Lisa Fithian, "Anti-Oppression Principles and Practices," *Organizing for Power, Organizing for Change*, accessed April 29, 2013, https://docs.google.com/document/d/1TnaLJXy6WSkJ-MQv4BlMhRXM1cc-4wBqNcgrD4W-VZQ/edit?pli = 1.

35. Nicole Burrowes, Morgan Cousins, Paula X. Rojas, and Ije Ude, "On Our Own Terms: Ten Years of Radical Community Building with Sista II Sista," in *The Revolution Will Not Be Funded: Beyond the Non-Profit Industrial Complex*, ed. INCITE! Women of Color Against Violence (Cambridge, MA: South End Press, 2007), 228.

36. LA Crew, "Ideas in Action: An LA Story," *Left Turn*, February 2009, 54.

37. Clare Bayard and Chris Crass, "Anti-Racism for Collective Liberation: An Interview with the Catalyst Project," *Infoshop.org*, May 23, 2006, http://www.infoshop.org/inews/article.php?story = 2006catalyst_interview. See also Chris Crass, *Towards Collective Liberation: Anti-Racist Organizing, Feminist Praxis, and Movement Building Strategy* (Oakland: PM Press, 2013), 17–18.

38. Sharmeen Khan, ed., "Roundtable on Anti-Oppression Politics in Anti-Capitalist Movements," *Upping the Anti* 1 (2005): 86.

39. The account in these opening paragraphs draws on Noam Chomsky, *Year 501: The Conquest Continues* (Boston: South End Press, 1993); Ward Churchill, *A Little Matter of Genocide: Holocaust and Denial in the Americas, 1492 to the Present* (San Francisco: City Lights Books, 1997); Frantz Fanon, *The Wretched of the Earth* (New York: Grove Press, 1963); Eduardo H. Galeano, *Open Veins of Latin America: Five Centuries of the Pillage of a Continent* (New York: Monthly Review Press, 1997); Butch Lee and Red Rover, *Night-Vision: Illuminating War and Class on the Neo-Colonial Terrain* (New York: Vagabond, 1993); Luxemburg, *The Accumulation of Capital*; Anne McClintock, Aamir Mufti, Ella Shohat, and Social Text Collective, *Dangerous Liaisons: Gender, Nation, and Postcolonial Perspectives* (Minneapolis: University of Minnesota Press, 1997); Midnight Notes Collective, *Midnight Oil*; Robinson, *Black Marxism*; Walter Rodney, *How Europe Underdeveloped Africa* (Washington, DC: Howard University Press, 1993).

40. On the Central American solidarity movement, see Van Gosse, "'The North American Front': Central American Solidarity in the Reagan Era," in *Reshaping the US Left: Popular Struggles in the 1980s*, ed. Mike Davis and Michael Sprinker (London: Verso, 1988), 1–43; Christian Smith, *Resisting Reagan: The U.S. Central America Peace Movement* (Chicago: University of Chicago Press, 1996); Becky Thompson, *A Promise and a Way of Life: White Antiracist Activism* (Minneapolis: University of Minnesota Press, 2001), chapter 8; Tony Vellela, *New Voices: Student Political Activism in the '80s and '90s*

(Boston: South End Press, 1988), chapter 4. On the anti-apartheid movement, see Janice Love, *The U.S. Anti-Apartheid Movement: Local Activism in Global Politics* (New York: Praeger, 1985); Henry Muhanika, "Anti-Apartheid Campaign in Canada," PhD dissertation, Carleton University, 1987; Vellela, *New Voices*, chapter 3.

41. See, for instance, Subcomandante Marcos, "A Death Has Been Decided," July 2003. http://struggle.ws/mexico/ezln/2003/marcos/deathJULY.html.

42. On this, see El Kilombo Intergaláctico, *Beyond Resistance*.

43. On the complexities of this kind of solidarity, see Alex Khasnabish, *Zapatismo Beyond Borders: New Imaginations of Political Possibility* (Toronto: University of Toronto Press, 2008), chapter 6.

44. John Ross, "Another Year Is Possible! Flashlights in the Tunnel of Hate," *Counterpunch*, December 24, 2006.

45. On Movement for Justice in El Barrio, see RJ Maccani, "Urban Zapatismo in NYC," *Left Turn*, May 2008.

46. This paragraph and the previous one draw on El Kilombo Intergaláctico, *Feliz Año Cabrones*, 28–36; Adjoa Jones de Almeida, Dana Kaplan, Paula Ximena Rojas-Urrutia, Eric Tang, and M. Mayuran Tiruchelvam, "Rethinking Solidarity," *Left Turn*, June 2006; Maccani, "'Be a Zapatista Wherever You Are': Learning Solidarity in the Fourth World War," *RESIST*, May 2008; Yuen, "Introduction," xix–xx.

47. For history and analysis of the occupation, see Noam Chomsky, *Fateful Triangle: The United States, Israel, and the Palestinians*, 2nd ed. (Cambridge, MA: South End Press, 1999); Norman Finkelstein, *Image and Reality of the Israel-Palestine Conflict* (London: Verso, 2003); Edward Said, *The Question of Palestine*, 2nd ed. (London: Vintage, 1992).

48. *Left Turn* magazine played a particularly important role in circulating information and analysis about this upsurge of Palestinian struggles as well as international solidarity efforts.

49. Probably the most well-known North American ISM activist was Rachel Corrie, who was killed in 2003 while attempting to prevent a Palestinian house from being bulldozed by the Israeli military in the Gaza Strip. For an introduction to the ISM as well as firsthand accounts, see Nancy Stohlman and Laurieann Aladin, eds., *Live from Palestine: International and Palestinian Direct Action Against the Israeli Occupation* (Cambridge, MA: South End Press, 2003).

50. On Anarchists Against the Wall, see Uri Gordon and Ohal Grietzer, eds., *Anarchists Against the Wall* (Oakland: AK Press, 2013).

51. Adam Hanieh, Hazem Jamjoum, and Rafeef Ziadah, "Challenging the New Apartheid: Reflections on Palestine Solidarity," *Left Turn*, June 2006, 61.

52. For the original call, see Council of National and Islamic Forces in Palestine, et al., "Palestinian Civil Society Calls for Boycott, Divestment and Sanctions Against Israel Until It Complies with International Law and Universal Principles of Human Rights," July 9, 2005, http://www.bdsmovement.net/call.

53. For more on these efforts and organizations, see Nora Barrows-Friedman, "Beyond Bil'in: BDS and Israel's Crackdown on the Palestinian Popular Struggle," *Left Turn*, April 2010; Coalition Against Israeli Apartheid, "Boycotting Israeli Apartheid in Toronto," *Left Turn*, February 2007; Noura Erakat and Monadel Herzallah, "National Popular Palestinian Conference," *Left Turn*, May 2008; Andrew Hugill, "Coalition Against Israeli Apartheid," *Left Turn*, May 2008; Jamal Jumaa, "'To Exist Is to Resist': From the Apartheid Wall in Palestine and Beyond," *Left Turn*, August 2008; Kole Kilibarda, "Confronting Apartheid: The BDS Movement in Canada," *Upping the Anti* 7 (2008): 131–43; Daniel Lang/Levitsky, "Jews Confront Zionism," *Monthly Review* 61, no. 2 (2009): 47–54; Robyn Letson, ed., "Coming Out Against Apartheid: A Roundtable About Queer Solidarity with Palestine," *Upping the Anti* 13 (2011): 137–51; Clare O'Connor and Caitlin Hewitt-White, "Labour Solidarity for Palestine: Unions and the BDS Movement," *Upping the Anti* 7 (2008): 145–60; Upping the Anti Editorial Committee, ed., "Perspectives on Palestine Solidarity Organizing," *Upping the Anti* 2 (2005): 103–26; Rafeef Ziadah, "60 Years of Israeli Apartheid and Occupation," *Left Turn*, May 2008.

54. One important site where anti-authoritarians began to engage this question was the 2005 Montreal conference Land, Decolonization and Self-Determination. As the conference organizers wrote, "We see decolonization as being only possible through active and collaborative efforts. This necessarily requires a parallel process of mutual self-determination and active solidarity between Indigenous and non-Indigenous communities, founded on a respect for the autonomy of all peoples, groups and individuals." Indigenous Peoples Solidarity Movement, "Land, Decolonization and Self-Determination," *A-Infos*, March 16, 2005, www.ainfos.ca/05/mar/ainfos00299.html.

55. For more on this, see Ramnath, *Decolonizing Anarchism.*

56. Upping the Anti Editorial Committee, ed.,"Perspectives on Palestine Solidarity Organizing," 118.

57. For further elaboration on this, see Harsha Walia, "Moving Beyond a Politics of Solidarity Toward a Practice of Decolonization," in *Organize! Building from the Local for Global Justice*, ed. Aziz Choudry, Jill Hanley, and Eric Shragge (Oakland: PM Press, 2012), 240–53.

58. The Palestinian National Authority is the very limited form of state-like government that was granted to Palestinians over parts of the occupied territories through the 1993 Oslo Accords between Palestine and Israel.

59. Singh made this comment while discussing a tendency in which anarchism "is cut off and simply stands in distant judgment of everything." He continued, "that happens sometimes with Palestine solidarity. People can't get beyond asking, 'So, what about this whole nation-state question?' I reply: 'You don't think that's a live discussion when you're doing Palestine solidarity organizing as an anarchist? You don't think that's a live discussion among Palestinian radicals themselves?' The key is to have those discussions within the context of the organizing and the struggle, not abstracted away from it."

60. In addition to those quoted, this paragraph draws on Ashanti Alston, "Beyond Nationalism But Not Without It," *Onward*, Spring 2002; Gordon, *Anarchy Alive!*, chapter 6; Maia Ramnath, "Anticolonialism and the Anarchist Imagination," *Perspectives on Anarchist Theory* 5 (2006): 79–86; Michael Staudenmaier, "Nationalism: Definitions and Clarifications," *Onward*, Spring 2002; Michael Staudenmaier, "What Good Are Nations? Anarchism and Nationalism," *Arsenal: A Magazine of Anarchist Strategy and Culture*, Spring 2001.

3. "ORGANIZING NOW THE WAY YOU WANT TO SEE THE WORLD LATER"

Epigraph: Andrea Smith, *Conquest: Sexual Violence and American Indian Genocide* (Cambridge, MA: South End Press, 2005), 187.

1. Scholar and activist Wini Brienes originally developed the term "prefigurative politics" to analyze the New Left. See Wini Breines, *Community and Organization in the New Left, 1962–1968: The Great Refusal* (Rutgers University Press, 1989).

2. The Team Colors Collective, perhaps more than anyone, has sharply articulated this critique. "Prefiguration," they write, " has come to justify the self-limited organizing that so frequently holds the attention of radicals. From this standpoint, any action, regardless of how self-referential and ineffectual, is considered a 'win,' simply because its very existence supposedly prefigures a world to come." Team Colors Collective, "Abandoning the Chorus: Checking Ourselves a Decade Since Seattle," *Groundswell* 1 (2010): 17–18. See also Team Colors Collective, *Wind(s) from Below: Radical Community Organizing to Make a Revolution Possible* (Portland, OR: Eberhardt Press, 2010), 79–82.

3. Andrew Cornell, *Oppose and Propose! Lessons from Movement for a New Society* (Oakland: AK Press, 2011), 161.

4. My discussion of different forms of prefigurative activity draws on Cornell, *Oppose and Propose!*, 161–65.

5. For more on this, see Francesca Polletta, *Freedom Is an Endless Meeting: Democracy in American Social Movements* (Chicago: University of Chicago Press, 2002), 8–10, 209–12.

6. This is only a thumbnail sketch of consensus decision-making process. For a detailed description, see C.T. Lawrence Butler and Amy Rothstein, *On Conflict and Consensus: A Handbook on Formal Consensus Decisionmaking*, 2nd ed. (Portland, ME: Food Not Bombs, 1991). For a history, see Andrew Cornell, "Consensus: What It Is, What It Isn't, Where It Comes From, and Where It Must Go," in *We Are Many: Reflections on Movement Strategy from Occupation to Liberation*, ed. Kate Khatib, Margaret Killjoy, and Mike McGuire (Oakland: AK Press, 2012), 163–73.

7. Even while acknowledging this limitation, we have to look at time in other ways too. Sarita Ahooja, who was active in migrant justice and international solidarity organizing in Montreal, raised this crucial point. She observed

that "the whole concept of time—that's really hard for us here in the North, but it's really important. . . . Many people say, 'Oh, it's so process-heavy, long meetings' and so on. Yeah, but sometimes it's like that." Pointing to her experiences of peoples' assemblies in Latin America and in Indigenous communities in North America, she continued, "sometimes people just go on and on and on, and some people repeat things. But it's like, the old lady, she gets to talk too, no?" Part of what I understand Ahooja to be discussing here is a different concept of time that people develop together in struggle. As John Holloway reminds us, the dominant notion of time—"clock time, tick-tick time, in which one tick is just the same as another"—is central to capitalist social relations, which regulate our lives and our labor by the clock. John Holloway, *Change the World without Taking Power*, 2nd ed. (London: Pluto, 2005), 58. Movements, however, are sometimes able to create an alternative sense of time—time in which we deliberate and imagine things together or time when other parts of our lives seem to stand still while history moves very quickly. General assemblies and other directly democratic meetings, especially during intense periods of struggle, can be places where we experience this different sense of time. But as Ahooja acknowledges, there are also plenty of instances when it just feels like people are droning on. One challenge is to develop processes that can work with these very different experiences of time. For some helpful reflections on this, see Holloway, "The Two Temporalities of Counter-Power and Anti-Power," 2005, http://info.interactivist.net/node/4232.

8. Marina Sitrin, *Horizontalism: Voices of Popular Power in Argentina* (Oakland: AK Press, 2006), vi.

9. The Another Politics Is Possible study group in New York usefully talks about this as "the non-material dimensions of oppression." These include "the ways [oppression] impacts our individual and collective emotional lives and the damage we inflict on each other and ourselves." Dan Berger and Chris Dixon, eds., "Navigating the Crisis: A Study Groups Roundtable," *Upping the Anti* 8 (2009): 166.

10. This discussion builds on Sitrin, *Horizontalism*, vii, 230–37.

11. Paula X. Rojas, "Are the Cops in Our Heads and Hearts?" in *The Revolution Will Not Be Funded: Beyond the Non-Profit Industrial Complex*, ed. INCITE! Women of Color Against Violence (Cambridge, MA: South End Press, 2007), 208.

12. Although not always acknowledged by organizers, this notion of "invisible labor" has especially grown from feminist interventions in Marxism during the 1970s. These interventions crucially highlighted women's unwaged reproductive labor as foundational for capitalism. For some germinal texts, see Mariarosa Dalla Costa and Selma James, *The Power of Women and the Subversion of the Community* (Bristol: Falling Wall Press, 1975); Ellen Malos, ed., *The Politics of Housework* (London: Allison and Busby, 1980). For more recent work that develops this line of analysis, see Mariarosa Dalla Costa and Giovanna F. Dalla Costa, *Women, Development, and the Labor of Reproduction: Struggles and Movements* (Trenton, NJ: Africa World Press, 1999); Silvia

Federici, *Caliban and the Witch: Women, the Body, and Primitive Accumulation* (Brooklyn: Autonomedia, 2004); Silvia Federici, *Revolution at Point Zero: Housework, Reproduction, and Feminist Struggle* (Oakland: PM Press, 2012); Maria Mies, *Patriarchy and Accumulation on a World Scale: Women in the International Division of Labor,* 2nd ed. (London: Zed Books, 1998).

13. For more on childcare collectives, see Bay Area Childcare Collective, "An Interview with the Bay Area Childcare Collective," *Left Turn,* May 2007; Heather Bowlan, "While Caregivers Organize, the Kids Are Throwin' Seed Bombs: Radical Childcare Collectives in the United States," *Make/shift,* Fall/Winter 2010/2011; Regeneración Childcare Collective, "Once Upon a Time in Brooklyn," *Left Turn,* May 2007.

14. Long-time Montreal organizer Helen Hudson made this point very strongly: "It's one thing to have childcare for a meeting and another to make time to homeschool your kid or deal with your kid's school or health problems. All of this goes beyond taking narrowly defined collective responsibility for childcare. So many parents—mostly moms—disappear when the wider community doesn't create space for children and parents." For more elaborated reflections on kids and movements, see Rahula Janowski, "Collective Parenting for Collective Liberation," *Left Turn,* February 2007; Victoria Law, "Where's My Movement? Contemporary Anarchist Mothers and Community Support," *Perspectives on Anarchist Theory* 13, no. 1 (2011): 19–30; Vikki Law, "Creating Space for Kids in Our Movements," *Left Turn,* August 2011; Victoria Law and China Martens, eds., *Don't Leave Your Friends Behind: Concrete Ways to Support Families in Social Justice Movements and Communities* (Oakland: PM Press, 2012); Cynthia Oka, "Moving the Movement: Towards a Multigenerational Ideal of Revolutionary Work," *Left Turn,* August 2011.

15. As Federici writes, "We go to demonstrations, we build events, and this becomes the peak of our struggle. The analysis of how we reproduce these movements, how we reproduce ourselves is not at the center of movement organizing. It has to be. We need to go to back to the historical tradition of working class organizing 'mutual aid' and rethink that experience, not necessarily because we want to reproduce it, but to draw inspiration from it for the present. We need to build a movement that puts on its agenda its own reproduction. The anti-capitalist struggle has to create forms of support and has to have the ability to collectively build forms of reproduction." Silvia Federici, "Precarious Labor: A Feminist Viewpoint," *In the Middle of a Whirlwind,* 2008, https://inthemiddleofthewhirlwind.wordpress.com/precarious-labor-a-feminist-viewpoint/. For further useful discussion of self-reproducing movements, see Team Colors Collective, *Wind(s) from Below,* 88–94.

16. See, for instance, David Stein, "Surviving Warfare, Practicing Resistance," in *Abolition Now! Ten Years of Strategy and Struggle Against the Prison Industrial Complex,* ed. CR-10 Publications Collective (Oakland: AK Press, 2008), 89.

17. Manissa McCleave Maharawal, "Reflections from the People of Color Caucus at Occupy Wall Street," in *We Are Many: Reflections on Movement*

Strategy from Occupation to Liberation, ed. Kate Khatib, Margaret Killjoy, and Mike McGuire (Oakland: AK Press, 2012), 178.

18. For some elaboration on this question within women of color organizing, see Andrea Smith, "Heteropatriarchy and the Three Pillars of White Supremacy: Rethinking Women of Color Organizing," in *Color of Violence: The INCITE! Anthology,* ed. INCITE! Women of Color Against Violence (Cambridge, MA: South End Press, 2006), 66–73.

19. See, for instance, Vasudha Desikan and Drew Franklin, "From Building Tents to Building Movements: Reflections from Occupy," *In Front and Center,* January 25, 2012, https://infrontandcenter.wordpress.com/2012/01/25/from-building-tents-to-building-movements-reflections-from-occupy-dc/#more-540"; McCleave Maharawal, "Reflections from the People of Color Caucus"; Lydia Pelot-Hobbs, "Reflections on Organizing Towards Collective Liberation at Occupy NOLA," *In Front and Center,* October 20, 2011, https://infrontandcenter.wordpress.com/2011/10/20/reflections-on-organizing-towards-collective-liberation-at-occupy-nola/.

20. This term also circulates widely in other parts of the left, from the non-profit and agency sectors to various forms of community organizing.

21. Who counts as "most impacted" is a source of ongoing discussion in CR. As Herzing said, "Internally, we have a lot of struggle around it, which I think is really healthy. For somebody like me, it doesn't mean only prisoners and it doesn't mean only former prisoners. So, for me, it means people who get hurt by cops or harassed by cops [and] not even hurt—family members of all those people, detainees, queer people, young people. There are a lot of different ways to be impacted. We imagine the prison industrial complex as a very broad network of things and people. And I think, from my perspective, if that's how we imagine this thing, then the people who are impacted by it are equally broad and complex."

22. For some different perspectives on this, see El Kilombo Intergaláctico, *Beyond Resistance: Everything* (Durham, NC: Paperboat Press, 2007), 1–20; Tom Keefer, "The Politics of Solidarity: Six Nations, Leadership, and the Left," *Upping the Anti* 4 (2007): 107–23.; Harsha Walia, "Moving Beyond a Politics of Solidarity Toward a Practice of Decolonization," in *Organize! Building from the Local for Global Justice,* ed. Aziz Choudry, Jill Hanley, and Eric Shragge (Oakland: PM Press, 2012), 240–53.

23. Vancouver migrant justice organizer Harsha Walia called this the "classist terminology" that often infuses anti-oppression politics. Jill Chettiar, an anti-poverty organizer in Vancouver, elaborated: "Many of the [anti-oppression] tools we use in terms of material can be pretty dense academic literature. Now, this is not a universal problem for people, poor or otherwise—not trying to make assumptions here about people's literacy one way or the other. However, the goal is to make all the information as accessible as possible. It's ironic that sometimes anti-oppression work has structural barriers written in, eh?"

24. Much of this paragraph draws on my understanding of a very rich internal organizing document that No One Is Illegal-Vancouver generously shared with me.

25. For useful criticisms of this tendency, see Michelle O'Brien, "Whose Ally? Thinking Critically About Anti-oppression Ally Organizing," Colours of Resistance Archive, accessed April 29, 2013, www.coloursofresistance.org/370/whose-ally-thinking-critically-about-anti-oppression-ally-organizing-part-1/; Stephanie Guilloud, "Letter on Oppression within the Movement," in *Letters from Young Activists,* ed. Dan Berger, Chesa Boudin, and Kenyon Farrow (New York: Nation Books, 2005), 120–26; Catherine Jones, "The Work Is Not the Workshop: Talking and Doing, Visibility and Accountability in the White Anti-Racist Community," Colours of Resistance Archive, accessed April 29, 2013, http://www.coloursofresistance.org/345/the-work-is-not-the-workshop-talking-and-doing-visibility-and-accountability-in-the-white-anti-racist-community/.

26. We can see this starkly in how attempts to deal with power relations get co-opted. If anti-oppression is treated as an individualized thing disconnected from broader struggles, Sharmeen Khan explained, "It becomes a very multicultural, 'just be nice' kind of politics, which is then very easy to [have] snatched up by the state and by different social work programs [which] have lots of anti-oppression stuff now." While this is perhaps an easier process in Canada, with its history of recuperating demands for justice and equality into an official state policy of so-called "multiculturalism," there are similar tendencies in the United States. Ultimately, this co-optation converts "transforming power relations" into "reorganizing power relations for more effective domination." For a sharp discussion of this, see CROATOAN, "Who Is Oakland: Anti-Oppression Activism, the Politics of Safety, and State Co-optation," *Escalating Identity,* April 2012, https://escalatingidentity.wordpress.com/2012/04/30/who-is-oakland-anti-oppression-politics-decolonization-and-the-state/.

27. McCleave Maharawal, "Reflections from the People of Color Caucus," 182.

28. My argument here builds on Andrew Cornell, "Who Needs Ends When We've Got Such Bitchin' Means?" *LiP,* Summer 2005.

29. Joshua Kahn Russell and Brian Kelly, "Giving Form to a Stampede: The First Two Years of the New Students for a Democratic Society," *Upping the Anti* 6 (2008): 84.

30. David Solnit, "The New Radicalism: Uprooting the System and Building a Better World," in *Globalize Liberation: How to Uproot the System and Build a Better World,* ed. David Solnit (San Francisco: City Lights, 2004), xxii–xxiii.

31. Solnit, "The New Radicalism," xxiii.

32. Anarchist scholar Richard Day advocates a prefigurative politics that, in large part, discards any concern for achieving large-scale social transformation. In his book *Gramsci is Dead,* Day argues for an approach based on constructing liberatory alternatives in the present. He calls this "structural renewal," helpfully using a term from the radical philosopher Martin Buber. However, Day not-so-helpfully couples this with a rejection of what he understands as the logic of hegemony at the heart of both revolutionary and reform-oriented struggles. As he describes it, this logic is based on "the assumption that effective

social change can only be achieved simultaneously and *en masse*, across an entire national or supranational space." Day contends, "Revolution and reform have failed to produce the goods, it is true, and neither the masses nor the mass have any political potential. However, what it seems cannot *ever* be done *for anyone at all* using hegemonic methods can perhaps be done *by* some of us, *here and now*." Day thus proposes "exodus"—a "leave-taking" from existing society. We should do this in the global North, he says, by constructing alternatives that help us "to meet our own needs locally, thereby limiting our participation in, and draining energy from, the neoliberal order." In short, Day seems to give up on winning much of anything and, instead, to settle for generally small attempts to somehow exit the dominant system. Most troubling, he suggests that this approach is central to "contemporary radical activism." Richard Day, *Gramsci Is Dead: Anarchist Currents in the Newest Social Movements* (London: Pluto Press, 2005), 91, 8, 210, 214. Certainly there are some activists, anarchists among them, who could be broadly characterized by the orientation Day lays out. But to suggest that this is a dominant perspective among radical organizers is wrong. Most of us are much more ambitious: we value prefigurative politics *and* we want a transformed world—the only real exit from the existing one.

33. Team Colors Collective, *Wind(s) from Below*, 92. Emphasis in original.

4. "DO YOU WANT TO HAVE A CHANCE AT WINNING SOMETHING?"

Epigraph: Madeline Gardner and Joshua Kahn Russell, "Praxis Makes Perfect: The New Youth Organizing," in *Real Utopia: Participatory Society for the 21st Century*, ed. Chris Spannos (Oakland: AK Press, 2008), 341.

1. This concern has developed most directly out of criticisms of Leninism on the one hand and liberalism and social democracy on the other hand. Anti-authoritarians tend to see Leninism as sacrificing genuine democracy for an ultimately flawed revolution and liberalism and social democracy as sacrificing genuinely transformative politics for a seat at the table of power. For an elaboration of these criticisms in theoretical terms, see John Holloway, *Change the World without Taking Power*, 2nd ed. (London: Pluto, 2005). For some useful reflections on social democracy, see Upping the Anti Editorial Committee, "Between a Rock and a Hard Place: Social Democracy and Anti-Capitalist Renewal in English Canada," *Upping the Anti* no. 5 (2007): 29–45.

2. On this point, see Andrew Cornell, "Who Needs Ends When We've Got Such Bitchin' Means?" *LiP*, Summer 2005.

3. For elaboration on this, see Ruckus Society, "The Symbolic Nature of Direct Action," accessed October 1, 2012, http://www.ruckus.org/article.php?id = 99.

4. Many (but not all) in the anti-authoritarian current embrace direct action based on the influence of anarchism. For a helpful historical account of direct action in anarchism, see Michael Schmidt and Lucien van der Walt, *Black*

Flame: The Revolutionary Class Politics of Anarchism and Syndicalism (Oakland: AK Press, 2009), 138–42. On direct action in more recent anarchist-influenced movements, see Uri Gordon, *Anarchy Alive! Anti-Authoritarian Politics from Practice to Theory* (London: Pluto Press, 2008); Kate Khatib, Margaret Killjoy, and Mike McGuire, eds., *We Are Many: Reflections on Movement Strategy from Occupation to Liberation* (Oakland: AK Press, 2012); Tom Malleson and David Wachsmuth, eds., *Whose Streets? The Toronto G20 and the Challenges of Summit Protest* (Toronto: Between the Lines, 2011); Notes from Nowhere, ed., *We Are Everywhere: The Irresistible Rise of Global Anticapitalism* (London: Verso, 2003).

   5. The black bloc is a tactic that involves activists moving together in a close formation, wearing black clothes and masks so that, ideally, no individual can be identified. Sometimes black bloc participants use this anonymity to engage in targeted acts of property destruction, such as smashing windows at corporate stores, or in physical confrontations with the police. The particular constellation of tactics associated with black blocs has its origins in autonomous movements in Germany during the 1980s. On this history, see Geronimo, *Fire and Flames: A History of the German Autonomist Movement* (Oakland: PM Press, 2012); George Katsiaficas, *The Subversion of Politics: European Autonomous Social Movements and the Decolonization of Everyday Life* (New Jersey: Humanities Press, 1997). Activists in North America began to use their own versions of these tactics in the early 1990s and the black bloc, as a form, gained more wide-spread attention during the Seattle WTO protests in 1999. For more on the use of black blocs in the global justice movement, see "Black Blocs for Dummies," accessed August 27, 2012, http://infoshop.org/page/Black-Blocs-for-Dummies; Claudio Albertani, "Paint It Black: Black Blocs, Tute Bianche and Zapatistas in the Anti-globalization Movement," *New Political Science* 24, no. 4 (2002): 579–95; David and X, eds., *The Black Bloc Papers: An Anthology of Primary Texts From the North American Anarchist Black Bloc, 1999–2001* (Baltimore: Insubordinate Editions, 2002).

   6. For an excellent discussion of this problem, see Gardner and Russell, "Praxis Makes Perfect," 338–39, 344. See also Ryan Harvey, "Are We Addicted to Rioting? Anarchists at the G20 Protests and Social Movement Strategy," *Indypendent Reader*, September 30, 2009.

   7. For a more detailed description of this dynamic in Montreal, see Chris Dixon, "Movements Where People Can Grow: An Interview with Helen Hudson," *Upping the Anti* 8 (2009): 90–91.

   8. Anti-authoritarian organizer and writer Andrea Gibbons, who worked with the tenant organization Strategic Actions for a Just Economy in Los Angeles, puts this another way: "In the face of desperate need, it is often diffi-cult to limit your own involvement. It is only through a commitment to the bigger picture that this becomes possible." Andrea Gibbons, "Driven From Below: A Look at Tenant Organizing and the New Gentrification," *Institute for Anarchist Studies*, 2009, http://www.anarchist-studies.org/node/321.

   9. Max Elbaum, letter to author, April 10, 2012.

10. Scott Neigh, email to author, February 8, 2010.

11. My argument in this section broadly draws on Dan Berger and Andy Cornell, "Ten Questions for Movement Building," *MRZine*, July 24, 2006; Chris Hurl, "Anti-Globalization and 'Diversity of Tactics'," *Upping the Anti* 1 (2005): 51–64; George Lakey, *Powerful Peacemaking: A Strategy for a Living Revolution* (Philadelphia: New Society Publishers, 1987); Hilary Moore and Joshua Kahn Russell, *Organizing Cools the Planet: Tools and Reflections to Navigate the Climate Crisis* (Oakland: PM Press, 2011); Joel Olson, "The Problem with Infoshops and Insurrection: US Anarchism, Movement Building, and the Racial Order," in *Contemporary Anarchist Studies: An Introductory Anthology of Anarchy in the Academy*, ed. Randal Amster, Abraham Deleon, Luis Fernandez, Anthony J. Nocella, and Deric Shannon (New York: Routledge, 2009), 35–45.

12. The term "ghetto" also has troubling racial connotations based on its origins in Nazi treatment of Jews and its now more widespread use to describe poor urban areas inhabited by people of color. For these reasons, I don't use the formulation "activist ghetto."

13. This sort of self-marginalization especially tends to develop in activist scenes rooted in subcultures. Punk rock activist scenes, frequently linked to anarchism, are one good example. For some sharp critical discussions of this dynamic, see Andy Cornell, "Dear Punk Rock Activism," in *Letters from Young Activists: Today's Rebels Speak Out*, ed. Dan Berger, Chesa Boudin, and Kenyon Farrow (New York: Nation Books, 2005), 69–75; Otto Nomous, "Race, Anarchy, and Punk Rock: The Impact of Cultural Boundaries Within the Anarchist Movement," Colours of Resistance Archive, accessed August 31, 2012, http://www.coloursofresistance.org/575/race-anarchy-and-punk-rock-the-impact-of-cultural-boundaries-within-the-anarchist-movement/.

14. For more on this, see Team Colors Collective, *Wind(s) from Below: Radical Community Organizing to Make a Revolution Possible* (Portland, OR: Eberhardt Press, 2010), 79–82.

15. Organizer and writer Jonathan Matthew Smucker and other contributors to the website *Beyond the Choir* have been particularly influential in highlighting these problems. See, for instance, Jonathan Matthew Smucker, "'Would You Like to Come to the Protest?' (What Prevents Radicals from Acting Strategically?)," *Beyond the Choir*, January 4, 2011.

16. For some theoretical elaboration on this, see Dimitris Papadopoulos, Niamh Stephenson, and Vassilis Tsianos, *Escape Routes: Control and Subversion in the 21st Century* (London: Pluto Press, 2008).

17. Scholar James C. Scott offers helpful conceptual tools for understanding these everyday forms of resistance in Scott, *Domination and the Arts of Resistance: Hidden Transcripts* (New Haven: Yale University Press, 1990); Scott, *Weapons of the Weak: Everyday Forms of Peasant Resistance* (New Haven: Yale University Press, 1985). For an excellent introduction, see Benjamin Holtzman and Craig Hughes, "Points of Resistance and Departure: An Interview with James C. Scott," *Upping the Anti* 11 (2010): 73–84. And for a relevant

application of these ideas to understanding African American freedom struggles, see Robin Kelley, *Race Rebels: Culture, Politics, and the Black Working Class* (New York: The Free Press, 1994), chapters 1–4.

18. Chris Crass, *Towards Collective Liberation: Anti-Racist Organizing, Feminist Praxis, and Movement Building Strategy* (Oakland: PM Press, 2013), 158.

19. Offering what I think is a helpful formulation, activist-scholar Peter Bohmer calls this "revolutionary patience." Peter Bohmer, "Panel Presentation on Activism," The Evergreen State College, February 3, 1998.

20. For some useful preliminary reflections on this point, see Members of Advance the Struggle and A New York City Revolutionary, "Unifying Revolutionary Forces in the Coming Year," *Advance the Struggle*, August 10, 2012.

21. For more on the CIW, see Coalition of Immokalee Workers, "Consciousness + Commitment = Change," in *Globalize Liberation: How to Uproot the System and Build a Better World*, ed. David Solnit (San Francisco: City Lights, 2004), 347–60; Elly Leary, "Immokalee Workers Take Down Taco Bell," *Monthly Review* 57, no. 5 (2005): 11–25; Marc Rodrigues, "Coalition of Immokalee Workers: McDonald's Campaign Escalates," *Left Turn*, February 2007; Marc Rodrigues, "Farmworker and Student Victory Over Burger King," *Left Turn*, November 2008; Marc Rodrigues, "Organizing After Victory: Immokalee Encuentro," *Left Turn*, November 2005; David Solnit, "The New Face of the Global Justice Movement: Taco Bell Victory—A Model of Strategic Organizing," *Left Turn*, September 2005.

22. For an introduction to campaigns, see Ruckus Society, "Action Strategy: A How-to Guide," accessed October 4, 2012, http://ruckus.org/article.php?id = 821.

23. Chris Crass, email to author, October 6, 2012.

24. For helpful frameworks and tools for doing this kind of planning, see Virginia Coover, Ellen Deacon, Charles Esser, and Christopher Moore, *Resource Manual for a Living Revolution: A Handbook of Skills and Tools for Social Change Activists*, 4th ed. (Philadelphia: New Society Publishers, 1985), part 1.

25. Stephanie Guilloud and the Executive Leadership Team of Project South, *The First U.S. Social Forum: Report from the Anchor Organization* (Atlanta: Project South, 2009), 1.

26. Kai Barrow, "Swan Song Manifesto," *Organizing Upgrade*, July 1, 2012.

5. "IN THE WORLD BUT NOT OF IT"

Epigraph: Jeremy Lazaou, "No Time Like the Present . . . ," *2 Eyes Open*, March 10, 2010.

1. Alston himself highlighted its Christian origins and the way that it was taken up in Black freedom struggles and cultural forms, specifically mentioning the Stevie Wonder song "As." In examining the decline of early twentieth-century socialist and communist politics in the United States, sociologist Daniel Bell used this phrase to describe ideological rigidity leading to political isola-

tion. Daniel Bell, *Marxian Socialism in the United States* (Princeton: Princeton University Press, 1967). Others have challenged this characterization. See, for instance, Irving Howe, *Socialism and America* (San Diego: Harcourt Brace Jovanovich, 1985); James Weinstein, *The Decline of Socialism in America, 1912–1925* (New York: Monthly Review Press, 1967).

2. Peter Marshall, *Demanding the Impossible: A History of Anarchism* (London: Fontana Press, 1993), 636.

3. Indeed, I believe there is strong resonance (though not sameness) between "in the world but not of it," as I discuss it in this chapter, and the for-mulation that radical theorist John Holloway regularly uses: "within, against, and beyond." See John Holloway, *Change the World without Taking Power,* 2nd ed. (London: Pluto, 2005), 216–45.

4. This question is a longstanding one in left politics and movements. For some of the classic lines of debate, see Eduard Bernstein, *Evolutionary Socialism: A Criticism and Affirmation* (New York: Schocken Books, 1961); Luigi Galleani, *The End of Anarchism?* (Orkney: Cienfuegos Press, 1982); Vladimir Ilyich Lenin, "What Is to Be Done?" *The Lenin Anthology,* ed. Robert C. Tucker (New York: W.W. Norton and Company, 1975), 12–114; Rosa Luxemburg, *Reform or Revolution* (New York: Pathfinder Press, 1973); Errico Malatesta, *Errico Malatesta: His Life and Ideas,* ed. Vernon Richards (London: Freedom Press, 1984); Leon Trotsky, *The Transitional Program for Socialist Revolution,* 3rd ed. (New York: Pathfinder Press, 1977).

5. Those influenced by the insurrectionary anarchist tradition have perhaps most clearly articulated this position. Insurrectionary anarchism rejects all attempts to win partial gains within the existing system, is deeply suspicious of formal organizations, and focuses primarily on encouraging ruptures with domi-nant institutions. For more on this, see Alfredo Maria Bonanno, *From Riot to Insurrection: Analysis for an Anarchist Perspective Against Post Industrial Capitalism* (London: Elephant Editions, 1988); Galleani, *The End of Anarchism?;* sasha k, "Some Notes on Insurrectionary Anarchism," *The Anarchist Library,* accessed October 30, 2012, http://theanarchistlibrary.org/library/sasha_k__ Some_notes_on_Insurrectionary_Anarchism.html. For a brief critical historical introduction to these ideas, see Michael Schmidt and Lucien van der Walt, *Black Flame: The Revolutionary Class Politics of Anarchism and Syndicalism* (Oakland: AK Press, 2009), 128–32. For a critical engagement with the contemporary trend, see Crimethinc., "Say You Want an Insurrection," accessed January 6, 2014, www. crimethinc.com/texts/rollingthunder/insurrection.php.

6. In the context of the campus occupations, this perspective was sometimes associated with the slogan "Occupy Everything, Demand Nothing," although it eventually took on more diverse meanings. See *Reclamations* at www.reclama-tionsjournal.org as well as Kelly Fritsch, ed., "Occupy Everything: A Roundtable on U.S. Student Occupations," *Upping the Anti* 10 (2010): 165–79; Research and Destroy, "Communiqué from an Absent Future: On the Terminus of Student Life," Revolution by the Book: The AK Press Blog, September 28, 2009, www. revolutionbythebook.akpress.org/communique-from-an-absent-future-the-

terminus-of-student-life/. On the influence of this insurrectionist-influenced view in the occupy movement, see Joshua Clover, "The Coming Occupation," in *We Are Many: Reflections on Movement Strategy from Occupation to Liberation*, ed. Kate Khatib, Margaret Killjoy, and Mike McGuire (Oakland: AK Press, 2012), 95–103.

7. On the problems and temptations of state-based logics, see Holloway, *Change the World*, 11–18, 216–45.

8. See, for instance, No One Is Illegal-Vancouver, "Our Vision," accessed April 29, 2013, http://noii-van.resist.ca/?page_id = 17. To understand the politics behind this focus, see Harsha Walia, *Undoing Border Imperialism* (Oakland: AK Press, 2013).

9. The CR publication *The Abolitionist* offers one of the best ways to learn more about this work. See also CR-10 Publications Collective, ed., *Abolition Now! Ten Years of Strategy and Struggle Against the Prison Industrial Complex* (Oakland: AK Press, 2008).

10. Critical Resistance, "Mission and Vision," accessed November 2, 2012, http://criticalresistance.org/about/.

11. On this history, see Davis, *Are Prisons Obsolete?* (New York: Seven Stories Press, 2003), chapter 3.

12. For some description of this proposed program, see Solidarity Across Borders, "STATUS FOR ALL!," accessed December 12, 2012, www.solidarity-acrossborders.org/en/revendications/status-for-all.

13. In this way, being "in the world" has some resonances with "social insertion," a strategy that has developed within the Latin American anarchist organizing approach known as *especifismo*. U.S.-based anarchist organizer Adam Weaver, who has played a leading role in spreading these ideas among English-speaking anarchists, explains: "Social insertion means anarchist involvement in daily fights of the oppressed and working classes. It does not mean acting within single-issue advocacy campaigns based around the involvement of traditional political activists, but rather within movements of people struggling to better their own condition, which come together not always out of exclusively materially-based needs, but also socially and historically rooted needs of resisting attacks of the state and capitalism." Adam Weaver, "Especifismo: The Anarchist Praxis of Building Popular Movements and Revolutionary Organization in South America," *The Northeastern Anarchist*, Spring 2006, 13. For more on *especifismo*, including a link to an informal reader on the topic, see Weaver, "Especifismo," *Machete 408*, accessed November 2, 2012, https://machete408.wordpress.com/especifismo/.

14. For a classic description of this focus, see Saul Alinsky, *Rules for Radicals: A Practical Primer for Realistic Radicals* (New York: Vintage Books, 1972), 113–25. For a more nuanced version, see Kim Bobo, Jackie Kendall, and Steve Max, *Organizing for Social Change: Midwest Academy Manual for Activists*, 3rd ed. (Santa Ana, CA: Seven Locks Press, 2001), chapter 3. For critiques of this focus from veteran community organizers, see Gary Delgado, "The Last Stop Sign," *Shelterforce*, December 1998; Tom Knoche, "Organizing

Communities: Building Neighborhood Movements for Radical Change," in *Globalize Liberation: How to Uproot the System and Build a Better World,* ed. David Solnit (San Francisco: City Lights Books, 2004), 293–98.

15. This abolitionist principle has some resonances with the strategy advocated by the New Left thinker André Gorz, which was based around what he called "non-reformist" or "structural" reforms. As Gorz argues, "a struggle for non-reformist reforms—for anti-capitalist reforms—is one which does not base its validity and its right to exist on capitalist needs, criteria, and rationales. A non-reformist reform is determined not in terms of what can be, but what should be." And further: "To fight for alternative solutions and for structural reforms (that is to say, for intermediate objectives) is not to fight for improvements in the capitalist system; it is rather to break it up, to restrict it, to create counter-powers which, instead of creating a new equilibrium, undermine its very foundations." André Gorz, *A Strategy for Labor: A Radical Proposal,* trans. Martin A. Nicolaus and Victoria Ortiz (Boston: Beacon Press, 1967), 7, 181. It is worth noting that Gorz's notion had an important influence on at least some early prison abolitionist work, as is evident in Thomas Mathiesen, *The Politics of Abolition* (New York: Wiley, 1974). For more recent thinking around this strategy, see Ruth Wilson Gilmore, *Golden Gulag: Prisons, Surplus, Crisis, and Opposition in Globalizing California* (Berkeley: University of California Press, 2007), chapter 6; Robin Hahnel, "Winnowing Wheat from Chaff: Social Democracy and Libertarian Socialism in the 20th Century," in *Real Utopia: Participatory Society for the 21st Century,* ed. Chris Spannos (Oakland: AK Press, 2008), 204–62; Yotam Marom, "Rome Wasn't Sacked in a Day: On Reform, Revolution, and Winning," in *We Are Many: Reflections on Movement Strategy from Occupation to Liberation,* ed. Kate Khatib, Margaret Killjoy, and Mike McGuire (Oakland: AK Press, 2012), 417–23; Julia Sudbury, "Maroon Abolitionists: Black Gender-oppressed Activists in the Anti-Prison Movement in the U.S. and Canada," *Meridians: Feminism, Race, Transnationalism* 9, no. 1 (2009): 1–29.

16. Joel Olson, "New Arizona," *Repeal Coalition,* accessed November 3, 2012, www.repealcoalition.org/new-arizona.html.

17. Luis Fernandez and Joel Olson, "To Live, Love and Work Anywhere You Please," *Contemporary Political Theory* 10, no. 3 (August 2011): 412–19.

18. Although what Singh argued is broadly consistent across NOII, individual collectives and organizers have some differences in how they relate to casework. On this, see Macdonald Scott, ed. "Fighting Borders: A Roundtable on Non-Status (Im)migrant Justice in Canada," *Upping the Anti* 2 (2005): 151–59.

19. Jeffrey Shantz, "Anarchy in the Unions: Contemporary Anarchists at Work," *WorkingUSA: The Journal of Labor and Society* 12, no. 3 (2009): 382.

20. For more on this, see Hilary Moore and Joshua Kahn Russell, *Organizing Cools the Planet: Tools and Reflections to Navigate the Climate Crisis* (Oakland: PM Press, 2011), 50.

21. The term "dual power" originally comes from Lenin's analysis of the Bolshevik revolution: Vladimir Ilyich Lenin, "The Dual Power," *The Lenin Anthology,* ed. Robert C. Tucker (New York: W.W. Norton and Company, 1975),

301–4. In recent decades, anarchists have put this concept to use in anti-statist and non-vanguardist ways. During the 1990s, Christopher Day, a leading figure in the U.S.-based Love and Rage Revolutionary Anarchist Federation, used it to understand the work of the Zapatistas and draw lessons for revolutionaries in the U.S.: Christopher Day, "Dual Power In the Selva Lacandon," in *A New World in Our Hearts: Eight Years of Writings from the Love and Rage Revolutionary Anarchist Federation,* ed. Roy San Filippo (Oakland: AK Press, 2003), 17–31. Building from the pivotal discussions at the 1996 Active Resistance conference in Chicago, anarchist organizer James Mumm made use of this concept, combining anarchist politics and community organizing approaches: James Mumm, "Active Revolution: New Directions in Revolutionary Social Change," *Common Struggle,* 1998, www.nefac.net/node/120. Activist and writer Brian Dominick, meanwhile, has used dual power to think about the role of counterinstitutions in a revolutionary project: Brian Dominick, "An Introduction to Dual Power Strategy," accessed November 7, 2012, http://left-liberty.net/?p = 265; Brian Dominick, "From Here to Parecon: Thoughts on Strategy for Economic Revolution," in *Real Utopia: Participatory Society for the 21st Century,* ed. Chris Spannos (Oakland: AK Press, 2008), 380–95. Perhaps seeking to more explicitly highlight the anarchist lineage of this approach, a number of anarchist scholars have more recently used the term "counterpower": David Graeber, *Fragments of an Anarchist Anthropology* (Chicago: Prickly Paradigm Press, 2004), 24–37; Schmidt and van der Walt, *Black Flame,* 65–67. For some other contributions to these discussions that don't explicitly use these terms, see Ezequiel Adamovsky, "Autonomous Politics and Its Problems: Thinking the Passage from the Social to Political," in *Real Utopia: Participatory Society for the 21st Century,* ed. Chris Spannos (Oakland: AK Press, 2008), 346–62; Errol Schweizer and Brielle Epstein, "People Get Ready! A Survival Handbook for Reality," Colours of Resistance Archive, accessed April 29, 2013, www.coloursofresistance.org/522/people-get-ready-a-survival-handbook-for-reality-2/; Malav Kanuga, "Bluestockings Bookstore and New Institutions of Self-Organized Work: The Space Between Common Notions and Common Institutions," in *Uses of A Whirlwind: Movement, Movements, and Contemporary Radical Currents in the United States,* ed. Team Colors Collective (Oakland: AK Press, 2010), 19–35; El Kilombo Intergaláctico and Michael Hardt, "Organizing Encounters and Generating Events," in *Uses of A Whirlwind: Movement, Movements, and Contemporary Radical Currents in the United States,* ed. Team Colors Collective (Oakland: AK Press, 2010), 245–57. I use "dual power" and "counterpower" more or less interchangeably.

22. Pat Korte and Brian Kelly, "Which Way for the New Left? Social Theory, Vision, and Strategy for a Revolutionary Youth and Student Movement," in *Real Utopia: Participatory Society for the 21st Century,* ed. Chris Spannos (Oakland: AK Press, 2009), 366.

23. Cindy Milstein, *Anarchism and Its Aspirations* (Oakland: AK Press, 2010), 70–74.

24. On this, see Andrew Cornell, *Oppose and Propose! Lessons from Movement for a New Society* (Oakland: AK Press, 2011), 162; Joel Olson, "The

Problem with Infoshops and Insurrection: US Anarchism, Movement Building, and the Racial Order," in *Contemporary Anarchist Studies: An Introductory Anthology of Anarchy in the Academy*, ed. Randal Amster, Abraham Deleon, Luis Fernandez, Anthony J. Nocella, and Deric Shannon (New York: Routledge, 2009), 35–45.

25. Regarding the limitations of infoshops, see Brad Sigal, "Demise of the Beehive Collective: Infoshops Ain't the Revolution," in *A New World in Our Hearts: Eight Years of Writings from the Love and Rage Revolutionary Anarchist Federation*, ed. Roy San Filippo (Oakland: AK Press, 2003), 69–76.

26. On this, see Ruth Wilson Gilmore, "In the Shadow of the Shadow State," in *The Revolution Will Not Be Funded: Beyond the Non-Profit Industrial Complex*, ed. INCITE! Women of Color Against Violence (Cambridge, MA: South End Press, 2007), 41–52.

27. For an overview of this critique, see Andrea Smith, "Introduction," in *The Revolution Will Not Be Funded: Beyond the Non-Profit Industrial Complex*, ed. INCITE! Women of Color Against Violence (Cambridge, MA: South End Press, 2007), 1–18. For a related critique from the global justice movement, see James Davis, "This Is What Bureaucracy Looks Like: NGOs and Anti-Capitalism," in *The Battle of Seattle: The New Challenge to Capitalist Globalization*, ed. Eddie Yuen, George Katsiaficas, and Daniel Burton Rose (New York: Soft Skull Press, 2001), 175–82. And for a critical perspective on the role of NGOs in Latin America, see James Petras and Henry Veltmeyer, *Globalization Unmasked: Imperialism in the 21st Century* (Halifax: Fernwood Publishing, 2001), 128–37.

28. For the beginnings of an effort to apply this critique to the Canadian context, see Chris Keefer, "Fighting the Co-optation of Resistance," *Upping the Anti* 6 (2008): 188–89. There have also been longstanding debates within the Canadian feminist movement about government funding. See Marjorie Griffin Cohen, "The Canadian Women's Movement," in *Canadian Women's Issues: Twenty-Five Years of Women's Activism in English Canada*, ed. Ruth Roach Pierson, Marjorie Griffin Cohen, Paula Bourne, and Philinda Masters (Toronto: James Lorimer & Company, 1993), 19–22; Roxana Ng, "State Funding to a Community Employment Center: Implications for Working with Immigrant Women," in *Community Organization and the Canadian State*, ed. Roxana Ng, Gillian Walker, and Jacob Muller (Toronto: Garamond Press, 1990), 165–83; Alicia Schreader, "The State-Funded Women's Movement," in *Community Organization and the Canadian State*, ed. Roxana Ng, Gillian Walker, and Jacob Muller (Toronto: Garamond Press, 1990), 184–89. And for a critique of the activities of Canadian NGOs in the global South, see Nikolas Barry-Shaw and Dru Oja Jay, *Paved with Good Intentions: Canada's Development NGOs from Idealism to Imperialism* (Halifax: Fernwood, 2012).

29. For more on this problem, see Tiffany Lethabo King and Ewuare Osayande, "The Filth on Philanthropy," in *The Revolution Will Not Be Funded: Beyond the Non-Profit Industrial Complex*, ed. INCITE! Women of Color Against Violence (Cambridge, MA: South End Press, 2007), 79–89; Amara H. Pérez, "Between Radical Theory and Community Praxis: Reflections on

Organizing and the Non-Profit Industrial Complex," in *The Revolution Will Not Be Funded: Beyond the Non-Profit Industrial Complex*, ed. INCITE! Women of Color Against Violence (Cambridge, MA: South End Press, 2007), 91–99.

30. Smith, "Introduction," 3. See also Paula X. Rojas, "Are the Cops in Our Heads and Hearts?" in *The Revolution Will Not Be Funded: Beyond the Non-Profit Industrial Complex*, ed. INCITE! Women of Color Against Violence (Cambridge, MA: South End Press, 2007), 197–214.

31. For critical analysis of service provision, see Paul Kivel, "Social Service or Social Change?" in *The Revolution Will Not Be Funded: Beyond the Non-Profit Industrial Complex*, ed. INCITE! Women of Color Against Violence. Cambridge (MA: South End Press, 2007), 129–49; David Wagner, *What's Love Got to Do with It? A Critical Look at American Charity* (New York: The New Press, 2000).

32. Some prominent examples include the Garment Worker Center in Los Angeles (www.garmentworkercenter.org), the Immigrant Workers' Centre in Montreal (http://iwc-cti.ca), Domestic Workers United (www.domesticworkersunited.org) and FIERCE (www.fiercenyc.org) in New York, People Organized to Win Employment Rights in San Francisco (www.peopleorganized.org), and the Downtown Eastside Women's Centre in Vancouver (www.dewc.ca).

33. Rinku Sen, "Domestic Workers," *Colorlines*, September 2, 2010, http://colorlines.com/archives/2010/09/domestic_workers_lead_the_way_toward_21st_century_labor_rights.html.

34. See, for instance, Team Colors Collective, *Wind(s) from Below: Radical Community Organizing to Make a Revolution Possible* (Portland, OR: Eberhardt Press, 2010).

35. For frank discussions of these problems by radicals engaged with NGOs, see Harmony Goldberg, "Building Power in the City: Reflections on the Emergence of the Right to the City Alliance and the National Domestic Workers Alliance," in *Uses of A Whirlwind: Movement, Movements, and Contemporary Radical Currents in the United States*, ed. Team Colors Collective (Oakland: AK Press, 2010), 97–108; The Rank-and-Filer, "Turning the Complex Upside Down: Rethinking Nonprofit Structures," *The Rank-and-Filer*, March 2011.

36. Rojas, "Are the Cops in Our Heads and Hearts?" 208.

37. At Liberty Square in New York and in some other encampments, activists tried to resolve this by calling for reducing or ending needs-based efforts. This was not only politically troubling but also counterproductive for the movement. For a critical analysis of this response, see Craig Hughes, *Occupied Zuccotti, Social Struggle, and Planned Shrinkage* (zine, New York, 2012), 4–23. See also Morrigan Phillips, "Room for the Poor," in *We Are Many: Reflections on Movement Strategy from Occupation to Liberation*, ed. Kate Khatib, Margaret Killjoy, and Mike McGuire (Oakland: AK Press, 2012), 137–45.

38. For some elaboration on this, see Barbara Ehrenreich, "Why Homelessness Is Becoming an Occupy Wall Street Issue," *Mother Jones*, October 24, 2011.

39. For an in-depth examination of Katrina and its aftermath, see Jordan Flaherty, *Floodlines: Community and Resistance from Katrina to the Jena Six*

(Chicago: Haymarket Books, 2010). For a collection of relevant readings, see Challenging White Supremacy Workshop, "A Katrina Reader," accessed November 28, 2012, http://katrinareader.org/.

40. On these CR efforts, see Flaherty, *Floodlines,* 139–46; Ms. Foundation for Women, "Mayaba Liebenthal," accessed November 22, 2012, http://ms .foundation.org/our_work/broad-change-areas/building-democracy/katrina-womens-response-fund/katrina-grantee-stories/mayaba-liebenthal.

41. On these INCITE! initiatives, see Alisa Bierria, Mayaba Liebenthal, and INCITE! Women of Color Against Violence, "To Render Ourselves Visible: Women of Color Organizing and Hurricane Katrina," in *What Lies Beneath: Katrina, Race, and the State of the Nation,* ed. South End Press (Cambridge, MA: South End Press, 2007), 31–47; Flaherty, *Floodlines,* 102–4; Rachel Luft, "Beyond Disaster Exceptionalism: Social Movement Developments in New Orleans After Hurricane Katrina," *American Quarterly* 61, no. 3 (September 2009): 499–527; Clyde Woods, "The Politics of Reproductive Violence: An Interview with Shana Griffin by Clyde Woods, March 12, 2009," *American Quarterly* 61, no. 3 (September 2009): 583–91.

42. For a discussion of this, see Luft, "Beyond Disaster Exceptionalism."

43. On CG, see Scott Crow, *Black Flags and Windmills: Hope, Anarchy, and the Common Ground Collective* (Oakland: PM Press, 2011); Sue Hilderbrand, Scott Crow, and Lisa Fithian, "Common Ground Relief," in *What Lies Beneath: Katrina, Race, and the State of the Nation,* ed. South End Press (Cambridge, MA: South, 2007), 80–98. For critical discussions based on firsthand experiences, see Ingrid Chapman, "Hearts on Fire: The Struggle for Justice in New Orleans," *Znet,* September 8, 2007; Flaherty, *Floodlines,* chapter 4; Rachel Luft, "Looking for Common Ground: Relief Work in Post-Katrina New Orleans as an American Parable of Race and Gender Violence," *NWSA Journal* 20, no. 3 (Fall 2008): 5–31.

44. For accounts of Occupy Sandy, see Tom Hintze, "How Occupy Sandy's Relief Machine Stepped Into the Post-Superstorm Void," *Alternet,* November 5, 2012; Allison Kilkenny, "Occupy Sandy Efforts Highlight Need for Solidarity, Not Charity," *The Nation,* November 5, 2012; Yotam Marom, "Occupy Sandy, from Relief to Resistance," *Waging Nonviolence,* November 13, 2012.

45. Hilderbrand, Crow, and Fithian, "Common Ground Relief," 80.

46. Sarah Jaffe, "Power to the People," *Jacobin,* November 3, 2012.

47. Flaherty, *Floodlines,* 109.

48. Lydia Pelot-Hobbs, "Preparing for Disaster from New Orleans to New York," *The Oyster Knife,* November 4, 2012.

49. Marom, "Occupy Sandy."

50. James Tracy, "Victory in Chinatown: The San Francisco Community Land Trust," *Left Turn,* May 2007, 62.

51. For a discussion of the strategic orientation of the SFCLT and its broader implications, see Tom Wetzel, "The Capitalist City or the Self-Managed City?" in *Globalize Liberation: How to Uproot the System and Build a Better World,* ed. David Solnit (San Francisco: City Lights Books, 2004), 361–80.

52. Bierria, Liebenthal, and INCITE! Women of Color Against Violence, "To Render Ourselves Visible," 45–46.

53. My discussion of these lessons builds on Cornell, *Oppose and Propose!*, 161–63.

54. Liz Samuels, David Stein, Alexis Pauline Gumbs, Andrea Smith, Ari Wohlfeiler, Rita Bo Brown, Dylan Rodríguez, et al., "Perspectives On Critical Resistance," in *Abolition Now! Ten Years of Strategy and Struggle Against the Prison Industrial Complex*, ed. CR-10 Publications Collective (Oakland: AK Press, 2008), 5. See also Angela Davis, *Abolition Democracy: Beyond Empire, Prisons, and Torture* (New York: Seven Stores Press, 2005), 73.

55. David Stein, "Surviving Warfare, Practicing Resistance," in *Abolition Now! Ten Years of Strategy and Struggle Against the Prison Industrial Complex*, ed. CR-10 Publications Collective (Oakland: AK Press, 2008), 89.

56. Sista II Sista, "Sistas Makin' Moves: Collective Leadership for Personal Transformation and Social Justice," in *Color of Violence: The INCITE! Anthology*, ed. INCITE! Women of Color Against Violence (Cambridge, MA: South End Press, 2006), 203.

57. For more on Sista's Liberated Ground, see Nadine Naber, Verónica Giménez, and Loira Limbal, "Transcript of Sista II Sista," *Global Feminisms: Comparative Case Studies of Women's Activism and Scholarship*, January 23, 2004, www.umich.edu/~glblfem/en/transcripts/us/SistaIISista_U_E_102806.pdf.

58. For more on these efforts, see Ching-In Chen, Jai Dulani, and Leah Lakshmi Piepzna-Samarasinha, eds., *The Revolution Starts at Home: Confronting Intimate Violence Within Activist Communities* (Brooklyn: South End Press, 2011); INCITE! Women of Color Against Violence, *Color of Violence: The INCITE! Anthology* (Cambridge, MA: South End Press, 2006); Ana Clarissa Rojas Durazo, Alisa Bierria, and Mimi Kim, eds., *Community Accountability: Emerging Movements to Transform Violence*, special issue of *Social Justice: A Journal of Crime, Conflict and World Order* 37, no. 4 (2011–2012); Rose City Copwatch, "Alternatives to Police," *Rose City Copwatch*, 2008, http://rosecitycopwatch.org/alternatives-to-police/.

59. See, for instance, El Kilombo Intergaláctico, "Zapatista Justice," *Left Turn*, May 2008; Puaz, "The Community Police: An Example of Popular Justice.," *Left Turn*, May 2008; Nadine Warbrick, "Criminal Justice in Aotearoa/ New Zealand," *Left Turn*, May 2008.

60. For a critical discussion of these kinds of efforts, see Andrea Smith, *Conquest: Sexual Violence and American Indian Genocide* (Cambridge, MA: South End Press, 2005), 139–42, 158–60.

61. Harm Free Zone Project, "Rethinking Restorative Justice: Harm Free Zones in New York," unpublished document in author's possession, New York, October 21, 2007.

62. Harm Free Zone Project, "General Framework," unpublished document in author's possession, New York, October 22, 2006. See also Rachel Herzing and Isaac Ontiveros, "Reflections from the Fight Against Policing," in *We Are Many: Reflections on Movement Strategy from Occupation to Liberation*, ed.

Kate Khatib, Margaret Killjoy, and Mike McGuire (Oakland: AK Press, 2012), 226.

63. For further elaboration, see Bierria, Liebenthal, and INCITE! Women of Color Against Violence, "To Render Ourselves Visible," 36; Smith, *Conquest*, 164.

64. Harm Free Zone Project, "General Framework."

65. Team Colors Collective, "Messy Hearts Made of Thunder: Occupy, Struggle, and Radical Community Organizing," in *We Are Many: Reflections on Movement Strategy from Occupation to Liberation*, ed. Kate Khatib, Margaret Killjoy, and Mike McGuire (Oakland: AK Press, 2012), 406.

66. Cindy Milstein, "Occupy Anarchism," in *We Are Many: Reflections on Movement Strategy from Occupation to Liberation*, ed. Kate Khatib, Margaret Killjoy, and Mike McGuire (Oakland: AK Press, 2012), 304.

67. This is partly based on a formulation from an unnamed Pittsburgh organizer by way of Dan Berger and Andy Cornell, "Ten Questions for Movement Building," *MRZine*, July 24, 2006.

6. "BRINGING PEOPLE TOGETHER TO BUILD THEIR POWER"

Epigraph: Rose Bookbinder and Michael Belt, "OWS and Labor Attempting the Possible: Building a Movement by Learning to Collaborate Through Difference," in *We Are Many: Reflections on Movement Strategy from Occupation to Liberation*, edited by Kate Khatib, Margaret Killjoy, and Mike McGuire (Oakland: AK Press, 2012), 267.

1. The distinction has developed through a variety of movement experiences. Within 1990s anarchism, community organizer James Mumm played an influential role in refining and popularizing it. In 1998, he self-published an essay that developed out of discussions at the 1996 Active Resistance conference in Chicago: James Mumm, "Active Revolution: New Directions in Revolutionary Social Change," *Common Struggle*, 1998, www.nefac.net/node/120. This thinking came to define how many understand activism and organizing. Within the global justice movement, Chris Crass, Pauline Hwang, and Helen Luu, cofounders of the Colours of Resistance network, all significantly contributed to a focus on organizing: Chris Crass, *Towards Collective Liberation: Anti-Racist Organizing, Feminist Praxis, and Movement Building Strategy* (Oakland: PM Press, 2013), 151–63; Pauline Sok Yin Hwang, "Anti-Racist Organizing: Reflecting On Lessons from Quebec City," in *Under the Lens of the People: Our Account of the Peoples' Resistance to the FTAA, Quebec City, April 2001*, ed. The Peoples Lenses Collective (Toronto: The Peoples Lenses Collective, 2003), 48–52; Helen Luu, "Discovering a Different Space of Resistance: Personal Reflections on Anti-Racist Organizing," in *Globalize Liberation: How to Uproot the System and Build a Better World*, ed. David Solnit (San Francisco: City Lights, 2004), 411–26. In 2001, leading global justice organizers Kim Fyke and Gabriel Sayegh drew much of this together and laid out key questions with which a whole cohort was grappling: Kim Fyke and Gabriel Sayegh, "Anarchism and the Struggle to Move

Forward," *Perspectives on Anarchist Theory* 5, no. 2 (2001). In the decade since, this distinction has become even more commonly used through popular activist training programs and movement writing. To mention just two examples, community organizer and anarchist Camilo Viveiros has spread the idea through his "activism to organizing" workshops, and climate justice organizers Hilary Moore and Joshua Kahn Russell have regularly used it in their trainings and writing: Moore and Russell, *Organizing Cools the Planet: Tools and Reflections to Navigate the Climate Crisis* (Oakland: PM Press, 2011). My discussion of this distinction draws on all of this work and my interviews, as well as Aziz Choudry, Jill Hanley, and Eric Shragge, "Introduction: Organize! Looking Back, Thinking Ahead," in *Organize! Building from the Local for Global Justice*, ed. Aziz Choudry, Jill Hanley, and Eric Shragge (Oakland: PM Press, 2012), 1–22; Andy Cornell, "Dear Punk Rock Activism," in *Letters from Young Activists: Today's Rebels Speak Out*, ed. Dan Berger, Chesa Boudin, and Kenyon Farrow (New York: Nation Books, 2005), 69–75.

2. Discussing NOII organizing, Harsha Walia echoes this: "The term 'self-organized' developed to distinguish immigrant/refugee based organizing that involves the participation and leadership of those from migrant backgrounds from immigrant serving organizations that replicate client-based relationships. But I think the term 'self-organized' is false in that it assumes that these movements or committees organically develop by themselves. Much of the ability to organize against deportation, detention, security measures, and regressive and racist border policies springs from the necessary support that activists provide. This support includes booking rooms, providing childcare, and articulating political demands." Quoted in Macdonald Scott, ed., "Fighting Borders: A Roundtable on Non-Status (Im)migrant Justice in Canada," *Upping the Anti* 2 (2005): 156.

3. On this, see Cornell, "Dear Punk Rock Activism," 75; Fyke and Sayegh, "Anarchism and the Struggle to Move Forward"; Moore and Russell, *Organizing Cools the Planet*, chapter 3.

4. For some more elaborated critical reflections on community, see Himani Bannerji, "A Question of Silence: Reflections on Violence against Women in Communities of Colour," in *Scratching the Surface: Canadian Anti-Racist Feminist Thought*, ed. Enakshi Dua and Angela Robertson (Toronto: Women's Press, 1999), 261–77; Gerald W. Creed, ed., *The Seductions of Community: Emancipations, Oppressions, Quandaries* (Santa Fe: School of American Research Press, 2006); Moore and Russell, *Organizing Cools the Planet*, 27–30; Clare O'Connor, "What Moves Us Now? The Contradictions of 'Community,'" in *Whose Streets? The Toronto G20 and the Challenges of Summit Protest*, ed. Tom Malleson and David Wachsmuth (Toronto: Between the Lines, 2011), 187–200.

5. In this sense, one crucial part of organizing is cultivating community as a space for collective deliberation and action. See El Kilombo Intergaláctico, *Feliz Año Cabrones: On the Continued Centrality Of the Zapatista Movement After 14 Years* (Durham, NC: El Kilombo Intergaláctico, 2008), 37.

6. On these models, see Nancy Naples, ed., *Community Activism and Feminist Politics: Organizing Across Race, Class, and Gender* (New York: Routledge, 1998); Benjamin Shepard, *Queer Political Performance and Protest: Play, Pleasure and Social Movement* (New York: Routledge, 2010).

7. See, for example, Damien Domenack and Rachael Leiner, "Toxic Connections: Coalition Strategies Against Jail Expansion," in *Abolition Now!: Ten Years of Strategy and Struggle Against the Prison Industrial Complex*, ed. CR-10 Publications Collective (Oakland: AK Press, 2008), 103–7; Ruth Wilson Gilmore and Craig Gilmore, "The Other California," in *Globalize Liberation: How to Uproot the System and Build Another World*, edited by David Solnit (San Francisco: City Lights Books, 2004), 381–96.

8. On this, see Clare Bayard, "Demilitarization as Rehumanization," *Left Turn*, May 2011.

9. For helpful historical engagements with these questions, see Andrew Cornell, "Consensus: What It Is, What It Isn't, Where It Comes From, and Where It Must Go," in *We Are Many: Reflections on Movement Strategy from Occupation to Liberation*, ed. Kate Khatib, Margaret Killjoy, and Mike McGuire (Oakland: AK Press, 2012), 163–73; Francesca Polletta, *Freedom Is an Endless Meeting: Democracy in American Social Movements* (Chicago: University of Chicago Press, 2002).

10. On this, see Marianne Garneau, "Austerity and Resistance: Lessons from the 2012 Quebec Student Strike," *Insurgent Notes*, October 15, 2012.

11. There are complicated reasons for why these kinds of instrumental organizing approaches have become so common in North America. At the most general level, there are significant ways in which such approaches mimic and reproduce dominant power relations. On this, see Holloway, *Change the World without Taking Power*, 2nd ed. (London: Pluto, 2005), 11–18, 123–32. How particular organizing initiatives have come to take up these sorts of instrumental approaches is a topic that needs more investigation.

12. See, for example, recent revelations about "pinksheeting"—"the practice of collecting and using personal information about staffers and workers in organizing drives"—in UNITE HERE, one of the leading unions in the United States and Canada. Arlen Jones and Greg Hoffman, "Pink Sheeting and Harmful Organizing Methods at UNITE HERE," *Labor Notes*, January 8, 2010, *www.labornotes.org/2009/12/pink-sheeting-part-harmful-organizing-methods-unite-here*. See also Steven Greenhouse, "Some Organizers Protest Their Union's Tactics," *New York Times*, November 18, 2009.

13. The Canadian Federation of Students, the national student organization in English Canada, offers many examples of this. See Caelie Frampton, "Strength in Numbers? Why Radical Students Need a New Organizing Model," *Upping the Anti* 5 (2007): 101–14.

14. For some elaboration on this, see Team Colors Collective, *Wind(s) from Below: Radical Community Organizing to Make a Revolution Possible* (Portland, OR: Eberhardt Press, 2010), 94–100.

15. Andrew Cornell, *Oppose and Propose! Lessons from Movement for a New Society* (Oakland: AK Press, 2011), 164.

16. See John Clarke, "Organizing in Crisis: Ten Years After the OCAP March on Queen's Park," *Upping the Anti* 11 (2010), 101–13; Shantz, "Fighting to Win: The Ontario Coalition Against Poverty," in *We Are Everywhere: The Irresistible Rise of Global Anticapitalism*, ed. Notes from Nowhere (London: Verso, 2003), 464–71.

17. See Matt, "Interview with the Seattle Solidarity Network," *Libcom*, September 29, 2010, http://libcom.org/library/seasol-interview.

18. On these efforts, see Laura Gottesdiener, "Occupying Homes, One Year On and Growing Daily," *Waging Nonviolence*, December 24, 2012, http://wagingnonviolence.org/2012/12/occupy-homes-one-year-on-and-growing-daily"; Max Rameau, *Take Back the Land: Land, Gentrification, and the Umoja Village Shantytown* (Oakland: AK Press, 2013).

19. Clarke, "Organizing in Crisis," 111–12.

20. Moore and Russell, *Organizing Cools the Planet*, 24.

21. The Zapatistas offer us one helpful model for creating such situations through their practice of *encuentro*. On this, see El Kilombo Intergaláctico, *Beyond Resistance: Everything* (Durham, NC: Paperboat Press, 2007), 12–13; El Kilombo Intergaláctico, *Feliz Año Cabrones*, 28–36.

22. For some influential thinking about popular education, see Paulo Freire, *Pedagogy of the Oppressed*, trans. Myra Berman Ramos (New York: Continuum, 1983); Myles Horton and Paulo Freire, *We Make the Road by Walking: Conversations on Education and Social Change*, ed. Brenda Bell, John Gaventa, and John Peters (Philadelphia: Temple University Press, 1990); Myles Horton, *The Myles Horton Reader: Education for Social Change*, ed. Dale Jacobs (Knoxville: University of Tennessee Press, 2003).

23. From some reflections from organizers in the anti-authoritarian current about popular education in their work, see Coalition of Immokalee Workers, "Consciousness + Commitment = Change," in *Globalize Liberation: How to Uproot the System and Build a Better World*, ed. David Solnit (San Francisco: City Lights, 2004), 347–60; Andrea Gibbons, "Driven From Below: A Look at Tenant Organizing and the New Gentrification," *Institute for Anarchist Studies*, 2009, www.anarchist-studies.org/node/321; Tamara Lynne, "Why Must We Be Small? Reflections on Political Development and Cultural Work in Brazil's Landless Movement," *Perspectives on Anarchist Theory* 13, no. 1 (Fall 2011), 41–50.

24. Providence-based community organizer Camilo Viveiros shared this important observation during an informal conversation with me.

7. "LEADERSHIP FROM BELOW"

Epigraph: Harsha Walia, "Letter to Occupy Together Movement," in *Dreaming in Public: Building the Occupy Movement*, ed. Amy Schrager Lang and Daniel Lang/Levitsky (Oxford: New Internationalist Publications, 2012), 169.

1. For writing from anti-authoritarian organizers on the topic of leadership, see Another Politics is Possible and Communities Organizing Liberation, *So That We May Soar: Horizontalism, Intersectionality, and Prefigurative Politics* (zine, New York and Los Angeles, 2010); Dan Berger and Chris Dixon, eds., "Navigating the Crisis: A Study Groups Roundtable," *Upping the Anti* 8 (2009): 159–77; Chris Crass, *Towards Collective Liberation: Anti-Racist Organizing, Feminist Praxis, and Movement Building Strategy* (Oakland: PM Press, 2013); Kim Fyke and Gabriel Sayegh, "Anarchism and the Struggle to Move Forward," *Perspectives on Anarchist Theory* 5, no. 2 (2001); Madeline Gardner and Joshua Kahn Russell, "Praxis Makes Perfect: The New Youth Organizing," in *Real Utopia: Participatory Society for the 21st Century*, ed. Chris Spannos (Oakland: AK Press, 2008), 338–46; Bruce Kokopeli and George Lakey, *Leadership for Change: Toward a Feminist Model* (Philadelphia: New Society Publishers, 1984); LA Crew, "Ideas in Action: An LA Story," *Left Turn*, February 2009; Starhawk, *Truth or Dare: Encounters with Power, Authority, and Mystery* (San Francisco: Harper and Row, 1987), 268–86; Starhawk, *Webs of Power: Notes from the Global Uprising* (Gabriola, B.C.: New Society Publishers, 2002), 174–78; Harsha Walia, *Undoing Border Imperialism* (Oakland: AK Press, 2013), 194–201. This chapter draws on these reflections, my interviews, and internal documents that the San Francisco Heads Up Collective and NOII-Vancouver generously shared with me.

2. On this, see Kokopeli and Lakey, *Leadership for Change*, 1–7.

3. Barbara Ransby, *Ella Baker and the Black Freedom Movement: A Radical Vision* (Chapel Hill: University of North Carolina Press, 2003), 188. Chapter 6 of Ransby's book describes Baker's ideas about leadership.

4. On this, see Nancy Adamson, Linda Briskin, and Margaret McPhail, *Feminists Organizing for Change: The Contemporary Women's Movement in Canada* (Toronto: Oxford University Press, 1988), chapter 7; Francesca Polletta, *Freedom Is an Endless Meeting: Democracy in American Social Movements* (Chicago: University of Chicago Press, 2002), chapter 6.

5. The nonviolent direct action movement played a particularly important role here. See Barbara Epstein, *Political Protest and Cultural Revolution: Nonviolent Direct Action in the 1970s and 1980s* (Berkeley: University of California Press, 1991), 71–75, 140–41.

6. For a carefully considered and somewhat sympathetic discussion of this understanding, see Uri Gordon, *Anarchy Alive! Anti-Authoritarian Politics from Practice to Theory* (London: Pluto Press, 2008), chapter 3. For a more critical engagement, see Crass, *Towards Collective Liberation*, 165–70.

7. For relevant discussions of this dynamic in the nonviolent direct action movement, see Andrew Cornell, *Oppose and Propose! Lessons from Movement for a New Society* (Oakland: AK Press, 2011), 46–47; Epstein, *Political Protest and Cultural Revolution*, 271–72.

8. Jo Freeman, "The Tyranny of Structurelessness," in *Quiet Rumors: An Anarcha-Feminist Reader*, ed. Dark Star Collective (Edinburgh: AK Press, 2002), 56. For critiques of Freeman, see Gordon, *Anarchy Alive!*, 61–65; Cathy

Levine, "The Tyranny of Tyranny," *Quiet Rumors: An Anarcha-Feminist Reader,* ed. Dark Star Collective (Edinburgh: AK Press, 2002), 63–66. For a useful discussion of Freeman's analysis in relation to direct action environmentalism, see Leith Kahl, "The Tyranny of Structurelessness and Earth First!" *Earth First! Journal* 21, no. 5 (2001).

9. For more on this, see Crass, *Towards Collective Liberation,* 165–70.

10. On this, see Crass, *Towards Collective Liberation,* 165–70.; Starhawk, *Truth or Dare,* 268–71.

11. Berger and Dixon, "Navigating the Crisis," 171. For a similar formulation, see Gardner and Russell, "Praxis Makes Perfect," 342.

12. Ella Baker, "Bigger Than a Hamburger," in *The Eyes on the Prize Civil Rights Reader: Documents, Speeches, and Firsthand Accounts from the Black Freedom Struggle,* ed. Clayborne Carson, David. J. Garrow, Gerald Gill, Vincent Harding, and Darlene Clark Hine (New York: Penguin Books, 1991), 121. Chris Crass has played a key role in directing anti-authoritarian attention toward Baker. See Crass, *Towards Collective Liberation,* 151–63. Some organizers have also been reading and discussing Barbara Ransby's *Ella Baker and the Black Freedom Movement.* For one result see, Reggie Gossett, "Organic Intellectual," *Left Turn,* June 2006.

13. Ransby, *Ella Baker and the Black Freedom Movement,* 188.

14. Crass, *Towards Collective Liberation,* 162. In my view, Crass' evaluation of contemporary anarchist approaches to leadership is largely accurate. There are important exceptions, however. For example, some sectors of what is called "class struggle anarchism" have developed more nuanced thinking around leadership, both in revolutionary organizations and broader movements. For example, Michael Schmidt and Lucien van der Walt, anarchist historians who come out of that milieu, argue that "there is a place for a *libertarian* form of leadership, one compatible with anarchism, in which positions of responsibility are undertaken in a democratic and mandated manner, the influence of anarchism and syndicalism reflects its ideological influence yet is not imposed from above through coercion or manipulation, and leadership facilitates the self-emancipation of the popular classes, rather than substitutes for it." Michael Schmidt and Lucien van der Walt, *Black Flame: The Revolutionary Class Politics of Anarchism and Syndicalism* (Oakland: AK Press, 2009), 261.

15. Crass, *Towards Collective Liberation,* 154. For a more developed framework for thinking about leadership in nonhierarchical groups, see Starhawk, *The Empowerment Manual: A Guide for Collaborative Groups* (Gabriola Island, BC: New Society Publishers, 2011), chapter 6.

16. On *mandar obedeciendo,* see El Kilombo Intergaláctico, *Beyond Resistance: Everything* (Durham, NC: Paperboat Press, 2007), 11.

17. In arguing for this, Mac Scott referenced his experience with the Ontario Coalition Against Poverty, a membership organization with a formally elected leadership. As he explained, "I see leadership as being below—for example, in a membership organization—the membership. So, in a truly democratic [organization]—which is easier to say than to do, right?—you would have a member-

ship that makes all your major decisions. What leadership does is it helps that organization to figure out what those decisions are and implement those decisions. And that leadership is also visible, elected through consensus or by voting, and hence also accountable. They're directed by the membership, they're accountable to the membership, and they're elected by the membership. And I think that's much preferable to the models we used to use and [that] are still used sometimes, of not having an elected leadership and just having one or two people really lead through charisma and sometimes just do whatever the hell they want and the group doesn't even know what that is."

18. Beyond rotational systems, we can also create and practice "complexes" of responsibilities—roles that include a balance of menial and empowering tasks, rote and stimulating labor. Radical theorists Michael Albert and Robin Hahnel have developed this idea through writing about what they call "participatory job complexes" in workplaces. Some collective workplaces have put this framework into practice, and many of these ideas are relevant for organizing too. See Michael Albert and Robin Hahnel, *Looking Forward: Participatory Economics for the Twenty-First Century* (Boston: South End Press, 1991), chapters 1–2.

19. This is a reference to Ella Baker's often quoted words: "I have always thought what is needed is the development of people who are interested not in being leaders as much as in developing leadership in others." Charles Payne, *I've Got the Light of Freedom: The Organizing Tradition and the Mississippi Freedom Struggle* (Berkeley: University of California Press, 1996), 93.

20. Longtime anti-authoritarian activist Jen Angel lays this out clearly: "It must be acknowledged that within groups, there are power inequities based on who has knowledge, skills, time, and experience. The answer to these inequities is not to fight that power, but to help everyone in the organization to gain the needed skills, experience, and knowledge." Jen Angel, *Becoming the Media: A Critical History of Clamor Magazine* (Oakland: PM Press, 2008), 32.

21. LA Crew, "Ideas in Action," 53.

22. LA Crew, "Ideas in Action," 53.

23. Berger and Dixon, "Navigating the Crisis," 164.

24. Along similar lines, Helen Hudson, a longtime anarchist organizer in Montreal, talked about the importance of what she called "membership development, so that people are doing the concrete tasks of organizing together while also learning how to do these tasks." She continued, "There are lots of tangible skills that you learn informally over time. But we need a systematic way of making sure that people learn, for example, how to make a speech, how to do a door-to-door campaign, how to design a poster, how to write effectively, how to mobilize a bunch of people to fight around a demand, how to facilitate a meeting."

25. For a glimpse into this culture of training, see Virginia Coover, Ellen Deacon, Charles Esser, and Christopher Moore, *Resource Manual for a Living Revolution: A Handbook of Skills and Tools for Social Change Activists,* 4th ed. (Philadelphia: New Society Publishers, 1985), 153–200.

26. The PowerShift conferences in Canada have arguably been more successful in this regard. See www.wearepowershift.ca.

27. These statements are available on the NOII-Vancouver website: http://noii-van.resist.ca.

28. See Berger and Dixon, "Navigating the Crisis."

29. Crass, *Towards Collective Liberation*, 169.

30. This paragraph significantly draws on my interview with Montreal-based anti-prison organizer Helen Hudson, published as Chris Dixon, "Movements Where People Can Grow: An Interview with Helen Hudson," *Upping the Anti* 8 (2009): 89–90. For other reflections on mentorship, see Chris Dixon, "Dear Older Activists," in *Letters from Young Activists: Today's Rebels Speak Out*, ed. Dan Berger, Chesa Boudin, and Kenyon Farrow (New York: Nation Books, 2005), 49–53; Paul Kivel, "Are You Mentoring for Social Justice?" *Racial Equity Tools*, 2004, www.racialequitytools.org/resourcefiles/kivel2.pdf

31. For more on the Freedom School, see Sista II Sista, "Sistas Makin' Moves: Collective Leadership for Personal Transformation and Social Justice," in *Color of Violence: The INCITE! Anthology*, ed. INCITE! Women of Color Against Violence (Cambridge, MA: South End Press, 2006), 201.

32. More information about these programs is available on the Project South and the Catalyst Project websites listed at the end of this book.

33. Although this formulation has circulated widely, I first encountered it through Occupy Wall Street organizer George Machado. Carwil Bjork-James and George Machado, "Is This Really What Democracy Looks Like? Self-Governance, Leadership, and Autonomy," presented at the Left Forum, New York, March 18, 2012.

34. Crass, *Towards Collective Liberation*, 162–63.

8. "VEHICLES FOR MOVEMENT-BUILDING"

Epigraph: Another Politics is Possible, and Communities Organizing Liberation, *So That We May Soar: Horizontalism, Intersectionality, and Prefigurative Politics* (zine, New York and Los Angeles, 2010), 15–16.

1. The most developed version of this perspective comes out of an anarchist current that significantly overlaps with insurrectionism. See Jason McQuinn, "Against Organizationalism: Anarchism as Both Theory and Critique of Organization," *Anarchy*, accessed January 30, 2013, http://flag.blackened.net/anarchynz/againstorganizationalism.htm; sasha k, "Some Notes on Insurrectionary Anarchism," *The Anarchist Library*, accessed October 30, 2012, http://theanarchistlibrary.org/library/sasha_k__Some_notes_on_Insurrectionary_Anarchism.html. For critiques, see Joe Black, "Anarchism, Insurrections and Insurrectionalism," *Anarkismo.net*, July 20, 2006, www.anarkismo.net/newswire.php?story_id = 3430; Joel Olson, "The Problem with Infoshops and Insurrection: U.S. Anarchism, Movement Building, and the Racial Order," in *Contemporary Anarchist Studies: An Introductory Anthology of Anarchy in the Academy*, ed. Randal Amster, Abraham Deleon, Luis Fernandez, Anthony J. Nocella, and Deric Shannon

(New York: Routledge, 2009), 35–45. For a critical engagement with these ideas historically, see Michael Schmidt and Lucien van der Walt, *Black Flame: The Revolutionary Class Politics of Anarchism and Syndicalism* (Oakland: AK Press, 2009), 240–42.

2. An enduring expression of this tendency is The Red Sunshine Gang, "Anti-Mass: Methods of Organizations for Collectives," *The Anarchist Library*, January 30, 2013, http://theanarchistlibrary.org/library/the-red-sunshine-gang-anti-mass. For a critique, see Upping the Anti Editorial Committee, "Becoming the Enemy They Deserve: Organizational Questions for a New 'New Left'," *Upping the Anti* 4 (2007): 21–33.

3. Myles Horton and Paulo Freire, *We Make the Road by Walking: Conversations on Education and Social Change*, ed. Brenda Bell, John Gaventa, and John Peters (Philadelphia: Temple University Press, 1990), 6.

4. For some anti-authoritarian reflections on this, see Chris Crass, "Beyond Voting: Anarchist Organizing, Electoral Politics and Developing Strategy for Liberation," Colours of Resistance Archive, 2004, www.coloursofresistance .org/508/beyond-voting-anarchist-organizing-electoral-politics-and-developing-strategy-for-liberation/; Scott Neigh, "Elections: All We Can Hope For?" *Linchpin*, November 2008.

5. On this, see Max Uhlenbeck, "Elections 2008" *Left Turn*, August 2008.

6. On this, see Crass, "Beyond Voting"; Steve Williams and James Tracy, "The Left and The Elections," *Left Turn*, May 2008.

7. On this history, see Vijay Prashad, *The Darker Nations: A People's History of the Third World* (New York: New Press, 2007).

8. For a history of U.S.-based Maoist party-building initiatives, see Max Elbaum, *Revolution in the Air: Sixties Radicals Turn to Lenin, Mao and Che* (London: Verso, 2002). For a brief analysis of party-building efforts in Canadian and Quebecois contexts, see Upping the Anti Editorial Committee, "Becoming the Enemy They Deserve," 27–28.

9. For examples, see Jodi Dean, *The Communist Horizon* (London: Verso, 2012); Freedom Road Socialist Organization, "Which Way Is Left? Theory, Politics, Organization and 21st-Century Socialism," *Freedom Road Socialist Organization*, 2007, www.freedomroad.org/images/stories/PDF/wwil.pdf; New Politics Initiative, "A Discussion Paper on The New Politics Initiative," *Studies in Political Economy* 66 (Autumn 2001): 143–56. For an anti-authoritarian response, see Elliott Liu, "Everybody Wants A New Old Left," *Lines That Divide, Lines That Connect* (blog), February 15, 2009. http://linesblog.com/?q = node/88.

10. Liu, "Everybody Wants A New Old Left."

11. For some elaboration, see John Holloway, *Change the World without Taking Power*, 2nd ed. (London: Pluto, 2005), 16–18, 128–32.

12. On this, see Elbaum, *Revolution in the Air*, 55–58.

13. Liu, "Everybody Wants A New Old Left."

14. On the development of this form, see Eric Tang, "Non-Profits and the Autonomous Grassroots," in *The Revolution Will Not Be Funded: Beyond the*

Non-Profit Industrial Complex, ed. INCITE! Women of Color Against Violence (Cambridge, MA: South End Press, 2007), 218–21.

15. 501c3 is the U.S. tax code for nonprofit organizations. For more of Guilloud's thinking on this, see Stephanie Guilloud and William Cordery, "Fundraising Is Not a Dirty Word: Community-Based Economic Strategies for the Long Haul," in *The Revolution Will Not Be Funded: Beyond the Non-Profit Industrial Complex*, ed. INCITE! Women of Color Against Violence (Cambridge, MA: South End Press, 2007), 107–11.

16. On affinity groups, see Murray Bookchin, *Post-Scarcity Anarchism*, 2nd ed. (Montréal: Black Rose Books, 1986), 243–44; Francesca Polletta, *Freedom Is an Endless Meeting: Democracy in American Social Movements* (Chicago: University of Chicago Press, 2002), 189–99; Starhawk, *Webs of Power: Notes from the Global Uprising* (Gabriola, B.C.: New Society Publishers, 2002), 16–20.

17. For a basic introduction to affinity groups and collectives, see Uri Gordon, *Anarchy Alive! Anti-Authoritarian Politics from Practice to Theory* (London: Pluto Press, 2008), 15–16.

18. On the encampment as an organizational form, see Rodrigo Nunes, "The Lessons of 2011: Three Theses on Organisation," *Mute*, June 7, 2012, www.metamute.org/editorial/articles/lessons-2011-three-theses-organisation.

19. On this, see Chris Dixon, "Movements Where People Can Grow: An Interview with Helen Hudson," *Upping the Anti* 8 (2009): 90–92.

20. On this, see also Dan Berger and Chris Dixon, eds., "Navigating the Crisis: A Study Groups Roundtable," *Upping the Anti* 8 (2009): 171.

21. Jerome Raza, "The History of the Quebec Student Movement and Combative Unionism," *Anarkismo*, November 26, 2012, www.anarkismo.net/article/24361.

22. Marianne Garneau, "Austerity and Resistance: Lessons from the 2012 Quebec Student Strike," *Insurgent Notes*, October 15, 2012, http://insurgent-notes.com/2012/10/austerity-and-resistance-lessons-from-the-2012-quebec-student-strike/.

23. Elise Thorburn, ed., "Squarely in the Red: Dispatches from the 2012 Quebec Student Strike," *Upping the Anti* 14 (2012): 111–12.

24. Sylvia Rivera Law Project, "About," accessed February 6, 2013, http://srlp.org/about/.

25. Rickke Mananzala and Dean Spade, "The Nonprofit Industrial Complex and Trans Resistance," *Sexuality Research and Social Policy* 5, no. 1 (2008): 65.

26. Sylvia Rivera Law Project, *SRLP Collective Member Handbook* (New York: Sylvia Rivera Law Project, n.d.), 10–13.

27. Mananzala and Spade, "The Nonprofit Industrial Complex," 68.

28. Sylvia Rivera Law Project, "About."

29. Mananzala and Spade, "The Nonprofit Industrial Complex," 68.

30. Chris Crass, ed., "Strategic Opportunities: White Anti-Racist Organizing and Building Left Organization and Movement," in *Towards Collective Liberation: Anti-Racist Organizing, Feminist Praxis, and Movement Building Strategy*, ed. Chris Crass (Oakland: PM Press, 2013), 181.

31. Crass, "Strategic Opportunities," 193. My description of Heads Up is also based on my interviews with former members Clare Bayard and Rahula Janowski as well as internal documents that they shared with me.

32. Longtime San Francisco housing organizer James Tracy talked about this in terms of leadership development, which he argued we should approach structurally. "It's not like we're just developing individual leaders," said Tracy. "First of all, [we have] to develop an organizational structure where people can take leadership in many different ways. So, it's not just turning out new articulate people, but that's just a step. But you're actually making a thing where, in this area, basically people are under her leadership on that area. There's of course process and voting and decision-making, but another area is somebody else's, where they can lead. So, [it's] developing a structure that can actually accommodate more than one leader, which is really hard. . . . The fact is, some people step up sooner than others. If somebody is ready to rumble and get involved with stuff, you don't be like, 'Oh, you can't be involved 'cause we don't have the whole community working horizontally together.' . . . But I think it has to be all about the structure. If an organization is developing leaders, but it doesn't have a structure to do it, it just disintegrates with everybody trying to run the show to the exclusion of other people instead of to the inclusion of other people."

33. On the concept of "political home," see Adam Weaver and S. Nappalos, "Fighting for the Future: The Necessity and Possibility of National Political Organization for Our Time," *Machete 408*, September 8, 2013, https://machete408.wordpress.com/2013/09/08/fighting-for-the-future-the-necessity-and-possibility-of-national-political-organization-for-our-time/.

34. The classic text on this is Vladimir Ilyich Lenin, "What Is to Be Done? Burning Questions of Our Movement," *The Lenin Anthology*, ed. Robert C. Tucker (New York: W.W. Norton and Company, 1975), 12–114 For some reflections on this organizational model in the United States during the 1970s and 1980s, see Elbaum, *Revolution in the Air*, 332–36; Michael Staudenmaier, *Truth and Revolution: A History of the Sojourner Truth Organization, 1969–1986* (Oakland: AK Press, 2012), 328–32. And for some reflections from one recent and influential effort, see Standing Together to Organize a Revolutionary Movement, *Reclaiming Revolution: History, Summation, and Lessons from the Work of Standing Together to Organize a Revolutionary Movement (STORM)* (San Francisco: STORM, 2004), 69–71.

35. This tendency is known as "platformism" or "class struggle anarchism." The first term references the *Organizational Platform of the Libertarian Communists*, a 1926 document developed by some leading anarchists in the wake of the Bolshevik Revolution in Russia: Nestor Makhno, Peter Arshinov, and Ida Mett, *Organizational Platform of the Libertarian Communists* (Montreal: Abraham Guillen Press/Arm the Spirit, 2002). Assessing what they saw as the weaknesses of the anarchist movement, the writers of the *Platform* called for building a focused anarchist organization founded on a common revolutionary politics and program. Over the last several decades, various

anarchist efforts have taken up the *Platform* and its prescriptions. For an historical perspective on this, see Michael Schmidt and Lucien van der Walt, *Black Flame: The Revolutionary Class Politics of Anarchism and Syndicalism* (Oakland: AK Press, 2009), chapter 8. For a discussion of this tendency in the United States and Canada more recently, see Tom Wetzel, "Anarchism, Class Struggle and Political Organization," *Znet*, July 22, 2009. www.zcommunications.org/anarchism-class-struggle-and-political-organization-by-tom-wetzel. For some recent theorizing about organization coming out of this tendency, see S. Nappalos, "Defining Practice: The Intermediate Level of Organization and Struggle," *RECOMPOSITION* (blog), August 29, 2010, https://recomposition-blog.wordpress.com/2010/08/29/defining-practice-the-intermediate-level-of-organization-and-struggle/.

36. To greater and lesser degrees, NOII collectives function this way too. Bring the Ruckus (BTR), an explicitly anarchist cadre organization that had members in a number of U.S. cities, was active from 2002 to 2012. For the argument behind the BTR structure, see Joel Olson, "Movement, Cadre, and Dual Power," *Perspectives on Anarchist Theory* 13, no. 1 (Fall 2011): 33–38.

37. For some recent examples of study groups, see Berger and Dixon, "Navigating the Crisis."

38. Adrie Naylor, Elise Thorburn, and Robyn Letson, "Notes on Spontaneity and Organization," *Upping the Anti* 14 (2012): 34.

CONCLUSION

Epigraph: Laura Leslie, "Meet Kai Barrow," *The State of Things*, WUNC, May 24, 2010.

1. Sharmeen Khan and Tyler McCreary, "Building Unlikely Alliances: An Interview with Andrea Smith," *Upping the Anti* 10 (2010): 41.

2. Ryan Harvey, "Occupy Before and Beyond," in *We Are Many: Reflections on Movement Strategy from Occupation to Liberation*, ed. Kate Khatib, Margaret Killjoy, and Mike McGuire (Oakland: AK Press, 2012), 132.

3. Andrew Cornell, *Oppose and Propose! Lessons from Movement for a New Society* (Oakland: AK Press, 2011), 165.

4. CR-10 Publications Collective, ed., *Abolition Now! Ten Years of Strategy and Struggle Against the Prison Industrial Complex* (Oakland: AK Press, 2008).

5. Alexis Pauline Gumbs, "Freedom Seeds: Growing Abolition in Durham, North Carolina," in *Abolition Now! Ten Years of Strategy and Struggle Against the Prison Industrial Complex*, ed. CR-10 Publications Collective (Oakland: AK Press, 2008), 153.

6. Shyam Khanna, "Mississippi Goddam: SNCC, Occupy, and Radical Community Organizing," *Tidal: Occupy Theory, Occupy Strategy* 4 (2013): 13.

7. David Graeber, "Where Does Occupy Go from Here?" *The Independent*, April 19, 2013.

8. This question comes out of Joel Olson, "The Problem with Infoshops and Insurrection: U.S. Anarchism, Movement Building, and the Racial Order," in

Contemporary Anarchist Studies: An Introductory Anthology of Anarchy in the Academy, ed. Randal Amster, Abraham Deleon, Luis Fernandez, Anthony J. Nocella, and Deric Shannon (New York: Routledge, 2009), 35–45; Michael Staudenmaier, *Truth and Revolution: A History of the Sojourner Truth Organization, 1969–1986* (Oakland: AK Press, 2012), 326–27.

9. Although I don't completely agree with their conclusions, this is a question partially posed in Team Colors Collective, "Abandoning the Chorus: Checking Ourselves a Decade Since Seattle," *Groundswell* 1 (2010): 13–18.

10. For some useful reflections that raise this question in various ways, see Chris Crass, "Beyond Voting: Anarchist Organizing, Electoral Politics and Developing Strategy for Liberation," Colours of Resistance Archive, 2004, www.coloursofresistance.org/508/beyond-voting-anarchist-organizing-electoral-politics-and-developing-strategy-for-liberation/; Cindy Milstein, "Hope in a Time of Elections," *Left Turn,* August 2008; Scott Neigh, "Elections: All We Can Hope For?" *Linchpin,* November 2008; Upping the Anti Editorial Committee, "Between a Rock and a Hard Place: Social Democracy and Anti-Capitalist Renewal in English Canada," *Upping the Anti* 5 (2007): 29–45.

Bibliography

INTERVIEWS

Unless otherwise noted, all interviews were conducted in person with the author.

Ahooja, Sarita. January 31, 2007. Montreal.
Alston, Ashanti. March 8, 2007. New York City.
Bayard, Clare. June 11, 2007; March 7, 2013. San Francisco.
Chettiar, Jill. October 29, 2006. Vancouver.
Cruz, Rosana. December 13, 2007. New Orleans.
Desroches, Mike. January 28, 2007. Toronto.
El-Amine, Rayan. June 13, 2007. San Francisco.
Fiorentini, Francesca. March 16, 2007. New York City.
Foster, Mary. February 5, 2007. Montreal.
Gill, Harjit Singh. June 7, 2007. Oakland.
Gomez, Tatiana. February 6, 2007. Montreal.
Grewal, Harjap. October 25, 2006. Vancouver.
Guilloud, Stephanie. December 16, 2007. Atlanta.
Herzing, Rachel. June 13, 2007; March 13, 2013. Oakland.
Hudson, Helen. February 2, 2007 (in person); February 19, 2013 (via email). Montreal.
Hwang, Pauline. January 25, 2007. Toronto.
Janowski, Rahula. June 8, 2007. San Francisco.
Jarrett, Tynan. February 4, 2007. Montreal.
Khan, Sharmeen. January 26, 2007. Toronto.
Lehman, Brooke. March 13, 2007. New York City.
Maccani, RJ. March 9, 2007. Brooklyn.
Maria, Andréa. January 24, 2007. Toronto.
Maschi, Pilar. March 14, 2007. Bronx.
Mehta, Sonya. June 10, 2007. San Francisco.

Miller, Amy. February 6, 2007. Montreal.

Mutis Garcia, Rafael. March 12, 2007. New York City.

O'Brien, Michelle. March 13, 2007 (in person); February 15, 2013 (via email). Brooklyn.

Paz, Adriana. October 28, 2006. Vancouver.

Pelot-Hobbs, Lydia. December 9, 2007. New Orleans.

Pourtavaf, Leila. February 5, 2007. Montreal.

Rojas-Urrutia, Paula Ximena. March 12, 2007. Brooklyn.

Russell, Joshua Kahn. June 15, 2007. Oakland.

Schoen, Sophie. February 2, 2007. Montreal.

Scott, Mac. January 30, 2007. Toronto.

Singh, Jaggi. February 3, 2007. Montreal.

Solnit, David. June 9, 2007; March 12, 2013. Berkeley and San Francisco.

Sweetman, Mick. January 30, 2007. Toronto.

Tracy, James. June 8, 2007. San Francisco.

Walia, Harsha. October 24, 2006 (in person); January 3, 2013 (via email). Vancouver.

Warner, Marika. January 29, 2007. Toronto.

Whitney, Jennifer. December 7, 2007. New Orleans.

Wise, Ora. March 9, 2007. Brooklyn.

MATERIALS REFERENCED

Abbs, Maryann, Caelie Frampton, and Jessica Peart, eds. "Going for Gold on Stolen Land: A Roundtable on Anti-Olympic Organizing." *Upping the Anti* 9 (2009): 141–57.

Abolitionist Editorial Collective. "Taking Stock of Critical Resistance." *The Abolitionist,* Summer 2011.

Abu-Jamal, Mumia. *We Want Freedom: A Life in the Black Panther Party.* Cambridge, MA: South End Press, 2004.

Adamovsky, Ezequiel. "Autonomous Politics and Its Problems: Thinking the Passage from the Social to Political." In *Real Utopia: Participatory Society for the 21st Century,* edited by Chris Spannos, 346–62. Oakland: AK Press, 2008.

Adams, Jason. "Nonwestern Anarchisms: Rethinking the Global Context," May 6, 2006. www.infoshop.org/texts/nonwestern.pdf.

Adamson, Nancy, Linda Briskin, and Margaret McPhail. *Feminists Organizing for Change: The Contemporary Women's Movement in Canada.* Toronto: Oxford University Press, 1988.

Aguilar, Ernesto, ed. *Our Culture, Our Resistance: Further Conversations with People of Color on Anarchism, Race, Class and Gender.* Houston: APOC, 2004.

———, ed. *Our Culture, Our Resistance: People of Color Speak Out on Anarchism, Race, Class and Gender.* Houston: APOC, 2004.

Albert, Michael, Leslie Cagan, Noam Chomsky, Robin Hahnel, Mel King, Lydia Sargent, and Holly Sklar. *Liberating Theory.* Boston: South End Press, 1986.

Albert, Michael, and Robin Hahnel. *Looking Forward: Participatory Economics for the Twenty-First Century.* Boston: South End Press, 1991.

Albertani, Claudio. "Paint It Black: Black Blocs, Tute Bianche and Zapatistas in the Anti-globalization Movement." *New Political Science* 24, no. 4 (2002): 579–95.

Alfred, Taiaiake. *Wasáse: Indigenous Pathways of Action and Freedom.* Peterborough, ON: Broadview Press, 2005.

Alinsky, Saul. *Rules for Radicals: A Practical Primer for Realistic Radicals.* New York: Vintage Books, 1972.

Allison, Aimee, and David Solnit. *Army of None: Strategies to Counter Military Recruitment, End War, and Build a Better World.* New York: Seven Stories Press, 2007.

Alston, Ashanti. "Beyond Nationalism But Not Without It." *Onward,* Spring 2002.

Andersen, Margaret L., and Patricia Hill Collins, eds. *Race, Class, & Gender: An Anthology.* 7th ed. Belmont, CA: Wadsworth Publishing, 2009.

Anderson, Benedict. *Under Three Flags: Anarchism and the Anti-Colonial Imagination.* London: Verso, 2005.

Angel, Jen. *Becoming the Media: A Critical History of Clamor Magazine.* Oakland: PM Press, 2008.

Another Politics is Possible, and Communities Organizing Liberation. *So That We May Soar: Horizontalism, Intersectionality, and Prefigurative Politics.* Zine, New York and Los Angeles: APP and COIL, 2010.

Antliff, Allan, ed. *Only A Beginning: An Anarchist Anthology.* Vancouver: Arsenal Pulp Press, 2004.

Anzaldúa, Gloria. *Borderlands/La Frontera: The New Mestiza.* San Francisco: Spinsters/Aunt Lute, 1987.

Aptheker, Herbert. *Abolitionism: A Revolutionary Movement.* Boston: Twayne Publishers, 1989.

Arsenault, Chris. "Native Leader Serving Six Months for Opposing Mine: Supporters Call Algonquin Leader a 'Political Prisoner'." *The Dominion,* March 16, 2008. www.dominionpaper.ca/articles/1754.

Austin, David. *Fear of a Black Nation: Race, Sex and Security in Sixties Montreal.* Toronto: Between the Lines, 2013.

Avery, Donald. *"Dangerous Foreigners": European Immigrant Workers and Labour Radicalism in Canada 1896–1932.* Toronto: McClelland and Stewart Limited, 1979.

Avicolli Mecca, Tommi, ed. *Smash the Church! Smash the State! The Early Years of Gay Liberation.* San Francisco: City Lights Press, 2009.

Baker, Ella. "Bigger Than a Hamburger." In *The Eyes on the Prize Civil Rights Reader: Documents, Speeches, and Firsthand Accounts from the Black Freedom Struggle,* edited by Clayborne Carson, David. J. Garrow, Gerald Gill, Vincent Harding, and Darlene Clark Hine, 120–22. New York: Peguin Books, 1991.

Bakunin, Mikhail. "Statism and Anarchy." In *No Gods, No Masters: An Anthology of Anarchism,* edited by Daniel Guérin, 164–66. San Francisco: AK Press, 1998.

Ball, David. "Idle No More Sweeps Canada and Beyond as Aboriginals Say Enough Is Enough." *Indian Country Today*, December 22, 2012. http://indiancountrytodaymedianetwork.com/article/idle-no-more-sweeps-canada-and-beyond-aboriginals-say-enough-enough-146516.

Bannerji, Himani. "A Question of Silence: Reflections on Violence Against Women in Communities of Colour." In *Scratching the Surface: Canadian Anti-Racist Feminist Thought*, edited by Enakshi Dua and Angela Robertson, 261–77. Toronto: Women's Press, 1999.

———. *Thinking Through: Essays on Feminism, Marxism and Anti-Racism.* Toronto: Women's Press, 1995.

Bari, Judi. *Timber Wars.* Monroe, ME: Common Courage Press, 1994.

Barrow, Kai. "Swan Song Manifesto." *Organizing Upgrade*, July 1, 2012. www.organizingupgrade.com/index.php/modules-menu/community-organizing/item/57-kai-barrow.

Barrows-Friedman, Nora. "Beyond Bil'in: BDS and Israel's Crackdown on the Palestinian Popular Struggle." *Left Turn*, April 2010.

Barry-Shaw, Nikolas, and Dru Oja Jay. *Paved with Good Intentions: Canada's Development NGOs from Idealism to Imperialism.* Halifax: Fernwood, 2012.

Bayard, Clare. "Demilitarization as Rehumanization." *Left Turn*, May 2011.

———. "Immigrant Justice Rising." *Left Turn*, September 2006.

Bayard, Clare, and Chris Crass. "Anti-Racism for Collective Liberation: An Interview with the Catalyst Project." *Infoshop.org*, May 23, 2006. www.infoshop.org/inews/article.php?story = 2006catalyst_interview.

Bay Area Childcare Collective. "An Interview with the Bay Area Childcare Collective." *Left Turn*, May 2007.

Bell, Daniel. *Marxian Socialism in the United States.* Princeton: Princeton University Press, 1967.

Berger, Dan. *Outlaws of America: The Weather Underground and the Politics of Solidarity.* Oakland: AK Press, 2006.

———. "Social Movements and Mass Incarceration: What Is to Be Done?" *Souls* 15, no. 1–2 (January 2013): 3–18.

———. "'We Are the Revolutionaries': Visibility, Protest and Racial Formation in 1970s Radicalism." PhD dissertation, University of Pennsylvania, 2010.

Berger, Dan, and Andy Cornell. "Ten Questions for Movement Building." *MRZine*, July 24, 2006. http://mrzine.monthlyreview.org/2006/bc240706.html.

Berger, Dan, and Chris Dixon, eds. "Navigating the Crisis: A Study Groups Roundtable." *Upping the Anti* 8 (2009): 159–77.

Bernstein, Eduard. *Evolutionary Socialism: A Criticism and Affirmation.* New York: Schocken Books, 1961.

Bevington, Douglas. "Earth First! in Northern California: An Interview with Judi Bari." In *The Struggle for Ecological Democracy: Environmental Justice Movements in the United States*, edited by Daniel J. Faber, 248–71. New York: Guilford Press, 1998.

———. *The Rebirth of Environmentalism: Grassroots Activism from the Spotted Owl to the Polar Bear.* Washington: Island Press, 2009.

———. "Strategic Experimentation and Stigmatization in Earth First!" In *Extreme Deviance,* edited by Erich Goode and D. Angus Vail, 189–96. Los Angeles: Pine Forge Press, 2008.

Bevington, Douglas, and Chris Dixon. "Movement-Relevant Theory: Rethinking Social Movement Scholarship and Activism." *Social Movement Studies* 4, no. 3 (2005): 185–208.

Bierria, Alisa, Mayaba Liebenthal, and INCITE! Women of Color Against Violence. "To Render Ourselves Visible: Women of Color Organizing and Hurricane Katrina." In *What Lies Beneath: Katrina, Race, and the State of the Nation,* edited by South End Press, 31–47. Cambridge, MA: South End Press, 2007.

Bird, Stewart, Dan Georgakas, and Deborah Shaffer, eds. *Solidarity Forever: An Oral History of the IWW.* Chicago: Lake View Press, 1985.

Bjork-James, Carwil, and George Machado. "Is This Really What Democracy Looks Like? Self-Governance, Leadership, and Autonomy." Presented at the Left Forum, New York, March 18, 2012.

Black, Joe. "Anarchism, Insurrections and Insurrectionalism." *Anarkismo.net,* July 20, 2006. www.anarkismo.net/newswire.php?story_id = 3430.

"Black Blocs for Dummies." *Infoshop.org.* Accessed August 27, 2012. http://infoshop.org/page/Black-Blocs-for-Dummies.

Block, Niko. "Prison Farms on Death Row." *The Dominion,* October 2010.

Bloom, Joshua, and Waldo Martin, Jr. *Black Against Empire: The History and Politics of the Black Panther Party.* Berkeley: University of California Press, 2013.

Bloom, Liza Minno, Hallie Boas, and Berkley Carnine. "Collective Liberation: Lesson Learned in Allyship with Indigenous Resistance at Black Mesa." *Left Turn,* August 2011.

Blumenkranz, Carla, Keith Gessen, Mark Greif, Sarah Leonard, Sarah Resnick, Nikil Saval, Eli Schmitt, and Astra Taylor, eds. *Occupy! Scenes from Occupied America.* London: Verso, 2011.

Bobo, Kim, Jackie Kendall, and Steve Max. *Organizing for Social Change: Midwest Academy Manual for Activists.* 3rd ed. Santa Ana, CA: Seven Locks Press, 2001.

Bohmer, Peter. "Panel Presentation on Activism." The Evergreen State College, February 3, 1998.

Bonanno, Alfredo Maria. *From Riot to Insurrection: Analysis for an Anarchist Perspective Against Post Industrial Capitalism.* London: Elephant Editions, 1988.

Bookbinder, Rose, and Michael Belt. "OWS and Labor Attempting the Possible: Building a Movement by Learning to Collaborate Through Difference." In *We Are Many: Reflections on Movement Strategy from Occupation to Liberation,* edited by Kate Khatib, Margaret Killjoy, and Mike McGuire, 263–73. Oakland: AK Press, 2012.

Bookchin, Murray. *Post-Scarcity Anarchism.* 2nd ed. Montréal: Black Rose Books, 1986.

Bordewich, Fergus. *Bound for Canaan: The Underground Railroad and the War for the Soul of America.* New York: Amistad, 2005.

Bowlan, Heather. "While Caregivers Organize, the Kids Are Throwin' Seed Bombs: Radical Childcare Collectives in the United States." *Make/shift,* Fall/Winter 2010/2011.

Breines, Wini. *Community and Organization in the New Left, 1962–1968: The Great Refusal.* New Brunswick, NJ: Rutgers University Press, 1989.

Breton, Émilie, Sandra Jeppesen, Anna Kruzynski, and Rachel Sarrasin. "Prefigurative Self-Governance and Self-Organization: The Influence of Antiauthoritarian (Pro)Feminist, Radical Queer, and Antiracist Networks in Quebec." In *Organize! Building from the Local for Global Justice,* edited by Aziz Choudry, Jill Hanley, and Eric Shragge, 156–73. Oakland: PM Press, 2012.

Brown, Elaine. *A Taste of Power: A Black Woman's Story.* New York: Pantheon Books, 1992.

Buhle, Paul, and Nicole Schulman, eds. *Wobblies! A Graphic History of the Industrial Workers of the World.* London: Verso, 2005.

Burrowes, Nicole, Morgan Cousins, Paula X. Rojas, and Ije Ude. "On Our Own Terms: Ten Years of Radical Community Building with Sista II Sista." In *The Revolution Will Not Be Funded: Beyond the Non-Profit Industrial Complex,* edited by INCITE! Women of Color Against Violence. 227–34. Cambridge, MA: South End Press, 2007.

Butler, C.T. Lawrence, and Keith McHenry. *Food Not Bombs: How to Feed the Hungry and Build Community.* Philadelphia: New Society Publishers, 1992.

Butler, C.T. Lawrence, and Amy Rothstein. *On Conflict and Consensus: A Handbook on Formal Consensus Decisionmaking.* 2nd ed. Portland, ME: Food Not Bombs, 1991.

Caffentzis, George, and Silvia Federici. "A Brief History of Resistance to Structural Adjustment." In *Democratizing the Global Economy: The Battle Against the World Bank and the International Monetary Fund,* edited by Kevin Danaher, 139–44. Monroe, ME: Common Courage Press, 2001.

Calvert, Greg. "A Left Wing Alternative." In *The Movement Toward A New America,* edited by Mitchell Goodman, 585–89. Philadelphia: Pilgrim Press, 1970.

Campbell, Jim. "Bulldozer/Prison News Service." In *Only A Beginning: An Anarchist Anthology,* edited by Allan Antliff, 74–81. Vancouver: Arsenal Pulp Press, 2004.

Carson, Clayborne. *In Struggle: SNCC and the Black Awakening of the 1960s.* 2nd ed. Cambridge, MA: Harvard University Press, 1995.

Carty, Linda. *And Still We Rise: Feminist Political Mobilizing in Contemporary Canada.* Toronto: Women's Press, 1993.

Catalyst Project. "Justice and Survival: A Forum on Building Movements to Stop War." *Left Turn,* August 2007.

Challenging White Supremacy Workshop. "A Katrina Reader." Accessed November 28, 2012. http://katrinareader.org/.

Chan, Wendy, and Kiran Mirchandani, eds. *Crimes of Colour: Racialization and the Criminal Justice System in Canada*. Toronto: University of Toronto Press, 2001.

Chang, Jen, Bethany Or, Eloginy Tharmendran, Emmie Tsumara, Steve Daniels, and Darryl Leroux, eds. *Resist! A Grassroots Collection of Stories, Poetry, Photos and Analyses from the Québec City FTAA Protests and Beyond*. Halifax: Fernwood Publishing, 2001.

Chapman, Ingrid. "Hearts on Fire: The Struggle for Justice in New Orleans." *Znet*, September 8, 2007. www.zcommunications.org/hearts-on-fire-the-struggle-for-justice-in-new-orleans-by-ingrid-chapman.

———. "We Can Do This: Direct Action Against Global Capitalism and U.S. Imperialism: An Interview with Ingrid Chapman," *Clamor Communique* 35 (December 2, 2003). www.clamormagazine.org/communique/communique35.pdf.

Chen, Ching-In, Jai Dulani, and Leah Lakshmi Piepzna-Samarasinha, eds. *The Revolution Starts at Home: Confronting Intimate Violence Within Activist Communities*. Brooklyn: South End Press, 2011.

Chomsky, Noam. *Fateful Triangle: The United States, Israel, and the Palestinians*. 2nd ed. Cambridge, MA: South End Press, 1999.

———. *Year 501: The Conquest Continues*. Boston: South End Press, 1993.

Chossudovsky, Michel. *The Globalization of Poverty: Impacts of IMF and World Bank Reforms*. Penang, Malaysia: Third World Network, 1997.

Choudry, Aziz, Jill Hanley, and Eric Shragge, "Introduction: Organize! Looking Back, Thinking Ahead." In *Organize! Building from the Local for Global Justice*, edited by Aziz Choudry, Jill Hanley, and Eric Shragge, 1–22. Oakland: PM Press, 2012.

Choudry, Aziz, and Dip Kapoor, eds. *Learning From the Ground Up: Global Perspectives on Social Movements and Knowledge Production*. New York: Palgrave Macmillan, 2010.

Churchill, Ward. *A Little Matter of Genocide: Holocaust and Denial in the Americas, 1492 to the Present*. San Francisco: City Lights Books, 1997.

———. "Indigenism, Anarchism, and the State." *Upping the Anti* 1, no. 1 (2005): 30–40.

Churchill, Ward, and Jim Vander Wall. *Agents of Repression: The FBI's Secret Wars Against the Black Panther Party and the American Indian Movement*. Boston: South End Press, 1988.

Clare, Eli. *Exile and Pride: Disability, Queerness and Liberation*. Cambridge, MA: South End Press, 2009.

Clarke, John. "Organizing in Crisis: Ten Years After the OCAP March on Queen's Park." *Upping the Anti* 11 (2010): 101–13.

Cleaver, Harry. *Reading Capital Politically*. San Francisco: AK Press, 2000.

Cleaver, Kathleen. "Women, Power, and Revolution." In *Liberation, Imagination, and the Black Panther Party: A New Look at the Panthers and*

Their Legacy, edited by Kathleen Cleaver and George Katsiaficas, 123–27. New York: Routledge, 2001.

Cleaver, Kathleen, and George Katsiaficas, eds. *Liberation, Imagination, and the Black Panther Party: A New Look at the Panthers and Their Legacy.* New York: Routledge, 2001.

Close, Laura. "Organizer + Catalyst = Laura Close." *Clamor*, August 2003.

Clover, Joshua. "The Coming Occupation." In *We Are Many: Reflections on Movement Strategy from Occupation to Liberation*, edited by Kate Khatib, Margaret Killjoy, and Mike McGuire, 95–103. Oakland: AK Press, 2012.

Coalition Against Israeli Apartheid. "Boycotting Israeli Apartheid in Toronto." *Left Turn*, February 2007.

Coalition of Immokalee Workers. "Consciousness + Commitment = Change." In *Globalize Liberation: How to Uproot the System and Build a Better World*, edited by David Solnit, 347–60. San Francisco: City Lights, 2004.

Cole, Luke, and Sheila Foster. *From the Ground Up: Environmental Racism and the Rise of the Environmental Justice Movement.* New York: New York University Press, 2001.

Collins, Patricia Hill. *Black Feminist Thought: Knowledge, Consciousness, and the Politics of Empowerment.* New York: Routledge, 1991.

Collins, Thatcher. "A Protestography." In *Confronting Capitalism: Dispatches from a Global Movement*, edited by Eddie Yuen, George Katsiaficas, and Daniel Burton Rose, xxxiv–xlviii. New York: Soft Skull Press, 2004.

Combahee River Collective. "The Combahee River Collective Statement." In *Home Girls: A Black Feminist Anthology*, edited by Barbara Smith, 272–82. New York: Kitchen Table: Women of Color Press, 1983.

Coover, Virginia, Ellen Deacon, Charles Esser, and Christopher Moore. *Resource Manual for a Living Revolution: A Handbook of Skills and Tools for Social Change Activists.* 4th ed. Philadelphia: New Society Publishers, 1985.

Cornell, Andrew. "Consensus: What It Is, What It Isn't, Where It Comes From, and Where It Must Go." In *We Are Many: Reflections on Movement Strategy from Occupation to Liberation*, edited by Kate Khatib, Margaret Killjoy, and Mike McGuire, 163–73. Oakland: AK Press, 2012.

———. *Oppose and Propose! Lessons from Movement for a New Society.* Oakland: AK Press, 2011.

———. "Who Needs Ends When We've Got Such Bitchin' Means?" *LiP*, Summer 2005.

Cornell, Andy. "Dear Punk Rock Activism." In *Letters from Young Activists: Today's Rebels Speak Out*, edited by Dan Berger, Chesa Boudin, and Kenyon Farrow, 69–75. New York: Nation Books, 2005.

Coulthard, Glen. "Beyond Recognition: Indigenous Self-Determination as Prefigurative Practice." In *Lighting the Eighth Fire: The Liberation, Resurgence, and Protection of Indigenous Nations*, edited by Leanne Simpson, 187–203. Winnipeg: Arbeiter Ring, 2008.

Council of National and Islamic Forces in Palestine, et al. "Palestinian Civil Society Calls for Boycott, Divestment and Sanctions Against Israel Until It

Complies with International Law and Universal Principles of Human Rights," July 9, 2005. www.bdsmovement.net/call.

Cox, Donald. "The Split in the Party." In *Repression Breeds Resistance: The Black Liberation Army and the Radical Legacy of the Black Panther Party*, edited by Kathleen Cleaver and George Katsiaficas, 118–22. New York: Routledge, 2001.

CR-10 Publications Collective, ed. *Abolition Now! Ten Years of Strategy and Struggle Against the Prison Industrial Complex*. Oakland: AK Press, 2008.

Crass, Chris. "Beyond Voting: Anarchist Organizing, Electoral Politics and Developing Strategy for Liberation." Colours of Resistance Archive, 2004. www.coloursofresistance.org/508/beyond-voting-anarchist-organizing-electoral-politics-and-developing-strategy-for-liberation/.

———. *Collective Liberation on My Mind: Essays by Chris Crass*. Montreal, QC: Kersplebdeb, 2001.

———, ed. "Strategic Opportunities: White Anti-Racist Organizing and Building Left Organization and Movement." In *Towards Collective Liberation: Anti-Racist Organizing, Feminist Praxis, and Movement Building Strategy*, 179–96. Oakland: PM Press, 2013.

———. *Towards Collective Liberation: Anti-Racist Organizing, Feminist Praxis, and Movement Building Strategy*. Oakland: PM Press, 2013.

Creed, Gerald W., ed. *The Seductions of Community: Emancipations, Oppressions, Quandaries*. Santa Fe: School of American Research Press, 2006.

Crenshaw, Kimberlé. "Mapping the Margins: Intersectionality, Identity Politics, and Violence Against Women of Color." *Stanford Law Review* 43, no. 6 (1991): 1241–99.

Crimethinc. "Say You Want an Insurrection." *Crimethinc*. Accessed January 6, 2014. www.crimethinc.com/texts/rollingthunder/insurrection.php.

Critical Resistance. "Mission and Vision." *Critical Resistance*. Accessed November 2, 2012. http://criticalresistance.org/about/.

———. "Not So Common Language." *Critical Resistance*. Accessed April 19, 2009. www.criticalresistance.org/article.php?id = 49.

Critical Resistance, and INCITE! Women of Color Against Violence. "Gender Violence and the Prison-Industrial Complex." In *Color of Violence: The INCITE! Anthology*, edited by INCITE! Women of Color Against Violence, 223–26. Cambridge, MA: South End Press, 2006.

CROATOAN. "Who Is Oakland: Anti-Oppression Activism, the Politics of Safety, and State Co-optation." *Escalating Identity*, April 2012. https://escalatingidentity.wordpress.com/2012/04/30/who-is-oakland-anti-oppression-politics-decolonization-and-the-state/.

Crow, Scott. *Black Flags and Windmills: Hope, Anarchy, and the Common Ground Collective*. Oakland: PM Press, 2011.

Curtin, Mary Ellen. *Black Prisoners and Their World, Alabama, 1865–1900*. Charlottesville: University Press of Virginia, 2000.

Dalla Costa, Mariarosa, and Giovanna F. Dalla Costa. *Women, Development, and the Labor of Reproduction: Struggles and Movements*. Trenton, NJ: Africa World Press, 1999.

Dalla Costa, Mariarosa, and Selma James. *The Power of Women and the Subversion of the Community.* Bristol: Falling Wall Press, 1975.

David, and X, eds. *The Black Bloc Papers: An Anthology of Primary Texts From the North American Anarchist Black Bloc, 1999–2001.* Baltimore: Insubordinate Editions, 2002.

Davis, Angela. *Abolition Democracy: Beyond Empire, Prisons, and Torture.* New York: Seven Stores Press, 2005.

———. *Are Prisons Obsolete?* New York: Seven Stories Press, 2003.

———. *Women, Race and Class.* New York: Vintage Books, 1981.

Davis, Angela, and Elizabeth Martinez. "Coalition Building Among People of Color." In *The Angela Y. Davis Reader,* edited by Joy James, 297–306. Malden, MA: Blackwell Publishers, 1998.

Davis, James. "This Is What Bureaucracy Looks Like: NGOs and Anti-Capitalism." In *The Battle of Seattle: The New Challenge to Capitalist Globalization,* edited by Eddie Yuen, George Katsiaficas, and Daniel Burton Rose, 175–82. New York: Soft Skull Press, 2001.

Davis, James, and Paul Rowley. "Internationalism Against Globalization." In *Confronting Capitalism: Dispatches from a Global Movement,* edited by Eddie Yuen, George Katsiaficas, and Daniel Burton Rose, xxx–xxxiii. New York: Soft Skull Press, 2004.

Davis, Mike. "Hell Factories in the Field: A Prison-Industrial Complex." *The Nation,* February 20, 1995.

Day, Christopher. "Dual Power In the Selva Lacandon." In *A New World in Our Hearts: Eight Years of Writings from the Love and Rage Revolutionary Anarchist Federation,* edited by Roy San Filippo, 17–31. Oakland: AK Press, 2003.

Day, Richard. *Gramsci Is Dead: Anarchist Currents in the Newest Social Movements.* London: Pluto Press, 2005.

Dean, Jodi. *The Communist Horizon.* London: Verso, 2012.

De Angelis, Massimo. *The Beginning of History: Value Struggles and Global Capital.* London: Pluto Press, 2006.

Delgado, Gary. "The Last Stop Sign." *Shelterforce,* December 1998. www.nhi.org/online/issues/102/stopsign.html.

De Marcellus, Olivier. "Peoples' Global Action: The Grassroots Go Global." In *We Are Everywhere: The Irresistible Rise of Global Anticapitalism,* edited by Notes from Nowhere, 97–101. London: Verso, 2003.

Desikan, Vasudha, and Drew Franklin. "From Building Tents to Building Movements: Reflections from Occupy." *In Front and Center* (blog), January 25, 2012. https://infrontandcenter.wordpress.com/2012/01/25/from-building-tents-to-building-movements-reflections-from-occupy-dc/#more-540.

Dissent Editorial Collective, ed. *Days of Dissent: Reflections on Summit Mobilisations.* London: Dissent! Network, 2004.

Dixon, Chris. "Dear Older Activists." In *Letters from Young Activists: Today's Rebels Speak Out,* edited by Dan Berger, Chesa Boudin, and Kenyon Farrow, 49–53. New York: Nation Books, 2005.

———. "Finding Hope After Seattle: Rethinking Radical Activism and Building a Movement." *Onward,* Spring 2001.

———. "Movements Where People Can Grow: An Interview with Helen Hudson." *Upping the Anti* 8 (2009): 81–94.

Domenack, Damien, and Rachael Leiner. "Toxic Connections: Coalition Strategies against Jail Expansion." In *Abolition Now! Ten Years of Strategy and Struggle against the Prison Industrial Complex,* edited by CR-10 Publications Collective, 103–7. Oakland: AK Press, 2008.

Dominick, Brian. "An Introduction to Dual Power Strategy." *Left-Liberty.net.* Accessed November 7, 2012. http://left-liberty.net/?p = 265.

———. "From Here to Parecon: Thoughts on Strategy for Economic Revolution." In *Real Utopia: Participatory Society for the 21st Century,* edited by Chris Spannos, 380–95. Oakland: AK Press, 2008.

Dua, Enakshi. "Canadian Anti-Racist Feminist Thought: Scratching the Surface of Racism." In *Scratching the Surface: Canadian Anti-Racist Feminist Thought,* edited by Enakshi Dua and Angela Robertson, 7–31. Toronto: Women's Press, 1999.

Dua, Enakshi, and Angela Robertson, eds. *Scratching the Surface: Canadian Anti-Racist Feminist Thought.* Toronto: Women's Press, 1999.

Duberman, Martin. *Stonewall.* New York: Plume, 1993.

Dubofsky, Melvin. *We Shall Be All: A History of the Industrial Workers of the World.* New York: Quadrangle, 1969.

Du Bois, W. E. B. *Black Reconstruction.* Millwood, N.Y: Kraus-Thomson Organization Ltd., 1976.

Dunbar-Ortiz, Roxanne. *Outlaw Woman: A Memoir of the War Years, 1960–1975.* San Francisco: City Lights, 2001.

Echols, Alice. *Daring to Be Bad: Radical Feminism in America 1967–1975.* Minneapolis: University of Minnesota Press, 1989.

Ehrenreich, Barbara. "Why Homelessness Is Becoming an Occupy Wall Street Issue." *Mother Jones,* October 24, 2011. www.motherjones.com/politics/2011/10/homelessness-occupy-wall-street.

Elbaum, Max. *Revolution in the Air: Sixties Radicals Turn to Lenin, Mao and Che.* London: Verso, 2002.

El Kilombo Intergaláctico. *Beyond Resistance: Everything.* Durham, NC: Paperboat Press, 2007.

———. *Feliz Año Cabrones: On the Continued Centrality Of the Zapatista Movement After 14 Years.* Durham, NC: El Kilombo Intergaláctico, 2008.

———. "Zapatista Justice." *Left Turn,* May 2008.

El Kilombo Intergaláctico, and Michael Hardt. "Organizing Encounters and Generating Events." In *Uses of A Whirlwind: Movement, Movements, and Contemporary Radical Currents in the United States,* edited by Team Colors Collective, 245–57. Oakland: AK Press, 2010.

Epstein, Barbara. "Notes on the Antiwar Movement." *Monthly Review* 55, no. 3 (2003): 109–16.

————. *Political Protest and Cultural Revolution: Nonviolent Direct Action in the 1970s and 1980s*. Berkeley: University of California Press, 1991.

Epstein, Barbara, and Chris Dixon. "A Politics and a Sensibility: The Anarchist Current on the U.S. Left." In *Toward a New Socialism*, edited by Anatole Anton and Richard Schmitt, 445–62. Lanham, MD: Lexington Books, 2007.

Erakat, Noura, and Monadel Herzallah. "National Popular Palestinian Conference." *Left Turn*, May 2008.

Evans, Sara. *Personal Politics: The Roots of Women's Liberation in the Civil Rights Movement and the New Left*. New York: Vintage Books, 1980.

Fanon, Frantz. *The Wretched of the Earth*. New York: Grove Press, 1963.

Farrell, Bryan. "The Eyes of Texas Are Upon You, Keystone XL." *Waging Nonviolence*, November 21, 2012. http://wagingnonviolence.org/feature/the-eyes-of-texas-are-upon-you-keystone-xl/.

————. "From the Tar Sands Action to Moving Planet." *Waging Nonviolence*, September 9, 2011. http://wagingnonviolence.org/2011/09/from-the-tar-sands-action-to-moving-planet/.

Farrell, James J. *The Spirit of the Sixties: Making Postwar Radicalism*. New York: Routledge, 1997.

Federici, Silvia. *Caliban and the Witch: Women, the Body, and Primitive Accumulation*. Brooklyn: Autonomedia, 2004.

————. "Precarious Labor: A Feminist Viewpoint." *In the Middle of a Whirlwind* (blog), 2008. https://inthemiddleofthewhirlwind.wordpress.com/precarious-labor-a-feminist-viewpoint/.

————. *Revolution at Point Zero: Housework, Reproduction, and Feminist Struggle*. Oakland: PM Press, 2012.

Feinberg, Leslie. *Trans Liberation: Beyond Pink or Blue*. Boston: Beacon Press, 1998.

Fenton, Cameron. "Changing the System." *The Dominion*, April 2011.

Fernandez, Luis, and Joel Olson. "To Live, Love and Work Anywhere You Please." *Contemporary Political Theory* 10, no. 3 (August 2011): 412–19.

Ferreira, Jason. "Medicine of Memory: Third World Radicalism in 1960s San Francisco and the Politics of Multiracial Unity." Presentation at University of California, Santa Cruz, February 23, 2005.

Fidler, Dick. *Red Power in Canada*. Toronto: Vanguard, 1970. www.socialisthistory.ca/Docs/1961-/Red%20Power/Red_Power_1970.htm.

Finkelstein, Norman. *Image and Reality of the Israel-Palestine Conflict*. London: Verso, 2003.

Fiorentini, Francesca, and Sasha Wright. "New Hope for the Anti-War Movement." *Left Turn*, November 2006.

Fithian, Lisa. "Anti-Oppression Principles and Practices." *Organizing for Power, Organizing for Change*. Accessed April 29, 2013. https://docs.google.com/document/d/1TnaLJXy6WSkJ-MQv4BlMhRXM1cc-4wBqNcgrD4W-VZQ/edit?pli = 1.

Flaherty, Jordan. *Floodlines: Community and Resistance from Katrina to the Jena Six*. Chicago: Haymarket Books, 2010.

Foucault, Michel. *Discipline and Punish: The Birth of the Prison.* Translated by Alan Sheridan. New York: Vintage Books, 1977.

Frampton, Caelie. "Strength in Numbers? Why Radical Students Need a New Organizing Model." *Upping the Anti* 5 (2007): 101–14.

Frampton, Caelie, Gary Kinsman, AK Thompson, and Kate Tilleczek, eds. *Sociology for Changing the World: Social Movements/Social Research.* Halifax: Fernwood Publishing, 2006.

Franco, Marisa. "How a Bus Full of Undocumented Families Could Change the Immigration Debate." *YES! Magazine,* November 30, 2012. www.yesmagazine.org/peace-justice/how-a-bus-full-of-undocumented-families-could-change-the-immigration-debate.

Freedom Road Socialist Organization. "Which Way Is Left? Theory, Politics, Organization and 21st-Century Socialism." New York: Freedom Road Socialist Organization, 2007. www.freedomroad.org/images/stories/PDF/wwil.pdf.

Freeman, Jo. "The Tyranny of Structurelessness." In *Quiet Rumors: An Anarcha-Feminist Reader,* edited by Dark Star Collective, 54–61. Edinburgh: AK Press, 2002.

Freire, Paulo. *Pedagogy of the Oppressed.* Translated by Myra Berman Ramos. New York: Continuum, 1983.

Fritsch, Kelly, ed. "Occupy Everything: A Roundtable on U.S. Student Occupations." *Upping the Anti* 10 (2010): 165–79.

Fyke, Kim, and Gabriel Sayegh. "Anarchism and the Struggle to Move Forward." *Perspectives on Anarchist Theory* 5, no. 2 (2001). http://flag.blackened.net/ias/10fyke&sayegh.htm.

Galeano, Eduardo H. *Open Veins of Latin America: Five Centuries of the Pillage of a Continent.* New York: Monthly Review Press, 1997.

Galleani, Luigi. *The End of Anarchism?* Orkney: Cienfuegos Press, 1982.

Gardner, Madeline, and Joshua Kahn Russell. "Praxis Makes Perfect: The New Youth Organizing." In *Real Utopia: Participatory Society for the 21st Century,* edited by Chris Spannos, 338–46. Oakland: AK Press, 2008.

Garneau, Marianne. "Austerity and Resistance: Lessons from the 2012 Quebec Student Strike." *Insurgent Notes,* October 15, 2012. http://insurgentnotes.com/2012/10/austerity-and-resistance-lessons-from-the-2012-quebec-student-strike/.

Geronimo. *Fire and Flames: A History of the German Autonomist Movement.* Oakland: PM Press, 2012.

Gibbons, Andrea. "Driven From Below: A Look at Tenant Organizing and the New Gentrification." *Institute for Anarchist Studies,* 2009. www.anarchist-studies.org/node/321.

Gilmore, Ruth Wilson. *Golden Gulag: Prisons, Surplus, Crisis, and Opposition in Globalizing California.* Berkeley: University of California Press, 2007.

———. "In the Shadow of the Shadow State." In *The Revolution Will Not Be Funded: Beyond the Non-Profit Industrial Complex,* edited by INCITE! Women of Color Against Violence, 41–52. Cambridge, MA: South End Press, 2007.

Gilmore, Ruth Wilson, and Craig Gilmore. "The Other California." In *Globalize Liberation: How to Uproot the System and Build Another World*, edited by David Solnit, 381–96. San Francisco: City Lights Books, 2004.

Goldberg, Harmony. "Building Power in the City: Reflections on the Emergence of the Right to the City Alliance and the National Domestic Workers Alliance." In *Uses of A Whirlwind: Movement, Movements, and Contemporary Radical Currents in the United States*, edited by Team Colors Collective, 97–108. Oakland: AK Press, 2010.

Goldman, Emma. "Prisons: A Social Crime and Failure." *Anarchism and Other Essays*, 109–26. New York: Dover Publications, 1969.

Gonzalez, Paulina. "The Strategy and Organizing Behind the Successful DREAM Act Movement." *Narco News*, July 10, 2012. http://narconews.com/Issue67/article4607.html.

Gordon, Uri. *Anarchy Alive! Anti-Authoritarian Politics from Practice to Theory*. London: Pluto Press, 2008.

Gordon, Uri, and Ohal Grietzer, eds. *Anarchists Against the Wall*. Oakland: AK Press, 2013.

Gorz, André. *A Strategy for Labor: A Radical Proposal*. Translated by Martin A. Nicolaus and Victoria Ortiz. Boston: Beacon Press, 1967.

Gosse, Van. "'The North American Front': Central American Solidarity in the Reagan Era." In *Reshaping the U.S. Left: Popular Struggles in the 1980s*, edited by Mike Davis and Michael Sprinker, 1–43. London: Verso, 1988.

Gossett, Reggie. "Organic Intellectual." *Left Turn*, June 2006.

Gottesdiener, Laura. "Occupy Homes, One Year On and Growing Daily." *Waging Nonviolence*, December 24, 2012. http://wagingnonviolence.org/2012/12/occupy-homes-one-year-on-and-growing-daily.

Gould, Deborah. *Moving Politics: Emotion and ACT UP's Fight Against AIDS*. Chicago: University of Chicago Press, 2009.

Gowan, Peter. *The Global Gamble: Washington's Faustian Bid for World Dominance*. London: Verso, 1999.

Graeber, David. *Fragments of an Anarchist Anthropology*. Chicago: Prickly Paradigm Press, 2004.

———. "The New Anarchists." *New Left Review* 13 (2002): 61–73.

———. "Where Does Occupy Go from Here?" *The Independent*, April 19, 2013. www.independent.co.uk/voices/comment/this-weeks-big-questions-where-does-occupy-go-from-here-should-thatcher-have-been-given-such-a-grand-funeral-8580342.html.

Green, James. *Taking History to Heart: The Power of the Past in Building Social Movements*. Amherst: University of Massachusetts Press, 2000.

Green, Joyce, ed. *Making Space for Indigenous Feminism*. Black Point, NS: Fernwood, 2007.

Greenhouse, Steven. "Some Organizers Protest Their Union's Tactics." *New York Times*, November 18, 2009.

Griffin Cohen, Marjorie. "The Canadian Women's Movement." In *Canadian Women's Issues: Twenty-Five Years of Women's Activism in English Canada*, edited by Ruth Roach Pierson, Marjorie Griffin Cohen, Paula Bourne, and Philinda Masters, 1–31. Toronto: James Lorimer and Company, 1993.

Groves, Tim. "Idle No More Across Turtle Island." *The Dominion*, April 2013.

Guilloud, Stephanie. "Letter on Oppression within the Movement." In *Letters from Young Activists,* edited by Dan Berger, Chesa Boudin, and Kenyon Farrow, 120–26. New York: Nation Books, 2005.

———. "Spark, Fire, and Burning Coals: An Organizer's History of Seattle." In *The Battle of Seattle: The New Challenge to Capitalist Globalization,* edited by Eddie Yuen, George Katsiaficas, and Daniel Burton Rose, 225–31. New York: Soft Skull Press, 2001.

———, ed. *Voices from the WTO: An Anthology of Writings from the People Who Shut Down the World Trade Organization.* Olympia, WA: The Evergreen State College, 2000.

Guilloud, Stephanie, and the Executive Leadership Team of Project South. *The First U.S. Social Forum: Report from the Anchor Organization.* Atlanta: Project South, 2009.

Guilloud, Stephanie, and William Cordery. "Fundraising Is Not a Dirty Word: Community-Based Economic Strategies for the Long Haul." In *The Revolution Will Not Be Funded: Beyond the Non-Profit Industrial Complex,* edited by INCITE! Women of Color Against Violence, 107–11. Cambridge, MA: South End Press, 2007.

Gumbs, Alexis Pauline. "Freedom Seeds: Growing Abolition in Durham, North Carolina." In *Abolition Now! Ten Years of Strategy and Struggle Against the Prison Industrial Complex,* edited by CR-10 Publications Collective, 145–55. Oakland: AK Press, 2008.

Gupta, A. K. "Moving Forward: UFPJ and the Anti-War Movement." *Left Turn,* March 2006.

Haddad, Bassam, Rosie Bsheer, and Ziad Abu-Rish, eds. *The Dawn of the Arab Uprisings: End of an Old Order?* London: Pluto Press, 2012.

Hahnel, Robin. "Winnowing Wheat from Chaff: Social Democracy and Libertarian Socialism in the 20th Century." In *Real Utopia: Participatory Society for the 21st Century,* edited by Chris Spannos, 204–62. Oakland: AK Press, 2008.

Hanieh, Adam, Hazem Jamjoum, and Rafeef Ziadah. "Challenging the New Apartheid: Reflections on Palestine Solidarity." *Left Turn,* June 2006.

Harm Free Zone Project. "General Framework." Unpublished document in author's possession. New York, October 22, 2006.

———. "Rethinking Restorative Justice: Harm Free Zones in New York." Unpublished document in author's possession. New York, October 21, 2007.

Harvey, David. *A Brief History of Neoliberalism.* New York: Oxford University Press, 2005.

Harvey, Ryan. "Are We Addicted to Rioting? Anarchists at the G20 Protests and Social Movement Strategy." *Indypendent Reader,* September 30, 2009. http://indyreader.org/content/are-we-addicted-rioting-anarchists-g20-protests-and-social-movement-strategy.

———. "Occupy Before and Beyond." In *We Are Many: Reflections on Movement Strategy from Occupation to Liberation*, edited by Kate Khatib, Margaret Killjoy, and Mike McGuire, 123–33. Oakland: AK Press, 2012.

Henaway, Mostafah, Nandita Sharma, Jaggi Singh, Harsha Walia, and Rafeef Ziadah. "Organizing for Migrant Justice and Self-Determination." *Infoshop .org*, October 22, 2007. http://news.infoshop.org/article.php?story= 20071029173229791.

Herzing, Rachel, and Isaac Ontiveros. "Reflections from the Fight Against Policing." In *We Are Many: Reflections on Movement Strategy from Occupation to Liberation*, edited by Kate Khatib, Margaret Killjoy, and Mike McGuire, 217–27. Oakland: AK Press, 2012.

Hewitt-White, Caitlin, ed. "Prison Abolition in Canada." *Upping the Anti* 4 (2007): 125–46.

Hilderbrand, Sue, Scott Crow, and Lisa Fithian. "Common Ground Relief." In *What Lies Beneath: Katrina, Race, and the State of the Nation*, edited by South End Press, 80–98. Cambridge, MA: South, 2007.

Hill, Gord. *500 Years of Indigenous Resistance*. Oakland: PM Press, 2009.

Hill, Hazel. "Sago from Grand River: Dispatches from the Six Nations Land Reclamation Struggle." *Left Turn*, August 2007.

Hilliard, David, and the Dr. Huey P. Newton Foundation. *The Black Panther Party: Service to the People Programs*. Albuquerque: University of New Mexico Press, 2008.

Hintze, Tom. "How Occupy Sandy's Relief Machine Stepped Into the Post-Superstorm Void." *Alternet*, November 5, 2012. www.alternet.org/occupy-wall-street/how-occupy-sandys-relief-machine-stepped-post-superstorm-void?paging = off.

Hirsch, Steven, and Lucien van der Walt, eds. *Anarchism and Syndicalism in the Colonial and Postcolonial World, 1870–1940: The Praxis of National Liberation, Internationalism, and Social Revolution*. Leiden: Brill, 2010.

Ho, Fred, ed. *Legacy to Liberation: Politics & Culture of Revolutionary Asian/Pacific America*. Oakland: AK Press, 2000.

Holloway, John. *Change the World without Taking Power*. 2nd ed. London: Pluto, 2005.

———. *Crack Capitalism*. London: Pluto, 2010.

———. "The Two Temporalities of Counter-Power and Anti-Power," 2005. http://info.interactivist.net/node/4232.

Holtzman, Benjamin, and Craig Hughes. "Points of Resistance and Departure: An Interview with James C. Scott." *Upping the Anti* 11 (2010): 73–84.

hooks, bell. *Feminist Theory from Margin to Center*. Boston, MA: South End Press, 1984.

Horton, Myles. *The Myles Horton Reader: Education for Social Change*. Edited by Dale Jacobs. Knoxville: University of Tennessee Press, 2003.

Horton, Myles, and Paulo Freire. *We Make the Road by Walking: Conversations on Education and Social Change*. Edited by Brenda Bell, John Gaventa, and John Peters. Philadelphia: Temple University Press, 1990.

Howe, Irving. *Socialism and America*. San Diego: Harcourt Brace Jovanovich, 1985.

Hsiao, Andrew. "Color Blind: Activists of Color Bring the Economic War Home, But Is the Movement Missing the Message?" In *The Battle of Seattle: The New Challenge to Capitalist Globalization*, edited by Eddie Yuen, George Katsiaficas, and Daniel Burton Rose, 343–46. New York: Soft Skull Press, 2001.

Hughes, Craig. *Occupied Zuccotti, Social Struggle, and Planned Shrinkage*. Zine. New York, 2012.

Hugill, Andrew. "Coalition Against Israeli Apartheid." *Left Turn*, May 2008.

Hurl, Chris. "Anti-Globalization and 'Diversity of Tactics'." *Upping the Anti* 1 (2005): 51–64.

Hwang, Pauline Sok Yin. "Anti-Racist Organizing: Reflecting On Lessons from Quebec City." In *Under the Lens of the People: Our Account of the Peoples' Resistance to the FTAA, Quebec City, April 2001*, edited by The Peoples Lenses Collective, 48–52. Toronto: The Peoples Lenses Collective, 2003.

INCITE! Women of Color Against Violence, ed. *Color of Violence: The INCITE! Anthology*. Cambridge, MA: South End Press, 2006.

———, ed. *The Revolution Will Not Be Funded: Beyond the Non-Profit Industrial Complex*. Cambridge, MA: South End Press, 2007.

INCITE! Women of Color Against Violence, and FIERCE! "Re-Thinking 'The Norm' In Police/Prison Violence and Gender Violence: Critical Lessons from the New Jersey 7." *Left Turn*, November 2008.

Indigenous Peoples Solidarity Movement. "Land, Decolonization and Self-Determination." *A-Infos*, March 16, 2005. www.ainfos.ca/05/mar/ainfos00299.html.

Industrial Workers of the World. "Preamble of the Industrial Workers of the World." In *Rebel Voices: An I.W.W. Anthology*, edited by Joyce Kornbluh, 12–13. Ann Arbor: University of Michigan Press, 1964.

Inouye, Kimiko, ed. "Home and a Hard Place: A Roundtable on Migrant Labour." *Upping the Anti* 7 (2008): 163–78.

Jacobs, Ron. *The Way the Wind Blew: A History of the Weather Underground*. London: Verso, 1997.

Jaffe, Sarah. "Power to the People." *Jacobin*, November 3, 2012. http://jacobin-mag.com/2012/11/power-to-the-people/.

James, Joy. *Resisting State Violence: Radicalism, Gender, and Race in U.S. Culture*. Minneapolis: University of Minnesota Press, 1996.

Janowski, Rahula. "Collective Parenting for Collective Liberation." *Left Turn*, February 2007.

Johnson Reagon, Bernice. "Coalition Politics: Turning the Century." In *Home Girls: A Black Feminist Anthology*, edited by Barbara Smith, 356–68. New York: Kitchen Table: Women of Color Press, 1983.

Jones, Arlen, and Greg Hoffman. "Pink Sheeting and Harmful Organizing Methods at UNITE HERE." *Labor Notes*, January 8, 2010. www.labornotes.org/2009/12/pink-sheeting-part-harmful-organizing-methods-unite-here.

Jones, Catherine. "The Work Is Not the Workshop: Talking and Doing, Visibility and Accountability in the White Anti-Racist Community." Colours of Resistance Archive. Accessed April 29, 2013. www.coloursofresistance. org/345/the-work-is-not-the-workshop-talking-and-doing-visibility-and-accountability-in-the-white-anti-racist-community/.

Jones, Charles E., ed. *The Black Panther Party (Reconsidered)*. Baltimore: Black Classic Press, 1998.

Jones de Almeida, Adjoa, Dana Kaplan, Paula Ximena Rojas-Urrutia, Eric Tang, and M. Mayuran Tiruchelvam. "Rethinking Solidarity." *Left Turn,* June 2006.

Jordan, June. *On Call: Political Essays.* Boston: South End Press, 1985.

Jumaa, Jamal. "'To Exist Is to Resist': From the Apartheid Wall in Palestine and Beyond." *Left Turn*, August 2008.

Juris, Jeffrey. "Spaces of Intentionality: Race, Class, and Horizontality at the United States Social Forum." In *Insurgent Encounters: Transnational Activism, Ethnography, and the Political,* edited by Jeffrey Juris and Alex Khasnabish, 39–65. Durham: Duke University Press, 2013.

k, sasha. "Some Notes on Insurrectionary Anarchism." *The Anarchist Library.* Accessed October 30, 2012. http://theanarchistlibrary.org/library/sasha_k__ Some_notes_on_Insurrectionary_Anarchism.html.

Kadi, Joanna, ed. *Food for Our Grandmothers: Writings by Arab-American and Arab-Canadian Feminists.* Boston: South End Press, 1994.

———. *Thinking Class: Sketches from a Cultural Worker.* Boston: South End Press, 1996.

Kahl, Leith. "The Tyranny of Structurelessness and Earth First!" *Earth First! Journal* 21, no. 5 (2001).

Kanuga, Malav. "Bluestockings Bookstore and New Institutions of Self-Organized Work: The Space Between Common Notions and Common Institutions." In *Uses of A Whirlwind: Movement, Movements, and Contemporary Radical Currents in the United States,* edited by Team Colors Collective, 19–35. Oakland: AK Press, 2010.

Kateel, Subhash. "Immigrant Rights Movement at the Crossroads." *Left Turn,* June 2006.

Katsiaficas, George. *The Imagination of the New Left: A Global Analysis of 1968.* Boston: South End Press, 1987.

———. "Seattle Was Not the Beginning." In *The Battle of Seattle: The New Challenge to Capitalist Globalization,* edited by Eddie Yuen, George Katsiaficas, and Daniel Burton Rose, 29–35. New York: Soft Skull Press, 2001.

———. *The Subversion of Politics: European Autonomous Social Movements and the Decolonization of Everyday Life.* New Jersey: Humanities Press, 1997.

Kauffman, L.A. "A Short History of Radical Renewal." In *From Act Up to the WTO: Urban Protest and Community Building in the Era of Globalization,* edited by Benjamin Shepard and Ronald Hayduk, 35–40. London: Verso, 2002.

———. "A Short Personal History of the Global Justice Movement." In *Confronting Capitalism: Dispatches from a Global Movement*, edited by Eddie Yuen, George Katsiaficas, and Daniel Burton-Rose, 375–88. New York: Soft Skull Press, 2004.

———. "Who Are Those Masked Anarchists?" In *The Battle of Seattle: The New Challenge to Capitalist Globalization*, edited by Eddie Yuen, Daniel Burton Rose, and George Katsiaficas, 124–29. New York: Soft Skull Press, 2001.

Keefer, Chris. "Fighting the Co-optation of Resistance." *Upping the Anti* 6 (2008): 184–89.

Keefer, Tom. "Declaring the Exception: Direct Action, Six Nations, and the Struggle in Brantford." *Upping the Anti* 7 (2008): 111–28.

———. "The Politics of Solidarity: Six Nations, Leadership, and the Left." *Upping the Anti* 4 (2007): 107–23.

———. "The Six Nations Land Reclamation." *Upping the Anti* 3 (2006): 135–67.

Kelley, Robin. *Freedom Dreams: The Black Radical Imagination.* Boston: Beacon Press, 2002.

———. *Hammer and Hoe: Alabama Communists During the Great Depression.* Chapel Hill: University of North Carolina Press, 1990.

———. *Race Rebels: Culture, Politics, and the Black Working Class.* New York: The Free Press, 1994.

Khan, Sharmeen, ed. "Roundtable on Anti-Oppression Politics in Anti-Capitalist Movements." *Upping the Anti* 1 (2005): 76–88.

Khan, Sharmeen, and Tyler McCreary. "Building Unlikely Alliances: An Interview with Andrea Smith." *Upping the Anti* 10 (2010): 40–52.

Khanna, Shyam. "Mississippi Goddam: SNCC, Occupy, and Radical Community Organizing." *Tidal: Occupy Theory, Occupy Strategy* 4 (2013): 12–13.

Khasnabish, Alex. *Zapatismo Beyond Borders: New Imaginations of Political Possibility.* Toronto: University of Toronto Press, 2008.

Khatib, Kate, Margaret Killjoy, and Mike McGuire, eds. *We Are Many: Reflections on Movement Strategy from Occupation to Liberation.* Oakland: AK Press, 2012.

Kilibarda, Kole. "Confronting Apartheid: The BDS Movement in Canada." *Upping the Anti* 7 (2008): 131–43.

Kilkenny, Allison. "Occupy Sandy Efforts Highlight Need for Solidarity, Not Charity." *The Nation* (blog), November 5, 2012. www.thenation.com /blog/171020/occupy-sandy-efforts-highlight-need-solidarity-not-charity.

King, Tiffany Lethabo, and Ewuare Osayande. "The Filth on Philanthropy." In *The Revolution Will Not Be Funded: Beyond the Non-Profit Industrial Complex*, edited by INCITE! Women of Color Against Violence, 79–89. Cambridge, MA: South End Press, 2007.

Kinsman, Gary. "AIDS Activism and the Politics of Emotion: An Interview with Deborah Gould." *Upping the Anti* 8 (2009): 65–80.

———. "Managing AIDS Organizing: 'Consultation,' 'Partnership,' and 'Responsibility' as Strategies of Regulation." In *Organizing Dissent:*

Contemporary Social Movements in Theory and Practice, edited by William K. Carroll, 213–39. Toronto: Garamond Press, 1997.

———. *The Regulation of Desire: Homo and Hetero Sexualities.* 2nd ed. Montreal: Black Rose Books, 1996.

Kinsman, Gary, and Patrizia Gentile. *The Canadian War on Queers: National Security as Sexual Regulation.* Vancouver: UBC Press, 2010.

Kirby, Jane. "Mass Protests and the Future of Convergence Activism: Is Summit-Hopping a Dying Tactic or the Next Olympic Sport?" *Briarpatch,* February 2010.

Kivel, Paul. "Are You Mentoring for Social Justice?" *Racial Equity Tools,* 2004. www.racialequitytools.org/resourcefiles/kivel2.pdf.

———. "Social Service or Social Change?" In *The Revolution Will Not Be Funded: Beyond the Non-Profit Industrial Complex,* edited by INCITE! Women of Color Against Violence, 129–49. Cambridge, MA: South End Press, 2007.

Klein, Naomi. *The Shock Doctrine: The Rise of Disaster Capitalism.* New York: Picador, 2008.

Knoche, Tom. "Organizing Communities: Building Neighborhood Movements for Radical Change." In *Globalize Liberation: How to Uproot the System and Build a Better World,* edited by David Solnit, 287–310. San Francisco: City Lights Books, 2004.

Kokopeli, Bruce, and George Lakey. *Leadership for Change: Toward a Feminist Model.* Philadelphia: New Society Publishers, 1984.

Kom'boa Ervin, Lorenzo. *Anarchism and the Black Revolution.* Philadelphia: Monkeywrench Press, 1994.

Kornbluh, Joyce, ed. *Rebel Voices: An I.W.W. Anthology.* Ann Arbor: University of Michigan Press, 1964.

Korte, Pat, and Brian Kelly. "Which Way for the New Left? Social Theory, Vision, and Strategy for a Revolutionary Youth and Student Movement." In *Real Utopia: Participatory Society for the 21st Century,* edited by Chris Spannos, 364–72. Oakland: AK Press, 2009.

Kostash, Myrna. *Long Way From Home: The Story of the Sixties Generation in Canada.* Toronto: James Lorimer and Company, 1980.

Kropotkin, Peter. "Prisons and Their Moral Influence on Prisoners." *Anarchist Archives,* 1927. http://dwardmac.pitzer.edu/Anarchist_Archives/kropotkin/revpamphlets/prisonsmoral.html.

Kruzynski, Anna, Rachel Sarrasin, and Sandra Jeppesen. "It Didn't Start with Occupy, and It Won't End with the Student Strike! The Persistence of Anti-authoritarian Politics in Quebec." *Wi Journal,* 2012. http://wi.mobilities.ca/it-didnt-start-with-occupy-and-it-wont-end-with-the-student-strike-the-persistence-of-anti-authoritarian-politics-in-quebec/.

Kulchyski, Peter. *The Red Indians: An Episodic, Informal Collection of Tales from the History of Aboriginal People's Struggles in Canada.* Winnipeg: Arbeiter Ring, 2007.

LA Crew. "Ideas in Action: An LA Story." *Left Turn,* February 2009.

Lafore, Beca, Helia Rasti, Jonathan Stribling-Uss, and Meddle Bolger. *Shutdown: The Rise and Fall of Direct Action to Stop the War*. Oakland: AK Press, 2009.

Lakey, George. *Powerful Peacemaking: A Strategy for a Living Revolution*. Philadelphia: New Society Publishers, 1987.

Lalonde, Julien, Murray Bush, and Brett Rhyno. "Many Pipelines, More Resistance." *The Dominion*, December 2012.

Lang, Amy, and Daniel Lang/Levitsky, eds. *Dreaming in Public: Building the Occupy Movement*. Oxford: New Internationalist Publications, 2012.

Lang/Levitsky, Daniel. "Jews Confront Zionism." *Monthly Review* 61, no. 2 (2009): 47–54.

Law, Victoria. "Protection Without Police: North American Community Responses to Violence in the 1970s and Today." *Upping the Anti* 12 (2011): 91–104.

———. "Where's My Movement? Contemporary Anarchist Mothers and Community Support." *Perspectives on Anarchist Theory* 13, no. 1 (2011): 19–30.

Law, Victoria, and China Martens, eds. *Don't Leave Your Friends Behind: Concrete Ways to Support Families in Social Justice Movements and Communities*. Oakland: PM Press, 2012.

Law, Vikki. "Creating Space for Kids in Our Movements." *Left Turn*, August 2011.

Lazaou, Jeremy. "No Time Like the Present . . . ." *2 Eyes Open*, March 10, 2010. http://2eyesopen.com/2010/03/10/no-time-like-the-present/.

Leary, Elly. "Immokalee Workers Take Down Taco Bell." *Monthly Review* 57, no. 5 (2005): 11–25.

Lee, Butch, and Red Rover. *Night-Vision: Illuminating War and Class on the Neo-Colonial Terrain*. New York: Vagabond, 1993.

Leier, Mark. *Where the Fraser River Flows: The Industrial Workers of the World in British Columbia*. Vancouver: New Star Books, 1990.

Lenin, Vladimir Ilyich. "The Dual Power." *The Lenin Anthology*, edited by Robert C. Tucker, 301–4. New York: W.W. Norton and Company, 1975.

———. "What Is to Be Done? Burning Questions of Our Movement." *The Lenin Anthology*, edited by Robert C. Tucker, 12–114. New York: W.W. Norton and Company, 1975.

Leslie, Laura. "Meet Kai Barrow." Interview. *The State of Things*. WUNC, May 24, 2010.

Letson, Robyn, ed. "Coming Out Against Apartheid: A Roundtable About Queer Solidarity with Palestine." *Upping the Anti* 13 (2011): 137–51.

Levine, Cathy. "The Tyranny of Tyranny." In *Quiet Rumors: An Anarcha-Feminist Reader*, edited by Dark Star Collective, 63–66. Edinburgh: AK Press, 2002.

Lichtenstein, Alex. *Twice the Work of Free Labor: The Political Economy of Convict Labor in the New South*. London: Verso, 1996.

Lipsitz, George. *A Life in the Struggle: Ivory Perry and the Culture of Opposition*. 2nd ed. Philadelphia: Temple University Press, 1995.

Liu, Elliott. "Everybody Wants A New Old Left." *Lines That Divide, Lines That Connect* (blog), February 15, 2009. http://linesblog.com/?q = node/88.

Loewe, B. "Turning the Tide: Migrant Rights, Barrio Defense, and New Directions." *Left Turn*, February 2011.

Lorde, Audre. *Sister Outsider*. Freedom, CA: The Crossing Press, 1996.

Louie, Steve, and Glenn Omatsu. *Asian Americans: The Movement and the Moment*. Los Angeles: UCLA Asian American Studies Center Press, 2001.

Love, Janice. *The U.S. Anti-Apartheid Movement: Local Activism in Global Politics*. New York: Praeger, 1985.

Loyd, Jenna, Matt Mitchelson, and Andrew Burridge, eds. *Beyond Walls and Cages: Prisons, Borders, and Global Crisis*. Athens, GA: University of Georgia Press, 2012.

Luft, Rachel. "Beyond Disaster Exceptionalism: Social Movement Developments in New Orleans After Hurricane Katrina." *American Quarterly* 61, no. 3 (September 2009): 499–527.

———. "Looking for Common Ground: Relief Work in Post-Katrina New Orleans as an American Parable of Race and Gender Violence." *NWSA Journal* 20, no. 3 (Fall 2008): 5–31.

Lukacs, Martin. "Canada's First Nations Protest Heralds a New Alliance." *The Guardian*, December 20, 2012. www.guardian.co.uk/commentisfree/2012/dec/20/canada-first-nations-new-alliance.

Luu, Helen. "Discovering a Different Space of Resistance: Personal Reflections on Anti-Racist Organizing." In *Globalize Liberation: How to Uproot the System and Build a Better World*, edited by David Solnit, 411–26. San Francisco: City Lights, 2004.

Luxemburg, Rosa. *The Accumulation of Capital*. Translated by Agnes Schwarzschild. London: Routledge, 2003.

———. *Reform or Revolution*. New York: Pathfinder Press, 1973.

Lynne, Tamara. "Why Must We Be Small? Reflections on Political Development and Cultural Work in Brazil's Landless Movement." *Perspectives on Anarchist Theory* 13, no. 1 (Fall 2011): 41–50.

Maccani, RJ. "Another Politics Is Possible!" *Zapagringo* (blog), June 25, 2007. http://zapagringo.blogspot.com/2007/06/another-politics-is-possible.html.

———. "'Be a Zapatista Wherever You Are': Learning Solidarity in the Fourth World War." *RESIST*, May 2008. www.resistinc.org/newsletters/articles/be-zapatista-wherever-you-are.

———. "Enter the Intergalactic: The Zapatistas' Sixth Declaration in the U.S. and the World." *Upping the Anti* 3 (2006): 105–21.

———. "From Below and to the Left: Zapatistas and the Other Campaign." *Left Turn*, June 2006.

———. "Urban Zapatismo in NYC." *Left Turn*, May 2008.

Makhno, Nestor, Peter Arshinov, and Ida Mett. *Organizational Platform of the Libertarian Communists*. Montreal: Abraham Guillen Press/Arm the Spirit, 2002.

Malatesta, Errico. *Errico Malatesta: His Life and Ideas.* Edited by Vernon Richards. London: Freedom Press, 1984.

Malleson, Tom, and David Wachsmuth, eds. *Whose Streets? The Toronto G20 and the Challenges of Summit Protest.* Toronto: Between the Lines, 2011.

Malos, Ellen, ed. *The Politics of Housework.* London: Allison and Busby, 1980.

Mananzala, Rickke, and Dean Spade. "The Nonprofit Industrial Complex and Trans Resistance." *Sexuality Research and Social Policy* 5, no. 1 (2008): 53–71.

Mao Tsetung. *Five Essays on Philosophy.* Peking: Foreign Languages Press, 1977.

Marcos, Subcomandante. "A Death Has Been Decided," July 2003. http://struggle.ws/mexico/ezln/2003/marcos/deathJULY.html.

Marom, Yotam. "Occupy Sandy, from Relief to Resistance." *Waging Nonviolence*, November 13, 2012. http://wagingnonviolence.org/2012/11/occupy-sandy-from-relief-to-resistance/.

———. "Rome Wasn't Sacked in a Day: On Reform, Revolution, and Winning." In *We Are Many: Reflections on Movement Strategy from Occupation to Liberation*, edited by Kate Khatib, Margaret Killjoy, and Mike McGuire, 417–23. Oakland: AK Press, 2012.

Marshall, Peter. *Demanding the Impossible: A History of Anarchism.* London: Fontana Press, 1993.

Martin, Henry. "A Border Runs Through It: Mohawk Sovereignty and the Canadian State." *Briarpatch*, August 2010.

Martinez, Elizabeth. *De Colores Means All of Us: Latina Views for a Multi-Colored Century.* Cambridge, MA: South End Press, 1998.

Martinez, Elizabeth (Betita). "Where Was the Color in Seattle? Looking for Reasons Why the Great Battle Was so White." *ColorLines* 3, no. 1 (2000): 11–12.

Marx, Karl. *Capital: A Critique of Political Economy.* Translated by Ben Fowkes. Vol. 1. London: Penguin Books, 1976.

———. *Early Writings.* Translated by Gregor Benton and Rodney Livingstone. New York: Vintage Books, 1975.

Marx, Karl, and Friedrich Engels. "Manifesto of the Communist Party." In *The Marx-Engels Reader*, edited by Robert C. Tucker, 469–500. New York: W.W. Norton and Company, 1978.

Mason, Paul. *Why It's Kicking Off Everywhere: The New Global Revolutions.* London: Verso, 2012.

Mathiesen, Thomas. *The Politics of Abolition.* New York: Wiley, 1974.

Matt. "Interview with the Seattle Solidarity Network." *Libcom.org*, September 29, 2010. http://libcom.org/library/seasol-interview.

Matthiessen, Peter. *In the Spirit of Crazy Horse.* New York: Viking Press, 1983.

Maynard, Robyn. "Double Punishment for Villanueva." *The Dominion*, July 2010.

Mazón, Alexis. "The U.S. Occupation of Border Communities." *Left Turn*, September 2006.

McCleave Maharawal, Manissa. "Reflections from the People of Color Caucus at Occupy Wall Street." In *We Are Many: Reflections on Movement*

Strategy from Occupation to Liberation, edited by Kate Khatib, Margaret Killjoy, and Mike McGuire, 177–83. Oakland: AK Press, 2012.

McClintock, Anne, Aamir Mufti, Ella Shohat, and Social Text Collective. *Dangerous Liaisons: Gender, Nation, and Postcolonial Perspectives.* Minneapolis: University of Minnesota Press, 1997.

McCormack, A. Ross. *Reformers, Rebels, and Revolutionaries: The Western Canadian Radical Movement 1899–1919.* Toronto: University of Toronto Press, 1977.

McCreary, Tyler. "Oil and Water Don't Mix: Dakelh Communities Defend Their Land and Watercourses from Enbridge's Northern Gateway Pipeline Project." *Briarpatch*, April 2011.

McKay, Ian. *Rebels, Red, Radicals: Rethinking Canada's Left History.* Toronto: Between the Lines, 2005.

McNally, David. *Global Slump: The Economics and Politics of Crisis and Resistance.* Oakland: PM Press, 2010.

McQuinn, Jason. "Against Organizationalism: Anarchism as Both Theory and Critique of Organization." *Anarchy.* Accessed January 30, 2013. http://flag .blackened.net/anarchynz/againstorganizationalism.htm.

McSorley, Tim. "Reprieve in Barriere Lake Forestry Battle." *The Dominion*, October 2012.

Melendez, Miguel. *We Took the Streets: Fighting for Latino Rights with the Young Lords.* New York: St. Martin's Press, 2003.

Members of Advance the Struggle, and A New York City Revolutionary. "Unifying Revolutionary Forces in the Coming Year." *Advance the Struggle*, August 10, 2012. http://advancethestruggle.wordpress.com/2012/08/10 /building-revolutionary-organization-in-2012/.

Meyer, Matt, ed. *Let Freedom Ring: A Collection of Documents from the Movements to Free U.S. Political Prisoners.* Oakland: PM Press, 2008.

Midnight Notes and Friends. *Promissory Notes: From Crises to Commons.* Jamaica Plain, MA: Midnight Notes, 2009. http://midnightnotes.org /Promissory%20Notes.pdf.

Midnight Notes Collective, ed. *Auroras of the Zapatistas: Local and Global Struggles of the Fourth World War.* Brooklyn: Autonomedia, 2001.

———, ed. *Midnight Oil: Work, Energy, War, 1973–1992.* Brooklyn: Autonomedia, 1992.

Mies, Maria. *Patriarchy and Accumulation on a World Scale: Women in the International Division of Labor.* 2nd ed. London: Zed Books, 1998.

Mills, Sean. *The Empire Within: Postcolonial Thought and Political Activism in Sixties Montreal.* Montreal and Kingston: McGill-Queens University Press, 2010.

Milstein, Cindy. *Anarchism and Its Aspirations.* Oakland: AK Press, 2010.

———. "Hope in a Time of Elections." *Left Turn*, August 2008.

———. "Occupy Anarchism." In *We Are Many: Reflections on Movement Strategy from Occupation to Liberation*, edited by Kate Khatib, Margaret Killjoy, and Mike McGuire, 291–305. Oakland: AK Press, 2012.

Mitchell, Dave Oswald. "Killers in High Places: Drugs, Gangs, and Harper's War on the Poor." *Briarpatch*, February 2013.

Monaghan, Jeff, and Kevin Walby. "The Green Scare Is Everywhere: The Importance of Cross-Movement Solidarity." *Upping the Anti* 6 (2008): 115–34.

Moore, Hilary. "An Ethic of Care: A Relationship-Based Approach to Climate Justice Organizing in the Bay Area." MA thesis, Institute for Social Ecology, 2010.

Moore, Hilary, and Joshua Kahn Russell. *Organizing Cools the Planet: Tools and Reflections to Navigate the Climate Crisis*. Oakland: PM Press, 2011.

Moraga, Cherríe. *Loving in the War Years: Lo Que Nunca Pasó Por Sus Labios*. Boston: South End Press, 1983.

Moraga, Cherríe, and Gloria Anzaldúa, eds. *This Bridge Called My Back: Writings by Radical Women of Color*. New York: Kitchen Table, Women of Color Press, 1983.

Ms. Foundation for Women. "Mayaba Liebenthal." Accessed November 22, 2012. http://ms.foundation.org/our_work/broad-change-areas/building-democracy/katrina-womens-response-fund/katrina-grantee-stories/mayaba-liebenthal.

Muhanika, Henry. "Anti-Apartheid Campaign in Canada." PhD dissertation, Carleton University, 1987.

Mumm, James. "Active Revolution: New Directions in Revolutionary Social Change." *Common Struggle*, 1998. www.nefac.net/node/120.

Muñoz, Carlos. *Youth, Identity, Power: The Chicano Movement*. 2nd ed. London: Verso, 2007.

Muñoz Ramírez, Gloria. *The Fire and the Word: A History of the Zapatista Movement*. San Francisco: City Lights Books, 2008.

Muntaqim, Jalil. *On the Black Liberation Army*. Paterson, NJ: NJ ABC-BG, 1998.

Naber, Nadine, Verónica Giménez, and Loira Limbal. "Transcript of Sista II Sista." *Global Feminisms: Comparative Case Studies of Women's Activism and Scholarship*, January 23, 2004. www.umich.edu/~glblfem/en/transcripts/us/SistaIISista_U_E_102806.pdf.

Nail, Thomas, ed. "Building Sanctuary City: NOII-Toronto on Non-Status Migrant Justice Organizing." *Upping the Anti* 11 (2010): 147–60.

Nann, Nrinder Nindy Kaur. "Grounding Power: An Interview with Nrinder Nindy Kaur Nann." Colours of Resistance Archive, December 2, 2003. www.coloursofresistance.org/542/grounding-power-an-interview-with-nrinder-nindy-kaur-nann/.

Naples, Nancy, ed. *Community Activism and Feminist Politics: Organizing across Race, Class, and Gender*. New York: Routledge, 1998.

Nappalos, S. "Defining Practice: The Intermediate Level of Organization and Struggle." *RECOMPOSITION* (blog), August 29, 2010. https://recompositionblog.wordpress.com/2010/08/29/defining-practice-the-intermediate-level-of-organization-and-struggle/.

Naylor, Adrie, Elise Thorburn, and Robyn Letson. "Notes on Spontaneity and Organization." *Upping the Anti* 14 (2012): 23–37.

Neigh, Scott. "Elections: All We Can Hope For?" *Linchpin,* November 2008. http://linchpin.ca/collections+/+left+/+Elections-all-we-can-hope.

————. *Gender and Sexuality: Canadian History Through the Stories of Activists.* Black Point, NS: Fernwood Publishing, 2012.

————. *Resisting the State: Canadian History Through the Stories of Activists.* Black Point, NS: Fernwood Publishing, 2012.

Nelson, Alondra. *Body and Soul: The Black Panther Party and the Fight Against Medical Discrimination.* Minneapolis: University of Minnesota Press, 2011.

New Politics Initiative. "A Discussion Paper on The New Politics Initiative." *Studies in Political Economy* 66 (Autumn 2001): 143–56.

Newton, Huey P. *Revolutionary Suicide.* New York: Harcourt Brace Jovanovich, 1973.

Ng, Roxana. "State Funding to a Community Employment Center: Implications for Working with Immigrant Women." In *Community Organization and the Canadian State,* edited by Roxana Ng, Gillian Walker, and Jacob Muller, 165–83. Toronto: Garamond Press, 1990.

Night, Austin, Emily Night, and David Night. "From Here to the Free State: Building the Bridge in Minneapolis." *Arsenal: A Magazine of Anarchist Strategy and Culture,* Spring 2001.

Nomous, Otto. "Race, Anarchy, and Punk Rock: The Impact of Cultural Boundaries within the Anarchist Movement." Colours of Resistance Archive. Accessed August 31, 2012. www.coloursofresistance.org/575/race-anarchy-and-punk-rock-the-impact-of-cultural-boundaries-within-the-anarchist-movement/.

No One Is Illegal-Montreal. "No One Is Illegal-Montreal's Basis of Unity." December 27, 2006. http://nooneisillegal-montreal.blogspot.com/2006/12/no-one-is-illegal-montreals-basis-of.html.

No One Is Illegal-Vancouver. "Our Vision." Accessed April 29, 2013. http://noii-van.resist.ca/?page_id = 17.

Notes from Nowhere. "Emergence: An Irresistible Global Uprising." In *We Are Everywhere: The Irresistible Rise of Global Anticapitalism,* edited by Notes from Nowhere, 19–29. London: Verso, 2003.

————, ed. *We Are Everywhere: The Irresistible Rise of Global Anticapitalism.* London: Verso, 2003.

Nunes, Rodrigo. "The Lessons of 2011: Three Theses on Organisation." *Mute,* June 7, 2012. www.metamute.org/editorial/articles/lessons-2011-three-theses-organisation.

O'Brien, Michelle. "Whose Ally? Thinking Critically About Anti-oppression Ally Organizing." Colours of Resistance Archive. Accessed April 29, 2013. www.coloursofresistance.org/370/whose-ally-thinking-critically-about-anti-oppression-ally-organizing-part-1/.

O'Connor, Clare. "What Moves Us Now? The Contradictions of 'Community.'" In *Whose Streets? The Toronto G20 and the Challenges of Summit Protest,* edited by Tom Malleson and David Wachsmuth, 187–200. Toronto: Between the Lines, 2011.

O'Connor, Clare, and Caitlin Hewitt-White, eds. "Labour Solidarity for Palestine: Unions and the BDS Movement." *Upping the Anti* 7 (2008): 145–60.

Oka, Cynthia. "Moving the Movement: Towards a Multigenerational Ideal of Revolutionary Work." *Left Turn*, August 2011.

Olson, Joel. *The Abolition of White Democracy.* Minneapolis: University of Minnesota Press, 2004.

———. "Movement, Cadre, and Dual Power." *Perspectives on Anarchist Theory* 13, no. 1 (Fall 2011): 33–38.

———. "New Arizona." *Repeal Coalition.* Accessed November 3, 2012. www .repealcoalition.org/new-arizona.html.

———. "The Problem with Infoshops and Insurrection: U.S. Anarchism, Movement Building, and the Racial Order." In *Contemporary Anarchist Studies: An Introductory Anthology of Anarchy in the Academy,* edited by Randal Amster, Abraham Deleon, Luis Fernandez, Anthony J. Nocella, and Deric Shannon, 35–45. New York: Routledge, 2009.

Omi, Michael, and Howard Winant. *Racial Formation in the United States: From the 1960s to the 1990s.* 2nd ed. New York: Routledge, 1994.

Ontiveros, Isaac, and Rachel Herzing. "Repression Breeds Resistance: Reflections on 10 Years of the Prison Industrial Complex." *Left Turn,* May 2011.

———. "Resisting the War on Gangs (Inside and Out)." *The Abolitionist,* Summer 2012.

"Our Way or the Highway: Inside the Minnehaha Free State." In *The Struggle Is Our Inheritance: A Radical History of Minnesota,* 70–74. Zine, Minneapolis, 2008. http://twincities.indymedia.org/files/mn_radical_ history_zine.pdf.

Papadopoulos, Dimitris, Niamh Stephenson, and Vassilis Tsianos. *Escape Routes: Control and Subversion in the 21st Century.* London: Pluto, 2008.

Parenti, Christian. *Lockdown America: Police and Prisons in the Age of Crisis.* London: Verso, 2000.

Pasternak, Shiri. "'They're Clear-Cutting Our Way of Life': Algonquins Defend the Forest." *Upping the Anti* 8 (2009): 125–41.

Pate, Kim. "A Canadian Journey into Abolition." In *Abolition Now! Ten Years of Strategy and Struggle Against the Prison Industrial Complex,* edited by CR-10 Publications Collective, 77–85. Oakland: AK Press, 2008.

Payne, Charles. *I've Got the Light of Freedom: The Organizing Tradition and the Mississippi Freedom Struggle.* Berkeley: University of California Press, 1996.

Pelot-Hobbs, Lydia. "Preparing for Disaster from New Orleans to New York." *The Oyster Knife,* November 4, 2012. www.theoysterknife.com/2012/11/04/ guest-post-preparing-for-disaster-from-new-orleans-to-new-york/.

———. "Reflections on Organizing Towards Collective Liberation at Occupy NOLA." *In Front and Center,* October 20, 2011. https://infrontandcenter. wordpress.com/2011/10/20/reflections-on-organizing-towards-collective-liberation-at-occupy-nola/.

Peoples' Global Action. "Hallmarks of Peoples' Global Action." 2001. http://nadir.org/nadir/initiativ/agp/free/pga/hallm.htm.

Peoples Lenses Collective, ed. *Under the Lens of the People: Our Account of the Peoples' Resistance to the FTAA, Quebec City, April 2001*. Toronto: The Peoples Lenses Collective, 2003.

Pérez, Amara H. "Between Radical Theory and Community Praxis: Reflections on Organizing and the Non-Profit Industrial Complex." In *The Revolution Will Not Be Funded: Beyond the Non-Profit Industrial Complex*, edited by INCITE! Women of Color Against Violence, 91–99. Cambridge, MA: South End Press, 2007.

Petras, James. "The Rise of the Migrant Workers Movement." *Left Turn*, September 2006.

Petras, James, and Henry Veltmeyer. *Globalization Unmasked: Imperialism in the 21st Century*. Halifax: Fernwood Publishing, 2001.

Pharr, Suzanne. *Homophobia: A Weapon of Sexism*. Inverness, CA: Chardon Press, 1988.

Phillips, Morrigan. "Room for the Poor." In *We Are Many: Reflections on Movement Strategy from Occupation to Liberation*, edited by Kate Khatib, Margaret Killjoy, and Mike McGuire, 137–45. Oakland: AK Press, 2012.

Piven, Frances Fox, and Richard Cloward. *Poor People's Movements: Why They Succeed, How They Fail*. New York: Vintage Books, 1977.

Podur, Justin. "Canada's Newest Political Prisoners: Indigenous Leaders Jailed for Protesting Mining Exploration on Their Lands." *The Dominion*, October 23, 2008. www.dominionpaper.ca/articles/2051.

Polletta, Francesca. *Freedom Is an Endless Meeting: Democracy in American Social Movements*. Chicago: University of Chicago Press, 2002.

Potter, Will. *Green Is the New Red: An Insider's Account of a Social Movement Under Siege*. San Francisco: City Lights Publishers, 2011.

Prashad, Vijay. *The Darker Nations: A People's History of the Third World*. New York: New Press, 2007.

Prisoners' Justice Day Committee. "History of Prisoners' Justice Day." *Prisonjustice.ca*, 2001. www.vcn.bc.ca/august10/politics/1014_history.html.

Prison Research Action Project. *Instead of Prisons: A Handbook for Abolitionists*. Syracuse, NY: Prison Research Action Project, 1976.

Puaz. "The Community Police: An Example of Popular Justice." *Left Turn*, May 2008.

Pulido, Laura. *Black, Brown, Yellow, and Left: Radical Activism in Los Angeles*. Berkeley: University of California Press, 2006.

Raider Nation Collective, ed. *From the January Rebellions to Lovelle Mixon and Beyond*. Oakland: Raider Nation, 2010.

Rajah, Colin. "Globalism and Race at A16 in D.C." *ColorLines*, Fall 2000.

Rameau, Max. *Take Back the Land: Land, Gentrification, and the Umoja Village Shantytown*. Oakland: AK Press, 2013.

Ramnath, Maia. "Anticolonialism and the Anarchist Imagination." *Perspectives on Anarchist Theory* 5 (2006): 79–86.

————. *Decolonizing Anarchism.* Oakland: AK Press, 2011.

————. *Haj to Utopia: How the Ghadar Movement Charted Global Radicalism and Attempted to Overthrow the British Empire.* Berkeley: University of California Press, 2011.

The Rank-and-Filer. "Turning the Complex Upside Down: Rethinking Nonprofit Structures." *The Rank-and-Filer,* March 2011. www.rankandfiler.net/turning-the-complex-upside-down/.

Ransby, Barbara. *Ella Baker and the Black Freedom Movement: A Radical Vision.* Chapel Hill: University of North Carolina Press, 2003.

Raza, Jerome. "The History of the Quebec Student Movement and Combative Unionism." *Anarkismo,* November 26, 2012. www.anarkismo.net/article/24361.

Rebick, Judy. *Ten Thousand Roses: The Making of a Feminist Revolution.* Toronto: Penguin, 2005.

The Red Sunshine Gang. "Anti-Mass: Methods of Organizations for Collectives." *The Anarchist Library,* January 30, 2013. http://theanarchistlibrary.org/library/the-red-sunshine-gang-anti-mass.

Regeneración Childcare Collective. "Once Upon a Time in Brooklyn." *Left Turn,* May 2007.

Research and Destroy. "Communiqué from an Absent Future: On the Terminus of Student Life." *Revolution by the Book: The AK Press Blog,* September 28, 2009. www.revolutionbythebook.akpress.org/communique-from-an-absent-future-the-terminus-of-student-life/.

Rich, Adrienne. "Compulsory Heterosexuality and Lesbian Existence." In *Blood, Bread, and Poetry: Selected Prose 1979–1985,* 23–75. New York: W.W. Norton and Co., 1986.

Richie, Beth. "Standing with Duanna Johnson Against Police Brutality: A Challenge for the Gay and Civil Rights Movements." *Left Turn,* May 2009.

Robinson, Cedric. *Black Marxism: The Making of the Black Radical Tradition.* London: Zed Books, 1983.

Rodney, Walter. *How Europe Underdeveloped Africa.* Washington, DC: Howard University Press, 1993.

Rodrigues, Marc. "Coalition of Immokalee Workers: McDonald's Campaign Escalates." *Left Turn,* February 2007.

————. "Farmworker and Student Victory Over Burger King." *Left Turn,* November 2008.

————. "Organizing After Victory: Immokalee Encuentro." *Left Turn,* November 2005.

Rodriguez, Dylan, Nancy Stoller, Rita Bo Brown, Terry Kupers, Andrea Smith, and Julia Sudbury. "Reflections on Critical Resistance." *Social Justice: A Journal of Crime, Conflict and World Order* 27, no. 3 (Fall 2000): 180–94.

Roediger, David. *The Wages of Whiteness: Race and the Making of the American Working Class.* 2nd ed. London: Verso, 1999.

Rojas, Paula X. "Are the Cops in Our Heads and Hearts?" In *The Revolution Will Not Be Funded: Beyond the Non-Profit Industrial Complex,* edited by

INCITE! Women of Color Against Violence, 197–214. Cambridge, MA: South End Press, 2007.

Rojas Durazo, Ana Clarissa, Alisa Bierria, and Mimi Kim, eds. "Community Accountability: Emerging Movements to Transform Violence." Special Issue, *Social Justice: A Journal of Crime, Conflict and World Order* 37, no. 4 (2011–2012).

Rolbin-Ghanie, Maya. "'It's All About The Land': Native Resistance to the Olympics." *The Dominion*, March 1, 2008. www.dominionpaper.ca/articles /1738.

Rose City Copwatch. "Alternatives to Police." *Rose City Copwatch.* 2008. http://rosecitycopwatch.org/alternatives-to-police/.

Rosemont, Franklin. *Joe Hill: The IWW and the Making of a Revolutionary Workingclass Counterculture.* Chicago: Charles H. Kerr Publishing Company, 2003.

Rosen, Ruth. *The World Split Open: How the Modern Women's Movement Changed America.* New York: Penguin Books, 2007.

Rosenblatt, Elihu, ed. *Criminal Injustice: Confronting the Prison Crisis.* Boston: South End Press, 1996.

Ross, John. "Another Year Is Possible! Flashlights in the Tunnel of Hate." *Counterpunch*, December 24, 2006. www.counterpunch.org/ross12222006 .html.

———. *The War Against Oblivion: Zapatista Chronicles, 1994–2000.* Monroe, ME: Common Courage Press, 2000.

Roth, Benita. *Separate Roads to Feminism: Black, Chicana, and White Feminist Movements in America's Second Wave.* Cambridge: Cambridge University Press, 2004.

Ruckus Society. "Action Strategy: A How-to Guide." *Ruckus Society.* Accessed October 4, 2012. http://ruckus.org/article.php?id = 821.

———. "The Symbolic Nature of Direct Action." *Ruckus Society.* Accessed October 1, 2012. www.ruckus.org/article.php?id = 99.

Rusche, Georg, and Otto Kirchheimer. *Punishment and Social Structure.* New York: Russell and Russell, 1968.

Russell, Joshua Kahn, and Brian Kelly. "Giving Form to a Stampede: The First Two Years of the New Students for a Democratic Society." *Upping the Anti* 6 (2008): 75–94.

Said, Edward. *The Question of Palestine.* 2nd ed. London: Vintage, 1992.

Sale, Kirkpatrick. *SDS.* New York: Random House, 1973.

Salerno, Salvatore. *Red November, Black November: Culture and Community in the Industrial Workers of the World.* Albany: State University of New York Press, 1989.

Samuels, Liz. "Improvising on Reality: The Roots of Prison Abolition." In *The Hidden 1970s: Histories of Radicalism,* edited by Dan Berger, 21–38. New Brunswick, NJ: Rutgers University Press, 2010.

Samuels, Liz, David Stein, Alexis Pauline Gumbs, Andrea Smith, Ari Wohlfeiler, Rita Bo Brown, Dylan Rodríguez, et al. "Perspectives On Critical Resistance."

In *Abolition Now!: Ten Years of Strategy and Struggle Against the Prison Industrial Complex*, edited by CR-10 Publications Collective, 1–14. Oakland: AK Press, 2008.

Sandoval, Chela. *Methodology of the Oppressed*. Minneapolis: University of Minnesota Press, 2000.

San Filippo, Roy, ed. *A New World in Our Hearts: Eight Years of Writings from the Love and Rage Revolutionary Anarchist Federation*. Oakland: AK Press, 2003.

Sayegh, Gabriel. "Redefining Success: White Contradictions in the Anti-Globalization Movement." Colours of Resistance Archive. Accessed April 29, 2013. www.coloursofresistance.org/298/redefining-success-white-contradictions-in-the-anti-globalization-movement/.

Scher, Abby. "Anarchism Faces the '90s." *Dollars and Sense*, April 1999.

Schmidt, Michael, and Lucien van der Walt. *Black Flame: The Revolutionary Class Politics of Anarchism and Syndicalism*. Oakland: AK Press, 2009.

Schreader, Alicia. "The State-Funded Women's Movement: A Case of Two Political Agendas." In *Community Organization and the Canadian State*, edited by Roxana Ng, Gillian Walker, and Jacob Muller, 184–89. Toronto: Garamond Press, 1990.

Schweizer, Errol, and Brielle Epstein. "People Get Ready! A Survival Handbook for Reality." Colours of Resistance Archive. Accessed April 29, 2013. http://www.coloursofresistance.org/522/people-get-ready-a-survival-handbook-for-reality-2/.

Scott, James C. *Domination and the Arts of Resistance: Hidden Transcripts*. New Haven: Yale University Press, 1990.

———. *Weapons of the Weak: Everyday Forms of Peasant Resistance*. New Haven: Yale University Press, 1985.

Scott, Macdonald, ed. "Fighting Borders: A Roundtable on Non-Status (Im)migrant Justice in Canada." *Upping the Anti* 2 (2005): 151–59.

Seale, Bobby. *Seize the Time: The Story of the Black Panther Party and Huey P. Newton*. New York: Random House, 1970.

Sen, Rinku. "Domestic Workers Lead the Way to 21st Century Labor Rights." *Colorlines*, September 2, 2010. http://colorlines.com/archives/2010/09/domestic_workers_lead_the_way_toward_21st_century_labor_rights.html.

Shah, Sonia, ed. *Dragon Ladies: Asian American Feminists Breathe Fire*. Boston: South End Press, 1997.

Shantz, Jeff. "Fighting to Win: The Ontario Coalition Against Poverty." In *We Are Everywhere: The Irresistible Rise of Global Anticapitalism*, edited by Notes from Nowhere, 464–71. London: Verso, 2003.

———. "Reclamation: The Role of Solidarity in the Six Nations Struggle for Their Land." *The Northeastern Anarchist*, Winter 2007.

Shantz, Jeffrey. "Anarchy in the Unions: Contemporary Anarchists at Work." *WorkingUSA: The Journal of Labor and Society* 12, no. 3 (2009): 371–85.

Shapiro, Tricia. *Mountain Justice: Homegrown Resistance to Mountaintop Removal, For the Future of Us All*. Oakland: AK Press, 2010.

Shepard, Benjamin. "DIY Politics and Queer Activism." In *Uses of A Whirlwind: Movement, Movements, and Contemporary Radical Currents in the United States,* edited by Team Colors Collective, 163–82. Oakland: AK Press, 2010.

———. *Queer Political Performance and Protest: Play, Pleasure and Social Movement.* New York: Routledge, 2010.

Shepard, Benjamin, and Ronald Hayduk, eds. *From ACT UP to the WTO: Urban Protest and Community Building in the Era of Globalization.* London: Verso, 2002.

Shiva, Vandana. *Biopiracy: The Plunder of Nature and Knowledge.* Boston: South End Press, 1997.

———. *Staying Alive: Women, Ecology and Development.* London: Zed Books, 1988.

———. *Stolen Harvest: The Hijacking of the Global Food Supply.* Cambridge, MA: South End Press, 2000.

Shukaitis, Stevphen, David Graeber, and Erika Biddle, eds. *Constituent Imagination: Militant Investigations, Collective Theorization.* Oakland: AK Press, 2007.

Sigal, Brad. "Demise of the Beehive Collective: Infoshops Ain't the Revolution." In *A New World in Our Hearts: Eight Years of Writings from the Love and Rage Revolutionary Anarchist Federation,* edited by Roy San Filippo, 69–76. Oakland: AK Press, 2003.

Silliman, Jael Miriam, Marlene Gerber Fried, Loretta Ross, and Elena Gutiérrez, eds. *Undivided Rights: Women of Color Organize for Reproductive Justice.* Cambridge, MA: South End Press, 2004.

Singh, Jaggi. "Resisting Global Capitalism in India." In *The Battle of Seattle: The New Challenge to Capitalist Globalization,* edited by Eddie Yuen, George Katsiaficas, and Daniel Burton Rose, 48–50. New York: Soft Skull Press, 2001.

Singh, Nikhil Pal. *Black Is a Country: Race and the Unfinished Struggle For Democracy.* Cambridge, MA: Harvard University Press, 2004.

Sista II Sista. "Sistas Makin' Moves: Collective Leadership for Personal Transformation and Social Justice." In *Color of Violence: The INCITE! Anthology,* edited by INCITE! Women of Color Against Violence, 196–207. Cambridge, MA: South End Press, 2006.

Sitrin, Marina. *Horizontalism: Voices of Popular Power in Argentina.* Oakland: AK Press, 2006.

———. " 'Walking We Ask Questions': An Interview with John Holloway." *Perspectives on Anarchist Theory* 8, no. 2 (2004): 8–11.

Sivesind, Sonja. "Combating White Privilege in the Anti-Globalization Movement." *Clamor,* April 2002.

Smith, Andrea. "Against the Law: Indigenous Feminism and the Nation-State." *Affinities: A Journal of Radical Theory, Culture, and Action* 5, no. 1 (2011): 56–69.

———. "Beyond Inclusion: Recentering Feminism." *Left Turn,* June 2006.

———. *Conquest: Sexual Violence and American Indian Genocide.* Cambridge, MA: South End Press, 2005.

———. "Heteropatriarchy and the Three Pillars of White Supremacy: Rethinking Women of Color Organizing." In *Color of Violence: The INCITE! Anthology,* edited by INCITE! Women of Color Against Violence, 66–73. Cambridge, MA: South End Press, 2006.

———. "Introduction." In *The Revolution Will Not Be Funded: Beyond the Non-Profit Industrial Complex,* edited by INCITE! Women of Color Against Violence, 1–18. Cambridge, MA: South End Press, 2007.

Smith, Barbara, ed. *Home Girls: A Black Feminist Anthology.* New York: Kitchen Table, Women of Color Press, 1983.

———. *The Truth That Never Hurts: Writings on Race, Gender, and Freedom.* New Brunswick, NJ: Rutgers University Press, 1998.

Smith, Christian. *Resisting Reagan: The U.S. Central America Peace Movement.* Chicago: University of Chicago Press, 1996.

Smith, Nat, and Eric A. Stanley, eds. *Captive Genders: Trans Embodiment and the Prison Industrial Complex.* Oakland: AK Press, 2011.

Smith, Paul Chaat, and Robert Allen Warrior. *Like a Hurricane: The Indian Movement from Alcatraz to Wounded Knee.* New York: New Press, 1996.

Smucker, Jonathan Matthew. "'Would You Like to Come to the Protest?' (What Prevents Radicals from Acting Strategically?)." *Beyond the Choir,* January 4, 2011. www.beyondthechoir.org/diary/22/would-you-like-to-come-to-the-protest-what-prevents-radicals-from-acting-strategically.

Solidarity Across Borders. "STATUS FOR ALL!" Accessed December 12, 2012. http://www.solidarityacrossborders.org/en/revendications/status-for-all.

Solnit, David. "Active Resistance at the Democratic Convention: Planting Seeds for an Anarchist Movement." *Fifth Estate,* Fall 1996.

———. "The New Face of the Global Justice Movement: Taco Bell Victory—A Model of Strategic Organizing." *Left Turn,* September 2005.

———. "The New Radicalism: Uprooting the System and Building a Better World." In *Globalize Liberation: How to Uproot the System and Build a Better World,* edited by David Solnit, xi–xxiv. San Francisco: City Lights, 2004.

Sonnie, Amy, and James Tracy. *Hillbilly Nationalists, Urban Race Rebels, and Black Power: Community Organizing in Radical Times.* Brooklyn: Melville House, 2011.

South End Press, ed. *What Lies Beneath: Katrina, Race, and the State of the Nation.* Cambridge, MA: South End Press, 2007.

Springer, Kimberly. *Living for the Revolution: Black Feminist Organizations, 1968–1980.* Durham: Duke University Press, 2005.

Standing Together to Organize a Revolutionary Movement. *Reclaiming Revolution: History, Summation, and Lessons from the Work of Standing Together to Organize a Revolutionary Movement (STORM).* San Francisco: STORM, 2004.

Starhawk. *The Empowerment Manual: A Guide for Collaborative Groups.* Gabriola Island, BC: New Society Publishers, 2011.

———. *Truth or Dare: Encounters with Power, Authority, and Mystery.* San Francisco: Harper and Row, 1987.

———. *Webs of Power: Notes from the Global Uprising.* Gabriola, BC: New Society Publishers, 2002.

Staudenmaier, Michael. "Nationalism: Definitions and Clarifications." *Onward,* Spring 2002.

———. *Truth and Revolution: A History of the Sojourner Truth Organization, 1969–1986.* Oakland: AK Press, 2012.

———. "What Good Are Nations? Anarchism and Nationalism." *Arsenal: A Magazine of Anarchist Strategy and Culture,* Spring 2001.

Stein, David. "Surviving Warfare, Practicing Resistance." In *Abolition Now! Ten Years of Strategy and Struggle Against the Prison Industrial Complex,* edited by CR-10 Publications Collective, 87–90. Oakland: AK Press, 2008.

Stein, Marc. *Rethinking the Gay and Lesbian Movement.* New York: Routledge, 2012.

Stern, Jessica. "Transforming Justice." *Left Turn,* February 2008.

Stohlman, Nancy, and Laurieann Aladin, eds. *Live from Palestine: International and Palestinian Direct Action Against the Israeli Occupation.* Cambridge, MA: South End Press, 2003.

Style, Sophie. "People's Global Action." *Z Magazine,* January 2002.

Sudbury, Julia. *Global Lockdown: Race, Gender, and the Prison-Industrial Complex.* New York: Routledge, 2005.

———. "Maroon Abolitionists: Black Gender-Oppressed Activists in the Anti-Prison Movement in the U.S. and Canada." *Meridians: Feminism, Race, Transnationalism* 9, no. 1 (2009): 1–29.

Sycamore, Matt Bernstein, ed. *That's Revolting: Queer Strategies for Resisting Assimilation.* Brooklyn: Soft Skull Press, 2004.

Sylvia Rivera Law Project. "About." Accessed February 6, 2013. http://srlp.org/about/.

———. *SRLP Collective Member Handbook.* New York: Sylvia Rivera Law Project, n.d.

Tang, Eric. "Non-Profits and the Autonomous Grassroots." In *The Revolution Will Not Be Funded: Beyond the Non-Profit Industrial Complex,* edited by INCITE! Women of Color Against Violence, 215–25. Cambridge, MA: South End Press, 2007.

Team Colors Collective. "Abandoning the Chorus: Checking Ourselves a Decade Since Seattle." *Groundswell* 1 (2010): 13–18.

———. "Messy Hearts Made of Thunder: Occupy, Struggle, and Radical Community Organizing." In *We Are Many: Reflections on Movement Strategy from Occupation to Liberation,* edited by Kate Khatib, Margaret Killjoy, and Mike McGuire, 399–407. Oakland: AK Press, 2012.

———. *Wind(s) from Below: Radical Community Organizing to Make a Revolution Possible.* Portland, OR: Eberhardt Press, 2010.

Theberge, Steve. "Vibrant, Young, and Relevant: Reflections on the Counter Military Recruitment Movement." *Left Turn,* November 2005.

Thomas-Muller, Clayton. "Tar Sands: The World's Largest Climate Crime." *Left Turn*, February 2010.

Thompson, Becky. *A Promise and a Way of Life: White Antiracist Activism.* Minneapolis: University of Minnesota Press, 2001.

Thompson, Fred, and Jon Bekken. *The I.W.W.: Its First One Hundred Years, 1905–2005.* Cincinnati: Industrial Workers of the World, 2006.

Thorburn, Elise, ed. "Squarely in the Red: Dispatches from the 2012 Quebec Student Strike." *Upping the Anti* 14 (2012): 107–21.

Thuma, Emily. "'Not a Wedge, But a Bridge': Prisons, Feminist Activism, and the Politics of Gendered Violence, 1968–1987." PhD dissertation, New York University, 2010.

Tokar, Brian. "Toward a Movement for Climate Justice." In *Uses of A Whirlwind: Movement, Movements, and Contemporary Radical Currents in the United States*, edited by Team Colors Collective, 135–48. Oakland: AK Press, 2010.

Torres, Andrés, and José Velázquez. *The Puerto Rican Movement: Voices from the Diaspora.* Philadelphia: Temple University Press, 1998.

Tracy, James. "Victory in Chinatown: The San Francisco Community Land Trust." *Left Turn*, May 2007.

Trotsky, Leon. *The Transitional Program for Socialist Revolution.* 3rd ed. New York: Pathfinder Press, 1977.

Uhlenbeck, Max. "A Light Within." *Left Turn*, August 2007.

———. "The Antiwar Movement and the 2008 Elections." *Left Turn*, February 2008.

———. "Elections 2008." *Left Turn*, August 2008.

Umoja, Akinyele Omowale. "Repression Breeds Resistance: The Black Liberation Army and the Radical Legacy of the Black Panther Party." In *Liberation, Imagination, and the Black Panther Party: A New Look at the Panthers and Their Legacy*, edited by Kathleen Cleaver and George Katsiaficas, 3–19. New York: Routledge, 2001.

Upping the Anti Editorial Committee. "Becoming the Enemy They Deserve: Organizational Questions for a New 'New Left'." *Upping the Anti* 4 (2007): 21–33.

———. "Between a Rock and a Hard Place: Social Democracy and Anti-Capitalist Renewal in English Canada." *Upping the Anti* 5 (2007): 29–45.

———. "Breaking the Impasse." *Upping the Anti* 2 (2006): 14–21.

———. "Editorial." *Upping the Anti* 1 (2005): 7–14.

———. "Growing Pains: The Anti-Globalization Movement, Anti-Imperialism and the Politics of the United Front." *Upping the Anti* 3 (2006): 27–44.

———, ed. "Perspectives on Palestine Solidarity Organizing." *Upping the Anti* 2 (2005): 103–26.

Varon, Jeremy. *Bringing the War Home: The Weather Underground, the Red Army Faction, and Revolutionary Violence in the Sixties and Seventies.* Berkeley: University of California Press, 2004.

Vellela, Tony. *New Voices: Student Political Activism in the '80s and '90s.* Boston: South End Press, 1988.

Viehmeyer, Doug. "Steppin' It Up: The New SDS." *Left Turn,* May 2007.

Wagner, David. *What's Love Got to Do with It? A Critical Look at American Charity.* New York: The New Press, 2000.

Walia, Harsha. "Letter to Occupy Together Movement." In *Dreaming in Public: Building the Occupy Movement,* edited by Amy Schrager Lang and Daniel Lang/Levitsky, 164–70. Oxford: New Internationalist Publications, 2012.

——. "Moving Beyond a Politics of Solidarity Toward a Practice of Decolonization." In *Organize! Building from the Local for Global Justice,* edited by Aziz Choudry, Jill Hanley, and Eric Shragge, 240–53. Oakland: PM Press, 2012.

——. "Resisting Displacement, North and South: Indigenous and Immigrant Struggles." *Znet,* August 12, 2003. www.zmag.org/content/showarticle. cfm?SectionID = 30&ItemID = 4039.

——. *Undoing Border Imperialism.* Oakland: AK Press, 2013.

Walia, Harsha, and Stefan Christoff. "Resistance Without Reservation!" *Znet,* August 5, 2004. www.zmag.org/content/showarticle.cfm?SectionID = 30&ItemID = 5996.

Warbrick, Nadine. "Criminal Justice in Aotearoa/New Zealand." *Left Turn,* May 2008.

Warner, Tom. *Never Going Back: A History of Queer Activism in Canada.* Toronto: University of Toronto Press, 2002.

Weaver, Adam. "Especifismo." *Machete 408.* Accessed November 2, 2012. https://machete408.wordpress.com/especifismo/.

——. "Especifismo: The Anarchist Praxis of Building Popular Movements and Revolutionary Organization in South America." *The Northeastern Anarchist,* Spring 2006.

Weaver, Adam, and S. Nappalos. "Fighting for the Future: The Necessity and Possibility of National Political Organization for Our Time." *Machete 408,* September 8, 2013. https://machete408.wordpress.com/2013/09/08 /fighting-for-the-future-the-necessity-and-possibility-of-national-politi- cal-organization-for-our-time/.

Wei, William. *The Asian American Movement.* Philadelphia: Temple University Press, 1993.

Weinstein, James. *The Decline of Socialism in America, 1912–1925.* New York: Monthly Review Press, 1967.

Wet'suwet'en, Toghestiy. "A Wet'suwet'en Grassroots Alliance." *The Dominion,* May 2011.

Wetzel, Tom. "Anarchism, Class Struggle and Political Organization." *Znet,* July 22, 2009. www.zcommunications.org/anarchism-class-struggle-and- political-organization-by-tom-wetzel.

——. "The Capitalist City or the Self-Managed City?" In *Globalize Liberation: How to Uproot the System and Build a Better World,* edited by David Solnit, 361–80. San Francisco: City Lights Books, 2004.

White, Roger. *Post Colonial Anarchism: Essays on Race, Repression and Culture in Communities of Color, 1999–2004.* Oakland: Jailbreak Press, 2004.

Williams, Steve, and James Tracy. "The Left and the Elections." *Left Turn*, May 2008.

Wong, Kristine. "Shutting Us Out: Race, Class, and the Framing of a Movement." In *Confronting Capitalism: Dispatches from a Global Movement*, edited by Eddie Yuen, George Katsiaficas, and Daniel Burton Rose, 204–14. New York: Soft Skull Press, 2004.

Wood, Lesley J. "Organizing Against the Occupation: U.S. and Canadian Anti-war Activists Speak Out." *Social Movement Studies* 3, no. 2 (2004): 241–57.

———, ed. "Roundtable on Anti-War Organizing in Canada." *Upping the Anti* 2 (2005): 127–50.

Woodcock, George. *Anarchism: A History of Libertarian Ideas and Movements.* Cleveland: Meridian Books, 1962.

Woodroffe, Jessica, and Mark Ellis-Jones. *States of Unrest: Resistance to IMF Policies in Poor Countries.* World Development Movement, September 2000.

Woods, Clyde. "The Politics of Reproductive Violence: An Interview with Shana Griffin by Clyde Woods, March 12, 2009." *American Quarterly* 61, no. 3 (September 2009): 583–91.

Wright, Sasha. "The Second Superpower: Prospects for the Anti-War Movement." *Left Turn*, October 2004.

Yates, Michael D., ed. *Wisconsin Uprising: Labor Fights Back.* New York: Monthly Review Press, 2012.

Yuen, Eddie. "Introduction." In *Confronting Capitalism: Dispatches from a Global Movement*, edited by Eddie Yuen, George Katsiaficas, and Daniel Burton Rose, vii–xxix. New York: Soft Skull Press, 2004.

Yuen, Eddie, George Katsiaficas, and Daniel Burton Rose, eds. *The Battle of Seattle: The New Challenge to Capitalist Globalization.* New York: Soft Skull Press, 2001.

———, eds. *Confronting Capitalism: Dispatches from a Global Movement.* New York: Soft Skull Press, 2004.

Zapatista Army of National Liberation. "Sixth Declaration of the Selva Lacandona." *Enlace Zapatista*, June 2005. http://enlacezapatista.ezln.org .mx/sdsl-en/.

Ziadah, Rafeef. "60 Years of Israeli Apartheid and Occupation." *Left Turn*, May 2008.

Index

Occupy Our Homes, 1 *fig.*, 55, 169, 240. *See also* direct action support work

Occupy Sandy, 55, 145–46, 240

Occupy Wall Street, 2, 12, 53–55, 145

October League, 32

Olson, Joel, 134

Ontario Coalition Against Poverty, 135–36, 157 *fig.*, 169, 213, 240, 300n17

organization: and accountability, 207, 214–15; ad hoc activist groups, 205, 218; affinity groups, 204–5; anti-authoritarian critiques of, 200; and anti-oppression, 96, 207, 208, 210, 212; cadre groups, 217, 306n36; in Coalition large de l'Association pour une solidarité syndicale étudiante, 211; collectives, 204, 208, 212–14; in Critical Resistance, 214; electoral parties, 201–2; and "entry points" for participation, 215–16; fetishization of forms of, 200, 205–6, 210; and flexibility, 207, 208–9; in Heads Up Collective, 213; in INCITE!, 214; and "in the world but not of it," 217–19; and leadership, 300–301n17; and leadership development, 207, 210, 212, 305n32; membership-based, 213, 300–301n17; movement building approach to, 200–201, 206–14, 217–19, 232; and movements, 203, 206, 217–19; nongovernmental organizations, 204; and nonhierarchical decision-making, 210; nonhierarchical organizations, 204–14; in No One Is Illegal, 205, 214; organizational longings, 214–17; and "political home," 216–17; and prefigurative politics, 209–10; revolutionary parties, 202–3, 217; and ruts, 201–6; and strategy, 209–10, 216; in Sylvia Rivera Law Project, 211–12; and transmitting lessons, 230–31

Organization for a Free Society, 217, 240

organizing, 158, 160–61, 163; vs. activism, 159–62, 163, 295–96n1; affective, 90–92, 167; and "against-and-beyond," 158–59; anti-authoritarian, 165–69, 232; community, 164, 167–68; and counterpower, 148, 227; in crisis mode, 114–15, 121, 229–30; and empowerment, 135–36; and feminism, 165; and humility, 171; Indigenous solidarity, 45, 79–80, 128, 277n54; instrumental, 297nn11,12; and "in the world but not of it," 8, 153–54, 173–74, 226–27; and leadership development, 164; and material realities, 225; and movement-building, 118–19, 163; noninstrumental, 167–69; in No One Is Illegal, 163, 296n2; as an orientation, 162–65; as a political commitment, 158; and popular education, 171–72; practices, 169–73; and prefigurative politics, 165–69, 231–32; as a principle, 7; and prison abolitionism, 165; queer, 37, 41–42, 165, 178, 211–12; and relationship-building, 170–71; vision-based, 6–7, 132–37, 284n8; and women of color feminism, 170. *See also* labor organizing; migrant justice organizing; nonhierarchical organizing

pacifism, 27–28

Palestine, 78–80

Palestine solidarity organizing, 78–80, 213, 277n59

parties, electoral, 201–2. *See also* organization

parties, revolutionary, 32, 202–3, 217. *See also* organization

patience, 119, 226, 286n19

patriarchy, 32, 34, 71; and activist norms, 89–91, 115, 120, 144, 170–71, 191; and caring labor, 91,

Vancouver Olympics, 51
van der Walt, Lucien, 300n14
vanguardism, 66–67, 172, 203, 217,
    272n16
Villanueva, Fredy, 52
violence: gender-based, 35–37, 40,
    149–50; intimate, 35–37, 225; state,
    30, 35, 37, 52–53, 149, 151
violence against women. *See* gender-
    based violence
vision, 66, 120, 137, 222–23, 227. *See
    also* vision-based organizing
vision-based organizing, 6–7, 109,
    132–37, 284n8. *See also* "in the
    world but not of it"; organizing
Viveiros, Camilo, 296n1, 298n24

Walia, Harsha, 248–49; on anarchism,
    64; on anti-oppression, 281n23;
    on leadership, 175, 181, 186,
    187–88; on organizing, 158, 161,
    296n2; on reform struggles,
    128–29, 136; on transmitting
    lessons, 230
"walking we ask questions," 19–20,
    231. *See also* Zapatistas
Warner, Marika, 249; on leadership,
    187; on nonvanguardism, 66; on
    organizing, 160, 161; on
    prefigurative politics, 6, 89–90
War on Terror, 46–47, 213
war resisters. *See* GI resisters
War Resisters League (WRL), 27–28
War Resisters Support Campaign, 47,
    241
War Times, 47
Weather Underground, 32
Weaver, Adam, 288n13
White, Roger, 64
white supremacy. *See* racism
Whitney, Jennifer, 58, 207, 209, 249
Williams, Nastassia, 211
winning, 110, 132, 133, 233

Wisconsin state capitol occupation, 53,
    120
Wise, Ora, 79, 80, 172, 186, 249
Women of All Red Nations, 35
women of color feminism, xiii, 34–37;
    and anti-oppression, 35–36, 72;
    conceptions of coalition and
    difference, 36; impact on prison
    abolitionism, 40; intersectionality,
    35; and leadership development,
    195–96; and organizing, 170; and
    prefigurative politics, 36, 89–90;
    significance for anti-authoritarian
    current, 37, 55–56; and women's
    liberation movement, 33, 34–35. *See
    also* anti-racist feminism
Women's Health and Justice Initiative,
    146, 241
women's liberation movement, 32–33;
    impact on nonviolent direct action
    movement, 41; and leadership, 33,
    178; racism and class elitism within,
    33; and women of color feminism,
    34–35. *See also* feminism
Workers Solidarity Alliance, 217, 241
workshops, 96, 184, 193–94. *See also*
    leadership development; political
    education; popular education;
    skillshares; training
writing with movements, xii, 13,
    19–20. *See also* movement-based
    research

Young Lords, 35
Young Workers United, 47, 214, 241

Zapatistas, 43; and anti-authoritarian
    current, 5; *encuentro,* 43, 96;
    mandar obedeciendo, 188, 272n16;
    and solidarity, 77; and synthetic
    political approach, 61; "walking we
    ask questions," 19–20, 231
Ziadah, Rafeef, 78